GRADE 2

English Language Learner Resource Book

Macmillan/McGraw-Hill

Program Author
Dr. Diane August
Educational Researcher
• Principal Investigator, Developing Literacy in Second-Language Learners:
  Report of the National Literacy Panel on Language-Minority Children and Youth
• Member of the New Standards Literacy Project, Grades 4-5

Program Consultant
Dr. Cheryl Dressler
Literacy Consultant
English Learners

A

The *McGraw·Hill* Companies

 Macmillan/McGraw-Hill

Published by Macmillan/McGraw-Hill, of McGraw-Hill Education, a division of The McGraw-Hill Companies, Inc.,
Two Penn Plaza, New York, New York 10121.

Printed in the United States of America

1 2 3 4 5 6 7 8 9 10 DUB 13 12 11 10 09

Table of Contents

Unit 1 Planner — 2–3

Week 1
David's New Friends............ 4
Field Trip to an Aquarium...... 12
Glossary/Book Talk 14–15

Week 2
Mr. Putter & Tabby Pour
the Tea........................ 16
Cat Kisses 28
Glossary/Book Talk 30–31

Week 3
TIME Family Farm: Farming Then
and Now..................... 32
Glossary/Book Talk 34–35

Week 4
Meet Rosina 36
You-Tú........................ 46
Glossary/Book Talk 48–49

Week 5
My Name Is Yoon.............. 50
New Americans in Texas 64
Glossary/Book Talk 66–67

Unit 2 Planner — 68–69

Week 1
Babu's Song................... 70
Where in the World Is
Tanzania?..................... 84
Glossary/Book Talk 86–87

Week 2
Doña Flor 88
Henrietta Chamberlain King .. 104
Glossary/Book Talk 106–107

Week 3
TIME A Tall Tale: How Does Texas Honor
the Battle of San Jacinto?..... 108
Glossary/Book Talk 110–111

Week 4
One Grain of Rice 112
Same Story, Different Culture 126
Glossary/Book Talk 128–129

Week 5
African-American Inventors... 130
Inventors Time Line 140
Glossary/Book Talk 142–143

Unit 3 Planner — 144–145

Week 1
The Alvin Ailey Kids: Dancing
as a Team 146
You'll Sing a Song and I'll Sing
a Song 156
Glossary/Book Talk 158–159

Week 2
Abuelo and the Three Bears .. 160
The Three Bears 172
Glossary/Book Talk 174–175

Week 3
TIME Music of the Stone Age....... 176
Glossary/Book Talk 178–179

Week 4
Click, Clack, Moo:
Cows That Type 180
Early Ranching in Texas....... 192
Glossary/Book Talk 194–195

Week 5
Stirring up Memories........ 196
Brush Dance/Crayons 204
Glossary/Book Talk 206–207

Unit 4 Planner — 208–209

Week 1
Head, Body, Legs: A Story
from Liberia.................. 210
Watch It Move!............... 224
Glossary/Book Talk 226–227

Week 2
Officer Buckle and Gloria 228
Fire Safety 240
Glossary/Book Talk 242–243

Week 3
TIME A Trip to the Emergency
Room........................ 244
Glossary/Book Talk 246–247

Week 4
A Harbor Seal Pup Grows Up.. 248
The Puppy 258
Glossary/Book Talk 260–261

Week 5
Mice and Beans 262
Rosa María's Rice and Beans .. 278
Glossary/Book Talk 280–281

Unit 5 Planner — 282–283

Week 1
The Tiny Seed 284
Plant Parts 296
Glossary/Book Talk 298–299

Week 2
The Ugly Vegetables 300
The Water Cycle 312
Glossary/Book Talk 314–315

Week 3
TIME Meet the Super Croc 316
Glossary/Book Talk 318–319

Week 4
Farfallina and Marcel 320
Butterflies 332
Glossary/Book Talk 334–335

Week 5
Nutik, the Wolf Pup........... 336
Wolves....................... 346
Glossary/Book Talk 348–349

Unit 6 Planner — 350–351

Week 1
Dig Wait Listen: A Desert
Toad's Tale 352
The Sonoran Desert 364
Glossary/Book Talk 366–367

Week 2
Splish! Splash! Animal Baths .. 368
Ant and Grasshopper......... 380
Glossary/Book Talk 382–383

Week 3
TIME A Way to Help Planet Earth ... 384
Glossary/Book Talk 386–387

Week 4
Super Storms 388
It Fell in the City............. 400
Glossary/Book Talk 402–403

Week 5
Pushing Up the Sky 404
Getting to Know Joseph
Bruchac...................... 412
Glossary/Book Talk 414–415

**Oral Language Proficiency
Benchmark Assessment**. R1-R7

How to Use This Book

Purpose and Structure

The **English Language Learner Resource Book** provides additional language and concept support for the English language learners using the *Treasures* Reading/Language Arts program.

This **ELL Resource Book** is organized by units to follow the organization of the *Treasures* program. Each unit begins with a **Unit Planner** that identifies the weekly support, which includes:

- Interactive Question-Response Guide

The Unit Planner identifies pages from the **English Language Learner Practice Book** which provides ELLs practice on the target weekly skills taught in *Treasures*.

The **ELL Resource Book** also includes an **Oral Language Proficiency Benchmark Assessment** to help you monitor children's oral language proficiency growth.

Interactive Question-Response Guide

A question-response guide is provided for each main selection and paired selection. Each lesson focuses on the weekly theme, key skills, strategies, concepts, and vocabulary. This conversational, interactive instruction creates context and provides opportunities for children to learn how information builds and connects. The interactive scripts help children use what they already know as they add new knowledge. This instruction also provides ample opportunities for children to speak and use new language learned.

Instructional Techniques and Learning Strategies

The scripted lessons are easy to navigate: each page is divided into labeled sections that correspond to the child's page. The lessons provide language and vocabulary support in a variety of ways. Instructional techniques include:

- providing a brief "set purpose" statement at the beginning of a new section
- connecting to prior lessons and literature
- presenting extra background or context

- defining vocabulary using simple language or including synonyms (circumlocution) within the flow of instruction to clarify new words
- asking the right types of questions that focus on the basic meaning of the text and build overall understanding
- using visual elements for support to clarify or elicit language
- supporting text features, such as captions, sidebars, illustrations, and charts

English Language Learner Practice Book

Use the activities in the **English Language Learner Practice Book** to provide practice opportunities for the target skill or strategy taught each week:

- Phonics
- Vocabulary
- Grammar
- Writing
- Book Talk

Week 1

Selections	Vocabulary		ELL Practice Book
	Key Selection Words/ Cognates	**Academic Language/Cognates**	
David's New Friends *A Field Trip to an Aquarium*	groan excited whisper carefully different *diferente*	character setting story structure dictionary/abc order statements and questions complete sentence	• Phonics, pp. 1–2 • Vocabulary, p. 3 • Grammar, p. 4 • Book Talk, p. 5

Week 2

Selections	Vocabulary		ELL Practice Book
	Key Selection Words/ Cognates	**Academic Language/Cognates**	
Mr. Putter & Tabby Pour the Tea *Cat Kisses*	share enjoyed wonderful thinning delighted company *compañía*	plot story structure word parts command punctuation *puntuación* exclamation *exclamación*	• Phonics, pp. 6–7 • Vocabulary, p. 8 • Grammar, p. 9 • Book Talk, p. 10

Week 3

TIME FOR KIDS	Vocabulary		ELL Practice Book
	Key Selection Words/ Cognates	**Academic Language/Cognates**	
Family Farm: Then and Now	harvest crops regrow machines *máquinas* irrigate *irrigar*	main idea/details summarize subject prefix *prefijo*	• Phonics, pp. 11–12 • Vocabulary, p. 13 • Grammar, p. 14 • Book Talk, p. 15

Week 4

Selections	Vocabulary		ELL Practice Book
	Key Selection Words/ Cognates	**Academic Language/Cognates**	
Meet Rosina *You—Tú*	deaf signing relatives celebrate *celebrar* cultures *culturas*	summarize main idea/details comma dictionary *diccionario* predicate *predicado*	• Phonics, pp. 16–17 • Vocabulary, p. 18 • Grammar, p. 19 • Book Talk, p. 20

Week 5

Selections	Vocabulary		ELL Practice Book
	Key Selection Words/ Cognates	**Academic Language/Cognates**	
My Name Is Yoon *New Americans in Texas*	wrinkled settled cuddle patient *paciente* practiced *practicar* favorite *favorito/-a*	summarize make predictions confirm predictions subject *sujeto* predicate *predicado* inflected verb *verbo*	• Phonics, pp. 21–22 • Vocabulary, p. 23 • Grammar, p. 24 • Book Talk, p. 25

Student Response Strategies

Use the following strategies to help English Language Learners move to the next proficiency level.

✔ **WAIT** Give children ample time.

- Let children know that they can respond in different ways depending on their levels of proficiency, but all should be encouraged to answer questions related to the main point of the picture or text.

- Allow children to respond in their native language if they are very limited proficient. Ask a more proficient ELL student to repeat the answer in English.

✔ **REPEAT** If the child's response is correct, the teacher can repeat what the child has said. The teacher should repeat in a clear, loud voice that all can hear and at a slower pace.

✔ **REVISE for FORM** Generally the teacher will be repeating what the child has said but with corrections for grammar and pronunciation. The correction can be implicit or explicit (where teacher calls attention to the correction).

✔ **REVISE for MEANING** Teachers should also correct for meaning.

✔ **ELABORATE** Here, the teacher elaborates on a child's response or states the response in another way in order to more fully develop children's comprehension and oral language proficiency.

✔ **ELICIT** Finally, the teacher can also elicit a more comprehensive response from the child by prompting the child for further information.

Newcomers

Basic and Social Language Each week you will be focusing on an important aspect of classroom communication to teach or reinforce with your newcomers. Children will expand and internalize initial English vocabulary by learning and using routine language needed for classroom communication.

Introduce Self Teach children how to introduce themselves, ask for other classmates' names, and say *Hello/Goodbye.* Use the sentence frames *My name is _____* and *What is your name?* Model dialogues, such as Hello. *My name is <insert name>. What is your name?* Have children repeat and practice with a partner.

Basic Requests Teach children sentence frames for basic requests, such as *I need _____, I want _____,* and *Do you have _____ ?* In addition, teach them how to ask for permission, such as *May I use the restroom, please?* and to respond with *thank you.* Provide daily opportunities to model and practice each request. Reinforce *please* and *thank you.*

Classroom Items Teach children the names of commonly used classroom items, such as *pencil, paper, book, chair,* and *desk.* Reinforce each using the sentence frames *This is my _____, That is your _____* and *This is a _____.* These sentence frames focus on possession. Provide daily practice, for example, *This is my book. That is your book.*

LOG ON Have children use **Newcomer Games** to expand and internalize language needed for classroom communication.
www.macmillanmh.com

David's New Friends

Prior to reading the selection with children, they should have listened to the selection on **StudentWorks Plus**, the interactive eBook. In addition, selection vocabulary should have been pretaught using the **Visual Vocabulary Resources**.

Access Core Content

Teacher Note Pose the questions after you read the paragraph or page indicated.

Pages 10–11

Title

- *This is the title of the story:* David's New Friends. *Let's read the title together:* David's New Friends.

Illustration

- *Find David in the picture.*

- *It looks like David's mother has dropped him off somewhere. He is carrying a backpack. Where might David be?* (at school)

- *Let's remember the title of the story. What is it?* (David's New Friends) *Where do you think David might find new friends?* (Responses will vary.)

Page 12

Illustration

- (Point to the boy.) *Who is this?* (David) (Point to the woman.) *Who is this?* (David's mother)

- *Where are David and his mother?* (at home, or in the kitchen)

Text

- *This page tells us about tomorrow. It will be the first day of school. David is a student. David's mother is a teacher. David is thinking about the first day of school.*

Text, Choral Reading

- *Let's read this page together.*

Pages 10–11

Comprehension

Genre
Fiction is a story with made-up characters and events.

Story Structure
Character and Setting
As you read, use your Character and Setting Chart.

Character	Setting

Read to Find Out
What is David like? Think about what he says and does in the story.

10

Pages 12–13

"Tomorrow is the first day of school, David," Mom says. "Are you glad?"
"I guess."
My mom is a teacher. She really likes school. I like school, too, but the first day is **different**. Everything is new.

12

Main Selection

DAVID'S NEW FRIENDS

by Pat Mora

illustrated by
Ed Martinez

Illustration

- (Point to the girl.) *Who is this?* (David's sister, Linda)

Text

- (Write the word *lizards* on the board.) *Linda likes lizards. Let's say it together:* lizards.

 This page tells us something about David's character. It tells us something he doesn't like. What is it? (lizards)

- *David doesn't like lizards. How do you know this?* (He says, "Ugh." He groans. He says, "I don't like creepy lizards.")

- *Let's groan about lizards, like David:* Ugh, lizards. (Exaggerate a groaning tone of voice.)

 Linda likes lizards. David doesn't like lizards. Do you like lizards? Talk to your partner. Name three animals that you like. Then name three animals that you don't like.

Non-verbal Cues

Remind children that they can use non-verbal cues to share information when they are not able to do so verbally. Encourage children to use sounds or pantomime.

My sister Linda asks me to read to her. She hands me a book about lizards.

"Ugh," I **groan**. "Let's read about tigers. I don't like creepy lizards."

I read to my sister, but I think about school, too. Will I like my teacher? Will I meet new friends?

13

The next morning, Grandma hands me my backpack. "You are a big boy now," she says. "You're in second grade!"

I try to act big. Then I give her a hug. Mom drives me to school.

"Aren't you **excited**, David? You're going to see your school friends."

"Yes," I answer. But also I hope I'll meet some new ones, too.

14

Page 14

Illustration

- (Point to the mother.) *Who is getting into the car?* (David's mother)

- (Point to the girl.) *Who is waving to the mother?* (Linda, David's sister)

- (Point to the grandma). *Who is giving David a hug?* (his grandma)

Text

- *Now it is the first day of school. David is going to school. He is excited. Can you think of times when you have felt excited?*

- *Why is David excited?* (He will see his friends in school. He hopes he will meet new friends, too.)

Page 15

Illustration

- *There are three children looking at a fish tank. Point to the fish tank. What do you usually see in a fish tank?* (fish)

- *Look at David's face. What do you think he is saying?* (ugh; groaning sound)

Text

- *David likes his new classroom because it is full of neat stuff—things he likes. He sees his friends Ron and Josie. (Point to Ron and Josie in the illustration.)*

- *David sees one thing he doesn't like. What is it?* (a lizard)

 Talk with your partner. Name some neat stuff, or things you like, in your classroom.

Formal and Informal English

When children encounter a word used in a formal setting in the text, discuss other ways the character would communicate with more informal language. For example: *Mr. Roy / David*

Our teacher is standing by the chalkboard. "Good morning, girls and boys," he says. "I'm your new teacher, Mr. Roy." He gives the class a big grin.

Then he looks around. "Where's the chalk?" he asks.

16

My new classroom is full of neat stuff. Maybe this year *will* be fun.

I see Ron and Josie near the fish tank. I want to tell them about my trip to the zoo. Then I see the lizard. Ugh! I sit on the other side of the room.

> ✔ **Character and Setting**
> Who is the main character? How does the setting make him feel?

15

I get up and hand him some chalk.
Mr. Roy smiles. "Thanks, David."
"Okay," Mr. Roy says. "Let's begin!" He looks around. "Now, where are my glasses?"
I point to his head.
"What are you doing up there?" he asks his glasses. Everyone laughs. Mr. Roy gives me a wink.
I like this teacher.

17

Page 16

Text

- *David meets his new teacher. What is the teacher's name?* (Mr. Roy)

- *Mr. Roy gives a big grin, or smile.* (Demonstrate grinning.) *He is looking for something. What is it?* (chalk)

Illustration

- (Write the word *chalk* on the board.) *Mr. Roy is looking for the chalk. David is holding it. Point to the chalk in the picture. Let's say it together:* chalk. (Hold up a piece of chalk and point to it as you say the word together.)

- (Write the word *chalkboard* on the board.) *Mr. Roy is standing by the chalkboard. Point to the chalkboard in the picture. Let's say it together:* chalkboard. (Point to the chalkboard as you say the word together.)

- (Write the word *glasses* on the board.) *Mr. Roy has glasses. Point to his glasses in the picture. Let's say it together:* glasses.

Page 17

Text

- *David gives the chalk to Mr. Roy, and Mr. Roy smiles.* (Demonstrate smiling.)

- *Now Mr. Roy is looking for something else. What is it?* (his glasses) *David points to the glasses on Mr. Roy's head.* (Point to the top of your head) *Mr. Roy winks.* (Demonstrate winking.)

 David learns about Mr. Roy's character on this page. David likes Mr. Roy. Mr. Roy is nice. How does David know this? (He smiles. He winks. He does funny things.)

Page 18

Illustration

- *Point to David in the picture. Point to Mr. Roy. What are they looking at?* (Mr. Roy's shoes/slippers/feet)

Text

- (Write the word *snack* on the board.) *After math class, the children have a snack. Let's say it together:* snack.

- *What do the children have for a snack?* (juice) *Name another snack that children might eat at school.* (Answers will vary.)

- *Mr. Roy spills his juice on his shoes!* (Mime spilling juice on your shoes.)

- *There is something funny about Mr. Roy's shoes. They are slippers. Slippers are shoes that we wear in the house. We don't wear slippers to school or to work. Mr. Roy forgot to take off his slippers and put on his school shoes.* (Mime taking off and putting on.)

Page 19

Illustration

- *Point to the lizard in the picture. What is the lizard's name?* (Slim)

Text

- *Mr. Roy shows his friend to the class. His friend is a lizard. The lizard's name is Slim. Slim is another word for* thin. *Both the lizard and Mr. Roy are thin, not fat.*

- *When the children hear Slim's name, they giggle. Giggle is another word for* laugh. *Let's say it together:* giggle. *Now, let's giggle together.* (Demonstrate giggling, and encourage the children to imitate you.)

- *Look at the picture. How do you think David feels about Slim? Does David like Slim? How can you tell?* (No, he doesn't like lizards. He is making a face.)

We finish math at 10:00. Then it's snack time. Everyone gets juice to drink. Mr. Roy spills some on his shoes. I give him my napkin.

Mr. Roy says to me, "Oh no, David! These are my slippers. I was so excited this morning, I forgot to put on my shoes!" We laugh together.

18

Just then, Slim slips out of Mr. Roy's hand. Everyone starts yelling.
Slim is as fast as a whip.

20

"Okay, girls and boys," says Mr. Roy. "It's time to meet a friend of mine." He picks up the lizard.

"Oh no!" I say to myself. "Not the lizard!"

"His name is Slim," says Mr. Roy. "He's thin like me."

The class giggles.

Mr. Roy says, "I hold him **carefully** so I don't hurt him."

> ✓ Character and Setting
> How do you think the main character feels about Slim? Use story details.

19

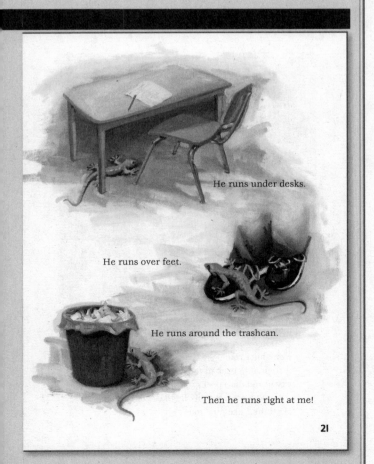

He runs under desks.

He runs over feet.

He runs around the trashcan.

Then he runs right at me!

21

Page 20

Illustration
- *Point to Slim in the picture. What is he doing?* (He is jumping out of Mr. Roy's hands.)

Text
- *Slim slips out of Mr. Roy's hands. Slips out means that he jumps out or runs away. He is very fast.*

- *The children are excited about Slim. How do you know they are excited?* (They yell.)

Text, Choral Reading
- *Let's read this page together.*

Page 21

Text
- *Slim ran everywhere in the classroom. Let's show how Slim ran.* (Demonstrate how Slim ran, and encourage children to imitate you. Use one hand as Slim and the other hand as the objects.)
  Slim ran under desks. (one hand under the other)
  Slim ran over feet. (one hand over the other)
  Slim ran around the trashcan. (one hand around the other)
  Slim ran right at me! (one hand toward your face.)

-
  > **Directionality**
  > Ask children to place their finger where you start reading (top left). Ask where you finish reading on this page (bottom right).

Page 22

Text

- *Mr. Roy tells David to catch Slim.* (Demonstrate catching something with your hand.)

- *Does David like lizards?* (no) *David tries to catch Slim. Everybody watches him. How do you think David feels?* (afraid; excited; not happy)

Page 23

Text

- *David whispers to Slim. Remember,* whisper *means "to speak very quietly." Let's whisper with David:* Here, Slim. I won't hurt you.

- *Why does David whisper?* (He doesn't want to scare Slim.)

- *David gets close to Slim.* (Use your hands to demonstrate: move one hand close to the other.)

- *Then he grabs, or catches, Slim.* (Use your hands to demonstrate: grab one hand with the other.)

"Catch him, David!" yells Mr. Roy.
I take a deep breath and drop to my knees.
All the kids stay very still. Everyone is watching me.

22

I feel Slim wiggle in my hands. I can tell that he's afraid.
"Don't worry, Slim," I say quietly. "We won't hurt you."
I put Slim back in the tank. He runs under a twig and then peeks out. He winks at me!
Mr. Roy says, "I think he likes you, David."
I think I like him, too.

24

"Here, Slim," I **whisper**. "I won't hurt you."
I move very slowly. I get closer and closer.
I look into Slim's bright eyes, and then—
I GRAB HIM!

23

At the end of the day, Mr. Roy stops me at the door. "Thanks for your help today, my friend," he says smiling.

Grandma and Linda are waiting for me after school.

"Wow!" I say. "I have a great new teacher. He's my friend. And guess what?"

"What?" asks Linda.

"I have another friend, too. His name is Slim. He's a lizard!"

25

Text

- *David holds Slim, and Slim wiggles. Let's wiggle with Slim.* (Demonstrate wiggling.) *Say it with me:* wiggle.

- *David puts Slim in the fish tank. Slim runs under a twig.* (Use your hands to demonstrate *under*.) *A twig is a very small branch from a tree.*

- *Slim winks at David! Let's wink together.* (Demonstrate winking.)

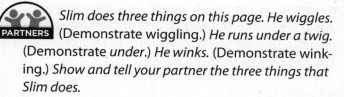 *Slim does three things on this page. He wiggles.* (Demonstrate wiggling.) *He runs under a twig.* (Demonstrate *under*.) *He winks.* (Demonstrate winking.) *Show and tell your partner the three things that Slim does.*

- *Does David like lizards now?* (yes)

Illustration

- *Point to David.*

- *Point Mr. Roy.*

- *Point to David's grandma.*

- *Point to Linda.*

Text

- *It is the end of the day. Mr. Roy thanks David. Linda and Grandma are waiting for David. He tells them about his new friends.*

- *David has two new friends. Who are they?* (Mr. Roy and Slim)

✓ *We learn about David's character in this story. We learn about things he likes. Let's remember some things that David likes.* (school, new friends, old friends, his teacher, lizards)

✓ *A story happens in a place. The place is called the setting. This story has two settings, or places. Let's remember the beginning of the story. What is the setting at the beginning?* (David's house) *What is the other setting in the story?* (David's school)

Field Trip to an Aquarium

Access Core Content

Teacher Note Pose the questions after you read the paragraph or page indicated.

Page 28

Text

- *This story tells us about a trip to an aquarium. Let's say it together:* aquarium. *An aquarium is like a museum about the ocean. At an aquarium, you can see ocean animals. They live in big tanks. You can see fish swim. You can be close to the animals.*

Photo and Caption

- *Do you see a big fish in the picture? Point to the fish. That fish is a shark. Let's say it together:* shark. *Sharks need lots of room to swim. They need big tanks.*

- *Sometimes we call a tank an aquarium. So, an aquarium can be two things. It is a place where you can see animals in tanks. It is also a tank. This shark lives in a big tank.*

Page 29

Paragraph 1

- *This paragraph tells us that an aquarium is like an ocean habitat. Say it with me:* habitat. *A habitat is the place an animal lives. It has food and everything else the animal needs.*

- *What kind of water is in the tank and in the ocean?* (salt water)

Paragraph 2

- *This paragraph tells us about sea animals in an aquarium.* Sea *is another word for* ocean. *Sea animals need three things. What are they?* (food, light, and air)

Caption

- *Let's read the caption together.*

- *The caption tells us two things about the sun and the ocean. The sun gives the ocean light. The sun warms the ocean.*

Pages 28–29

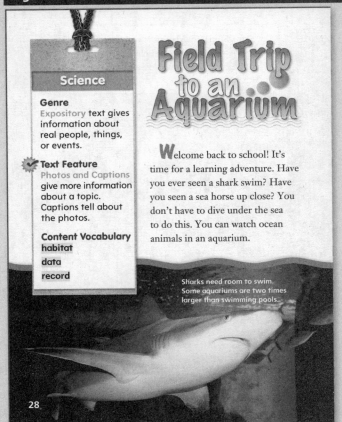

Science

Genre
Expository text gives information about real people, things, or events.

✔ **Text Feature**
Photos and Captions give more information about a topic. Captions tell about the photos.

Content Vocabulary
habitat
data
record

Field Trip to an Aquarium

Welcome back to school! It's time for a learning adventure. Have you ever seen a shark swim? Have you seen a sea horse up close? You don't have to dive under the sea to do this. You can watch ocean animals in an aquarium.

Sharks need room to swim. Some aquariums are two times larger than swimming pools.

28

Pages 30–31

Scientists study aquarium animals. They see how life in an aquarium changes. There may be changes in eating habits. Scientists ask questions. How do sea animals act in summer? Does this change in winter? Scientists gather **data**, or information. They **record** what they find.

Maybe one day your class will have an aquarium.

▲ Scientists study sea animals. Some scientists treat sick animals.

▼ These children do what scientists do. They take care of the aquarium and observe.

30

Science

An aquarium is a model of an ocean **habitat**. It has everything that ocean animals need to live and grow. In an aquarium, sea animals swim in big glass tanks filled with salt water. There are waves and caves.

Sea animals need food, light, and air. In an aquarium, workers feed the animals. Lamps light the tanks. Filters clean the water. Heaters warm it. Air bubbles flow into the tanks so the animals can breathe.

The sun warms the ocean and gives it light. In an aquarium, lamps light the water.

29

The tank may not be big, but it can be a model of an ocean habitat. You can study fish and plants that live under water. You can see an underwater world at work!

Coral look like rock, but they ▶ are tiny sea animals. Millions of them can form a reef.

 Connect and Compare

1. What is coral? Where did you find the information to answer the question?
   Photos and Captions

2. Think about the story *David's New Friends*. What might David and the class think about having an aquarium of fish in the room?
   Reading/Writing Across Texts

 Science Activity
Research two different kinds of coral. Make a chart listing how they are the same and how they are different.

LOG ON • FIND OUT Science Aquariums
www.macmillanmh.com

31

■ *Does the aquarium have light from the sun?* (no) *What gives the aquarium light?* (lamps) *What warms the aquarium?* (heaters)

Page 30

Top Photo and Caption

■ *This woman is a scientist. Let's say it together:* scientist. *She studies sea animals.*

■ *Let's read the caption together.*

Bottom Photo and Caption

■ *This girl is observing, or looking at, the aquarium. Let's read the caption together.*

🧑‍🤝‍🧑 PARTNERS *The girl can see many things in the aquarium. What can she see? Tell your partner.* (water, fish, lamp, heater, plants, sand)

Text

■ *This page tells us about scientists. They study aquarium animals. They watch the animals' habits—the things the animals do every day. Sometimes animals' habits change. They do different things in summer and in winter. Scientists watch aquarium animals to learn about these different things.*

Page 31

Photo and Caption

■ *Do these look like trees? They aren't trees. They are hard like rocks, but they aren't rocks. Let's read the caption together.*

■ *These are not trees and they are not rocks. What are they?* (tiny sea animals)

🧑‍🤝‍🧑 PARTNERS *In an aquarium, you can watch fish. You can study their habits. What do fish do? Tell your partner.* (swim, eat, sleep, fight, hide)

Name_____

Use the word chart to study this week's vocabulary words.
Write a sentence using each word in your writer's notebook.

Word	Context Sentence	Illustration
groan _____	Sam let out a <u>groan</u> when he spilled his milk.	
excited _____	I like school and am <u>excited</u> to be here.	**Describe how you feel when you are excited.**
whisper _____	I <u>whisper</u> a secret to my friend.	
carefully _____	I gave him the glass <u>carefully</u> so the juice would not spill.	**What do you do carefully?**
different _____	I am wearing two <u>different</u> shoes!	

© Macmillan/McGraw-Hill

Name _____

Read each question and prompt. Discuss the answers with your group. Use your Leveled Reader to find details to support your answers. Then write your answers on the blank lines or on another sheet of paper.

1. Describe the school in your book.

   _____

2. Tell about a class project in the story you read.

   _____

3. Explain how someone showed a special talent.

   _____

4. Talk about how friends help one another in your book.

   _____

5. What surprised you in the story you read?

   _____

6. Write one question about the book to ask your group.

   _____

   _____

Mr. Putter & Tabby Pour the Tea

Prior to reading the selection with children, they should have listened to the selection on **StudentWorks Plus**, the interactive eBook. In addition, selection vocabulary should have been pretaught using the **Visual Vocabulary Resources**.

Access Core Content

Teacher Note Pose the questions after you read the paragraph or page indicated.

Pages 38–39

Whole Spread

- *Let's read the title together:* Mr. Putter & Tabby Pour the Tea. *Let's pretend we are pouring tea.* (Demonstrate pouring, as if from a teapot.)

- *Now look at the title. This symbol means "and."* (Point to the ampersand in the title and write *& = and* on the board.)

- *Who do you think Mr. Putter and Tabby are?* (They are the characters in the story.)

- *Look at the illustration. I see a teapot on the stove. Let's point to the teapot. I see a set of dishes used for serving tea.*

- *Besides having a beginning, middle, and end, some stories have sections, or chapters. How many chapters are there in this story?* (three) *Let's read the names of the chapters together:* Mr. Putter, Tabby, Mr. Putter and Tabby.

Pages 38–39

Comprehension

Genre
Fiction is a story with made-up characters and events.

Story Structure
Plot
As you read, use your Story Map.

Beginning
↓
Middle
↓
End

Read to Find Out
What happens to Mr. Putter in the beginning, middle, and end of this story?

38

Pages 40–41

40

Page 40

Illustration

- *Look at the picture of Mr. Putter sitting in front of his house. How do you think he feels?* (He feels alone because he is sitting by himself; it looks like he is waiting for someone or something.)

Page 41

 Let's read this first page of Chapter 1 together: Before he got his fine cat, Tabby, Mr. Putter lived all alone. *Ask your partner some questions that this sentence makes you think of.* (How did Mr. Putter get his cat Tabby? What made him get a cat instead of any other pet? Why is Tabby called a "fine cat"?)

Request Assistance

Remind children of expressions they can use to request assistance from the teacher or their partners, such as *Can you repeat that, please? How do you say this?*

Chapter
1

Mr. Putter

Before he got his fine cat, Tabby, Mr. Putter lived all alone.

41

Mr. Putter & Tabby Pour the Tea

Page 42

Illustration

- *Point to Mr. Putter. Let's pretend we are Mr. Putter and show how he is feeling.* (Demonstrate drooping shoulders, sad face, big sigh.) *How is he feeling? Why?* (He is feeling sad because he is all alone.)

Pages 42–43

Text

- *Which words tell you that Mr. Putter is alone?* (no one to share his English muffins; no one to share his tea; no one to tell his stories to)

- *Look at the last sentence on page 43. Let's read it together:* And he had the most wonderful stories to tell.

- *Say* wonderful *again with me.* (Say the word with feeling to model reading with expression.) *Wonderful is another word for* great, *or* amazing.

-

> **Directionality**
>
> Ask children to place their finger where you start reading (top left). Ask where you finish reading on this page (bottom right).

In the mornings he had no one
to **share** his English muffins.
In the afternoons he had no one
to share his tea.

42

Pages 44–45

All day long as Mr. Putter
clipped his roses
and fed his tulips
and watered his trees,
Mr. Putter wished for
some **company**.

44

And in the evenings
there was no one
Mr. Putter could
tell his stories to.
And he had the
most **wonderful**
stories to tell.

43

Page 44

Text

- *What did Mr. Putter do in his garden all day?* (He cut his roses, fed his tulips, and watered his trees.)

- *Mr. Putter clipped his roses.* Clipped *is another word for* cut. (Write *clipped = cut* on the board. Use your fingers to demonstrate clipping something.)

Illustration

- *Mr. Putter fed his tulips. A tulip is a kind of flower. What do you think Mr. Putter fed his tulips?* (water, plant food) *Look at the picture. I see a bag of plant food. Point to it.*

Page 45

Illustration

- *Look at the table. What is on Mr. Putter's plate?* (an English muffin) *An English muffin is a kind of breakfast food. Like toast, you can put jam or butter on it. What do you think is in the jar on the table?* (jam for the muffin) *What do you think is in the pot?* (tea)

- *Why does Mr. Putter want a cat?* (A cat would keep him company.)

PARTNERS *Have you ever wished for some company? What kind of pet would you want to keep you company?* (Question is open.)

He had warm muffins to eat.
He had good tea to pour.
And he had wonderful stories to tell.
Mr. Putter was tired of living alone.
Mr. Putter wanted a cat.

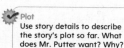
Plot
Use story details to describe the story's plot so far. What does Mr. Putter want? Why?

45

Page 46

Whole Page

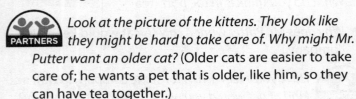

Now we are ready to begin reading Chapter 2. This is the middle chapter. Remember, a plot has a beginning, a middle, and an end. What might happen in the middle of this story? (Mr. Putter will meet Tabby the cat.)

- *How did Mr. Putter feel when the pet store lady told him she had 14 cats?* (delighted) Delighted *is another word for* happy. *Let's pretend to be delighted about something.* (Model looking delighted.)

- *How did Mr. Putter feel when he looked into the cage with all the kittens?* (not happy; not delighted) *Show me what that looks like.* (Children demonstrate with various facial expressions.)

Page 47

Whole Page

Look at the picture of the kittens. They look like they might be hard to take care of. Why might Mr. Putter want an older cat? (Older cats are easier to take care of; he wants a pet that is older, like him, so they can have tea together.)

- *The pet store lady says that cats are not peppy.* Peppy *is another word for* playful, *or* bouncy. *Let's pretend to be peppy.*

Formal and Informal English

When children encounter a word, such as *sir*, used in a formal setting in the text discuss other situations in which that word may be used.

Chapter

2

Tabby

Mr. Putter went to the pet store.
"Do you have any cats?" he asked the pet store lady.
"We have fourteen," she said.
Mr. Putter was **delighted.**
But when he looked into the cage, he was not.

46

Mr. Putter himself had not been cute and peppy for a very long time.
He said, "I want a cat."
"Then go to the shelter, sir," said the pet store lady.
"You are sure to find a cat."

48

"These are kittens," he said.
"I was hoping for a cat."
"Oh, no one wants cats, sir,"
said the pet store lady.
"They are not cute.
They are not peppy."

47

Mr. Putter went to the shelter.
"Have you any cats?"
he asked the shelter man.
"We have a fat gray one,
a thin black one,
and an old yellow one," said the man.
"Did you say old?" asked Mr. Putter.

49

Page 48

Whole Page

■ *Point to the word* shelter *on this page. A shelter is a place where homeless pets are taken care of until they can find new homes. What kinds of animals might you find at a shelter?* (dogs, cats, puppies, kittens, rabbits)

■ *When I say that I am "sure to" do something, like Mr. Putter is "sure to find a cat," what do you think that means? Why?* (The word *sure* means *certain*, so it means something will definitely happen.)

Page 49

Illustration

■ *Look at the way Mr. Putter is walking. His shoulders are slumped.* (Model what *slumped* means.) *How do you think Mr. Putter is feeling as he walks into the shelter?* (discouraged; worried that he won't find a new friend)

Text

■ *Let's read the last sentence together.* "Did you say old?" asked Mr. Putter. (Model an eager voice as you read the sentence.) *How do you think Mr. Putter is feeling now?* (He is feeling excited.)

■ *Which cat do you think Mr. Putter might adopt? Why?* (He will probably adopt the old yellow cat, because they are both old.)

Page 50

Text, Choral Reading

- *Let's read the lines on this page that describe the old cat:* Its bones creaked, its fur was thinning, and it seemed a little deaf. *Let's make creaking sounds together.* (Demonstrate a creaking noise using the word *creak*.) The word sounds just like the sound we are making. *What kinds of things creak?* (doors, floorboards, new shoes)

- *If someone's hair is thinning, it means he or she is losing hair or going bald. Why is the cat's hair thinning, or falling out?* (The cat is old.) *Why is Mr. Putter's hair thinning?* (He is getting old, too.)

Page 51

Text

- *On this page the last sentence lets us know that something new is about to begin. Let's read the last sentence together:* And that is how their life began. *This sentence tells us that we will now read about Mr. Putter and Tabby's life together.*

Tell your partner what you think Mr. Putter and Tabby might do together. (They might have English muffins and tea together. They might garden together.)

The shelter man brought Mr. Putter
the old yellow cat.
Its bones creaked,
its fur was **thinning**,
and it seemed a little deaf.
Mr. Putter creaked,
his hair was thinning,
and he was a little deaf, too.

50

Chapter
3
Mr. Putter and Tabby

In the mornings
Mr. Putter and Tabby liked to share
an English muffin.
Mr. Putter ate his with jam.
Tabby ate hers with cream cheese.

52

So he took the old yellow cat home.
He named her Tabby.
And that is how their life began.

51

In the afternoons
Mr. Putter and Tabby
liked to share tea.
Mr. Putter took his with sugar.
Tabby took hers with cream.

53

Pages 52–53

Text

- Mr. Putter and Tabby seem to be getting along well. How do we know this? (They are doing things together. They like to share English muffins and tea.)

Page 53

Illustration

- *Look at this picture. How can you tell Mr. Putter and Tabby are happy together?* (Mr. Putter is smiling. The cat is also smiling.)

Text

- *Look at the last two sentences. Let's read them together.* Mr. Putter took his with sugar. Tabby took hers with cream. *Another word for* took *in these sentences is* drank.

Page 54

Text

- *We have learned that when you say the word* creak, *it sounds just like the noise you are trying to describe. There is another word like this on this page. The word is* purr. *This is a sound that cats make when they are happy. Let's purr together.*

Page 55

Text

- *What does it mean to "warm their old bones in the sun"?* (They sat in the sunshine to get warm.) *Yes, when you warm your bones, you get near something very warm.*

- *Opera is a kind of play in which all of the characters sing instead of talk. Opera singers sing very loudly so that their voices can be heard. Show me what an opera singer might sound like.*

Illustration

- *Point to Mr. Putter and Tabby. What are they doing in this picture?* (singing along with the opera music)

And in the evenings
they sat by the window,
and Mr. Putter told stories.
He told the most wonderful stories.
Each story made Tabby purr.

54

Mr. Putter could not remember
life without Tabby.
Tabby could not remember
life without Mr. Putter.
They lived among their
tulips and trees.

56

On summer days they warmed their
old bones together in the sun.
On fall days they took
long walks through the trees.
And on winter days they turned
the opera up *very* loud.

55

They ate their muffins.

They poured their tea.

57

Page 56

Illustration

- *Point to Tabby in this picture. Where is she?* (on the roof, above Mr. Putter's head)

- *What is Mr. Putter carrying?* (a tray with a teapot on it)

- *Let's read what it says on the mailbox:* Putter & Tabby. *Remember that this symbol means "and."* (Point to the ampersand written on the board.)

Text, Choral Reading

- *Let's read the first two sentences together to find out how Mr. Putter and Tabby feel about each other:* <u>Mr. Putter could not remember life without Tabby.</u> <u>Tabby could not remember life without Mr. Putter.</u> *What does it mean that they "could not remember life without" each other?* (They are so happy together that it seems like they have always been together.)

Page 57

Illustration

- *Look at the illustration on page 57. What are Mr. Putter and Tabby sharing together?* (muffins and tea)

PARTNERS

Pretend you are sharing muffins and tea with your partner. Show how you would pour the tea. What would you say to each other as you share the muffins and tea? ("please" and "thank you")

Page 58

Text

■ *Let's make a list of all of the things that Tabby and Mr. Putter do together.* (eat breakfast, drink tea, garden, sing opera, share stories) *Do you think they are happy together?* (yes)

Illustration

■ *Point to the photo album in the bottom left corner. Photo albums are used to save and share happy memories. Why do you think this is here?* (The photo album shows pictures of Mr. Putter and Tabby enjoying their lives together.)

They turned up the opera, and **enjoyed** the most perfect company of all— each other.

Plot
Think about the story's plot. What does Mr. Putter do in each chapter of this story? Use illustrations and story details.

58

59

Illustration

- *Look at the picture. How does the story end?* (Mr. Putter and Tabby live happily together.)

Whole Story

Remember, a plot has a beginning, a middle, and an end. Tell me something that happened at the beginning of the story. (Mr. Putter was lonely. He was sad because he had no one to share his life with.) *Tell me something that happened in the middle of the story.* (He went to the shelter to find a cat.) *Tell me what happened at the end of the story.* (Mr. Putter and Tabby became good friends and were happy together.)

Cat Kisses

Access Core Content

Teacher Note Pose the questions after you read the poem on this page together with the class.

Pages 62–63

Illustration

■ *Today we are reading a poem about a cat in a little girl's life. Look at this picture and point to the little girl. What is the cat doing?* (licking her face)

Lines 1–4

■ *Let's read the first four lines together. Listen to the words. Some of the words sound the same; they rhyme. What are the rhyming words in these lines?* (chin and begin) *Read the lines again, and this time clap your hands when you hear the rhyming words.* (Model reading the lines and clapping your hands when the children read the rhyming words.)

Lines 5–6

■ *Now let's read the next two lines together:* Sandpaper kisses / a cuddle, a purr. *Have you ever had a cat lick your hand? How did it feel?* (The cat's tongue felt rough or scratchy.)

■ *We use sandpaper to scratch off paint from something. It is very rough. The poet is comparing a cat's tongue to sandpaper, so you can get an idea of how a cat's tongue feels.*

Pages 62–63

Poetry

Genre
A Rhyming Poem has lines that end with the same rhyming sounds.

Literary Elements
Rhythmic Patterns are sounds and words that repeat to give a song or poem a certain rhythm.

Words that Rhyme begin with different sounds but end with the same sound.

Rhyme, rhythm, and repetition help create images in poetry.

Cat Kisses

by Bobbi Katz

Sandpaper kisses
on a cheek or a chin
that is the way
for a day to begin!
Sandpaper kisses
a cuddle, a purr.
I have an alarm clock
that's covered with fur.

62

Poetry

Connect and Compare

1. What are some pairs of words that rhyme in this poem? **Rhyme**

2. Think about Mr. Putter and Tabby. Do you think the person in this poem feels the same way about her cat that Mr. Putter does about Tabby? Explain why or why not.
Reading/Writing Across Texts

LOG ON ▸ FIND OUT **Poetry**
www.macmillanmh.com

63

Lines 7–8

- *Let's read the last two lines together:* I have an alarm clock / that's covered with fur. *Can an alarm clock be covered with fur?* (no)

- *Who or what in this poem is covered with fur?* (the cat) *What do you see in your mind when you read this?* (The cat licks the girl's face to wake her up in the morning.) *So who is the alarm clock?* (The cat is the alarm clock because he wakes up the girl by licking her.)

- *Now let's read the last four lines aloud again. Clap when you hear the rhyming words:* Sandpaper kisses / a cuddle, a purr. / I have an alarm clock / that's covered with fur. *What are the rhyming words?* (*purr* and *fur*)

Name _____

Use the word chart to study this week's vocabulary words.
Write a sentence using each word in your writer's notebook.

Word	Context Sentence	Illustration
share _____	We can <u>share</u> the ice cream.	
enjoyed _____	We <u>enjoyed</u> the ice cream.	
wonderful _____	The ice cream tastes <u>wonderful</u>.	**What food tastes wonderful to you?**
thinning _____	The crowd is <u>thinning</u> out as people leave the game.	
delighted _____	I am <u>delighted</u> to see you!	
company _____	My cat keeps me <u>company</u> at night.	

© Macmillan/McGraw-Hill

Name_____

Read each question and prompt. Discuss the answers with your group. Use your Leveled Reader to find details to support your answers. Then write your answers on the blank lines or on another sheet of paper.

1. Describe some places where people can make a garden.

   _____

2. Tell what happens when people share the hard work of making a garden.

   _____

3. Give examples of things people must do to get a garden started.

   _____

4. List some of the plants that can grow in a garden.

   _____

5. Tell how people can learn more about gardens.

   _____

6. Write one question about the book to ask your group.

   _____

   _____

Family Farm: Then and Now

Prior to reading the selection with students, they should have listened to the selection on **StudentsWorks**, the interactive eBook. In addition, selection vocabulary should have been pretaught using the **Visual Vocabulary Resources**.

Access Core Content

Teacher Note Pose the questions after you read the paragraph or page indicated.

Page 70

Title

- *Let's read the title of this article together:* Family Farm Then and Now. *We are going to read about farms from a long time ago and about farms now. On a farm, people grow vegetables. Corn is a vegetable. Do you like corn?*

Tell your partner the names of three vegetables that you like.

Illustration

- *Look at this picture of a farm from long ago. The farmer is using animals to pull a plow. The plow digs up the ground. Point to the plow. Point to the animals.*

Text

- *Lets read the question under the title together:* How did farming begin in the United States?

- *The first farmers were Native Americans. They grew vegetables like corn and beans. They used irrigation. Say it with me:* irrigation. *That means they brought water from rivers to their farms.*

Page 71

Paragraph 1

- *New people came to North America. They were from Europe. (Show Europe and North America on a map.) The American Indians helped the new people.*

- *The Native Americans had a lot of knowledge about farming. Knowledge means they knew a lot. Say it with me:* knowledge. *They shared their knowledge with the Europeans. Then the Europeans could grow crops, too*

Real World Reading

Comprehension

Genre
Expository text gives information about real people, places, and events.

✓ **Summarize**
Main Idea and Details
The main idea is what an article is mostly about. Details and facts give more information about the main idea.

FAMILY FARM Then and Now

How did farming begin in the United States?

Thousands of years before people from Europe and Africa arrived in North America, Native Americans were successful farmers. They grew beans, corn, squash, and cotton. In the dry Southwest, Native Americans dug canals to bring water from rivers to their **crops**. Bringing water to crops is called irrigation.

Animals such as horses and oxen helped farmers plow the land and plant crops.

70

New Settlers

As more and more settlers arrived, they moved further west to get land of their own. They crossed the Mississippi River and kept going. The government helped them claim large pieces of land. They built houses, cleared the land, and began farming.

Farmland was passed down from family to family. Children whose parents were farmers usually grew up to become farmers. Family members did most of the work themselves. They earned money by selling their crops. They also sold milk and meat from the farm animals they raised.

Families worked together to farm the land and sell their crops.

72

When Europeans arrived, they learned about farming from the Native Americans. They learned to grow and **regrow** the crops they needed for food.

Native American and European farmers had very different ideas about owning land. Most Native American groups believed that the land belonged to everyone. Land was to be used by any family that was willing to work on it. The Europeans believed that one person or family should own the land. The owner could keep the land or sell it. This difference often caused trouble between the Native Americans and settlers.

Native Americans and new settlers share the land.

71

Machines help today's farmers clear fields, plant seeds, and harvest crops.

Today there are fewer family farms. The family farms that remain are bigger. Modern ways of farming make it easier to grow more crops. Electric pumps **irrigate** huge fields. **Machines** help farmers clear fields, plant seeds, and **harvest** crops.

Many farms today are owned by companies. The people who work on these farms are employees of the company.

Every year the number of family farms gets smaller. Children move away. Farmland is sold. Family farming may become a thing of the past, but it will always be an important part of American history.

Think and Compare

1. Who were the first successful farmers?

2. Why is farming land as important today as it was in the past?

3. What is the main idea of this selection?

4. Based on "A Nutty State" and "Family Farm," how have machines changed farming?

73

Paragraph 2

- *The Native Americans and Europeans had different ideas about land. The Native Americans believed that land belonged to everyone. Did the Europeans believe this, too?* (no) *The Europeans believed that people could own land.*

Illustration

- *Look at this illustration. This picture is from long ago.* (Point to Native Americans.) *These Native Americans have lived here for a very long time.* (Point to Europeans.) *These Europeans are new. They just arrived.*

Page 72

Paragraph 1

- *Many European settlers came to this country. What did they do with the land? Let's read the last sentence of this paragraph:* They settled down, built houses, cleared the land, and began farming.

- *Many families stayed on their land for many years. They did most of the work themselves. Children helped, too.*

Illustration

- *Look at this picture of a family working on their farm. When you clear the land, you cut down trees to make room for crops.* (Point to the stumps.) *Did this family clear the land?* (yes) *Did they build a house?* (yes) *What else did they build?* (a fence)

 With your partner, pretend you are clearing land, building a house, or planting seeds. Tell your classmates what you are doing.

Page 73

Photograph

- *Look at this big machine. It is called a tractor. Does this photo show a farm from long ago or from now?* (It's a farm from now.)

Text

- *Farms are different now. There are still family farms. They have machines to help do the work. Some farms belong to companies. They are businesses.*

 What is the same about all farmers, both long ago and now? (They grow crops to eat and to sell to other people.)

 Would you like to live on a farm with your family? Why or why not? Talk about it with your partner.

Use the word chart to study this week's vocabulary words.
Write a sentence using each word in your writer's notebook.

Word	Context Sentence	Illustration
harvest _____	The apples are red and ready to <u>harvest</u>.	
crops _____	Some farmers sell their <u>crops</u> at the market.	**What other crops might you find at the market?**
knowledge _____	My <u>knowledge</u> about dinosaurs comes from books.	
machines _____	Some families have these <u>machines</u> in the basement.	**What are these machines used for?**
irrigate _____	Pipes bring water to <u>irrigate</u> the field.	

© Macmillan/McGraw-Hill

Read each question and prompt. Discuss the answers with your group. Use your Leveled Reader to find details to support your answers. Then write your answers on the blank lines or on another sheet of paper.

1. List some ways to find out about families long ago.

_____

2. Tell how a family's life may change over time and from place to place.

_____

3. Explain why it is important to learn about family history.

_____

4. Give some examples of family traditions.

_____

5. How can you learn about your own family history? Share some ideas with your classmates.

_____

6. Write one question about the book to ask your group.

_____

Meet Rosina

Pages 82–83

Prior to reading the selection with children, they should have listened to the selection on **StudentWorks Plus**, the interactive eBook. In addition, selection vocabulary should have been pretaught using the **Visual Vocabulary Resources**.

Access Core Content

Teacher Note Pose the questions after you read the paragraph or page indicated.

Page 83

Title and Text

- *Let's read the title of the book together:* Meet Rosina. *Who is Rosina? Point to Rosina in the photograph.*

- *Tell what we have learned about sign language.* (Sign language is a way that people can talk to one another without speaking.)

- *In sign language, people talk to each other by showing words and letters with their hands and fingers. This is called signing. Point to Rosina again. What do you think she is doing?* (She is signing a word.)

Page 84

Whole Page

- *Let's look at the girl in these photographs. Do you remember who she is?* (The girl is Rosina.)

Photo 1 and Caption

- *Rosina is signing the word* Hi *in this photograph. Let's sign the word with her as we read the word together:* Hi! (Demonstrate signing the word.)

Photo 2 and Caption

- *Now Rosina is signing the word* I'm. *That means "I am." Let's sign the word with her as we read the word together:* I'm. (Demonstrate signing the word.)

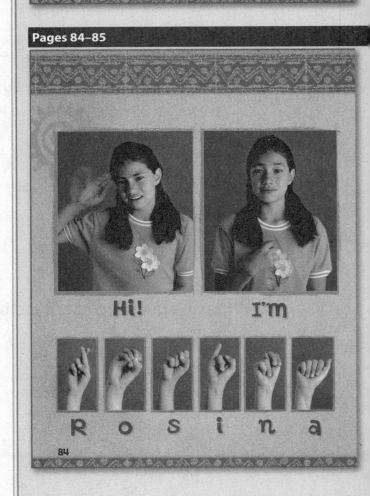

Pages 82–83

Comprehension

Genre
Expository A photo essay uses mostly photographs to give information about a topic.

Summarize
✓ Main Idea and Details As you read, use your Main Idea and Details Web.

Detail	Detail	Detail

Main Idea

Read to Find Out
Who is Rosina? Tell what details you find out about her.

82

Pages 84–85

Hi!   I'm

R o s i n a

84

Main Selection

Meet Rosina
by George Ancona

83

I am **deaf**, so I talk with my hands.

85

Photos 3–8 and Captions

■ *These photographs show Rosina's hand as she spells out a word with her fingers. Let's sign the letters with her as we read them: R, o, s, i, n, a. (Demonstrate signing each letter.) What do the letters R, o, s, i, n, a spell? (They spell Rosina.)*

Whole Page

■ *Let's sign with Rosina as we read this whole page together:* Hi! I'm R-o-s-i-n-a. *(Demonstrate signing.) Now let's read the page without signing:* Hi! I'm Rosina.

Page 85

Whole Page

■ *Point to Rosina in this photograph. Read Rosina's words with me:* I am deaf, so I talk with my hands. *Who remembers what it means to be deaf? (Someone who is deaf cannot hear.) Yes, a person who is deaf cannot hear. What is the name of the special language that deaf people use to show words and letters with their hands and fingers? (The language is called sign language.)*

Today we will read about Rosina. Rosina will tell us in her own words what her life is like. What do you think life is like for a person who cannot hear? Tell your partner what you think. (Question is open.)

Seek Clarification

Some children may be confused by unfamiliar words. Encourage children to always seek clarification when they encounter a word or phrase that does not make sense to them.

Meet Rosina

Page 86

Paragraph 1

- *What is special about Rosina's school?* (It is a school for children who are deaf.)

Paragraph 2

One important idea, or main idea, is that Rosina's school is a lot like our own school. What do Rosina and the other children do that we also do? (They study math, writing, reading, and art. They play sports.)

Page 87

Text

- *Recess is the time that we spend away from class in the middle of the day. Children can play games outside during recess. Say* recess *with me:* recess. *What do you like to do during recess?* (Question is open.)

- *When you play basketball you dribble the ball and shoot it up through a hoop.* (Demonstrate dribbling and shooting an imaginary basketball.) *Have you ever played basketball? Show me and tell me what you did.*

Photo

- *Can you find Rosina in this photograph? Point to Rosina. Now point to Rosina's brother. Who else do you see in the picture?* (A girl who is a school friend is in the picture.)

Page 88

Paragraph 1

- *Rosina is deaf. She cannot hear. Who else is deaf?* (Rosina's mom and aunt are deaf, too.)

-

Directionality

Ask children to place their finger where you start reading (top left). Ask where you finish reading on this page (bottom right).

I go to the New Mexico School for the Deaf. All of our teachers teach with American Sign Language. We call this **signing**.

We study math, writing, reading, and art. We also play sports. It's the same as in other schools.

✓ Main Idea and Details
Use facts and details from the selection to describe Rosina's school.

86

My mom and aunt are deaf, too. They work at the school. Mom is a teacher's helper.

Mom came from Mexico when she was little. She had to learn American Sign Language so that she could learn English. That's because each country has its own way of signing.

88

My brother Emilio also goes to my school. After lunch, we play basketball during recess.

87

Aunt Carla's job is to help students and teachers learn about different **cultures**. She also takes care of the school museum.

In the museum there are pictures of our **relatives** who went to the school. Aunt Carla often tells me fun stories about when my parents were younger. She told me that my parents met each other at a high school dance.

89

Paragraph 2

- *This paragraph tells about Rosina's mother. Rosina's mother came to America when she was young. She learned American Sign Language so she could speak English. American Sign Language is the sign language used in the United States. American Sign Language is different from other sign languages.*

Photo

- *Point to Rosina's mother in the photograph. Where is she?* (She is at school.) *Why is she at school?* (She is a teacher's helper.)

Page 89

Photo

- *This picture shows Rosina and Aunt Carla. Point to Rosina. Point to Aunt Carla. Show me what they are doing with their hands. What are they doing?* (They are using sign language to talk to each other.)

Paragraph 1

- *Aunt Carla helps children and teachers learn how other people live. She helps children and teachers learn about different cultures. Say* cultures *with me:* cultures.

- *Now say the word* museum *with me:* museum. *A museum is a place where important things are kept and put out for people to look at. What does Aunt Carla do at the school museum?* (Aunt Carla takes care of the school museum.)

Paragraph 2

- *Relatives are people who are members of the same family. Whose relatives are in the pictures at the school museum?* (Rosina's relatives are in the pictures.) *Who are some of your own relatives?* (Question is open.)

 Aunt Carla tells stories about Rosina's parents. Rosina thinks the stories are fun to hear. What fun stories do you enjoy hearing about your own relatives? Tell your partner some of those stories. (Question is open.)

Page 90

Text

- *A librarian is a person who works in a library. Say the word with me:* librarian. *The librarian in Rosina's school is named Hedy.*

- *Do we have a librarian in our school library? Who is our librarian?* (Help children recall and pronounce the name of your school librarian or librarians.)

Photo

- *Hedy the librarian tells stories by signing them for the children. Point to Hedy signing a story. Now can you find Rosina in the picture? Point to Rosina.*

Page 91

Whole Page

- *Show me how you look when you feel sad.* (Demonstrate a sad expression.) *Show me how you look when you feel scared.* (Demonstrate a scared expression.) *Show me how you look when you are worried.* (Demonstrate a worried expression.) *Now show me how you look when you are happy.* (Demonstrate a happy expression.) *The children feel all these things when Hedy tells stories. Hedy makes the children feel as if they are in the stories.*

Page 92

Text

- *Let's read this page together:* I love going to art class. I like to paint using watercolors. Here I am painting a picture of myself!

- *Watercolors are paints that are mixed with water. Say the word with me:* watercolors.

Photo

Look at the photograph of Rosina. Rosina is using watercolors to paint a picture of herself. What have you painted with watercolors? (Question is open.)

Pages 90–91

Sometimes we go to the school library. Our librarian, Hedy, signs stories from the books in the library.

90

Pages 92–93

I love going to art class. I like to paint using watercolors. Here I am painting a picture of myself!

92

Hedy is very good at telling stories. She makes us feel as if we're in the story. The story can make us feel sad, scared, worried, or happy.

91

When we were in second grade, our class made up a story. It was about a deaf dad who woke up one day with four arms. We wrote it and did all the drawings. Then we made it into a book called *Too Many Hands*.

Our book was published! Today we had a book signing. We wrote our names in the books that people bought.

93

Page 93

Paragraph 1

- *In second grade, Rosina's class made up a story. What was the story about?* (The story was about a deaf dad.) *How many arms did the deaf dad have?* (The deaf dad had four arms.) *What was the name of the book?* (The name of the book was *Too Many Hands*.)

 Why might it be good for a deaf dad to have four arms? Think about what a deaf dad could do with all those arms. (It would be good for a deaf dad to have four arms because he could sign words and do other things at the same time.)

Paragraph 2

- *When a book is published, it is printed. Copies are made to sell to people.*

- *The word* signing *can mean "using your hands and fingers to show words and letters." But the word also has another meaning. What did the children do at their book signing?* (They wrote their names in books that people bought.) *The word* signing *can also mean "writing your name."*

Photos

- *The big picture shows the children at their book signing.* (Point to the main photograph.) *The little photograph shows the cover of their book.* (Point to the inset photograph.) *Let's read aloud the name of the book, or the title of the book:* Too Many Hands.

 When you summarize, you retell the important parts of a selection in your own words. Let's look at the pictures in the story again. (Page back through the photographs with children.) *Let's summarize what we have learned about Rosina so far.* (Rosina is deaf. She uses sign language. She goes to a special school for deaf children. Her mother and aunt are deaf, too. They work at the school. Rosina's class published a book called *Too Many Hands*.)

Page 94

Text

- *In rugby, players try to tag the person on the other team who is carrying the ball. Turn to a classmate and gently tag that person.* (Demonstrate the action.) *How do you score in rugby?* (You score by taking the ball across the goal line.)

Photo

- *What is Rosina doing in this photograph?* (Rosina is playing rugby. She is tagging a player.)

Page 95

Paragraph 1

- *A trophy is something given to a winning sports team. A trophy may look like a cup, or it may have a small statue of a player on it. Have you ever seen or won a trophy? What did it look like?* (Question is open.)

Top Photo

- *This photograph shows Rosina's rugby team after wining their big trophy. Look at the players. How do you think they feel?* (The players feel happy and excited.)

Paragraph 2

- *Let's read this paragraph together:* Then we wanted to celebrate. We splashed our coach with cold water. Some of us got wet, too. We were just joking, so no one got mad.

Bottom Photo

- *Look at the bottom photograph. The players are splashing water on their coach. A coach is someone who leads a team and helps the players win. Point to the coach in the photograph.*

Page 96

Whole Page

- *Rosina's mom likes to fix her hair. What do you think that means?* Fix *can mean "to repair something or put it back together when it's broken." But to fix someone's hair means to brush and style someone's hair.*

- *A bun can be something to eat, like a hot dog bun. A bun can also be a knot of hair. Look at the photograph. What kind of a bun is Rosina's mother making?* (Rosina's mother is putting Rosina's hair in a knot called a bun.)

Pages 94–95

I like sports. This year I am playing rugby. The way we play is to tag the person carrying the ball. Then he or she throws it to another player on the team. By running fast we can get away and cross the goal line.

94

Pages 96–97

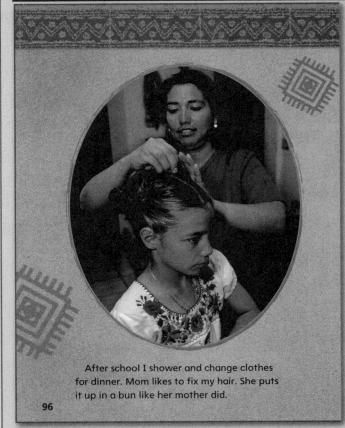

After school I shower and change clothes for dinner. Mom likes to fix my hair. She puts it up in a bun like her mother did.

96

Our team played other schools at the end of the year. We beat all the other teams and won a big trophy.

Then we wanted to **celebrate**. We splashed our coach with cold water. Some of us got wet, too. We were just joking, so no one got mad.

95

At home we all help Mom cook Mexican meals. While I chop the lettuce, Emilio cuts up cheese. Dad makes the guacamole. Then I fry the tacos.

97

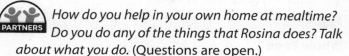

Page 97

Text

- *What kind of meals does Rosina eat at home?* (Rosina eats Mexican meals.)

- *Let's say the words* guacamole *and* tacos: guacamole, tacos. *Guacamole is mashed avocados. Guacamole can be used as a dip, in salads, and in tacos. Who likes guacamole? Why do you like it? Who has eaten tacos? What do you put in your tacos?* (Questions are open.)

Photos

- *Imagine that you are Rosina. You are helping your family make a meal. Show me how you would chop the lettuce. Chop, chop, chop!* (Demonstrate the action.) *Now pretend that you are frying the tacos in a pan. Sizzle, sizzle, sizzle! !* (Demonstrate the action.) *Don't forget to flip the tacos!*

PARTNERS *How do you help in your own home at mealtime? Do you do any of the things that Rosina does? Talk about what you do.* (Questions are open.)

Patterns in Language

Some grammatical structures, such as the ending –s in the present tense, pose difficulties to ELLs. Point out that there are several examples of words ending in -s in this selection, such as *likes, puts, cuts, makes.* Help children find a pattern.

Page 98

Text

- *Rosina plays chess with her dad. Chess is a game that is played on a board. Each player tries to capture the other player's game pieces. It can be a hard game to play, and it takes thought and skill. Rosina knows how to play chess. What does that tell you about Rosina?* (Rosina is a smart girl.)

Photo

- *Point to the chessboard in the photograph.*

Whole Page

- *An important idea, or main idea, is that Rosina does a lot of things during her day. Look back at the photographs from the story. What things would you enjoy doing, too? Point to the photographs and tell me.* (Question is open.)

Page 99

Whole Page

- *Let's read this page together and point to the people in the photograph as we read:* Mom, Dad, Emilio, and me. (Point to each person as you name him or her.) That's my family—but there are many more, too.

- *Think about what you know about families. Who do you think Rosina is talking about when she says "but there are many more, too"?* (Her family might include grandmothers, grandfathers, aunts, uncles, and cousins.)

Page 100

Photo

- *Look at all the people in Rosina's family! Does Rosina have a big family or a small family?* (Rosina has a big family.)

Paragraph 1

- *If members of Rosina's family came to New Mexico 500 years ago, they would have arrived in the early 1500s. That's a long time ago!* (Demonstrate by subtracting 500 from the current year to give the approximate year in which family members arrived in New Mexico.)

Pages 98–99

After dinner, Dad and I play a game of chess. Emilio roots for me. He's hoping that I win, but Dad wins anyway.

Main Idea and Details
Think about Rosina's day. What are three details you find interesting? Why?

98

Pages 100–101

We are a big family. I have lots of uncles, aunts, cousins, grandpas, and grandmas. My father's family was among the first Spanish people that came to New Mexico. That was 500 years ago.

Most of my mom's family is deaf. My whole family uses sign language to talk to each other.

100

Mom, Dad, Emilio, and me. That's my family—but there are many more, too.

99

This is how we sign "goodbye."

101

- *Retell in your own words what makes Rosina's father's family special.* (People in the family were some of the first Spanish people to live in New Mexico. They came to New Mexico many, many years ago.)

Paragraph 2
- *Why does the whole family use sign language?* (Most people in Rosina's mom's family are deaf.)

Page 101
Text
- *Let's read this last sentence together:* This is how we sign "goodbye."

Photo
- *Now it's time to say goodbye to Rosina. Hold your hand like Rosina is holding her hand. Let's sign goodbye as we say the word together:* Goodbye!

 What would you say to Rosina if you met her in real life? Tell your partner what you would say. (Question is open.)

Whole Selection

 One of the most important ideas in this selection is that Rosina is like other kids in many ways. Summarize what Rosina does that is just like other kids. (Rosina goes to school. She likes art class. She plays sports. She helps at home. She likes being with her family.)

You—Tú

Access Core Content

Page 104

Title

- *Now we are going to read a rhyming poem. Point to the title of the poem. Let's read the title together:* You–Tú.

- *The word* tú *is a Spanish word for* you. *The words* you *and* tú *rhyme. Words that rhyme begin with different sounds but end with the same sound. Let's read the title together again and listen for the rhyme:* You–Tú.

Illustration

- *Point to the boy looking at himself in the mirror. The boy is talking to his reflection. A reflection is what you see in a mirror. Point to what the boy says as I read his words aloud:* Who are you? *Now say the words with me:* Who are you?

 Imagine looking in a mirror and asking Who are you? *What answer would you give? Tell your partner what your answer would be.* (Question is open.)

Page 105

Whole Page

- *This poem is written in English and Spanish. Point to the English words. Now point to the Spanish words.*

English Version, Lines 1–3

- *I will read aloud the first three lines in English. Follow the words as I read them:* You are you. / Not me, / But you. *Now let's read the first three lines together:* You are you. / Not me, / But you.

English Version, Lines 4–8

- *Now listen as I read the rest of the poem in English. Follow along in the poem as I read:* Look in the mirror / Peek-a-boo / The face that you see / Isn't me— / It's you.

Poetry

You are you.	Tú eres tú.
Not me,	No yo,
But you.	Pero tú.
Look in the mirror	Mira al espejo
Peek-a-boo	Peek-a-boo
The face that you see	La cara que miras
Isn't me—	No soy yo—
It's you.	Eres tú.

✔ Connect and Compare

1. Where are the rhyming words in this poem? **Rhyme**
2. Think about the poem and *Meet Rosina*. How do you think Rosina would feel about this poem? Explain why. **Reading/Writing Across Texts**

LOG ON ▶ FIND OUT **Poetry** Rhyming Poems
www.macmillanmh.com

105

- *Have you ever played peek-a-boo with a baby? Show me how to play peek-a-boo.* (Demonstrate the actions by covering your face with your hands, uncovering your face suddenly, and saying "Peek-a-boo!") *Imagine looking in a mirror. What happens? Your face shows up all at once just like when you play peek-a-boo!*

English Version, Whole Poem

- *Now let's read the whole poem together:* You are you. / Not me, / But you. / Look in the mirror / Peek-a-boo / The face that you see / Isn't me— / It's you.

Spanish Version, Whole Poem

- *The Spanish words have the same meaning as the English words. We know that tú is Spanish for you. Do you see any other words that you recognize in the Spanish version of the poem?* (The word *peek-a-boo* is also in the Spanish poem.) *Yes. The word* peek-a-boo *is the same in both languages.*

Teacher Note If you have Spanish-speaking children in the group, have them read aloud the poem to the other children.

Read aloud the English version of the poem to your partner. Then have your partner read aloud the poem to you. Talk about what makes each of you special.

**Use the word chart to study this week's vocabulary words.
Write a sentence using each word in your writer's notebook.**

Word	Context Sentence	Illustration
cultures _____	These people come from many cultures.	**What culture do you come from?**
deaf _____	She cannot hear because she is deaf.	
signing _____	She is signing the words "I love you."	
relatives _____	My aunt and other relatives came for dinner.	
celebrate _____	They came to celebrate my birthday.	**How do you celebrate a special time?**

Name _____

Read each question and prompt. Discuss the answers with your group. Use your Leveled Reader to find details to support your answers. Then write your answers on the blank lines or on another sheet of paper.

1. Explain what a hero does.

   _____

2. Tell how Jane Addams helped poor immigrant families.

   _____

3. List some ways Martin Luther King, Jr. fought to change laws he knew were wrong.

   _____

4. Describe how César Chávez worked to help migrant workers.

   _____

5. Tell how an ordinary person can become a hero.

   _____

6. Write one question about the book to ask your group.

   _____

   _____

My Name Is Yoon

Pages 112–113

Prior to reading the selection with children, they should have listened to the selection on **StudentWorks Plus**, the interactive eBook. In addition, selection vocabulary should have been pretaught using the **Visual Vocabulary Resources**.

Access Core Content

Teacher Note Pose the questions after you read the paragraph or page indicated.

Page 113

Title and Illustration

- *Let's read the title of the story together:* My Name Is Yoon. *Now point to the girl in the picture. The girl's name is Yoon. Yoon is from a country called Korea. Say the girl's name with me:* Yoon.

- *In the vocabulary story, we read about a boy who moved to America from the country of Argentina. The boy could hardly wait to get to America. But when he got to America, he found that things were different from his home in Argentina. Now we are going to read what happens when Yoon moves to America from Korea.*

 What things can be different in different countries? (Language, school, food, and people might all be different.)

Page 114

Paragraph 1

- *Yoon is telling this story about herself. We can tell this because Yoon uses the word* I. *Yoon says she came from Korea. Korea is a long way from the United States.*

Paragraph 2

- *Point to the word* settled. *When you settle, you move in and unpack. The word* settled *ends with the letters* -ed. *Words that end in* -ed *tell about things that happened in the past. What happened in the past?* (Yoon and her family moved in and unpacked.)

Pages 112–113

Comprehension

Genre
Fiction is a story with made-up characters and events.

Summarize
Make and Confirm Predictions
As you read, use your Predictions Chart.

What I Predict	What Happens

Read to Find Out
How does Yoon feel about her new class?

112

Pages 114–115

My name is Yoon. I came here from Korea, a country far away.

It was not long after we **settled** in that my father called me to his side.

"Soon you will go to your new school. You must learn to print your name in English," he said. "Here. This is how it looks."

YOON

I **wrinkled** my nose. I did not like YOON. Lines. Circles. Each standing alone.

"My name looks happy in Korean," I said. "The symbols dance together.

114

My Name Is Yoon

by HELEN RECORVITS

illustrated by GABI SWIATKOWSKA

Main Selection

113

115

■ *The story says that Yoon's father called her to his side. When you call someone to your side, you ask him or her to come over to you.*

Paragraph 3

■ *Let's trace the letters in Yoon's name as we read them together: Y, O, O, N, YOON.*

Paragraph 4

■ *Yoon wrinkled her nose because she did not like her name in English. Pretend you are Yoon, and wrinkle your nose. (Model wrinkling your nose.)*

■ *Which letters in Yoon's name have lines?* (The letters *Y* and *N* have lines.) *Which letters are circles?* (The two *O*s are circles.)

Paragraph 5

■ *Point to Yoon's name as it is written in Korean. People from Korea have a different way of writing. They do not use the same alphabet, or letters, we use in English.*

■ *Trace over Yoon's name written in Korean. Each part of the name is called a symbol.*

■ *Yoon thinks her name looks happy in Korean. She thinks the symbols dance together. Do you think the name looks happy? Do you think the symbols dance together? Tell why. (Questions are open.)*

Page 115

Illustration

When you summarize, you retell the important parts of a story in your own words. Say summarize *with me: summarize. Now use this picture to summarize the beginning of the story.* (Yoon came to America from Korea. She will go to a new school soon. Her father shows her how to print her name in English.

■

Directionality

Ask children to place their finger where you start reading (top left). Ask where you finish reading on this page (bottom right).

Page 116

Paragraph 2

- *Yoon's name means "Shining Wisdom." If you have wisdom, you know a lot and you have good sense. The word* shining *can mean "very good" or "outstanding." So Yoon's name means "outstanding wisdom." It is a name she likes a lot.*

Paragraph 3

- *Why doesn't Yoon like America?* (Everything is different. America is not like Korea.)

- *When Yoon's father handed her the pencil, his eyes said "Do-as-I-say." Show me what a "Do-as-I-say" look might be like.* (Demonstrate the expression.) *What does Yoon's father want her to do?* (He wants Yoon to print the letters of the English alphabet.)

- *Yoon practiced writing the letters, as her father told her to do. What does it mean to practice something?* (When you practice something, you do it many times in order to be good at it.)

Paragraph 6

- *Yoon wrinkled her nose when she first saw her name spelled in English, because she did not like it. Now she wrinkles her nose again. What doesn't she like now?* (Yoon doesn't like the idea of being a student in an American school.)

Page 117

Illustration

- *Point to Yoon in the picture. Point to Yoon's mother. Now point to Yoon's father. What is Yoon doing?* (Yoon is practicing writing letters in the English alphabet.)

 Yoon's name means "Shining Wisdom." Does your name have a meaning? Tell your partner what your name means. If you don't know what your name means, tell your partner what you would like for it to mean. (Question is open.)

"And in Korean my name means Shining Wisdom. I like the Korean way better."

"Well, you must learn to write it this way. Remember, even when you write in English, it still means Shining Wisdom."

I did not want to learn the new way. I wanted to go back home to Korea. I did not like America. Everything was different here. But my father handed me a pencil, and his eyes said Do-as-I-say. He showed me how to print every letter in the English alphabet. So I **practiced**, and my father was very pleased.

"Look," he called to my mother. "See how well our little Yoon does!"

"Yes," she said. "She will be a wonderful student!"s

I wrinkled my nose.

116

My first day at school I sat quietly at my desk while the teacher talked about CAT. She wrote CAT on the chalkboard. She read a story about CAT. I did not know what her words meant, but I knew what the pictures said. She sang a song about CAT. It was a pretty song, and I tried to sing the words, too.

Later she gave me a paper with my name on it.

"Name. Yoon," she said. And she pointed to the empty lines underneath.

I did not want to write YOON. I wrote CAT instead. I wrote CAT on every line.

118

Page 118

Paragraph 1

- *How can you tell that Yoon does not know a lot of English?* (She did not know what the words of the story meant.)

Paragraph 3

- *The paper has Yoon's name printed on it. Under the name are empty lines. What does the teacher want Yoon to write on the empty lines?* (She wants Yoon to write her name.)

Paragraph 4

- *Why does Yoon write CAT on every line of the paper instead of her own name?* (Yoon does not like her name spelled in English letters.)

Page 119

Illustration

- *Let's look at the picture now. Point to the word CAT on the chalkboard in the picture. Let's say the letters and the word together:* C, A, T, CAT.

- *Look at the cats on the chalkboard. The cats aren't really in the classroom. The artist drew the cats to show what Yoon thinks about when she hears the word cat.*

- *Which cat in the picture do you like best? Why do you like that cat?* (Questions are open.)

Analyze Sayings and Expressions

Help children recognize that *his eyes said Do-as-I-say* is a saying that means that the person wants you to do something. Help them create other examples using this expression.

Pages 120–121

Text

- *When you cuddle up with someone, you get very close to that person. Cuddling up makes you feel good. It makes you safe and warm. Now pretend you are a little cat cuddling up next to your mother. Close your eyes and mew quietly.*

- *Why do you think Yoon wants to be a cat hiding in a corner and cuddling up with her mother?* (Yoon is unhappy and scared. She doesn't want to be at the new school.)

Illustration

- *Look at the picture of Yoon. She has ears just like a cat in this picture. Did Yoon turn into a cat? Why does she have cat ears in this picture?* (Yoon didn't really turn into a cat. The picture shows what Yoon wants to be. Yoon wants to be a cat hiding and then cuddling with her mother.)

- *Point to the words that Yoon writes. Let's read them together:* CAT, CAT, CAT.

Page 122

Paragraph 1

- *What did Yoon write on her paper?* (Yoon wrote *CAT.*) *Yoon's teacher knows that Yoon's name is not Cat. So she shakes her head and frowns. She wants Yoon to write her real name, so she asks, "So you are CAT?"*

Paragraph 2

- *A ponytail is long hair that is tied at the back of the head. A ponytail can look like the tail of a pony, or a small horse.*

- *"The ponytail girl" means "the girl with a ponytail." The girl with a ponytail thinks what the teacher says is funny, so she giggles. Pretend you are the ponytail girl. Giggle like you think something is funny.* (Model giggling.)

Pages 120–121

120

Pages 122–123

The teacher looked at my paper. She shook her head and frowned. "So you are CAT?" she asked.

The ponytail girl sitting behind me giggled.

After school I said to my father, "We should go back to Korea. It is better there."

"Do not talk like that," he said. "America is your home now."

 Make and Confirm Predictions
Do you predict that Yoon will make a friend in her new school? Use pictures or other details from the story to help make predictions.

122

I wanted to be CAT. I wanted to hide in a corner. My mother would find me and **cuddle** up close to me. I would close my eyes and mew quietly.

CAT CAT CAT

121

Page 122

Paragraph 4

- *After school, Yoon tells her father that they should go back to Korea. Why does Yoon want to go back to Korea?* (Yoon thinks it is better in Korea. Yoon is unhappy at her new school.)

 Yoon might be happier at her new school if she had a friend there. Who could be Yoon's friend at school? (One of the children at Yoon's new school might become her friend. The girl with the ponytail might become her friend.)

Page 123

Illustration

 Look at the picture of the teacher talking to Yoon. Do you think the teacher is angry because Yoon wrote CAT on her paper? Tell your partner what you think and tell why you think that. (The teacher probably isn't angry. She is smiling at Yoon.)

Monitor Oral Production

Remember to model self-corrective techniques on a regular basis as you speak to children. Pretend to mispronounce words and self-correct.

Page 124

Paragraph 1

- *A robin is a kind of bird. The little robin Yoon sees is hopping in the yard. Let's hop around the classroom together.*

- *Let's read what Yoon thinks about the robin. Read the words in the quotation marks with me:* "He is all alone, too. He has no friends. No one likes him."

- *Is it true that the robin and Yoon are all alone? Is it true that no one likes them? Tell me why.* (It is not true. Birds fly with other birds, and many people like birds a lot. Yoon has parents, a teacher, and classmates around her. Yoon's parents like her, and so does her teacher.)

Paragraph 4

- *What does Yoon's father say about Yoon's bird drawing? Let's read his words together:* Oh, this makes me happy.

- *What word does Yoon write under her drawing?* (Yoon prints the word *BIRD* under her drawing.)

Paragraph 5

- *Yoon is back in school. What word does Yoon print on her paper now instead of her name?* (Yoon prints *BIRD* instead of her name.) *Why do you think Yoon prints* BIRD? (Yoon likes the bird she saw. Yoon's father liked the bird she drew. Yoon wants to be like a bird.)

Page 125

Illustration

- *Look at the bird that Yoon drew. Point to the bird's head in the drawing. Point to the bird's tail. Point to the bird's legs. Let's all draw birds like the one Yoon drew.*

Page 126

Paragraph 1

- *Where would Yoon fly if she were a bird?* (She would fly back to Korea.) *Why do you think she would fly back to Korea?* (Yoon was happy in Korea.)

Pages 124–125

I sat by the window and watched a little robin hop, hop in the yard. "He is all alone, too," I thought. "He has no friends. No one likes him."

Then I had a very good idea. "If I draw a picture for the teacher, then maybe she will like me."

It was the best bird I had ever drawn. "Look, Father," I said proudly.

"Oh, this makes me happy," he said. "Now do this." And he showed me how to print BIRD under the picture.

The next day at school the teacher handed me another YOON paper to print. But I did not want to print YOON. I wrote BIRD instead. I wrote BIRD on every line.

124

Pages 126–127

I wanted to be BIRD. I wanted to fly, fly back to Korea. I would fly to my nest, and I would tuck my head under my little brown wing.

The teacher looked at my paper. Again she shook her head. "So you are BIRD?" she asked.

Then I showed her my special robin drawing. I patted my red dress, and then I patted the red robin. I lowered my head and peeked up at her. The teacher smiled.

126

125

127

Paragraph 2

- *What does the teacher ask Yoon when she sees that Yoon has printed BIRD on her paper? Let's read the teacher's word together: "So you are BIRD?"*

Paragraph 3

- *Yoon pats her dress and then the robin to show the teacher that she is like the bird. Show me how you pat something. (Demonstrate the action.) Then Yoon lowers her head and peeks up at the teacher. Pretend that you are Yoon. Lower your head and peek up at me. (Demonstrate the actions.)*

- *The teacher smiles at Yoon again. This tells us that the teacher really does like Yoon.*

Page 127

Illustration

- *Look at Yoon in this picture. What do you think she is doing? (She is pretending she is flying like a bird.) Pretend that you are a bird.*

- *Show me how you would fly. (Demonstrate the action.) Now show me how you would sit in your nest and tuck your head under your little wing. (Demonstrate the action.)*

PARTNERS *Where would you fly if you could fly anywhere like a bird? Tell you partner why you would fly there. What do you think you would see? (Questions are open.)*

Page 128

Paragraphs 1–4

- *Where is Yoon now? How do you know?* (Yoon is back home again. She is talking with her mother.)

Paragraph 5

- (Point to the word *patient*.) *When you are patient, you are good at waiting for something to happen.*

What do Yoon and her mother say to each other? Use your own words to tell me the most important things they say. (Yoon says that she thinks her teacher likes her, but at her old school she was the teacher's favorite and had many friends. Yoon's mother tells her she must be patient. She says Yoon will be a good student and will make friends.)

Page 129

Illustration

- *Look at the picture of Yoon and her mother. Point to Yoon. Now point to Yoon's mother.*

 Pretend that you are Yoon and her mother. Act out what they are saying and doing.

Page 130

Paragraph 1

- *Do you remember the ponytail girl? What did the ponytail girl do in class when Yoon wrote* CAT *on her paper?* (The girl giggled.) *What does the ponytail girl do now?* (The girl runs over to Yoon. The girl gives Yoon a cupcake. The girl giggles again.)

- *A cupcake is a small cake. Point to the word* cupcake *in the story. Let's read the word together:* CUPCAKE.

- *What does Yoon do when the ponytail girl gives her a cupcake and then giggles?* (Yoon giggles, too.) *Why do you think Yoon giggles?* (Yoon is happy. She likes the girl.)

Paragraph 2

- *Now what does Yoon write on her paper instead of her name?* (Yoon writes *CUPCAKE* instead of her name.)

Pages 128–129

"How was school today, my daughter?" my mother asked.

"I think the teacher likes me a little," I said.

"Well, that is good!" my mother said.

"Yes, but at my school in Korea, I was my teacher's **favorite**. I had many friends. Here I am all alone."

"You must be **patient** with everyone, including yourself," my mother said. "You will be a fine student, and you will make many new friends here."

128

Pages 130–131

The next day at recess, I stood near the fence by myself. I watched the ponytail girl sitting on the swing. She watched me, too. Suddenly she jumped off the swing and ran over to me. She had a package in her hand. The wrapper said CUPCAKE. She opened it and gave me one. She giggled. I giggled, too.

When we were back in school, the teacher gave us more printing papers. I did not want to write YOON. I wrote CUPCAKE instead.

130

129

131

- *Why do you think Yoon writes* CUPCAKE *instead of her name?* (Yoon likes the cupcake that the ponytail girl gave her. She likes the ponytail girl, too.)

Page 131

Illustration

- *This picture shows the ponytail girl giving Yoon the cupcake. We cannot see the girl's ponytail in the picture, but we can see the cupcake. Point to the cupcake in the ponytail girl's hand.*

Page 132

Paragraph 1

- *Yoon wants to be CUPCAKE. Let's read aloud what she thinks the kids in class would say if she were CUPCAKE:* <u>"CUPCAKE! Here is CUPCAKE!"</u>

Paragraph 2

- *The teacher likes Yoon more and more each day. Smile a very big smile like the teacher smiling at Yoon. (Demonstrate a big smile.) The teacher's eyes show how she feels. Show me what you would look like if you had an "I-like-this-girl-Yoon" look in your eyes. (Demonstrate a kind expression.)*

Page 133

Illustration

- *Let's look at the picture to see what Yoon would look like as a cupcake. Point to the real Yoon in the picture. Now point to what she would look like as a cupcake.*

- *What would you say if you saw a cupcake kid in class? What would you do? (Question is open.)*

Page 134

Paragraph 1

- *What did Yoon do when she got home after school? (Yoon told her mother about her ponytail friend. She sang a song in English for her father.) We can tell that Yoon is learning the new language because she sang in English. Yoon has also made a friend—the ponytail girl!*

Paragraph 3

- *Yoon's mother says, "You make us so proud, little Yoon." When you are proud of someone, you feel very pleased because that person has done something well.*

- *How do you know that Yoon is feeling better about school and about living in America? (Yoon says that maybe America will be a good home and that maybe different is good, too.)*

Pages 132–133

I wanted to be CUPCAKE. The children would clap their hands when they saw me. They would be excited. "CUPCAKE!" they would say. "Here is CUPCAKE!"

The teacher looked at my paper. "And today you are CUPCAKE!" she said. She smiled a very big smile. Her eyes said I-like-this-girl-Yoon.

132

Pages 134–135

After school I told my mother about my ponytail friend. I sang a new song for my father. I sang in English.

"You make us so proud, little Yoon," my mother said.

"Maybe America will be a good home," I thought. "Maybe different is good, too."

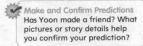

Make and Confirm Predictions
Has Yoon made a friend? What pictures or story details help you confirm your prediction?

134

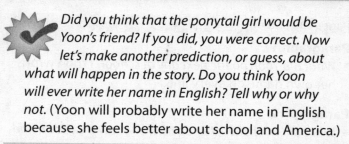

Did you think that the ponytail girl would be Yoon's friend? If you did, you were correct. Now let's make another prediction, or guess, about what will happen in the story. Do you think Yoon will ever write her name in English? Tell why or why not. (Yoon will probably write her name in English because she feels better about school and America.)

Page 135

Illustration

■ *Point to Yoon in the picture. Now point to Yoon's mother. Where is Yoon's father? Point to him. What part of the story do you think this picture shows? (The picture shows Yoon singing to her father.)*

Talk to your partner about songs you have learned in school. Name some of your favorite songs. Which songs have you sung to people in your family?

Paragraph 1

- *What did Yoon do the next day at school?* (Yoon wrote her own name on every line.)

Paragraph 2

- *What did Yoon's teacher do after she saw that Yoon had written her name on every line?* (She gave Yoon a big hug. She said, "You are YOON!")

Illustrations

- *Look at the picture of the teacher hugging Yoon. How do you think the teacher feels?* (The teacher feels happy that Yoon has written her name.)

- *Now look at the picture of Yoon holding up her name. Point to the letters and read them with me:* Y, O, O, N, YOON. *Look at Yoon's face. How do you think Yoon feels about writing her name in English?* (Yoon feels happy and proud.)

136

The next day at school, I could hardly wait to print. And this time I wrote YOON on every line.

When my teacher looked at my paper, she gave me a big hug. "Aha! You are YOON!" she said.

Yes. I am YOON.

I write my name in English now. It still means Shining Wisdom.

YOON

137

Whole Page

- *Now let's read this whole page together.* (Read the page chorally with children, using appropriate pacing, intonation, and expression.)

Did you predict that Yoon would finally write her name in English? What clues from the story helped you predict this? (Yoon decided that America would be a good home. She thought that different could be good, too. She was learning more English, and she was ready to write her name in her new language.)

PARTNERS *What part of this story did you like the best? Use your own words to retell that part of the story to your partner. Then listen to the part of the story that your partner liked best.*

New Americans in Texas

Access Core Content

Teacher Note Pose the questions after you read the paragraph or page indicated.

Page 140

Title
- *Let's read the title together:* New Americans in Texas.

Photo
- *Look at the photo. Do you see a picture of a family? Point to it. They are immigrants. Say it with me:* immigrants. *They came from another place, another country, and now they live in Texas.*

Text
- *Immigrants come to Texas for different reasons. Some immigrants come because they have friends and family here. What's another reason that they come here?* (Because they want to work here.) *Immigrants come from different countries. Say it with me:* countries. *Mexico is a country. Canada is a country. The United States is a country, too. Texas is a state in the United States of America.*

Do you know the names of different countries? Tell your partner the names of two countries.

Page 141

Paragraph 1
- *Some immigrants travel a long way to get to Texas. Countries like Vietnam and India are very far away.* (Point to the distance.) *Some immigrants come from closer countries, like Mexico and Guatemala.* (Bring hand close to you.) *But they still have to travel. How do immigrants travel?* (by boat, plane, train, bus, car)

Paragraph 2
- *In Texas, there are people from many countries. They have different cultures. Say it with me:* cultures. *Culture means "a way of life." Food is a big part of culture. Tamales are food from Mexico. What's another food from Mexico? Name a food from another country.* (Answers will vary.)

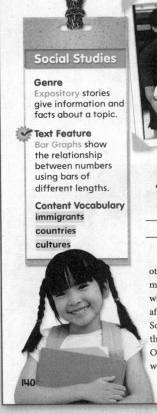

Social Studies

Genre
Expository stories give information and facts about a topic.

Text Feature
Bar Graphs show the relationship between numbers using bars of different lengths.

Content Vocabulary
immigrants
countries
cultures

New Americans in Texas

By Ken Lee

Immigrants have come from other **countries** to live in Texas for many years. Immigrants are people who come to live in one country after they have left another country. Some immigrants come because they have family or friends in Texas. Others come because they want to work in America.

140

Immigrants coming to America have brought many interesting things with them. They have brought wonderful new kinds of music and clothes. Immigrants have also brought new words for Americans to speak and write. For example, *banana* and *poncho* are Spanish words.

Many tasty foods that we enjoy have been brought to the United States by immigrants, too. Have you ever eaten a grapefruit? Grapefruits came from the Caribbean and are now grown in Texas, too.

Grapefruits are a tasty kind of fruit that grow well in Texas.

142

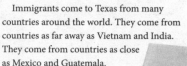

Social Studies

Immigrants come to Texas from many countries around the world. They come from countries as far away as Vietnam and India. They come from countries as close as Mexico and Guatemala.

Texas has a mix of people from all over the world. Because of this, people here have many different backgrounds and **cultures**. They have ideas and ways of life that they share with one another.

Countries Texas Immigrants Come From

This bar graph shows the countries that some immigrants come from. Use the bars to compare how many people come from each of these countries to live in Texas.

141

Some of the music we listen to comes here from other countries. Reggae is music from Jamaica. A lot of popular music and dances are from Mexico.

Immigrants and people in the United States learn many new things from each other.

Mexican music is popular.

Connect and Compare

1. From which country on the bar graph have the most immigrants come to Texas? **Bar Graphs**
2. Think about this article and *My Name Is Yoon*. What changes happen in the lives of immigrants when they come to a new country? Use details from the selections to help explain. **Reading/Writing Across Texts**

Social Studies Activity

Use a map or globe to locate one of the countries listed on the graph. Research and write a paragraph about the country.

 **Immigration**
www.macmillanmh.com

143

Graph

 Let's read the title of the graph together: Countries Texas Immigrants Come From.

- (Point to numbers.) *These numbers tell us how many immigrants come from each country. (Point to country names.) These are the names of some countries. Say them after me. (Read country names and have children repeat.)*

- *Point to the Philippines. That bar is short. The fewest people come from there. Point to Mexico. That bar is tall. The most people come from there. How many people come to Texas from Mexico? Read the number after me:* one million five hundred thousand.

Page 142

Paragraph 1

- *The culture of a group of people includes their music, their clothing, and the language they speak. Many immigrants in Texas speak Spanish. Some Spanish words are now used by everyone. What are two examples?* (banana and poncho)

Paragraph 2

- *Immigrants bring interesting foods to their new homes. Look at the photo and point to the fruit you see. Grapefruits came from another country, and now they grow in Texas. A grapefruit grows on a tree and looks like a large yellow orange. Raise your hand if you have eaten grapefruit.*

Page 143

Photo

- *Let's look at the photo. These are musicians. That means they play music. How many musicians do you see?* (three) *They are playing music from Mexico. Let's read the caption together:* Mexican music is popular. Popular *means "many people like it." Say it with me:* popular.

Text

- *The musicians in the photo may be immigrants from Mexico. Immigrants bring many new kinds of music to the United States. Reggae music is from Jamaica. It is very popular, too. People like to dance to reggae music. Stand up if you like to dance.*

- *Immigrants bring their cultures to share with new friends in Texas. And people in Texas share their culture with these new Americans.*

Name _____

Use the word chart to study this week's vocabulary words.
Write a sentence using each word in your writer's notebook.

Word	Context Sentence	Illustration
patient _____	We are patient as we wait to slide.	
practiced _____	I practiced writing my name in English.	
favorite _____	Mom made my favorite meal.	**What is your favorite meal?**
wrinkled _____	My dog has a wrinkled face.	
settled _____	I am settled in a chair with a good book.	
cuddle _____	I like to cuddle my dog.	

© Macmillan/McGraw-Hill

Read each question and prompt. Discuss the answers with your group. Use your Leveled Reader to find details to support your answers. Then write your answers on the blank lines or on another sheet of paper.

1. Tell about the main character in your book.

_____

2. Explain what problem the family has.

_____

3. Describe the family's journey on a boat or ship.

_____

4. Tell who helps the family when the boat or ship arrives in America.

_____

5. Share your ideas about a new chapter for your book.

_____

6. Write one question about the book to ask your group.

_____

_____

Week 1

Selections	Vocabulary		ELL Practice Book
	Key Selection Words/Cognates	Academic Language/Cognates	
Babu's Song Where in the World Is Tanzania?	concern exclaimed *exclamó* vendors *vendedores* figure *figura* collection *colección*	monitor comprehension reread character, setting, plot noun context clues	• Phonics, pp. 26–27 • Vocabulary, p. 28 • Grammar, p. 29 • Book Talk, p. 30

Week 2

Selections	Vocabulary		ELL Practice Book
	Key Selection Words/Cognates	Academic Language/Cognates	
Doña Flor Henrietta Chamberlain King	rattled tangle shivering advice respected *respetado/-a* commotion *conmoción*	monitor comprehension context clues plural nouns cause *causa* effect *efecto*	• Phonics, pp. 31–32 • Vocabulary, p. 33 • Grammar, p. 34 • Book Talk, p. 35

Week 3

Selections	Vocabulary		ELL Practice Book
	Key Selection Words/Cognates	Academic Language/Cognates	
TIME FOR KIDS A Tall Tale: How Does Texas Honor the Battle of San Jacinto?	independence landmark state government *gobierno* symbol *símbolo*	main idea and details word parts proper nouns monitor comprehension	• Phonics, pp. 36–37 • Vocabulary, p. 38 • Grammar, p. 39 • Book Talk, p. 40

Week 4

Selections	Vocabulary		ELL Practice Book
	Key Selection Words/Cognates	Academic Language/Cognates	
One Grain of Rice Same Story, Different Culture	collectors store reward clever amount double *doble*	generate questions inferences *inferencias* suffix *sufijo* possessive nouns *posesivo*	• Phonics, pp. 41–42 • Vocabulary, p. 43 • Grammar, p. 44 • Book Talk, p. 45

Week 5

Selections	Vocabulary		ELL Practice Book
	Key Selection Words/Cognates	Academic Language/Cognates	
African-American Inventors Inventors Time Line	allowed powerful invented *inventar* instrument *instrumento* products *productos* design *diseño*	generate questions compare *comparar* contrast *contrastar* suffix *sufijo* plurals *plural* possessives *posesivo*	• Phonics, pp. 46–47 • Vocabulary, p. 48 • Grammar, p. 49 • Book Talk, p. 50

Student Response Strategies

Use the following strategies to help English Language Learners move to the next proficiency level.

✔ **WAIT** Give children ample time.

- Let children know that they can respond in different ways depending on their levels of proficiency, but all should be encouraged to answer questions related to the main point of the picture or text.

- Allow children to respond in their native language if they are very limited proficient. Ask a more proficient ELL student to repeat the answer in English.

✔ **REPEAT** If the child's response is correct, the teacher can repeat what the child has said. The teacher should repeat in a clear, loud voice that all can hear and at a slower pace.

✔ **REVISE for FORM** Generally the teacher will be repeating what the child has said but with corrections for grammar and pronunciation. The correction can be implicit or explicit (where teacher calls attention to the correction).

✔ **REVISE for MEANING** Teachers should also correct for meaning.

✔ **ELABORATE** Here, the teacher elaborates on a child's response or states the response in another way in order to more fully develop children's comprehension and oral language proficiency.

✔ **ELICIT** Finally, the teacher can also elicit a more comprehensive response from the child by prompting the child for further information.

Newcomers

Basic and Social Language Each week you will be focusing on an important aspect of classroom communication to teach or reinforce with your newcomers. Children will expand and internalize initial English vocabulary by learning and using routine language needed for classroom communication.

School, People, and Places Take children on a tour of the school. Teach the names of important people and places. Use sentence frames such as, *Hello, Mrs. Sanchez. How are you?* Also verbalize these people and place names throughout the day, for example, *We are going to the library. Mrs. Gonzalez works there. She is our librarian.*

Commands/Imperatives Teach and reinforce basic classroom commands, such as *Sit down; Stand up; Listen, please; Line up; Stop!; Be careful;* and *Take out a pencil*. Model each and have children repeat. Use hand gestures as appropriate, for example, cup your ear when you say *Listen, please*.

Adjectives Teach basic adjectives related to feelings and color. Use the dialogue frames, *How are you? I am _____* or *I feel _____* for feeling words. Use the frames *The _____ is _____* for color, shape, and size adjectives. Use props, such as classroom objects and Photo Cards, to teach each frame and adjective.

LOG ON ▶ Have children use **Newcomer Games** to expand and internalize language needed for classroom communication. **www.macmillanmh.com**

Babu's Song

Pages 160–161

Prior to reading the selection with children, they should have listened to the selection on **StudentWorks Plus**, the interactive eBook. In addition, selection vocabulary should have been pretaught using the **Visual Vocabulary Resources.**

Access Core Content

Teacher Note Pose the questions after you read the paragraph or page indicated.

Pages 160–161

Illustration

The picture shows the characters in the book. The characters are a boy and his grandfather. The grandfather's name is Babu. Point to him.

Page 162

- *What do you know about soccer?* (It is a game. Two teams try to kick a ball into nets at the end of a field.) *What do you remember about the game from reading the emails Aki and Grandmother wrote?* (Soccer players wear special clothing and things that keep them safe.)

- *Bernardi's arms were pumping, or going up and down.* (Demonstrate a pumping motion with your arms.) *His heart was racing, or beating fast.* (Use your hand on your chest to demonstrate your heart beating fast.) *Why were Bernardi's arms pumping and his heart racing?* (He was playing soccer. He was trying hard to score a goal.)

- *Tell me what a uniform is.* (A special set of clothes worn by children who go to a certain school or people who do a certain job.) *The story says that Bernardi does not have a uniform. Point to Bernardi. How do you know which one he is?* (The other two boys are wearing the same thing. Bernardi is not.)

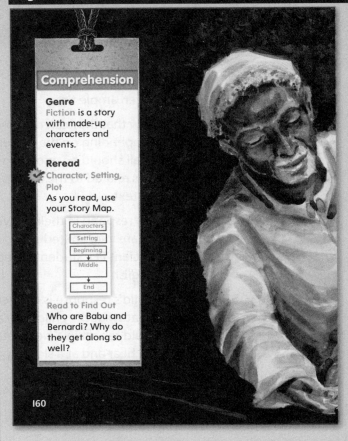

Comprehension

Genre
Fiction is a story with made-up characters and events.

Reread
Character, Setting, Plot
As you read, use your Story Map.

Characters
Setting
Beginning
↓
Middle
↓
End

Read to Find Out
Who are Babu and Bernardi? Why do they get along so well?

160

Pages 162–163

Bernardi ran hard, kicking the ball toward the goal. His arms pumping and his heart racing, he didn't care that he was the only boy on the field not wearing a school uniform.

162

Main Selection

by
Stephanie Stuve-Bodeen

illustrated by
Aaron Boyd

161

He loved soccer and his one **concern** was making a goal. With a final kick so powerful that it knocked him on his back, Bernardi sent the ball flying past the goalie and into the net.

163

Page 163

- *Point to the goalie in the picture. What does a goalie do?* (A goalie tries to keep the ball from going in the net.)

 Do you think Bernardi is a good soccer player? Why or why not? (He is good. He is fast, and he kicks hard. He gets the ball into the net.)

- *Shake your head* yes (demonstrate) *or* no (demonstrate) *to show me whether you think Bernardi would say each of the following ideas: Soccer is not fun.* (no) *Soccer is a great game.* (yes) *I would like to be on a soccer team.* (yes) *I do not care whether I win or lose.* (no) *Explain your answers.*

Seek Clarification

Some children may be confused by unfamiliar words, such as *powerful*. Encourage children to always seek clarification when they encounter a word that does not make sense to them. For example, *What does powerful mean?*

Page 164

Paragraph 1

- *Now we know why Bernardi was not wearing a uniform. Why?* (He does not go to school like the other children. His family does not have enough money to send him to school.) *In our country, families do not have to pay for school. Anyone can go to a public school for free. Some places in other countries do not have public schools.*

Remember, the setting of a story is where the story takes place. Does this part of the story happen inside or outside? (outside) *How do you know?* (People play soccer outside. We can see grass and bushes in the picture.)

Page 165

Illustration

We can use what the author says and what the pictures show to decide how Bernardi feels. Use your body and face to show how he felt. What clues did you use? (Children walk slowly and frown. The author says he walked home slowly. The picture shows him looking sad.)

Page 166

Paragraph 1

- *Babu had a sickness. Now, he cannot talk. Point to the part of the body that Babu probably had an illness in.* (throat, mouth)

Paragraph 2, Echo Reading

- *Listen as I read what Bernardi said to Babu. I will read it as Bernardi would say it. Echo after me. Say it the same way I say it:* "Hello, Babu," Bernardi said. "I made a goal today."

Bernardi lay on the grassy field, catching his breath. A boy helped him up, then ran after the others going into the school. Bernardi wished he could go to school like the other children. He liked to learn, and thought he could be a good student. Besides, then he could play soccer every day, not just when the schoolboys needed an extra player. Bernardi lived with his grandfather, Babu, and they did not have enough money for school.

Slowly Bernardi walked home.

164

When Bernardi walked in, Babu gave him a hug. This was how he said hello, because an illness had taken his voice a long time ago.

"Hello, Babu," Bernardi said. "I made a goal today." Bernardi loved telling Babu his soccer stories.

166

165

Babu held up a **figure** made of wood. He pulled a string, and the figure's jointed arms and legs popped up and down, making Bernardi laugh. Babu was a toy maker. He had only to look at an object and he knew what toy it would become, such as an airplane from a tin can or a whistle from a scrap of wood.

After Babu made his toys Bernardi would sell them. Together they made enough money to live on.

 Character, Setting, Plot
How does the setting affect Bernardi's feelings and actions?

167

Page 167

Paragraph 1

■ *Listen as I read about Babu's new toy:* Babu held up a figure made of wood. He pulled a string, and the figure's jointed arms and legs popped up and down, making Bernardi laugh. *Look at the picture. What has Babu made?* (a doll)

■ *The text says that the figure has jointed arms and legs. Jointed means "hinged," or "bendable." Point to the joints in your arms and legs.* (Demonstrate bending your elbows and knees as you define *jointed*.)

■ *Babu made toys out of other things. Look around the classroom. What are some things in our room that someone could use to make toys?* (Question is open.)

Paragraph 2

■ *Babu and Bernardi sold toys to get money to live. Did they make a lot of money? How do we know? Look back at page 164 for a clue.* (No, they did not make a lot of money. They did not have enough money for Bernardi to go to school.)

 Where does this part of the story happen? (inside Babu and Bernardi's home) *How do you know?* (Bernardi left the game to come home. We see Babu's things that he makes at home.)

■

Directionality

Ask children to place their finger where you start reading (top left). Ask where you finish reading on this page (bottom right).

Page 168

Whole Page

- *Bernardi was going to the market. A market is a place where people sell things they make or grow. What kinds of things might be sold at a market?* (Question is open.)

- *Humming is closing your lips and singing the tune of a song without using words.* (Demonstrate humming a tune that is familiar to the children.) *Hum along with me.* (Hum the tune again with children.)

- *Bernardi was sad that Babu could not use his voice. Why did Bernardi wish that Babu still had his voice?* (Babu could not sing the song that Bernardi like to hear.)

Page 169

Paragraph 1, Choral Reading

- *A vendor is someone who sells things at a market. Let's read together what Bernardi asked the vendors. Raise your voice at the end to show we are asking a question:* "Anything for Babu?"

Paragraph 2

- *Why do you think the vendors gave things to Babu?* (They wanted to help Babu and Bernardi.)

- *Mama Valentina gave Bernardi a gunnysack. Say the word with me:* gunnysack. *Let's figure out what it means. The word part* sack *is a clue. A gunnysack is a kind of sack, or bag. The picture helps, too. The woman gives Bernardi a bag. A gunnysack is a certain kind of bag. It is made of threads, or fibers, from plants.*

- *Let's read together what Bernardi did when the vendor gave him the gunnysack:* Bernardi thanked her as he stuffed it into his bag, even though he didn't think Babu could use it. *What does this tell us about the kind of character Bernardi is? Why?* (He is polite, because he thanks her.)

Pages 168–169

Babu made tea for Bernardi and himself. After they finished Bernardi took an old bag from beside the door, waved good-bye to Babu, and set off for the market. As he walked, Bernardi hummed a tune. It was a song that Babu had sung when he had his voice. Humming it made Bernardi wish Babu could still speak.

168

Pages 170–171

As Bernardi walked home, he passed a shop downtown and stopped to look in the window. There among the bright bolts of cloth and shiny pots was a new soccer ball. It was just what he had always wanted. Bernardi pressed his face against the window and looked at the price. It was more than it cost to go to school!

Slowly Bernardi backed away from the window. He did not hum as he walked home.

170

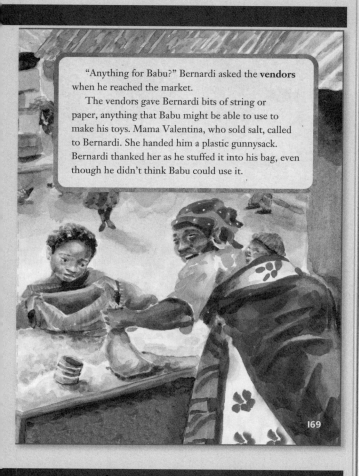

"Anything for Babu?" Bernardi asked the **vendors** when he reached the market.

The vendors gave Bernardi bits of string or paper, anything that Babu might be able to use to make his toys. Mama Valentina, who sold salt, called to Bernardi. She handed him a plastic gunnysack. Bernardi thanked her as he stuffed it into his bag, even though he didn't think Babu could use it.

169

171

Paragraph 1

Point to the pieces of cloth Bernardi saw. Point to the pot he saw. Point to the soccer ball he saw. Describe for your partner what Bernardi saw in the store window.

- *What are some things Bernardi may have said to himself as he looked into the window? (This is a great soccer ball. I wish I could buy that ball. I don't have enough money.)*

Paragraph 2

- *Bernardi stopped humming. Bernardi backed away from the window. Show with your face how Bernardi was feeling. (Children model frowning.) Why did he feel that way? (He wanted the ball but could not have it.)*

Synonyms and Circumlocution

Remind children that they can ask for synonyms to help clarify words or expressions they do not understand. Ask, *What is another word for "shop"?* (store)

Babu's Song

Page 172

Pretend to be Bernardi and Babu. Show what they did. (The child playing Babu pretends to hand something to the one playing Bernardi's part. Bernardi looks at what Babu gave him, pretends to open its lid, and acts as if he or she hears something.)

- *A tinkling sound is a soft ringing sound. A small bell is an example of something that makes a tinkling sound.*

Page 173

- *A music box is a box that has a little machine inside that plays music. When you open the top of the box, the music plays. Point to Bernardi's music box. It is made of a tin box that used to have food in it.*

Paragraph 1, Echo Reading

- *I will read what Bernardi said about the gift. I will read it the way Bernardi would say it:* "A music box!" exclaimed Bernardi. *Did you notice how I made my voice sound? I made it sound excited because Bernardi was excited. Now you try reading the sentence.*

Paragraph 2, Choral Reading

- *What is Babu's song? Let's go back to page 168 to remind ourselves. Let's reread the part together.* As he walked, Bernardi hummed a tune. It was a song that Babu had sung when he had his voice.

- *Do you think Bernardi likes the gift? Why or why not?* (Yes, because he misses Babu's song, and now he can hear it again.)

That evening Babu and Bernardí ate beans and rice by the light of the kerosene lamp. Babu put something by Bernardí's plate. Bernardí picked it up and held it closer to the light. It looked like a tin of lard. He opened the lid and heard a small tinkling.

172

The next Saturday was a busy one for Bernardi, as it was the day he sold toys to tourists. He set up shop on his favorite corner downtown, arranging the toys on the curb.

Bernardi cranked the music box and listened to Babu's song tinkle out. He had sold a few things when a woman picked up the music box. She asked how much it was, but Bernardi said it wasn't for sale.

174

"A music box!" Bernardi **exclaimed**, and listened again. It was rough and tinny, but he recognized the tune. It was Babu's song.

Bernardi hugged Babu, and together they listened to the music. That night, for the first time in many nights, Bernardi fell asleep listening to Babu's song.

173

The woman did not give up. She told Bernardi that she wanted the music box for her **collection**, but still Bernardi shook his head. The woman held out a handful of money. Bernardi's eyes widened. It would be more than enough to buy the ball in the store window.

175

Page 174

Paragraph 1

 Explain to a partner what Bernardi does on Saturday. Tell where he goes. Tell what he does. Tell why he does it. (He goes to a street corner in the city. He tries to sell the toys that Babu makes. He sells them to get money to live.)

Paragraph 2

■ *Does Bernardi want to sell the music box?* (no) *Why not?* (It is the only way he can hear Babu's song.) *Why do you think he brought it with him?* (He loves the box and wants to listen to it while he works.)

Page 175

■ *Show me what Bernardi does when the woman does not give up.* (Children will shake their heads *no*.) *What does this mean?* (It means *no*.)

 Pretend to be Bernardi and the woman. Think about what Bernardi probably said. Think about what the woman probably said. Show what they said and did.

Page 177

Paragraph 1

- *Did Bernardi sell the music box to the woman? How do you know?* (Yes, he took the money from the woman and gave the box to her.) *What is he going to do with the money?* (He wants to buy the soccer ball.)

Paragraphs 1 and 2

Tell your partner whether you think Bernardi should have sold the music box. (Question is open.)

Pages 178–179

Paragraph 2

- *Point to the tear on Bernardi's face. What does it mean?* (He feels sad.) *Do you think he is sad because the music box is gone? Explain.* (Yes, now he can't listen to Babu's song.)

Page 179

Paragraph 1

- *Bernardi sniffled. Here is what a sniffle sounds like.* (Demonstrate sniffling.) *He sniffled because he was crying. Let's read what Bernardi said to Babu. Let's sniffle as we read it:* "I couldn't buy the ball, Babu. (sniffle) It's your money."

Pages 176–177

Pages 178–179

When Bernardi got home, Babu was cleaning. He looked up at Bernardi holding the empty bag.

"I sold everything, Babu!" Bernardi said, trying to sound cheerful, but then a tear rolled down his face. Babu went over to Bernardi. He wiped his grandson's face and waited. He knew Bernardi would tell him what was wrong.

Bernardi picked up the music box. He thought about the brand-new ball and how it would feel when he kicked it. Surely Babu could make another music box.

Bernardi swallowed hard and took the money.

After Bernardi sold all the toys he did not go home. He took the money and headed for the shops down the street.

177

Bernardi sniffled. He told Babu about the music box and the soccer ball. Then he handed the money to Babu. "I couldn't buy the ball, Babu. It's your money."

Babu patted Bernardi's head. Then he placed the money in Bernardi's hand and held it, to show him that the money belonged to both of them.

179

Paragraph 2, Choral Reading

Now let's read what Babu did: Babu patted Bernardi's head. Then he placed the money in Bernardi's hand and held it, to show him that the money belonged to both of them. *With a partner, show what Babu did to Bernardi. Is Babu upset with Bernardi? How do you know?* (He is not upset. He is trying to make Bernardi feel better. He is trying to let him know it is okay that he wanted the ball.)

Do you think Babu is a good grandfather? Explain. (Yes, Babu loves Bernardi. Babu understands Bernardi.)

Page 180

Whole Page

Brainstorm ideas about where Babu might be going. Think of as many ideas as you can. (to the store to buy the ball, to get another music box)

Page 182

Paragraph 1

Was it day or night when Babu got home? How do you know? (It was night, because Bernardi was sitting in the lamplight.) *Use the picture on page 181 to decide whether Babu was gone a long time or a short time.* (He was gone a long time, because in the picture it is light outside. When he comes home, it is night.)

- *What might be in the bag?* (soccer ball, music box, things to make a toy)

Paragraph 2

- *The story says that Bernardi was trying not to sob. A sob is a very loud cry. What made Bernardi cry?* (His feelings about Babu bringing him something.)

Pages 180–181

Bernardi hung his head. "I don't want the ball anymore." He held out the money. "Take it, Babu. You decide what to do with the money."

Babu took the money and looked thoughtfully at Bernardi for a long time. Then he broke into a smile, signaled to Bernardi to wait, and walked out the door.

Bernardi sat quietly in the room as he waited for Babu. He wished he still had the music box. How could he have sold it?

180

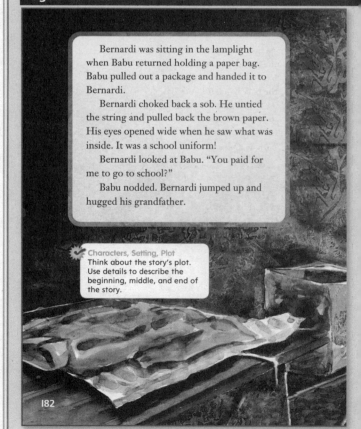

Pages 182–183

Bernardi was sitting in the lamplight when Babu returned holding a paper bag. Babu pulled out a package and handed it to Bernardi.

Bernardi choked back a sob. He untied the string and pulled back the brown paper. His eyes opened wide when he saw what was inside. It was a school uniform!

Bernardi looked at Babu. "You paid for me to go to school?"

Babu nodded. Bernardi jumped up and hugged his grandfather.

Characters, Setting, Plot
Think about the story's plot. Use details to describe the beginning, middle, and end of the story.

182

Page 182

Paragraph 2, Choral Reading

Let's read the part that tells about Bernardi opening the gift: He untied the string and pulled back the brown paper. His eyes opened wide when he saw what was inside. It was a school uniform!

Paragraph 2

- *Why was Bernardi excited about getting a school uniform? Look back at page 164 to help you remember.* (He was excited because it meant he could go to school. He wanted to go to school to learn and play with the other boys.)

Paragraph 3

- *How do you think Babu got the money to pay for school?* (He used the money the woman gave Bernardi for the music box.)

Paragraph 4

- *How does Bernardi feel? How do you know?* (He feels happy and excited. He wants to thank his grandfather. He hugs Babu.)

Page 184

Text

- *Why does Babu hold something behind his back?* (He doesn't want Bernardi to see what he has. He wants to surprise Bernardi.)

- *What was the surprise? Did Babu get it from the store?* (It was a soccer ball. No, he made it.)

 Tell your partner how you think someone could make a soccer ball with a bag and string. (Children might say that Babu could have stuffed something into the bag and then used the string to sew it closed.)

Page 185

Paragraph 1 and Illustration

- *Was the ball a real soccer ball? How was it like a real soccer ball? How was it different?* (No, it was round and it could bounce like a soccer ball. It was different because it was made out of a bag and string.)

Paragraph 2, Choral Reading

- *How did Bernardi feel about the ball? How do you know?* (He said it was wonderful. He said it was better than a real ball.) *Let's read together what Bernardi said to Babu. He was excited, so let's sound excited:* "Thank you, Babu. It's wonderful!"

Page 186

Text

 With your partner, draw the three things Babu gave Bernardi. (uniform, soccer ball, music box)

- *How does Bernardi feel at the end of the story? What story detail lets you know?* (He feels happy. He hums Babu's song.)

While Bernardi held the new uniform to his chest, Babu went back outside. He returned holding something behind his back. With a flourish Babu held out a soccer ball made from string and Mama Valentina's gunnysack.

184

Babu pulled one more surprise from the paper bag. It was an empty lard tin. As Babu began to make another music box, Bernardi put the water on the stove to boil. Then Bernardi hummed Babu's song as they sat in the lamplight and waited for their tea.

186

Bernardi put down his uniform and held the ball. He bounced it on one knee and it felt like the real thing.

"Thank you, Babu. It's wonderful!" Bernardi said to his grandfather and gave him a hug. Babu beamed. Bernardi decided that the ball was even better than the real thing.

185

187

Page 187

Illustration

■ *How do Babu and Bernardi feel about each other? How do you know?* (They love each other very much. They are smiling at each other. They are holding hands.)

Page 161

Title

■ *Let's go back and look at the title of the story. It is* Babu's Song. *Why is that a good title for this story?* (The song that Babu used to sing is an important part of the story. It is what Bernardi misses when Babu stopped speaking. It is what the music box plays. It is what Bernardi hums at the end when he is happy again.)

This story is realistic fiction. Tell me what that means. (Realistic fiction is a made-up story. It tells about things that could happen.) *Why is this realistic fiction?* (The things that happen to Babu and Bernardi could happen in real life.)

Where in the World Is Tanzania?

Access Core Content

Teacher Note Pose the questions after you read the paragraph or page indicated.

Title

- *Let's read the title of this article together:* "Where in the World Is Tanzania?" *Tanzania is a country in Africa. We will find out about this place.*

Paragraph 1 and Map

- *A continent is one of the seven big pieces of land on earth. Look at the map. This is a map of the continent of Africa. Tanzania is painted red. Point to it.*

- *I am going to say the names of some places and point to them on the map on page 191. Repeat the names of the places after me, and point to them on your map.* (Point to Africa, the Atlantic Ocean, the Pacific Ocean, and the Mediterranean Sea.)

- *Is the climate where we live hotter than the climate in Africa? How do you know?* (No, because Africa has the hottest weather. That means no other weather is hotter.)

Paragraph 2

- *Let's look at the map on page 191 again. Point to Tanzania. Say the name of the capital city with me:* Dodoma.

Paragraph 1

- *Point to the coast of Tanzania, or the part closest to the water. If you were in that part of the country, what ocean would you see?* (Indian Ocean)

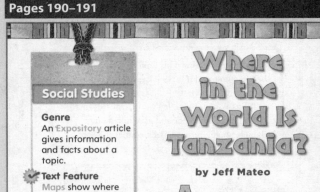

Social Studies

Genre
An Expository article gives information and facts about a topic.

Text Feature
Maps show where places are located.

Content Vocabulary
climate
capital
democracy

190

Where in the World Is Tanzania?

by Jeff Mateo

Africa is the second largest continent. It is so big that the United States could fit in it three times! Africa is between the Atlantic and Indian Oceans. It is south of the Mediterranean Sea. Africa has the hottest **climate** on Earth. This means the weather is hotter there than on any other continent.

There are 53 countries in Africa. Tanzania is a country in southeast Africa. Dodoma is its **capital** city. This is where the government is found. It is a **democracy**. This means that the people can vote for their leaders.

More than 33 million people live in Tanzania. There are 120 different tribes of people and each has its own customs and beliefs. The national language is Kiswahili. Tanzanians may speak English as well as the languages of their tribes.

Each tribe, such as the Makonde and Masai, has its own traditions and dances. Visitors come to learn about the people and watch the dances. The dances tell exciting stories.

Many people in Tanzania are farmers and miners. They dig minerals and gems, such as gold and diamonds, out of the ground.

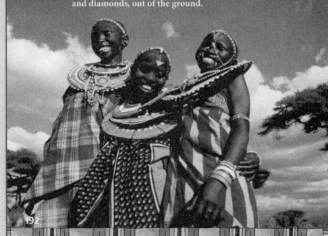

192

■ *Point to the part of Tanzania where you would see trees and tall grasses. Let's say the word for the kind of land in the middle of the country:* plateau.

 Let's say the name of the highest mountain: Mount Kilimanjaro. *There is something on the map that will tell us where the mountains are. The author tells us they are in the west. Look at the star shape on the left side of the map. (Point to the compass rose.) The W stands for "west." Point to it. West is toward the left of the map. Let's point to the western part of Tanzania. That is where the mountains are.*

Whole Page

 Name the three types of land in Tanzania. Have your partner point to each place.

Page 192

Paragraphs 1 and 2

■ *A tribe is a group of people who have the same way of living. Let's say the names of some tribes:* Makonde, Masai. *Let's say the name of Tanzania's language:* Kiswahili.

Paragraphs 2 and 3

 *Show what kind of work you might do if you lived in Tanzania. Have your partner guess what you are doing. (Children demonstrate an activity related to either farming or mining.)*

Page 193

Paragraph 2, Choral Reading

■ *Let's read together about the animals in Tanzania.*

Whole Page

 A tourist is a visitor to a place. One partner will pretend to be a Tanzanian. His or her job is to show visitors special things about the country. Use the ideas on this page and other things you learned about Tanzania in this article to tell the visitor what he or she will see. The other person will be the visitor and ask questions.

Tanzania has three types of land. The coastal area is long and flat. It is found along the Indian Ocean.

The plateau is large and flat. It is found in the middle of the country. It is covered in trees and tall grasses. A large part of it is the Great Rift Valley.

The mountains are in the west. The highest point is on Mount Kilimanjaro, which stands more than 19,000 feet tall.

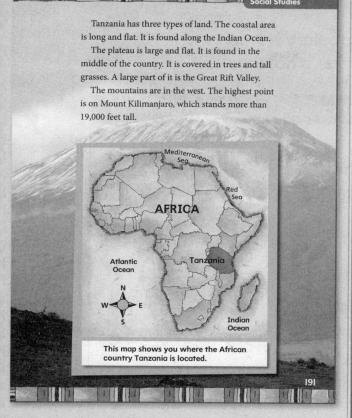

Mediterranean Sea

Red Sea

AFRICA

Atlantic Ocean

Tanzania

N W E S

Indian Ocean

This map shows you where the African country Tanzania is located.

191

Other Tanzanians help the tourists who come to visit the country. They work in hotels and give tours. Some Tanzanians make and sell crafts to tourists. Tourism is a big business in Tanzania. People come from all over the world to see the amazing wildlife.

Tanzania has many wild animals, such as lions, zebras, giraffes, and baboons. Many live in national parks, which are animal sanctuaries. The workers help protect the animals and the places where they live.

Connect and Compare

1. Which ocean is next to Tanzania? **Map**
2. Think about this article and *Babu's Song*. What new information does the article give you about life in Tanzania? **Reading/Writing Across Texts**

Social Studies Activity

Research Tanzania using a different source. Use the table of contents, index, and headings to locate information. Record a list of facts you learn.  **Social Studies** Africa www.macmillanmh.com

193

Name _____

Use the word chart to study this week's vocabulary words.
Write a sentence using each word in your writer's notebook.

Word	Context Sentence	Illustration
exclaimed _____	"She scored another goal!" Dad <u>exclaimed</u>.	
concern _____	My mother's <u>concern</u> was that I broke my leg.	**When might you have concern for someone?**
vendors _____	The food <u>vendors</u> sold hot dogs, ice cream, and popcorn.	HOT DOGS ICE CREAM POPCORN
figure _____	The prize was a <u>figure</u> of a soccer player scoring a goal.	
collection _____	My brother has a <u>collection</u> of stamps from all over the world.	**What kind of a collection would you rather have —stamps or shells?**

© Macmillan/McGraw-Hill

Name_____

Read each question and prompt. Discuss the answers with your group. Use your Leveled Reader to find details to support your answers. Then write your answers on the blank lines or on another sheet of paper.

1. Tell what sport kids in your book play.

_____

2. Explain the problem the main character in your book has.

_____

3. Tell who helped the main character in your book.

_____

4. Describe what the main character in your book learned to do.

_____

5. Tell who in your book is a hero, and explain why.

_____

6. Write one question about the book to ask your group.

_____

_____

Doña Flor

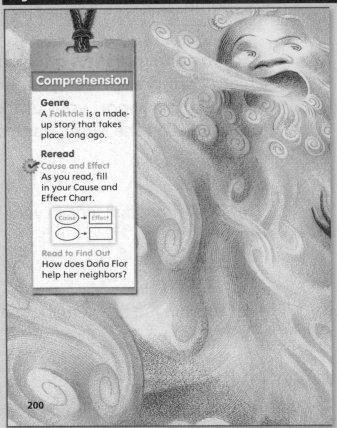

200

Pages 200–201

Prior to reading the selection with students, they should have listened to the selection on **StudentsWorks**, the interactive eBook. In addition, selection vocabulary should have been pretaught using the **Visual Vocabulary Resources**.

Access Core Content

Teacher Note Pose the questions after you read the paragraph or page indicated.

Pages 200–201

Title and Illustration

- *Let's read the title of the story together:* Doña Flor. *Look at this woman.* (Point to the woman in the illustration.) *Her name is Doña Flor.* (Point to the town.) *Look at the houses in the town. Is Doña Flor bigger than the houses or smaller than the houses?* (She is bigger than the houses.) *Doña Flor is very, very big. She is a giant. Say it with me:* giant.

- *What is Doña Flor doing?* (She is hugging the wind.)

- *Let's read the rest of the title together:* A Tall Tale About a Giant Woman with a Great Big Heart. (Put your hand over your heart.) *My heart is inside here. Say it with me:* heart. *Put your hand over your heart. Doña Flor has a great big heart. She has a lot of love.*

Page 202

Illustration

- (Point to Doña Flor.) *Who is this?* (She is Doña Flor.) (Point to the mountain.) *Look, she is bigger than the mountain!* (Point to the snow.) *Look at the snow. It's white and cold. Say it with me:* snow.

202

Comprehension

Genre
A **Folktale** is a made-up story that takes place long ago.

Reread
Cause and Effect
As you read, fill in your Cause and Effect Chart.

Cause → Effect

Read to Find Out
How does Doña Flor help her neighbors?

Main Selection

DOÑA FLOR

A Tall Tale About a Giant Woman with a Great Big Heart

By Pat Mora
Illustrated by Raul Colón

Award Winning Author

201

Every winter morning when the sun opened one eye, Doña Flor grabbed a handful of snow from the top of a nearby mountain. *"Brrrrrrrrr,"* she said, rubbing the snow on her face to wake up.

Long, long ago, when Flor was a baby, her mother sang to her in a voice sweet as river music. When Flor's mother sang to her corn plants, they grew tall as trees, and when she sang to her baby, her sweet flower, well, Flor grew and grew, too.

203

Page 203

Paragraph 1

■ *When Doña Flor wakes up every morning, she grabs some snow and rubs it on her face.* (Demonstrate grabbing and rubbing snow on face.) *Say and do it with me.* (Repeat gestures and encourage students to imitate you. Say the words *grab* and *rub* with the gestures.) *Does snow feel hot or cold?* (cold)

 What do you do when you wake up in the morning? Do you do this (stretch arms), *or this* (yawn and pat mouth)*? What do you do? Show your partner.*

Paragraph 2

■ *When Doña Flor was a baby, her mother liked to sing. She sang to the corn plants, and they grew and grew.* (Hold hand close to floor, then move it slowly up to demonstrate growing.) *She sang to baby Doña Flor, and she grew and grew.* (Repeat growing gesture.) *Say it with me:* Flor grew and grew.

 Now Doña Flor is a giant. Why is she so big? (She is big because her mother sang to her.)

■ *Do you grow when your mother sings to you? Real children don't grow when their mothers sing. This happens only to children in stories.*

Request Assistance

Remind children of expressions they can use to request assistance from the teacher or their partners, such as *Can you show me in the picture? Can you repeat it, please?*

Some children laughed at her because she was different. "*¡Mira!* Look! Big Foot!" they called when she walked by.

"Flor talks funny," they whispered, because Flor spoke to butterflies and grasshoppers. She spoke every language, even rattler.

But soon Flor's friends and neighbors asked her for help. Children late for school asked, "*Por favor,* Flor, could you give us a ride?" She took just one of her giant steps and was at the school door. Of course, the *escuela* shook and the windows rattled.

204

Page 204

Illustration

- *Do you see a giant foot in the picture? Point to it. Whose foot is it?* (It's Doña Flor's foot.)

Paragraph 1

- *The children in this story speak Spanish. Here they say a Spanish word.* Mira *means "look" in Spanish. How many of you know Spanish?*

- (Point to the children's words.) *Let's read together what the children said:* Mira! Look! Big Foot!

Paragraph 2

- *The children whispered about Flor, like this.* (Demonstrate whispering.) *Say it with me:* whisper. *Let's whisper with the children:* Flor talks funny.

- *Flor spoke to butterflies and grasshoppers. Those are insects you can see in a garden or a park. She even spoke to a rattler.* Rattler *is another name for a rattlesnake. A rattlesnake rattles like this.* (Shake some pencils together to make a rattling sound.)

- *What do you think Flor talked about with the rattlesnake?* (Answers will vary.)

Paragraph 3

- *The children asked Flor to take them to school. The school shook and rattled when Flor carried the children there.* (Shake hand and rattle pencils together.)

 Why did the school shake and rattle? (Because Flor was so big and heavy.)

Page 205

Illustration

- (Point to Doña Flor.) *Who is this?* (Doña Flor) (Point to children.) *Who are they?* (the children) *Where is Flor taking the children?* (to school) *Do you think going to school that way looks fun or scary?* (Answers will vary.)

206

205

When Flor finally stopped growing, she built her own house, *una casa* big as a mountain and open as a canyon. She scooped a handful of dirt and made herself a valley for mixing clay, straw, and water. She added some *estrellas*. The stars made the adobe shine. When she worked, Flor sang, and birds came and built nests in her hair. Flor wanted everyone to feel at home in her house. *"Mi casa es su casa,"* she said to people, animals, and plants, so they knew they were always welcome. Everyone called her *Doña* Flor because they respected her.

No one needed an alarm clock in Doña Flor's pueblo. When her hands, wide as plates, started pat-pat-patting tortillas, everyone in the village woke up. So her neighbors would have plenty to eat, she stacked her tortillas on the huge rock table in front of her house.

207

Page 206

Illustration

- *Point to Doña Flor in the picture. What is she doing?* (She is singing.)

Page 207

Paragraph 1

- *Doña Flor made a very big house, a giant house. She sang while she worked on her house. Do you like to sing while you work?*

- (Point to birds in illustration.) *When Flor sang, the birds came. They made nests in her hair. Do you think Flor liked that?* (Answers will vary.) *I think she liked it because she was friends with all the animals.*

- *Doña Flor welcomed everyone in to her house.* (Wave both hands toward yourself as if inviting people in.) *Everyone respected her. They wanted to be good to her and treat her right. Say it with me:* respected. *They said* Doña *in front of her name,* Flor, *to show that they respected her.*

- *How do you show respect to your teachers?* (We say *Miss, Mrs.,* or *Mr.* in front of their names.)

Paragraph 2

- *Doña Flor made tortillas every morning. Tortillas are a kind of flat bread made from cornmeal. Do you like to eat tortillas? When Doña Flor made tortillas with her giant hands, the noise was very loud. Let's make tortillas like Doña Flor.* (Pat hands together loudly as if making tortillas and encourage children to imitate you.) *Doña Flor stacked the tortillas. She put them in a big pile. Let's stack the tortillas with Doña Flor.* (Make a stacking motion and encourage children to imitate you.)

 Doña Flor was a giant woman. How big do you think her tortillas were? Were they this big? (Hold hands close together.) *Or this big?* (Hold hands a little farther apart.) *Bigger? How big do you think they were? Show your partner.*

 What made people in the village wake up in the morning? (Doña Flor was making tortillas.)

Paragraph 1

- *Doña Flor stocked tortillas in front of her house. Her neighbors came to eat her tortillas every day. Doña Flor's tortillas were so big, people even used them as roofs to cover their houses!*

Paragraphs 2–5

- *Nobody came to get tortillas from Doña Flor. Nobody wanted to leave their houses because they were afraid of the puma. A puma is a wild cat, like a tiger or a lion. Doña Flor went to look for her friends.*

- *Let's pretend we are in the town.* (Divide the class into three groups. Point to each group as you explain.) *You are Doña Flor. You are the people in their houses. You are the puma. What does Doña Flor say?* (What's the matter?) (Point to group 1 and have students repeat.) *What do the people in their houses say?* (The puma! Listen!) (Point to group 2 and have students repeat.) *What does the puma say?* (Rrrrroar!) (Point to group 3 and have students repeat.)

Illustration

- *Point to Doña Flor's eye. What is she looking at?* (Answers will vary.)

Non-verbal Cues

Remind children that they can use non-verbal cues to share information when they are not able to do so verbally. Encourage children to use pantomime or draw.

Flor's tortillas were the biggest, bestest tortillas in the whole wide world. People used the extra ones as roofs. *Mmmm*, the houses smelled corn-good when the sun was hot. In the summer, the children floated around the pond on tortilla rafts.

One warm spring day, while a family of lizards swept her house, Doña Flor brought out her stacks of fresh tortillas. Nobody came. *Hmmmmmmm*, thought Flor. She started knocking on doors and calling to her neighbors.

"*¿Qué pasa?* What's the matter?" she asked, bending down to peer into their small doors to see where they were hiding.

"*¿El puma!*" they whispered. "The children have heard a huge mountain lion circling the village. Listen!"

Flor listened, and sure enough, she heard a terrible "*Rrrr-oarrr!*"

208

210

209

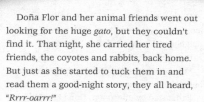

Doña Flor and her animal friends went out
looking for the huge *gato*, but they couldn't
find it. That night, she carried her tired
friends, the coyotes and rabbits, back home.
But just as she started to tuck them in and
read them a good-night story, they all heard,
"*Rrrr-oarrr!*"

"Where is that darn cat?" asked Flor, but the
scared animals were shaking and shivering
under their sheets. She gave each a giant kiss.

SMACK! The sound echoed and woke the
grumpy wind, who stormed up and down the
hills a-grumblin' and a-growlin'. That night,
the wind got so angry that he blew the trees and
houses first to the left and then to the
right, again to the left and then to the right.

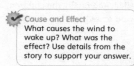 **Cause and Effect**
What causes the wind to
wake up? What was the
effect? Use details from the
story to support your answer.

211

Page 210

Illustration

- *Point to Doña Flor in the picture. Point to the animals. Remember, Doña Flor is friends with plants and animals. Here, she is carrying her friends the coyotes and the rabbits.* (Point out coyotes and rabbits as you name them.)

Page 211

Paragraph 1

- *Doña Flor and her animal friends looked for the puma, but they could not find it. Is a puma a wild cat or a wild dog?* (a wild cat) *How do we say* cat *in Spanish?* (gato)

- *Doña Flor carried her friends home. Suddenly they heard the puma. What did the puma say?* ("Rrrrroar!")

Paragraph 2

- *Are you scared of a puma?* (Answers will vary.) *Doña Flor's animal friends were scared. They were shivering, like this.* (Demonstrate shivering.) *Say and do it with me:* shivering.

- *Doña Flor gave each animal a giant kiss, like this.* (Make a loud kissing noise.)

 Doña Flor tucked her friends in for the night and started to read them a story. Show your partner how you would tuck in the animals for bed and read them a story.

Paragraph 3

 The wind was very angry. Why was he so angry? (Because the sound of Doña Flor's giant kiss woke him up.)

Choral Reading

- *Let's read the last sentence together.*

- *Let's blow like the wind. The wind blew the trees and houses to the left. Then he blew the trees and houses to the right. Do it with me. Whoosh! Whoosh!* (Make a whooshing sound as you wave your arms from side to side. As the children imitate the wind, repeat the words from the story: <u>first to the left, then to the right, again to the left and then to the right.</u>)

Page 212

Text

- *The wind made a lot of noise, like this.* (Make a whooshing noise.) *The puma, the wild cat, made a lot of noise, like this.* (Make a roaring noise.)

- *Let's make the noises that Doña Flor heard all night.* (Divide the class into two groups. Point to each group as you explain.) *You are the wind. What noise do you make?* (whooshing noise) *You are the puma. What noise do you make?* (roaring noise) *Now, wind and puma, make your noises.*

- *What a commotion you made!* Commotion *means "a lot of noise." Say it with me:* commotion.

- *Can you sleep when you hear loud noises like that?* (Answers will vary.) *Doña Flor couldn't sleep. Nobody in the town could sleep.*

Page 213

Illustration

- *Point to Doña Flor. Point to the wind. Doña Flor is hugging the wind.* (Demonstrate hugging.) *Say it with me:* hugging. *Where have you seen this picture before?* (on the cover page) *Why was she hugging the wind?* (Answers will vary.)

Text

- *In the morning, everybody looked outside.* (Point to illustration.) *What did they see?* (Doña Flor hugging the wind) *Doña Flor wanted the wind to be quiet.*

- *What did Doña Flor do after she hugged the wind?* (She started her chores.)

Pages 212–213

Now, Doña Flor liked her sleep, so she wasn't smiling when she heard the wind spinnin' round and around the village. Together, the wind and the giant cat roared all night, and nobody got much sleep.

212

Pages 214–215

Doña Flor had work to do. But first she looked around the village. Where were her neighbors? Then she heard, *"Rrrr-oarrr! Rrrr-oarrr!"*

Flor stomped off to find the puma that was bothering her *amigos.*

Exhausted by afternoon, Doña Flor still hadn't found that cat, so she sat outside the library for a rest. She was too big to fit inside, so she just reached in the window for books. You see, Flor was probably the fastest reader ever. Why, she could read the whole encyclopedia in five minutes. She liked to sit in the shade and read stories and poems nice and slow to the children and animals that climbed all over her soft body. Today, she called and called, and finally the children came, but they were scared.

214

As the sun rose, Flor's neighbors, shaking at the commotion, peered out their windows. Tired-looking Flor was giving that wind a big hug to quiet him down. Then she started her morning chores.

213

215

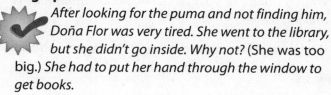

Page 215

Paragraphs 1 and 2

- Amigos *means "friends" in Spanish. Doña Flor's friends are also her neighbors.*

- *Doña Flor couldn't see her friends, but she heard the puma. What noise did the puma make?* ("Rrrroar!") *Doña Flor went to look for the puma.*

Paragraph 3

 After looking for the puma and not finding him, Doña Flor was very tired. She went to the library, but she didn't go inside. Why not? (She was too big.) *She had to put her hand through the window to get books.*

- *Doña Flor likes to read stories to the children and animals. Who reads stories to you?* (Answers will vary.)

 The children came to hear Doña Flor read stories, but they were scared. Why were they scared? (They were scared of the puma.)

What books do you like to read? Tell your partner the names of two books that you like.

Page 215

Illustration

- *Point to Doña Flor. What does she have in her hand?* (a book) *Doña Flor likes to read. What books do you think she likes to read?* (Answers will vary.)

Page 216

Illustration

- (Hold out your thumb.) *This is my thumb. Say it with me:* thumb. *Show me your thumb. Now look at the picture. Point to Doña Flor's thumb. Point to the people. Doña Flor's thumb is as big as the people, isn't it? She has a giant thumb.*

- *Do you see a river in the picture? Show your partner. What is Doña Flor doing with her giant thumb?* (She is making a river.)

- *Why is Doña Flor making a river? Let's read to find out.*

Page 217

Text

- *Doña Flor made the river because she wanted her friends to be happy.*

- *Did the river make a scary sound or a pretty sound?* (a pretty sound)

- *Doña Flor smiled when she saw and heard the river. Did her friends smile, too?* (no) *Why didn't they smile?* (They were scared of the mountain lion.)

- *Doña Flor's friends are scared of the mountain lion. Remember, the mountain lion has some other names. What other names does it have?* (puma, cat, gato) *What sound does it make?* ("Rrrroar!") *Is that a scary sound or a pretty sound?* (a scary sound)

Pages 216–217

216

Pages 218–219

That's it! thought Doña Flor, and again she stomped off to look for the giant puma, but she still couldn't find him. She went home to think and work in her garden. It was like a small forest on the edge of the *pueblo*, a tangle of poppies, morning glories, roses, luscious tomatoes, and *chiles*. Whatever she planted grew so fast, you could hear the roots spreading at night. Her neighbors used the sunflowers as bright yellow umbrellas. She gave the school band her hollyhocks to use as trumpets. The music smelled like spring.

"My plants grow that big because I sing to them like my mother did," Doña Flor told the children when they came three at a time to carry home an ear of corn. But today, the children ran home when they heard, *"Rrrr-oarrr!"* The sound rattled all the plates in the pueblo. Flor's neighbors' teeth started rattling, too.

218

What can I do to cheer my friends up? wondered Flor as she saw their frightened faces. She thought and thought. Now, Flor knew that her village needed *un río,* a river, so to make her neighbors happy, Doña Flor scratched a new riverbed with her thumb. When the water trickled down the stones for the first time, Flor called out, "Just listen to that! Isn't that the prettiest sound you've ever heard?" She smiled, and her smile was about as big as her tortillas, but today her neighbors could barely smile back. They were too worried about the mountain lion, and sure enough, suddenly there was a terrible *"Rrrr-oarrr! Rrrr-oarrr!"*

217

219

Illustration

- *Point to the children at the bottom of the page. Point to the flowers. Those are giant flowers! Whose flowers do you think they are?* (Doña Flor's)

- *(Point to the sunflower.) This flower has a name: sunflower. This child is holding it like an umbrella. Let's pretend we are carrying a giant sunflower umbrella.* (Demonstrate by holding a hand up as if carrying an umbrella.)

- *(Point to the hollyhocks.) These children are using the flowers like trumpets. They are making music. Let's pretend we are making music with giant flowers, like these children are.* (Demonstrate by holding a hand in front of your mouth as if playing a trumpet.)

Paragraph 1

- *Everybody was scared of the puma, and that made Doña Flor angry. She stomped away, like this.* (Demonstrate stomping.) *Say and do it with me:* stomp.

- *Doña Flor didn't want to feel angry, so she went to work in her garden.*

Paragraph 2

 All the flowers and vegetables in Doña Flor's garden were very big. Why were they so big? (They were big because Doña Flor sang to them.)

- *The children liked to visit Doña Flor's garden, but today they were scared. What scared them?* (the puma's roar)

Illustration

- *Show your partner Doña Flor. Show your partner Doña Flor's giant feet. What is she walking in?* (the river)

- *Look at how Doña Flor is walking. She is stomping. She is angry at the puma.*

 Doña Flor stomped because she was angry. With your partner, stomp through the river looking for the puma.

Illustration

- *Point to Doña Flor in the picture.* (Point to the deer.) *This animal is a deer. Point to the deer. Do you see a snake? Point to it. Point to the rabbit. What other animals do you see in the picture?* (cow, birds, horse) *All these animals are Doña Flor's friends.*

Paragraph 1

- *Roses are pretty flowers. Do you like roses? Doña Flor likes roses. The smell of roses helps her think. She took a bath that smelled like roses. What did she want to think about?* (the puma)

Paragraph 2 and Dialogue

- *Doña Flor decided to ask her animal friends for help. Remember, she knows how to speak to animals. She asked the deer.* (Point to deer in illustration.) *The deer said, "Go quietly to the tallest mesa." Say it with me:* Go quietly to the tallest mesa. *Mesa means "table" in Spanish. A mesa is like a hill with a flat top. It looks like a table.*

- (Point to rabbit in illustration.) *The rabbit whispered, like this:* Go quietly to the tallest mesa. *Whisper it with me:* Go quietly to the tallest mesa.

- (Point to snake in illustration.) *The snake hissed, like this.* (Make a hissing sound.) *The snake hissed in Spanish.* (Reread the snake's words.) *What does that mean? It means "go quietly to the tallest mesa." Say it with me:* Go quietly to the tallest mesa.

- *What do you think Doña Flor will do now? Will she go quietly to the nearest mesa?* (Answers will vary.)

Where is that big monster gato? Doña Flor wondered. The smell of roses helped Flor think, so she went inside and took a long, hot bubble bath. Everyone knew Doña Flor was thinking when bubbles that smelled like roses began to rise from her chimney.

I know, thought Flor, *I'll go to my animal friends for help.* She stomped off again, and she started asking because, remember, she spoke every language, even rattler.

"Go quietly to the tallest mesa," said the deer.

"Vaya silencios-s-s-amente a la mes-s-s-a mas-s-s alta," hissed the snake.

"Go quietly to the tallest mesa," whispered the rabbits.

220

Knowing that animals are mighty smart, Doña Flor followed their advice. She walked very, very softly up to the tallest mesa. She looked around carefully for the giant cat. Then right near her she heard, *"Rrrr-oarrr! Rrrr-oarrr!"* Flor jumped so high, she bumped into the sun and gave him a black eye.

222

221

Flor looked around. All she saw was the
back of a cute little puma. She watched him
very quietly. Doña Flor began to tiptoe toward
the puma when all of a sudden he roared into
a long, hollow log. The sound became a huge
"*Rrrr-oarrr!*" that echoed down into the valley.

223

Pages 222–223

Illustration

- (Refer to illustration on both pages.) *Show your partner Doña Flor. Show your partner the puma. Show your partner the sun. Look at the sun's face. It has one hurt eye. Show your partner the hurt eye.*

 Somebody hurt the sun's eye. What do you think: who hurt the sun's eye? Tell your partner.

Page 222

Text

- *The animals gave Doña Flor advice. They told her something to do: to go to the tallest mesa. Doña Flor followed their advice. She went to the mesa. What noise did she hear?* ("Rrrrrroar!")

- *When Doña Flor heard that loud noise, what did she do?* (She jumped.) (Hold one hand flat in front of you and the other hand below it. Then "jump" the lower hand up to hit the higher hand.) *When Doña Flor jumped, she hit something. What did she hit?* (the sun) *Giant Doña Flor hit the sun and hurt its eye!* (Point to sun and hurt eye.)

Choral Reading

- *Let's read the last two lines together:* Flor jumped so high, she bumped into the sun and gave him a black eye.

Page 223

Text

Doña Flor saw the puma. It was very small. Then she heard the puma's roar. It was very loud. Why was the puma able to make such a loud noise? (It roared into the log.) *The log made a little roar into a very loud noise.*

- *Let's roar into a log like the little puma.* (Demonstrate by holding both hands in front of your mouth in a tube shape.)

Page 224

Paragraph 1

■ *The little puma liked making his big noise. He laughed and laughed. Let's laugh with the puma.* (Laugh.)

Paragraph 2

■ *When the little puma saw giant Doña Flor, he stopped laughing. He tried to look fierce, like this.* (Make a fierce face and claws.) *His eyes looked angry, like fire.* (Make angry eyes and face.) *Let's be fierce with the puma.* (Encourage children to imitate fierce gesture and angry eyes.)

 Then the fierce little puma tried to roar, but he didn't use the log. What did his roar sound like? (a little roar) *Why?* (Without the log, it was not as loud.) *Let's make a little roar with the puma.* (Make a little roaring noise and encourage children to imitate you.)

Paragraph 3

■ *Was Doña Flor scared of the little puma?* (no) *She scratched its ears. Scratch with me.* (Scratch your hand.) *The puma stopped roaring and started purring. Let's purr with the puma.* (Make purring noise.)

PARTNERS *Doña Flor whispered to the puma. She talked to it quietly. What do you think she said? Tell you partner.*

Page 225

Illustration

■ *Show your partner giant Doña Flor. Show your partner the little puma. Show your partner Doña Flor's hands. Doña Flor is scratching the puma.* (Demonstrate by scratching your hand.)

Pages 224–225

Now, the little puma thought the loud noise was so funny that he rolled on his back and started laughing and laughing—until he saw big Doña Flor.

Aha! thought Flor. "Are you the *chico* who's causing all the trouble?" she asked. The little puma tried to look very fierce. His eyes sizzled with angry sparks. He opened his mouth wide, and his teeth glinted. He roared his meanest roar. *"Rrrr-oarrr!"* he growled, but without the log, the growl wasn't really very fierce.

Doña Flor just smiled at that brave cat and said, "Why, you're just a kitten to me, Pumito," and she bent down and scratched that puma behind the ears, and she whispered to him in cat talk until that cat began to purr and *purrrrrrrrrr.* Pumito began to lick Flor's face with his wet tongue.

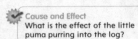
Cause and Effect
What is the effect of the little puma purring into the log?

224

Pages 226–227

226

Suddenly Flor heard a new noise. *"Doña Flor, ¿dónde estás?* Where are you?" called her worried neighbors. Even though they were frightened, they had all come, holding hands, looking for her.

"Meet my new *amigo,*" said Doña Flor, smiling at her thoughtful neighbors.

That evening, Flor plucked a star the way she always did and plunked it on the tallest tree so her friends in the *pueblo* could find their way home. She plucked *una estrella* to put above her door, too. Even the stars could hear Doña Flor humming.

Illustration

■ *Look at this picture. It is night and the sky is filled with stars. Point to giant Doña Flor. Point to the little puma. Point to Doña Flor's friends.*

■ (Point to big star.) *Look at this star. Say it with me:* star. *Doña Flor is plucking she star. She's taking it.* Pluck *means "to pull out something." Why does she want the star?* (Answers will vary.)

Paragraphs 1–2

■ *Doña Flor heard a noise, but it wasn't the puma. Who made the noise?* (her neighbors, or her friends) *The friends were saying, "Donde estas? Where are you?" Say it with me:* Where are you, Doña Flor?

■ *Doña Flor showed her new friend to her neighbors. How do we say* friend *in Spanish?* (amigo) *Doña Flor showed her new amigo, the puma, to her neighbors.*

Paragraph 3

■ *Doña Flor plucked a star from the sky and put it on top of a tree.* (Mime plucking star and placing it on top of a tree.) *The star gave light to the town.*

■ *How do we say* star *in Spanish?* (estrella) *Doña Flor plucked an estrella, a star, to put over her door.* (Mime plucking star and placing it over door.)

Page 228

Illustration

- (Refer to illustration on both pages.) *Look at Doña Flor. What is she doing?* (resting, or sleeping)

- (Point to clouds.) *Look at these big clouds. Are the clouds hard like a table* (knock on table), *or soft like a bed?* (soft, like a bed) *Do you see the puma? Point to it.*

 (Point to the animals in Doña Flor's lap.) *Doña Flor has her animal friends with her. I see a cow. What different animals do you see? Tell your partner.*

Text

- *Doña Flor reached up into the sky and got some soft clouds.* (Mime reaching up and pulling down clouds.) *Then she made a nice bed and got ready to sleep.* (Mime arranging clouds into bed. Then put head on folded hands as if sleeping.) *Let's make a bed like Doña Flor.* (Repeat gestures and encourage students to imitate you.)

Flor liked a fresh bed, so she reached up and filled her arms with clouds smelling of flowery breezes. She shaped the clouds into a soft, deep bed and into hills of puffy pillows. *"Mmmm,"* said Flor as she snuggled in the clouds.

228

"Tonight, I'm very tired after my adventure with the giant cat, right, Pumito?" chuckled Doña Flor. All the animals snuggled down with her, and Pumito stretched out over her big toes.

229

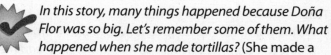

Page 229

Text

- *Doña Flor said good night to the little puma. She called him* Pumito. *That means "little puma" in Spanish.*

- *Doña Flor and all the animals went to sleep. Let's whisper good night to them: Good night, Doña Flor. Good night, Pumito. Good night, animals.*

In this story, many things happened because Doña Flor was so big. Let's remember some of them. What happened when she made tortillas? (She made a loud noise and everyone woke up.) *What happened when she kissed the animals?* (She made a loud noise and woke up the wind.) *What other things happened because Doña Flor was so big?* (Possible answers: The school shook when she walked by. She couldn't go inside the library. She made a river with her thumb. She touched the stars and the clouds.)

Henrietta Chamberlain King

Access Core Content

Teacher Note Pose the questions after you read the paragraph or page indicated.

Page 232

Title

- ■ *We are going to read about a famous Texas woman. (Point to title.) The title tells us her name. Let's read the title together:* Henrietta Chamberlain King.

Photo and Caption

- ■ *(Point to photo.) Is this a picture of Henrietta Chamberlain King? Let's read the caption together to find out:* Henrietta Chamberlain King was born in 1832 and died in 1925. *The caption tells us that this is a picture of Henrietta Chamberlain King.*

- ■ *The caption tells us that Henrietta was born in 1832. Say it with me:* 1832. *Point to 1832 in the caption. That was a long time ago. The caption also tells us that Henrietta died in 1925. Henrietta was 93 years old when she died. She was very old.*

- ■ *Henrietta is not living anymore. She is from the past. She is from history. Say it with me:* history.

Paragraph 1

- ■ *Henrietta was important in Texas history. She was a rancher. She lived on a ranch.* (Write *ranch* on the board.) *Say it with me:* ranch. *A ranch is a big farm with cows.* (Write *rancher* on the board.) *A rancher is a person who owns a ranch. Say it with me:* rancher.

Paragraph 2

- ■ *Henrietta and her husband had five children. Henrietta took care of her children, and she took care of the people who worked on the ranch.*

Social Studies

Genre
A Biography is the story of a person's life written by another person.

Text Feature
Photos and Captions give more information about a topic. Captions tell about the photos.

Content Vocabulary
education
acres
donated

Henrietta Chamberlain King

By Linda B. Ross

Henrietta King was an important person in Texas history. She was an excellent rancher and a woman who gave back to her community.

Henrietta and her husband, Richard, owned a ranch on the Santa Gertrudis Creek. Henrietta cared for her five children. She also managed the **education** and housing of all the Mexican American families who worked at the King Ranch.

In 1925, the King Ranch was 1,173,000 acres. It was larger than the state of Rhode Island!

232

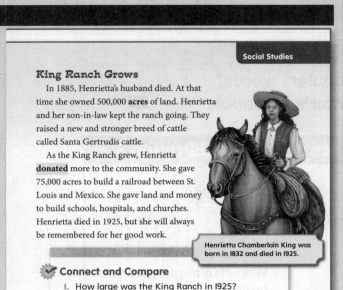

Social Studies

King Ranch Grows

In 1885, Henrietta's husband died. At that time she owned 500,000 **acres** of land. Henrietta and her son-in-law kept the ranch going. They raised a new and stronger breed of cattle called Santa Gertrudis cattle.

As the King Ranch grew, Henrietta **donated** more to the community. She gave 75,000 acres to build a railroad between St. Louis and Mexico. She gave land and money to build schools, hospitals, and churches. Henrietta died in 1925, but she will always be remembered for her good work.

Henrietta Chamberlain King was born in 1832 and died in 1925.

Connect and Compare

1. How large was the King Ranch in 1925? **Photographs and Captions**

2. Think about this biography and Doña Flor. What made Henrietta a local hero like Doña Flor? **Reading/Writing Across Texts**

Social Studies Activity

Research a hero who has helped your community. Make a poster that describes this person.

LOG ON — FIND OUT **Social Studies Heroes** www.macmillanmh.com

233

Photo and Caption

- (Point to photo.) *This is Henrietta's ranch. Let's read the caption together to find out the name of her ranch:* In 1925, the King Ranch was 1,173,000 acres. (Point to words *King Ranch*.) *The name of the ranch was King Ranch.*

- *King Ranch had a lot of acres.* Acres *describes a piece of land of a certain size. Say it with me:* acres. *Look at the caption. Do you see a number? Point to it. Let's read the number together:* one million one hundred seventy three thousand acres. *That's a lot of land. How much land is it? Let's read the rest of the caption together:* It was larger than the state of Rhode Island!

- *Texas is larger than Rhode Island.* (Show a map of the United States. Point to Texas and Rhode Island, and show how one can fit inside the other. Demonstrate "larger than" by holding up two classroom objects that are different sizes.)

 With your partner, look at things on your desk and in the classroom. Take turns telling your partner which objects in the classroom are larger than others.

Paragraph 1

- *Henrietta's husband died, but Henrietta kept working on the ranch. Her daughter's husband helped her. They made a new kind of cattle.* Cattle *means "a lot of cows." Say it with me:* cattle. *The new cattle were strong.*

Paragraph 2

- *Henrietta worked hard. The ranch grew. She had a lot of land and money. She wanted to share. She donated, or gave, land and money. She gave to a railroad, schools, hospitals, and churches.*

- *Do you think Henrietta was a nice person or a mean person? Why?* (She was a nice person, because she gave land and money to churches, schools, and hospitals.) *Do you think Henrietta was a lazy person or a busy person? Why?* (She was a busy person, because she took care of her children and ranch workers and because she worked hard on the ranch.)

Use the word chart to study this week's vocabulary words.
Write a sentence using each word in your writer's notebook.

Word	Context Sentence	Illustration
advice _____	The coach gave me good <u>advice</u>.	**Who else might give you advice?**
commotion _____	Our dog makes a <u>commotion</u> when the phone rings.	
rattled _____	The branches <u>rattled</u> against the window when the wind blew.	
respected _____	Everyone <u>respected</u> the famous scientist.	**Name someone you respect. Why?**
shivering _____	I was <u>shivering</u> in my thin jacket.	
tangle _____	The kittens turned the balls of yarn into a messy <u>tangle</u>.	

© Macmillan/McGraw-Hill

Name_____

Read each question and prompt. Discuss the answers with your group. Use your Leveled Reader to find details to support your answers. Then write your answers on the blank lines or on another sheet of paper.

1. What is a cowboy's job?

   _____

2. Explain why a cowboy's job could be hard.

   _____

3. Name two famous cowboys and tell why they became famous.

   _____

4. Describe how cowboys' jobs are different today.

   _____

5. Describe the clothing that cowboys wear and why they wear it.

   _____

6. Write one question about the book to ask your group.

   _____

A Tall Tale

Pages 240–241

Prior to reading the selection with students, they should have listened to the selection on **StudentsWorks**, the interactive eBook. In addition, selection vocabulary should have been pretaught using the **Visual Vocabulary Resources**.

Access Core Content

Teacher Note Pose the questions after you read the paragraph or page indicated.

Page 240

Title and Photo

■ *Let's read the title together:* A Tall Tale. *(Point to the photo.) This is a very tall monument. We build a monument to honor someone or to remember something important. Say it with me:* monument. *What monuments have you seen?*

Text

■ *This article is about a place called San Jacinto. San Jacinto is a Spanish name. Let's say it together:* San Jacinto.

■ *What is on top of the monument? (star) The star is a symbol. A symbol is a sign or a picture that stands for something else. The star is a symbol of the state of Texas.*

■ *Inside this monument is a museum. A museum is a place where objects of art or history can be seen. Say it with me:* museum. *What would you see in this museum?* (things about the Battle of San Jacinto)

Page 241

Text

Long ago, Texas was part of Mexico. Texans fought for independence, or to be free, from Mexico. Why was the Battle of San Jacinto important? (The Texans won the Battle of San Jacinto and got their independence.)

Photo

This picture shows scenes from the battle. Describe the battle scene to your partner.

Pages 240–241

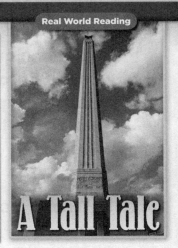

Comprehension

Genre
Expository text gives information about real people, places, and events.

Read Ahead
Main Idea and Details
The main idea is the most important idea in an article. Details and facts give more information.

Real World Reading

A Tall Tale

INDEPENDENCE FOR TEXAS

The San Jacinto (SAN jah–SIN–toh) Monument rises 570 feet into the Texas sky. At the top of the monument is a huge star. It is a **symbol** of Texas, the Lone Star State. Inside the monument is a museum. It tells the story of the Battle of San Jacinto. This amazing **landmark** stands on the spot where that battle was fought.

240

Pages 242–243

Workers from the community build each piece of the monument by hand.

BUILDING THE MONUMENT

The Texas **government** began building the San Jacinto Monument in 1936. First, workers had to make the base. It took 57 hours to pour the concrete for the foundation. After the base was ready, stones were placed on top to make the tower. Each stone weighed as much as 8,000 pounds. Work on the monument ended in 1939, but the hard work is always remembered. The people who made it possible were community worker heroes.

242

TIME FOR KIDS

Texas was once part of Mexico. Many people who lived in Texas came from the United States. They wanted Texas to break away from Mexico. In 1835, Texans fought against Mexico to form their own country. The Mexican army defeated the Texans in some battles. At San Jacinto the Texans won a big victory. Mexico had to give Texas its **independence**. These people are heroes to the community.

The huge monument tells the story of the Battle of San Jacinto.

The metal front doors of the San Jacinto Monument tell a story. The doors show six flags that flew over the **state** at different times. They are the flags of Spain, France, Mexico, the Republic of Texas, the Confederate States of America, and the United States. They show that Texas history is linked to world history.

The metal doors to the monument show the different flags flown over Texas.

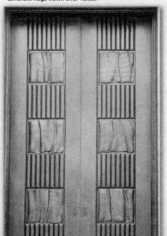

✔ Think and Compare

1. Where is the monument located?

2. Why was the monument built?

3. Use facts and other details from the text to state the main idea.

4. Think about "Lone Star Celebration" and this article. Why are Texas Independence Day and the San Jacinto Monument important to Texans?

243

Page 242

Text and Photos

- *The base of the monument at San Jacinto is made of concrete. Concrete is a mix of cement, water, and small stones. When it dries, it is very hard and strong.*

- *On top of the base, the workers placed huge stones to make the tower. Some of the stones weighted 8,000 pounds. Do you think that is light or heavy?* (heavy)

- (Point to the main photo on page 242.) *In this photo, we can see workers putting a big stone in place.* (Point to the inset photo.) *What does this photo show us?* (the star symbol)

- *Let's figure out how long it took to build the monument. Workers began in 1936. Their work ended in 1939. Let's count out the years they were working. Hold up one finger for each year:* 1936, 1937, 1938, 1939. *They worked on the monument for four years.*

Page 243

Text and Photo

- *This page tells us about the doors on the monument. Let's read this paragraph together.*

- *Now let's look at the photo of the metal doors. On the doors, can you see flags or stars?* (flags) *The flags are from different countries. They show that Texas history is part of world history.*

 What is this story mostly about? Is it mostly about a monument or a battle? (a monument) *Let's remember some details about the monument. Why did people want to build it?* (to remember the Battle of San Jacinto) *What does it look like?* (It's tall. It has a star on top. It's made of stone and concrete. It has metal doors.)

Monitor Oral Production

Remember to model self-corrective techniques on a regular basis as you speak to children. Pretend to mispronounce words and self-correct.

Use the word chart to study this week's vocabulary words.
Write a sentence using each word in your writer's notebook.

Word	Context Sentence	Illustration
independence _____	My dad walks to school with me. Teenagers have the <u>independence</u> to walk to school alone.	**How else do teenagers show their <u>independence</u>?**
landmark _____	Visitors take a boat to see this <u>landmark</u>.	
state _____	Texas is the name of the <u>state</u> where we live.	**What is the name of another <u>state</u>?**
government _____	The U.S. Capitol is an important <u>government</u> building.	
symbol _____	This <u>symbol</u> stands for "Poison."	

Name_____

Read each question and prompt. Discuss the answers with your group. Use your Leveled Reader to find details to support your answers. Then write your answers on the blank lines or on another sheet of paper.

1. Explain what a wildfire is.

   _____

2. What are two things wildfires need to begin?

   _____

3. Name two ways that firefighters fight wildfires.

   _____

4. Describe the big wildfires that happened in 1910, 1988, and 2003.

   _____

5. Explain how wildfires can help plants and animals.

   _____

6. Write one question about the book to ask your group.

   _____

   _____

© Macmillan/McGraw-Hill

One Grain of Rice

Pages 248–249

Prior to reading the selection with children, they should have listened to the selection on **StudentWorks Plus**, the interactive eBook. In addition, selection vocabulary should have been pretaught using the **Visual Vocabulary Resources**.

Access Core Content

Teacher Note Pose the questions after you read the paragraph or page indicated.

Pages 252–253

Title and Illustration

- *This is the title.* (Point to it.) *Let's read the main title together:* One Grain of Rice. *The subtitle is* A Mathematical Folktale.

- *This kind of story is called a folktale. A folktale is a made-up story that happened long ago.*

- *This story is a mathematical folktale. That means it has something to do with math. Do we work mostly with letters or numbers in math?* (numbers) *What number is in the title?* (one) *The number* one *may be important. Let's read to find out.*

Page 254

Text

- *Listen as I read the first sentence aloud:* Long ago in India, there lived a raja who believed that he was wise and fair, as a ruler should be.

- *A raja is a ruler of ancient India, or the India of long ago. Let's say* raja *together:* raja.

 What kinds of things does a wise and fair ruler do for people? Talk with your partner.

Illustration

- *Look at the top picture. Point to the raja. Now find the raja in the bottom picture.*

Pages 252–253

Comprehension

Genre
A Folktale is a made-up story that takes place long ago.

Ask Questions
Make Inferences
As you read, use your Inference Chart.

What I Read	What I Know

Inference

Read to Find Out
What important lesson does the raja learn from Rani?

252

Pages 254–255

Long ago in India, there lived a raja who believed that he was wise and fair, as a raja should be.

254

Main Selection

One Grain of Rice

A MATHEMATICAL FOLKTALE

Written and Illustrated by

Demi

253

The people in his province were rice farmers. The raja decreed that everyone must give nearly all of their rice to him.

"I will **store** the rice safely," the raja promised the people, "so that in time of famine, everyone will have rice to eat, and no one will go hungry."

255

Page 255

Paragraph 1, Choral Reading

- *Let's read this first paragraph together:* The people in his province were rice farmers. The raja decreed that everyone must give nearly all of their rice to him. Decreed *means "ordered." The raja ordered the people to give him nearly all of their rice.*

- Nearly all *means "almost all."* (Write *nearly all = almost all* on the board. Demonstrate *nearly all* by placing a group of pencils on the desk. Pick up almost all of the pencils.) *I picked up nearly all of the pencils.*

- *The people in the story have been ordered to give nearly all, or almost all, of their rice to the raja. Why do the people have to give their rice to the raja?* (because he is their ruler and he said they must)

Paragraph 2

- *The raja says he will store the rice safely. This means he will keep the rice safe.*

- *A time of famine is a time when people do not have enough to eat. The raja promises to keep the rice safe for a time of famine.*

- 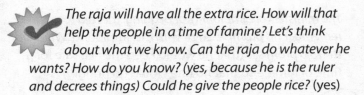 *The raja will have all the extra rice. How will that help the people in a time of famine? Let's think about what we know. Can the raja do whatever he wants? How do you know?* (yes, because he is the ruler and decrees things) *Could he give the people rice?* (yes)

-

Directionality
Ask children to place their finger where you start reading (top left). Ask where you finish reading on this page (bottom right).

Page 256

Paragraphs 1 and 2

- *Let's read the first paragraph together:* Each year, the raja's rice collectors gathered nearly all of the people's rice and carried it away to the royal storehouses. *The collectors took nearly all the rice. Was a lot left, or just a little?* (just a little)

- *The people were left with just enough rice to get by. When people are just getting by, they're having a hard time, not an easy time.*

Paragraph 3

- *Find a word that ends with -ly in this paragraph. What is it?* (badly) *The rice grew badly, which means that the rice grew in a bad way or not well.*

- *Read this sentence after me:* Then one year the rice grew badly, and there was famine and hunger. *Did the people have enough to eat?* (no)

Page 257

Illustration

- *Point to the people bowing in the picture. These people are the raja's ministers. Ministers help the raja run his kingdom.*

- *The ministers are imploring, or begging, the raja to remember his promise. Say it with me:* imploring. *What did the raja promise?* (that he would keep the rice safe for a time of famine so that no one would go hungry)

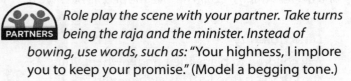
Role play the scene with your partner. Take turns being the raja and the minister. Instead of bowing, use words, such as: "Your highness, I implore you to keep your promise." (Model a begging tone.)

Text

- *Let's read the second paragraph together:* "No!" cried the raja. "How do I know how long the famine may last? I must have rice for myself. Promise or no promise, a raja must not go hungry!"

- *The raja does not want to go hungry. But there is enough rice saved for himself and his people. Why won't he share it?* (He says that he doesn't know how long the famine will last.)

- *The people grow more and more hungry as time goes on. Does the raja give them rice?* (no)

Each year, the raja's rice **collectors** gathered nearly all of the people's rice and carried it away to the royal storehouses.

For many years, the rice grew well. The people gave nearly all of their rice to the raja, and the storehouses were always full. But the people were left with only just enough rice to get by.

Then one year the rice grew badly, and there was famine and hunger. The people had no rice to give to the raja, and they had no rice to eat.

256

One day, the raja ordered a feast for himself and his court — as, it seemed to him, a raja should now and then, even when there is a famine.

A servant led an elephant from a royal storehouse to the palace, carrying two full baskets of rice.

258

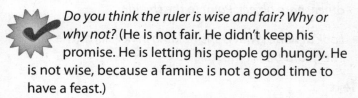

The raja's ministers implored him, "Your Highness, let us open the royal storehouses and give the rice to the people, as you promised."

"No!" cried the raja. "How do I know how long the famine may last? I must have rice for myself. Promise or no promise, a raja must not go hungry!"

Time went on, and the people grew more and more hungry. But the raja would not give out the rice.

257

A village girl named Rani saw that a trickle of rice was falling from one of the baskets. Quickly she jumped up and walked along beside the elephant, catching the falling rice in her skirt. She was **clever**, and she began to make a plan.

259

Page 258

Whole Page

- *In the middle of the famine, or great hunger, the raja decides to give himself a feast, which is a party with lots of food.*

- *Do you think the ruler is wise and fair? Why or why not?* (He is not fair. He didn't keep his promise. He is letting his people go hungry. He is not wise, because a famine is not a good time to have a feast.)

- *The servant brings rice into the palace, which is the raja's big house. How much rice does he bring?* (two baskets full)

Page 259

Whole Page

- *A village girl named Rani sees the elephant carrying the baskets of rice. She sees a trickle of rice falling from one of the baskets.* (Point to the word *trickle* on this page.)

- Trickle *means "to fall in drops or in a small amount." Point to the trickle of rice in the picture. Rice is falling out of the baskets, a few grains at a time. Do the grains look like a big stream of water or like drops of water?* (drops of water)

- *Rani is clever, or smart. A character in a story who is clever might trick someone else. Let's read to find out what Rani's plan is.*

Monitor Oral Production

Remember to model self-corrective techniques on a regular basis as you speak to children. Pretend to say the wrong word and self-correct.

Page 260

Illustration

- *A guard watches over the palace. Say the word after me:* guard. *Point to the guard in the picture. The guard is holding a shield, which can protect him from a sword or other sharp object. Point to the shield.*

- *Look at Rani. What is she holding in her skirt?* (the rice) *The guard thinks she stole it.*

Text

- *Let's pretend we are the guard. Let's show her that she can't come in.* (Demonstrate a halting action with an arm extended outward.) *What do you say to her?* (Children's responses include "Halt!" or "Halt, thief!")

- *Why is the guard calling Rani a thief?* (He thinks she is stealing the rice.)

- *Now let's read what Rani says to the guard:* "I am not a thief," Rani replied. "This rice fell from one of the baskets, and I am returning it now to the raja."

Page 261

Whole Page

- *When you do a good deed, you do something nice that helps another person. Rani did a good deed by returning the rice to the raja.*

- *The raja is happy that Rani gave the rice back to him. He wants to give her a reward. A reward is a prize or a gift that is given to someone who has done something nice, or done a good deed.*

 Pretend that you are Rani and the raja has just offered you a reward. Tell your partner what you would ask for, and why.

> **Formal and Informal English**
>
> When children encounter a word, such as *Your Highness*, used in a formal setting in the text discuss other situations in which that word may be used.

At the palace, a guard cried, "Halt, thief! Where are you going with that rice?"

"I am not a thief," Rani replied. "This rice fell from one of the baskets, and I am returning it now to the raja."

260

"Your Highness," said Rani, "I do not deserve any reward at all. But if you wish, you may give me one grain of rice."

"Only one grain of rice?" exclaimed the raja. "Surely you will allow me to reward you more plentifully, as a raja should."

262

When the raja heard about Rani's good deed, he asked his ministers to bring her before him. "I wish to **reward** you for returning what belongs to me," the raja said to Rani. "Ask me for anything, and you shall have it."

261

"Very well," said Rani. "If it pleases Your Highness, you may reward me in this way. Today, you will give me a single grain of rice. Then, each day for thirty days you will give me **double** the rice you gave me the day before. Thus, tomorrow you will give me two grains of rice, the next day four grains of rice, and so on for thirty days."

263

Text

- *We have read the words* one grain of rice *before. Where did we see them?* (in the title) *Rani asks for only one grain of rice as a reward.*

- *Let's read the second paragraph together to see what the raja says:* "Only one grain of rice?" exclaimed the raja. "Surely you will allow me to reward you more plentifully, as a raja should."

- *Why does the raja want to reward Rani plentifully, or in a big way?* (He thinks that's how a raja should act.)

Text

- *Rani agrees to ask for a bigger reward.*

- *Let's read what Rani says, starting at the end of the second line:* Today, you will give me a single grain of rice. Then, each day for thirty days you will give me double the rice you gave me the day before."

- Double *means "twice as much." Here is an example of what it means to double something.* (Demonstrate the concept of doubling by using small objects or by writing lines on the board.)

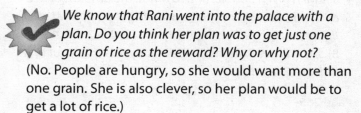 *We know that Rani went into the palace with a plan. Do you think her plan was to get just one grain of rice as the reward? Why or why not?* (No. People are hungry, so she would want more than one grain. She is also clever, so her plan would be to get a lot of rice.)

Illustration

- *The raja has many animals in his palace. Some of them will play a part in the story. Look at the animals in the picture. The birds are called peacocks. Say it with me:* peacocks. *Peacocks are known for their beautiful feathers. Now point to the elephants.*

Page 264

Whole Page

- *The raja thinks that Rani's reward is a modest, or small, reward. Do you think it is a small reward?* (Question is open.)

- *Look at the picture. Who is giving Rani her reward?* (one of the raja's birds)

- *Rani is presented with, or given, a single grain of rice. Single means "one."* (Hold up one finger.) *Is one grain of rice a lot or a little?* (a little)

Page 265

Whole Page

- *On day 2, Rani gets two grains of rice.* (Hold up two fingers.) *On day 3, she gets four grains of rice.* (Hold up four fingers.) *Each day Rani gets double, or two times the amount of rice.*

- *Look at the picture. What are the birds doing?* (giving Rani her reward)

- *In real life, birds would eat the rice. But in this story, birds are giving rice to Rani. Who would have told the birds to do this?* (the raja)

- *If Rani is given double, or two times, the amount of rice each day, how many grains will she get on day 4? Let's figure it out together.* (Write 1 + 1 = 2. 2 + 2 = 4. 4 + 4 = 8) *She will get 8 grains of rice on day 4. Is that a lot or a little rice?* (a little)

Page 266

Illustration

- *Look at the picture. The raja's lion and tiger are giving her the rice now. Let's point to the lion.* (Point to it.) *Let's point to the tiger.* (Point to it.)

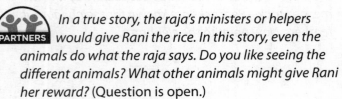 *In a true story, the raja's ministers or helpers would give Rani the rice. In this story, even the animals do what the raja says. Do you like seeing the different animals? What other animals might give Rani her reward?* (Question is open.)

"This seems still to be a modest reward," said the raja. "But you shall have it."

And Rani was presented with a single grain of rice.

264

On the ninth day, Rani was presented with two hundred and fifty-six grains of rice. She had received in all five hundred and eleven grains of rice, only enough for a small handful.

"This girl is honest, but not very clever," thought the raja. "She would have gained more rice by keeping what fell into her skirt!"

266

The next day, Rani was presented with two grains of rice.

And the following day, Rani was presented with four grains of rice.

On the twelfth day, Rani received two thousand and forty-eight grains of rice, about four handfuls. On the thirteenth day, she received four thousand and ninety-six grains of rice, enough to fill a bowl.

Make Inferences
Think about Rani's reward. Make an inference about why she asked for it in this special way.

Text
- *When someone gives you something, you receive it, or get it. On the ninth day, Rani receives, or gets, a handful of rice. (Use your hand to demonstrate handful.) Do you think this is very much rice?* (no)

- *The raja thinks she is honest but not clever. She had more than a handful of rice in her skirt!*

Page 267

Whole Page
- *On the twelfth day, Rani receives, or gets, about four handfuls of rice. (Demonstrate four handfuls by using your hands and a child's hands.)*

- *Let's read the first sentence together:* On the twelfth day, Rani received two thousand and forty-eight grains of rice, about four handfuls. *The sentence says* about four handfuls. About *means almost, or not exactly.*

- *On the thirteenth day she has enough rice to fill a bowl. (Cup your hands together to demonstrate a bowlful of rice.) Is that a lot of rice?* (no)

- *Let's think about the number of grains. On the second day, she had two grains. Now she has more than two thousand grains. Has the number grown a lot or a little?* (a lot)

 The raja thinks that Rani is not clever. He does not think she will get much rice from her plan. Why do you think she asked for her reward in this special way? (to fool him)

Page 268

Whole Page

- *On the sixteenth day, Rani has enough rice to fill two bags. (Hold up two fingers.) Point to the bag in the picture. Rani has enough rice to fill two of these bags.*

- *The raja says that he doesn't think her reward will amount to much more rice. This means that he doesn't think he will have to give her much more rice.*

- *It is now the sixteenth day. How many days are left? (fourteen) Do you think he will give her a lot more rice or a little more rice? (a lot more)*

Page 269

Paragraph 1, Echo Reading

- *Let's read the first paragraph. I'll read it first, then you repeat what I say.* <u>On the twentieth day, Rani was presented with sixteen more bags of rice.</u>

- *Sixteen bags of rice seems like a lot. Why is she getting more rice? (because the raja has to double the amount of rice each day)*

Paragraphs 2 and 3

- *By the twenty-fourth day Rani has enough rice to fill eight baskets. A basket is much bigger than a bag. A basket holds a lot more rice. Let's count the baskets on this page together. (Count the eight baskets with the children.)*

- *Rani now has eight million, three hundred eighty-four thousand, six hundred and eight grains of rice. What do you think of Rani's plan now? (Answers should reflect that Rani's plan is clever.)*

On the sixteenth day, Rani was presented with a bag containing thirty-two thousand, seven hundred and sixty-eight grains of rice. All together she had enough rice for two full bags.

"This doubling adds up to more rice than I expected!" thought the raja. "But surely her reward won't **amount** to much more."

268

On the twenty-seventh day, thirty-two Brahma bulls were needed to deliver sixty-four baskets of rice.

270

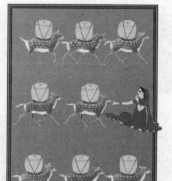

On the twentieth day, Rani was presented with sixteen more bags filled with rice.

On the twenty-first day, she received one million, forty-eight thousand, five hundred and seventy-six grains of rice, enough to fill a basket.

On the twenty-fourth day, Rani was presented with eight million, three hundred and eighty-eight thousand, six hundred and eight grains of rice—enough to fill eight baskets, which were carried to her by eight royal deer.

269

The raja was deeply troubled. "One grain of rice has grown very great indeed," he thought. "But I shall fulfill the reward to the end, as a raja should."

271

Page 270

Text, Choral Reading

- *Let's read this page together:* On the twenty-seventh day, thirty-two Brahma bulls were needed to deliver sixty-four baskets of rice.

 Rani now has sixty-four baskets of rice! Brahma bulls, which are like cows, carry the baskets of rice to Rani. How do you think Rani is feeling now? (Rani is happy with all the rice she is receiving for the people.)

Page 271

Text

- *Let's read the first sentence together.* The raja was deeply troubled. *Deeply troubled means "worried." Why do you think the raja is worried?* (because he is giving Rani so much rice)

- *The raja says that one grain of rice has grown very great indeed. This means that one grain of rice has turned into many, many grains of rice. Why is he giving Rani so many grains of rice now?* (because she asked for double the amount of rice each day)

- *The raja says that he will fulfill the reward to the end. This means that he will keep his promise to Rani. Do you think he will keep his promise to the end?* (Answers will vary.)

Illustration

 Find Rani on page 271 and show her to your partner. How do you think she is feeling now? Why does she feel that way? (She is so happy that she looks like she is dancing. She is happy to see the bulls. She is happy that he will fulfill the reward.)

Text

- *Listen as I read the paragraph on page 268:* <u>On the twenty-ninth day, Rani was presented with the contents of two royal storehouses.</u> *That is two times bigger than the day before.*

- *A storehouse is a big building that holds a lot of things, such as rice. If something is royal, it belongs to a ruler, such as a king or queen. Who do the storehouses in the story belong to?* (the raja)

Illustration

- *Look at the picture on pages 272–273. What animals are bringing the rice to Rani?* (camels) *Is Rani getting a lot of rice or a little?* (a lot)

Illustrations

- *Look at the pictures of all the elephants. They are crossing the province carrying rice.* Province *means "land or country." The elephants cross the land or country carrying the last of the rice to Rani.*

 Pretend that you and your partner live in the provinces. You haven't had a lot to eat for many years. Now here come so many elephants with rice for everyone! What would you say to your partner? (Response is open.)

On the twenty-ninth day, Rani was presented with the contents of two royal storehouses.

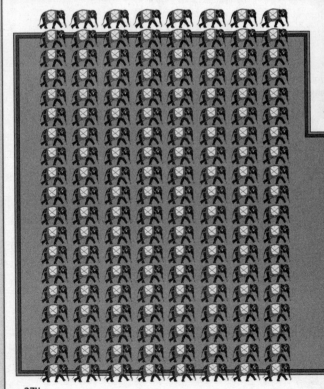

272

274

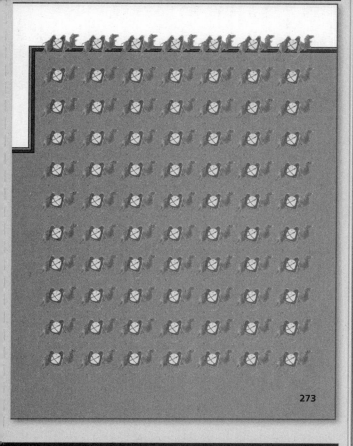

273

Text

- *Listen as I read aloud this sentence: 536, 870, 912. That is a huge amount of rice!* (Write 536,870,912.) *That is the contents, or what is inside, the last four royal storehouses.*

- *This is the last of the rice from the raja's storehouses. How do you think the raja feels now about the reward? Why do you think that?* (Question is open.)

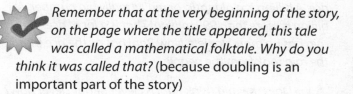 *Remember that at the very beginning of the story, on the page where the title appeared, this tale was called a mathematical folktale. Why do you think it was called that?* (because doubling is an important part of the story)

On the thirtieth and final day, two hundred and fifty-six elephants crossed the province, carrying the contents of the last four royal storehouses — five hundred and thirty-six million, eight hundred and seventy thousand, nine hundred and twelve grains of rice.

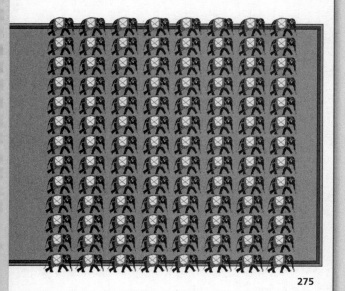

275

Page 276

Whole Page

- *Look at the mountains of grains of rice on this page! How do you think the people feel now? What makes you think so?* (happy, because they seem to be dancing and playing in all the rice)

- *Rani has now received more than one billion grains of rice. A billion is a gigantic, or really, really big number. A billion is more than 999 million! That is a lot of rice. The raja has no more rice left. Now Rani has all the rice that the raja took from the people.*

 Does the raja think Rani is clever or not clever now? Why? (clever because she had such a good plan to get the rice back)

All together, Rani had received more than one billion grains of rice. The raja had no more rice to give. "And what will you do with this rice" said the raja with a sigh, "now that I have none?"

 Make Inferences
Use details from the story and what you already know to make an inference about the lesson the raja learned.

276

"I shall give it to all the hungry people," said Rani. "And I shall leave a basket of rice for you, too, if you promise from now on to take only as much rice as you need."

"I promise," said the raja.

And for the rest of his days, the raja was truly wise and fair, as a raja should be.

277

Page 277

Whole Page

- *Rani says she will share a basket of rice with the raja. What does she make him promise?* (never to take more rice than he needs again)

- *Point to the very last sentence on page 277, and let's read it aloud:* And for the rest of his days, the raja was truly wise and fair, as a raja should be.

 What lesson do you think the raja has learned? (He has learned not to be greedy. He has learned to be fair and to think of others.)

Same Story, Different Culture

Access Core Content

Teacher Note Pose the questions after you read the paragraph or page indicated.

Page 280

Title

- *Let's read the title together:* Same Story, Different Culture. Culture *means "the traditions or beliefs of a group of people." Different countries have different cultures, or beliefs and traditions. This title means that the same story is told differently by different cultures, or groups of people.*

Text

- *The story of Cinderella is a famous fairy tale. Famous means that people all around the world have heard of the story. If something is famous, it is known by many people. Let's think of other things that are famous.* (movie stars, musicians, presidents.)

- *The story of Cinderella in our country, or culture, tells about a young girl who lives with her cruel, or mean stepmother and two mean stepsisters. She gets to go to the prince's ball, or big party, and the prince falls in love with her.*

- *In the end, Cinderella and the prince get married and live happily ever after. The story of Cinderella has a moral, or lesson, at the end. The moral of this story is that kindness is rewarded and cruelty, or meanness, is punished.*

- *What was the moral, or lesson, of the story* One Grain of Rice? (Kindness wins over cruelty and selfishness.)

- *The last sentence on this page tells us that we will read summaries of different Cinderella stories. Summaries are short retellings of a story.*

- *Summaries tell the main ideas in a story. Say the word with me:* summaries. *The summaries will introduce us to different versions of the Cinderella story .*

Pages 280–281

Social Studies

Genre
Expository text gives facts and information about a topic.

✿ **Text Feature**
Headings tell what information is found in the sections of an article.

Content Vocabulary
famous

moral

summaries

280

Same Story Different Culture

Children all over the world know the story of Cinderella. It is one of the most **famous** fairy tales of all time. However, people in different countries tell different versions of the story. No matter where they come from, Cinderella stories all have the same message. The **moral** is that kindness will be rewarded and cruelty will be punished. The text that follows has **summaries** of Cinderella stories from around the world.

Pages 282–283

A Chinese Cinderella

Yeh-Shen is a Cinderella story from China. Yeh-Shen's story is about 1,000 years older than the first known Cinderella story in Europe.

Like the Cinderella in the traditional story, Yeh-Shen grows up with a cruel stepmother. In this story, however, the stepmother kills Yeh-Shen's only friend, who is a fish. Yeh-Shen takes the fish's bones and buries them. The fish bones turn out to be very powerful.

When Yeh-Shen makes a wish to go to the spring festival, the fish bones give her a beautiful dress and golden slippers to wear. Unfortunately Yeh-Shen loses one of the slippers at the festival. The king finds the lost slipper and says that he wants to marry its owner.

Just like in the European version of the story, many women try on the golden slipper, but it fits only Yeh-Shen. Yeh-Shen marries the king and lives happily ever after.

282

An English Cinderella

In this tale from England, the main character is named Tattercoats instead of Cinderella. People call her Tattercoats because her clothing is so torn and ragged. In the traditional version of the story, Cinderella is mistreated by her stepmother and stepsisters. In this English version, Tattercoats lives with her grandfather, who does not treat her kindly.

In the middle of the story, Tattercoats's grandfather refuses to let Tattercoats go to the royal ball to meet the prince. Just like in the version of the story you know well, Tattercoats finds a way to go to the ball. At the party, she meets the prince. The prince falls in love and asks Tattercoats to marry him. The couple lives together happily, while Tattercoats's grandfather returns to his castle all alone.

281

Conclusion

The Cinderella character exists in many different cultures. In each story the main character may wear different clothes or go to different events. But one thing is the same in every culture. Cinderella always overcomes a difficult beginning to find a happy ending.

⚜ Connect and Compare

1. In which section would you find information about a Cinderella story in England? **Headings**

2. Think about *One Grain of Rice*. In what ways is the English version of Cinderella like *One Grain of Rice*? How are the stories different? **Reading/Writing Across Texts**

Social Studies Activity

Research a fairy tale from a country in Europe or Asia. Write a paragraph that compares that country's culture to your own culture. Share with your class. Speak clearly using correct language.

LOG ON ● FIND OUT **Social Studies** Fairy Tales
www.macmillanmh.com

283

Page 281

Whole Page

- *Headings tell what a section of an article will be about. What do you find out from this heading? (that this section is about an English version of* Cinderella*) An English story is a story from England.*

- *We know that the word* cinder *in Cinderella's name comes from the fact that she had to sleep in the fireplace. She'd lie down among the ashes and cinders in the fireplace to keep warm, so she is covered with cinders.*

- *If I say something is "in tatters," that object or piece of clothing is ready to be thrown away. It is so old and raggedy that you can't wear it anymore.*

PARTNERS *With your partner, talk about some ideas that would explain how Tattercoats got her name.*

- *Find other words on page 277 that remind you of things in the Cinderella version that you know. Point to them, and let's say them aloud:* ball, prince, castle, lives together happily.

Page 282

Whole Page

- *The heading on page 282 says* A Chinese Cinderella. *Chinese means from China.*

- *Find words or phrases in Yeh-Shen's story that remind you of the Cinderella story. (cruel stepmother, golden slippers, beautiful dress, lives happily ever after)*

Page 283

Whole Page

- *Point to the heading on this page. It is the* Conclusion, *or ending. It tells the main ideas of the selection.*

PARTNERS *Look at the picture on page 283. What part of the Conclusion does this show? (how the two Cinderella characters are different)*

- *The last sentence tells how the Cinderella character is the same in different versions. Let's read it together:* Cinderella always overcomes a difficult beginning to find a happy ending.

Name_____

Use the word chart to study this week's vocabulary words.
Write a sentence using each word in your writer's notebook.

Word	Context Sentence	Illustration
collectors _____	The collectors looked at the stamps they had gathered.	
store _____	In winter, I store my bike in the shed.	
clever _____	My clever dog brings her leash when she wants to walk.	
reward _____	I reward my dog with a hug when she obeys a command.	**Why might someone be rewarded?**
double _____	John has double the homework of Max.	
amount _____	What amount do I owe you?	

© Macmillan/McGraw-Hill

Read each question and prompt. Discuss the answers with your group. Use your Leveled Reader to find details to support your answers. Then write your answers on the blank lines or on another sheet of paper.

1. Name the characters in your book.

   _____

2. Describe what the characters in your book were like.

   _____

3. Explain what problem the main character has.

   _____

4. Explain why the main character in your book is rewarded.

   _____

5. Share something you learned from your book.

   _____

6. Write one question about the book to ask your group.

   _____

   _____

African-American Inventors

Pages 290–291

Prior to reading the selection with children, they should have listened to the selection on **StudentWorks Plus**, the interactive eBook. In addition, selection vocabulary should have been pretaught using the **Visual Vocabulary Resources**.

Access Core Content

Teacher Note Pose the questions after you read the paragraph or page indicated.

Pages 290–291

Title

- *We just read about young inventors in* Kid Inventors Then and Now. *What did the young people do? Why do we call them inventors?* (They made new things that no one had made before.) *In this selection, we will read about some other inventors.*

- *All the inventors in* Kid Inventors Then and Now *were children or teenagers. All the inventors in the selection we will read now are African Americans.*

Page 292

Text

- *Read the title of this page with me:* Introduction. *The introduction comes before the main part of a selection. It tells you what you are going to learn. It can also help you get interested.*

- *Let's read the last sentence of the paragraph together to find out the main idea:* Throughout our history, African Americans have invented many important things.

- *To invent is to make something no one has made before.* (Write *invent*, *inventor*, and *invention* on the board. Underline *invent* in each word.) *An invention is what someone invents. The person who invents is an inventor.*

Comprehension

Genre
A Biography is the story of a person's life written by another person.

Ask Questions
Compare and Contrast
As you read, use the Compare and Contrast Chart.

Different Alike Different

Read to Find Out
How are these inventors alike? How are they different?

290

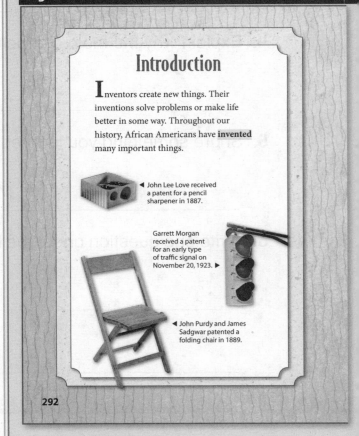

Introduction

Inventors create new things. Their inventions solve problems or make life better in some way. Throughout our history, African Americans have **invented** many important things.

◄ John Lee Love received a patent for a pencil sharpener in 1887.

Garrett Morgan received a patent for an early type of traffic signal on November 20, 1923. ▶

◄ John Purdy and James Sadgwar patented a folding chair in 1889.

292

Main Selection

African-American INVENTORS

by Jim Haskins
illustrated by Eric Velasquez

Award Winning Illustrator

ED STATES PATENT OFFICE

291

Benjamin Banneker

Benjamin Banneker was born on a farm in Maryland in 1731. At that time, Maryland was one of thirteen British colonies in North America.

Most African-American people in the colonies were enslaved, but Benjamin's parents were free. Because Benjamin was born to a free family, he could go to school.

▲ Benjamin Banneker grew up near Baltimore, Maryland, in the mid-1700s.

293

Captions and Art

- *Look at the art. Are these items ones you see often and use?* (yes) *The art and captions make the introduction lively. We can see right away that these inventors have made a difference in our lives.*

- *Let's read the first caption together:* John Lee received a patent for a pencil sharpener in 1887.

- *A patent is an official paper from the government. It says that the inventor of a certain invention is the only person allowed to make and sell that invention. Why would an inventor want a patent?* (so other people couldn't take the inventor's idea and pretend it was their own)

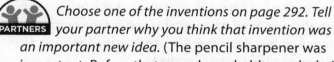 *Choose one of the inventions on page 292. Tell your partner why you think that invention was an important new idea.* (The pencil sharpener was important. Before that, people probably used a knife to sharpen pencils. A pencil sharpener is safer.)

Page 293

Whole Page

- *Say the name of this inventor with me:* Benjamin Banneker. *Now let's read the second paragraph together.*

- *The author says that most African Americans were enslaved. An enslaved person, or slave, is forced to work for someone without getting paid.*

- *Benjamin Banneker's parents were not slaves. How were their lives different from those of other African Americans?* (They got paid for their work. They were allowed to send Benjamin to school.)

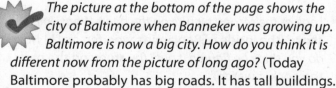 *The picture at the bottom of the page shows the city of Baltimore when Banneker was growing up. Baltimore is now a big city. How do you think it is different now from the picture of long ago?* (Today Baltimore probably has big roads. It has tall buildings. People use cars and trucks. People don't use ships like those in the pictures.)

Page 294

Whole Page

- *Benjamin went to a local school. That means he went to a school in his community. What are some other things in our community? Use the word* local *to tell me. Here is an example:* I shop at a local grocery store.

- *Benjamin was good at math. Which of the following things would a person who is very good at math do well: add numbers, measure things, sing, figure out problems, write stories?* (add numbers, measure things, figure out problems)

- *After he finished his education, or schooling, Benjamin worked on the family farm. How might he have used his math skills there?* (to measure food for the animals, to measure fences for building, to measure animals, to figure out how to pay for things)

 Benjamin would have learned other skills on the farm. Talk with your partner about the kinds of things he would have learned. (how to plant things, how to take care of animals, the importance of weather)

Page 295

Whole Page

- *Point to the picture of the pocket watch. This is a kind of watch people used long ago. They kept the watch in their pocket and pulled it out to tell the time*

- *Benjamin met a man who had a pocket watch that was made in Europe. He was interested in it, so the man gave it to him. Do you think Benjamin was interested in how the watch looked or how it worked?* (how it worked)

- *Look at the second picture on the page. What does it show?* (the inside of Benjamin's wooden clock) *How do you think he figured it out?* (by studying the parts of the pocket watch)

- *Let's read the second paragraph together to find out if we were right.*

Pages 294–295

In the 1700s many schoolhouses were one room. ▼

Benjamin went to a local school for boys. He was so good at math that he soon knew more than his teacher. After he finished his education, Benjamin worked on the family farm.

294

Pages 296–297

Benjamin used his clock to measure the movements of the stars. He used math to figure out the position of the stars, sun, moon, and planets. Years later, he wrote an almanac. An almanac is a book that lists the positions of the sun, moon, and planets for every day of the year.

▲ Benjamin published almanacs from 1792 to 1797.

296

Benjamin's life changed when he was twenty years old. He met a man who owned a pocket watch. The watch had been made in Europe. Benjamin was so interested in the watch that the man let him keep it.

Benjamin studied the watch, its parts, and the way it was made. He decided to make his own clock out of wood. It was the first clock ever made in North America.

◄ Benjamin Banneker's wooden clock worked perfectly for more than 40 years.

295

Benjamin wrote a new almanac every year for six years. People read it to find out when the sun and moon would rise and set. They read it to find out how the weather would change each season. Many farmers used Benjamin's almanacs so they would know when to plant their crops. He was as famous for his almanacs as he was for his clock.

▲ Farming in the 1700s was done by hand. Tractors and other farm machines had not been invented yet.

297

Page 296

Whole Page

- *Let's read the sentence that tells what an almanac is together.* An almanac is a book that lists the positions of the sun, moon, and planets for every day of the year. *It tells where the sun, moon, and planets are in the sky at different times each day.*

- *How did Benjamin figure out the postions?* (He used his math skills.)

- *Let's read the caption under the picture of the almanacs. For how many years did Benjamin publish his almanacs?* (six years)

Page 297

Whole Page

- *The information in the almanac was important for farmers. Why did they need to know when the sun and moon would rise and set?* (to plan their workdays)

- *Benjamin's almanac also predicted how the weather would change in each season. Why was this information important to farmers?* (The crops need rain and sun to grow. Farmers need to plan times for planting and picking their crops.)

- *Let's read the caption under the picture together to help us understand how different life was when Benjamin lived:* Farming in the 1700s was done by hand. Tractors and other farm machines had not been invented yet.

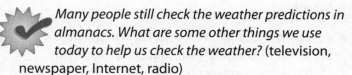 *Many people still check the weather predictions in almanacs. What are some other things we use today to help us check the weather?* (television, newspaper, Internet, radio)

- *Why was Benjamin Banneker important?* (He made the first clock in the United States. He wrote almanacs.)

Page 298

Whole Page

- *Let's read the first paragraph together. What do we know about Sarah E. Goode? (She was the first African-American woman to receive a patent for an invention.)*

- *Look at the caption next to the picture of Sarah and her patent. When did she receive it? (in 1885)*

- *Point to the words* cabinet-bed *near the top of the patent. (Point to* cabinet-bed.*) Now say* cabinet-bed *with me. Sarah invented a type of cabinet bed.*

- *You know what a bed is. A cabinet is a piece of furniture with drawers and shelves. People use cabinets to store things. What kinds of things might you store, or keep, in a cabinet? (clothing, dishes, paper, pencils)*

- *What do you think a cabinet bed might be? (a bed that fits into a cabinet, a bed that has a cabinet under it)*

- *Listen as I read the second paragraph. Now imagine that you have invented something. Why would you need a patent? (so no one else can say they invented it)*

Page 299

- *Let's read the caption at the top of the page:* Sarah Goode owned a furniture store in the 1880s. *What are some kinds of furniture? (bed, table, chair)*

- *Listen as I read the page aloud. Was Sarah born free or a slave? (a slave) When she became free, what did she do?* (She went to school. Later she owned her own business.)

- *Benjamin and Sarah were different in many ways. Benjamin lived in the 1700s, and Sarah lived in the _____. (1800s) Benjamin was born free, and Sarah was born a _____. (slave) Benjamin lived in Maryland, and Sarah lived in _____. (Chicago)*

- *Now tell me ways that Benjamin and Sarah were alike.* (They were African Americans. They went to school. They both were smart, and they worked hard. They became famous inventors.)

Sarah E. Goode

We know quite a bit about Benjamin Banneker. We know very little about Sarah E. Goode. What we do know is that she was the first African-American woman to receive a patent for an invention.

A patent is a legal paper. It is given out by the United States government in Washington, D.C. A person who invents something can get a patent to prove that he or she was the first to have made it. No one else can say they invented that same thing.

Sarah Goode received her patent in 1885. ▼

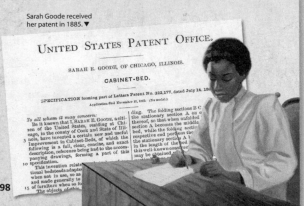

298

Many African-American people were moving from southern states to northern states in the 1870s and 1880s. They moved into apartment houses. Sometimes many people slept in one room. This was because many people did not have enough money to rent their own rooms.

Sarah had the idea of making a bed that could fit in a small space. It could fold up during the day and unfold at night. She worked out a **design**. Then she made a model.

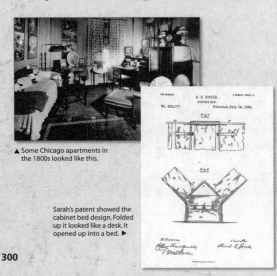

▲ Some Chicago apartments in the 1800s looked like this.

Sarah's patent showed the cabinet bed design. Folded up it looked like a desk. It opened up into a bed. ▶

300

Sarah Goode owned a furniture ▶
store in the 1880s.

▲ In the 1880s and 1890s many people moved to Chicago to find jobs.

Sarah was born in a southern state in 1850. She was born into slavery. When slavery ended, Sarah was a teenager. She was able to go to school once she was free. After she received her education, Sarah moved to Chicago, Illinois.

Sarah must have been smart and hard working. By the time she was 35 years old, she owned her own business. Sarah Goode was the owner of a furniture store.

299

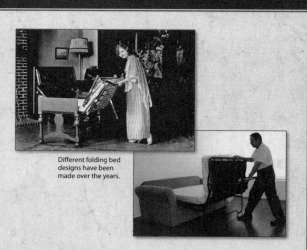
Different folding bed
designs have been
made over the years.

Sarah called her invention a "cabinet bed." When it was folded up, it could be used as a desk. There was even a place for keeping pens and paper.

Sarah did not want anyone else to copy her invention. She made sure of that by getting a patent.

We do not know how many cabinet beds Sarah made. We do know that her idea is still helpful for people. Folding beds are still in use today.

Compare and Contrast
Compare Benjamin Banneker's and Sarah Goode's inventions. How did they help people? Use story details.

301

Page 300

Whole Page

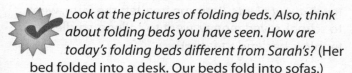
PARTNERS *Look at the picture of the kind of home many people had in Chicago in the 1800s. People did not have much space. Take turns with your partner naming things you see in this small room.*

■ *Let's read the second paragraph together.*

■ *Why did Sarah invent a cabinet-bed?* (It could fit in a small space. It could fold up during the day.)

Page 301

Whole Page

■ *What kind of cabinet was Sarah's bed when it folded up?* (a desk)

■ *Remember that a cabinet is a piece of furniture with drawers and shelves. Why is a desk a kind of cabinet?* (because a desk has drawers and it stores things)

✔ *Look at the pictures of folding beds. Also, think about folding beds you have seen. How are today's folding beds different from Sarah's?* (Her bed folded into a desk. Our beds fold into sofas.)

Patterns in Language
Some grammatical structures, such as past tense "ed," pose difficulties to ELLs. Point out that there are several examples of words ending in *-ed* in this selection, such as, *moved, worked, called, folded*. Help children find a pattern.

Page 302

Whole Page

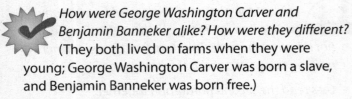

How were George Washington Carver and Benjamin Banneker alike? How were they different? (They both lived on farms when they were young; George Washington Carver was born a slave, and Benjamin Banneker was born free.)

■ *People called George the Plant Doctor. Why did they do so?* (He knew a lot about plants.)

■ *Look at the picture. What did people use in the 1870s instead of cars?* (horses and buggies, or carriages) *What were the roads made of?* (dirt) *Nowadays, roads are made of asphalt, which makes the ride much smoother. Also, today roads do not become muddy in the rain.*

Page 303

Whole Page

■ *Let's think of all the steps George went through to teach about plants.* (became free, left the farm, went to school, saved money, went to college, studied farming, became a teacher)

■ *Look at all that George did to become a teacher. What kind of person do you think he was?* (He was smart. He was a hard worker.)

■ *Let's read the caption under the photograph together:* George graduated from college in 1894. *Graduated means that he finished taking all the classes he needed to take. He finished his work in college.*

■

> **Directionality**
> Ask children to place their finger where you start reading (top left). Ask where you finish reading on this page (bottom right).

George Washington Carver

George Washington Carver was born in Missouri about 1861. Like Sarah E. Goode, he was born into slavery. His family was enslaved by a couple named Carver. George was raised by Mr. and Mrs. Carver.

George loved the Carver farm, with all of its plants and animals. He planted his own garden. Soon, he knew so much about plants that people called him the Plant Doctor.

▲ This is a painting of a typical farm in the 1870s.

302

▲ George taught at his college in Alabama.

George taught at Tuskegee Institute in Alabama. It was a college for African-American people. He studied plants at the college. George told farmers that peanuts and sweet potatoes were good crops to grow. He found that he could make 118 different **products** from the sweet potato. These included soap, coffee, and glue.

▲ George told farmers which vegetables were useful crops to grow.

304

▲ George Washington Carver at school.

George wanted to go to school to learn more about plants. Slavery was over, so he was free to leave the Carver farm. It took him twenty years to get enough education and save enough money to enter college.

George went to college in Iowa. He was the first African-American student at the school. He studied farming and learned even more about plants. When he graduated, he became a teacher.

▲ George graduated from college in 1894.

303

George learned that he could do even more with peanuts. He made over 300 different products from peanuts. Some of these were peanut butter, ice cream, paper, ink, shaving cream, and shampoo. George only received three patents for the products he invented. He believed that most of them should belong to everyone.

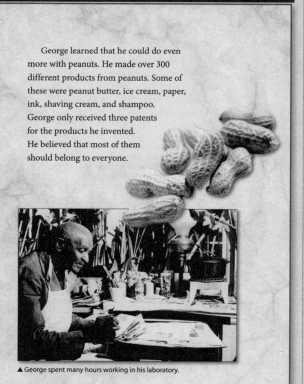

▲ George spent many hours working in his laboratory.

305

Page 304

Whole Page

- *Let's read together the sentences that tell what George learned about sweet potatoes:* He found that he could make 118 different products from the sweet potato. These included soap, coffee, and glue.

- *Your family probably does not make soap, coffee, and glue from sweet potatoes. What are some ways your family does use sweet potatoes?* (candied sweet potatoes, sweet potato pie, sweet potato fries)

- *Let's read the caption below the picture of George:* George told farmers which vegetables were useful crops to grow.

- *Pretend you are a farmer and you grow sweet potatoes. Would you be happy or sad to know that 118 products can be made from sweet potatoes? Why?* (happy, because I could sell lots of them and make money to live)

Page 305

Whole Page

- *Let's read together the sentences that tell what George learned about peanuts:* He made over 300 different products from peanuts. Some of these were peanut butter, ice cream, paper, ink, shaving cream, and shampoo.

- *Look at the picture of George in his laboratory. He was very hard working.*

- *George believed that most of his patents should belong to everyone. What does this tell you about him?* (He cared about people. He was generous.)

- **PARTNERS** *Make one web about sweet potatoes and one web about peanuts. (Show students how to make the webs and label the center circles.) Write the names of things that people make from them. You can use products from the selection and other ones you know about.*

Page 306

Whole Page

■ *Point to the heading on this page. It says* Patricia Bath, M.D. *The letters* M.D. *after a person's name mean "medical doctor." People call Patricia Bath "Dr. Bath." Who are some doctors you know?* (Question is open.)

Let's reread the first paragraph on page 299 together to help us remember about Sarah Goode. What is one way that Sarah Goode is different from Patricia Bath? (Sarah was born in a southern state. Patricia was born in a northern state.)

■ Disease *means "sickness." Say the word with me:* disease. *Cancer is one kind of disease.*

Page 307

Whole Page

■ *Say the word* cataract. *This is the name of the eye disease that Patricia wanted to cure.*

■ *Let's read together what the author tells us about cataracts:* Cataracts are like clouds on the lens of the eye. They make everything look cloudy.

■ *Think of something cloudy, like a big piece of ice. Would it be hard or easy to look at something through a big piece of ice?* (hard)

■ *Let's imagine a wet ball with a layer of ice all over it. How could we get the ice off? We could hit the ice with a big stick. The ice would break up and fall off. Patricia's invention works something like that. Instead of a stick, a strong light breaks up a cataract.*

Patricia Bath, M.D.

Patricia Bath was born more than 75 years after George Washington Carver. Patricia was born in a northern state. She grew up in the New York City neighborhood of Harlem.

Like George Washington Carver, she was still young when she began to study living things. Her special interest was human diseases. After high school, she got a job helping people who studied cancer.

306   ▲ Patricia Bath grew up in Harlem, New York, in the 1940s.

In 1988 Patricia received a patent for the instrument she invented. She was the first African-American woman to get a patent for a medical invention. Since then she has invented other eye instruments. Her work has **allowed** many people to see again.

Compare and Contrast
Compare and contrast Patricia Bath and George Washington Carver. How are their lives similar? How are they different? Use photos and story details.

◀ Dr. Patricia Bath has invented many eye instruments.

308

In college, Patricia studied chemistry. Then she went to medical school. She decided to study eye diseases. She wanted to find out how to remove cataracts.

Cataracts are like clouds on the lens of the eye. They make everything look cloudy. Patricia designed an **instrument** for removing cataracts. It gives off a **powerful** beam of light that breaks up the cataract. Then it can be removed.

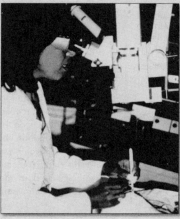

▲ Dr. Patricia Bath performing eye surgery.

307

Inventors Change the World

The stories of these four inventors show how African-American inventors have helped make life better for all Americans throughout history. Benjamin Banneker helped people keep time and know the positions of the stars and planets. Sarah Goode made furniture for people to use in small homes. George Washington Carver made hundreds of products from sweet potatoes and peanuts. Dr. Patricia Bath invented a cure for one kind of blindness. The world is better because of their work.

309

Page 308

Whole Page

- *Look at the picture. It shows another instrument, or tool, that Patricia invented for looking at eyes.*

- *Think about what Patricia has done. What kind of person do you think she is?* (smart, caring, hard working)

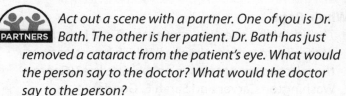 *Act out a scene with a partner. One of you is Dr. Bath. The other is her patient. Dr. Bath has just removed a cataract from the patient's eye. What would the person say to the doctor? What would the doctor say to the person?*

Page 309

Whole Page

- *Let's read the heading together:* Inventors Change the World. *Which invention do you think was the most important?* (Question is open.)

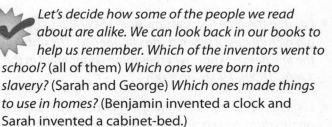 *Let's decide how some of the people we read about are alike. We can look back in our books to help us remember. Which of the inventors went to school?* (all of them) *Which ones were born into slavery?* (Sarah and George) *Which ones made things to use in homes?* (Benjamin invented a clock and Sarah invented a cabinet-bed.)

Seek Clarification

Some children may be confused by unfamiliar words, such as *throughout*. Encourage children to always seek clarification when they encounter a word or phrase that does not make sense to them. For example, *I don't understand the word "throughout."*

Inventors
Time Line

Access Core Content

Teacher Note Pose the questions after you read the paragraph or page indicated.

Pages 312–313

Whole Page

- *The title of this selection is* Inventors Time Line. *Look at the diagram of the time line. Which inventors from the selection are not shown on the time line?* (George Washington Carver and Sarah E. Goode)

- *Let's read the paragraph together.*

- *Now answer yes or no to each question: Does a time line tell what happened?* (yes) *Does it tell where things happen?* (no) *Does it tell when things happen?* (yes) *Does it tell how things happen?* (no)

- *Point to the dates on the time line. They help us get the big picture about when things happened. The dates on the line help us know whether things happened in the 1700s, 1800s, 1900s, or 2000s.*

- *Look at the date 1731. Something important happened on this date. Now point to the sentence beside it. This sentence tells what happened.*

- *Now point to 1792. What happened on this date? Benjamin Banneker published an almanac.*

- *Look at the sentences next to these dates: 1731, 1858, 1942. How are the sentences alike?* (They all tell when inventors were born.)

Social Studies

Genre
Expository text gives facts and information about real people and events.

✓ **Text Feature**
A Time Line is a line that shows dates of important events in the order in which they happened.

Content Vocabulary
predict
events
information

Inventors Time Line

1731 - Benjamin Banneker is born.

| 1700 | 1750 | 1800 |

1792 - Benjamin Banneker publishes an almanac. It helps predict weather for the coming year.

A time line is helpful for finding out when important **events** took place. The time line on these pages gives you **information** about some of the inventors you have read about this week. You can see when they were born and when they created their inventions.

312

Social Studies

1858 - Chester Greenwood is born.	**1942** - Patricia Bath is born.	**1988** - Dr. Bath receives a patent.	

1850	1900	1950	2000

1873 - Chester Greenwood invents earmuffs. **1983** - K-K Gregory is born. **1993** - K-K Gregory invents Wristies.

Connect and Compare

1. Which was invented first, earmuffs or Wristies? How do you know? **Time Line**

2. Think about this time line and *African-American Inventors*. Choose one inventor from the selection and make a time line of his or her life. **Reading/Writing Across Texts**

Social Studies Activity

Research another famous inventor. Make a time line that shows important events in his or her life.

LOG ON · FIND OUT **Inventors** www.macmillanmh.com

313

- Some of the dates and sentences are above the time line. Some are below it. The author did this to fit all the information on the time line.

PARTNERS Look at the time line and the inventions that are shown. Take turns pretending to be one of the inventors. Act out using the invention that is described. Partners should find the part of the time line that tells when that invention was invented and point to it.

- The time line does not show all that we learned about inventors. What detail could we add about Benjamin Banneker? (a sentence that explains that he made the first American clock)

- What detail could we add about Dr. Bath? (a sentence that tells what she invented)

Name _____

Use the word chart to study this week's vocabulary words. Write a sentence using each word in your writer's notebook.

Word	Context Sentence	Illustration
allowed _____	We are not <u>allowed</u> to wear baseball caps in school.	**Describe things you are not allowed to do in school.**
powerful _____	Many trees fell during the <u>powerful</u> winter storm.	
invented _____	Thomas Edison <u>invented</u> the light bulb.	
instrument _____	The dentist used a special <u>instrument</u> to clean my teeth.	
products _____	We bought paper <u>products</u> for the picnic.	
design _____	The mittens have a snowflake <u>design</u>.	

Name _____

Read each question and prompt. Discuss the answers with your group. Use your Leveled Reader to find details to support your answers. Then write your answers on the blank lines or on another sheet of paper.

I. Explain some ways that people use computers.

_____

2. Tell how computers have changed since the first computer was invented.

_____

3. List some things that contain computers.

_____

4. Describe how life would be different without computers.

_____

5. Share your ideas about how computers can help people in the future.

_____

6. Write one question about the book to ask your group.

_____

Weekly Planners

Week 1

Selections	Vocabulary		ELL Practice Book
	Key Selection Words/Cognates	Academic Language/Cognates	
The Alvin Ailey Kids: Dancing as a Team *You'll Sing a Song and I'll Sing a Song*	perform effort remember mood proud	summarize action verb visualize *visualizar* antonym *antónimo*	• Phonics, pp. 51–52 • Vocabulary, p. 53 • Grammar, p. 54 • Book Talk, p. 55

Week 2

Selections	Vocabulary		ELL Practice Book
	Key Selection Words/Cognates	Academic Language/Cognates	
Abuelo and the Three Bears *The Three Bears*	arrive argue stubborn noticed cozy medium *mediano*	summarize visualize present tense idiom context clue verb *verbo*	• Phonics, pp. 56–57 • Vocabulary, p. 58 • Grammar, p. 59 • Book Talk, p. 60

Week 3

TIME FOR KIDS®	Vocabulary		ELL Practice Book
	Key Selection Words/Cognates	Academic Language/Cognates	
Music of the Stone Age	pleasant impossible *imposible* treasures *tesoros* talent *talento*	generate questions multiple-meaning words past tense author's purpose *autor*	• Phonics, pp. 61–62 • Vocabulary, p. 63 • Grammar, p. 64 • Book Talk, p. 65

Week 4

Selections	Vocabulary		ELL Practice Book
	Key Selection Words/Cognates	Academic Language/Cognates	
Click, Clack, Moo: Cows That Type *Early Ranching in Texas*	demand impatient *impaciente* furious *furioso* emergency *emergencia* sincerely *sinceramente* neutral *neutral*	generate questions verb: have cause *causa* effect *efecto* thesaurus *tesauro* synonym *sinónimo*	• Phonics, pp. 66–67 • Vocabulary, p. 68 • Grammar, p. 69 • Book Talk, p. 70

Week 5

Selections	Vocabulary		ELL Practice Book
	Key Selection Words/Cognates	Academic Language/Cognates	
Stirring Up Memories *Brush Dance* and *Crayons*	memories glamorous creating *crear* familiar *familiar* occasions *ocasiones* imagination *imaginación*	generate questions draw conclusions roots combine sentences	• Phonics, pp. 71–72 • Vocabulary, p. 73 • Grammar, p. 74 • Book Talk, p. 75

Student Response Strategies

Use the following strategies to help English Language Learners move to the next proficiency level.

✔ **WAIT** Give children ample time.

- Let children know that they can respond in different ways depending on their levels of proficiency, but all should be encouraged to answer questions related to the main point of the picture or text.

- Allow children to respond in their native language if they are very limited proficient. Ask a more proficient ELL student to repeat the answer in English.

✔ **REPEAT** If the child's response is correct, the teacher can repeat what the child has said. The teacher should repeat in a clear, loud voice that all can hear and at a slower pace.

✔ **REVISE for FORM** Generally the teacher will be repeating what the child has said but with corrections for grammar and pronunciation. The correction can be implicit or explicit (where teacher calls attention to the correction).

✔ **REVISE for MEANING** Teachers should also correct for meaning.

✔ **ELABORATE** Here, the teacher elaborates on a child's response or states the response in another way in order to more fully develop children's comprehension and oral language proficiency.

✔ **ELICIT** Finally, the teacher can also elicit a more comprehensive response from the child by prompting the child for further information.

Newcomers

Basic and Social Language Each week you will be focusing on an important aspect of classroom communication to teach or reinforce with your newcomers. Children will expand and internalize initial English vocabulary by learning and using routine language needed for classroom communication.

Place and Position Introduce the sentence frames *Where is the _____? It is _____*. Teach the position and location words *on, off, under, over, in, out, up,* and *down*. Model each using classroom objects. Then ask questions about the position of objects, and ask children to respond. Finally, prompt children to ask classmates about the position or location of objects.

More Commands/Instructions Teach and reinforce the classroom commands and instructions such as *Listen, Repeat, Can*

you _____? and *Do you understand?* Model for children how to respond in complete sentences using yes or no, for example, *Yes, I understand.*

Action Words Teach the sentence frame *I can _____* and a series of action words to complete the sentence such as *clap, read, run, smile, sleep,* and *stand*. Have children practice with a partner, saying *I can _____. Can you _____?*

LOG ON Have children use **Newcomer Games** to expand and internalize language needed for classroom communication.
www.macmillanmh.com

The Alvin Ailey Kids: Dancing as a Team

Pages 330–331

Prior to reading the selection with children, they should have listened to the selection on **StudentWorks Plus**, the interactive eBook. In addition, selection vocabulary should have been pretaught using the **Visual Vocabulary Resources**.

Access Core Content

Teacher Note Pose the questions after you read the paragraph or page indicated.

Pages 330–331

Title and Photos

- *Point to the title. This story has a long title. Let's read the first part of the title together:* The Alvin Ailey Kids. *Let's read the next part together:* Dancing as a Team.

- *These kids are students at the Alvin Ailey School. What do you think they learn there?* (dancing)

- *Look at their shoes. These are special shoes for a special dance. It is called a tap dance. Tap means a sound like this.* (Make a tapping sound.) *These shoes make a tapping sound when the children dance.*

Page 332

Whole Page

- *Look at the girls in the picture. What kind of dance are they doing?* (tap)

- *This page tells us about the Alvin Ailey School. Where is this school?* (in New York) *When do the students take classes?* (after school and on Saturday)

- *Hundreds of students dance at the school.* (Write hundreds *on board.*) Hundreds *means a lot. Find the word* hundreds *on this page.*

- *Let's read this page together.*

Comprehension

Genre
Expository text gives information and facts about a topic.

Visualize
Summarize
As you read, use the Summarize Chart.

Main Idea
Main Idea → Summary
Main Idea

Read to Find Out
Who are the Alvin Ailey kids and what do they do?

330

Alvin Ailey Kids

At The Alvin Ailey School in New York City, kids study dance. They take dance classes after school. They take classes on Saturday. Hundreds of students dance at the school.

332

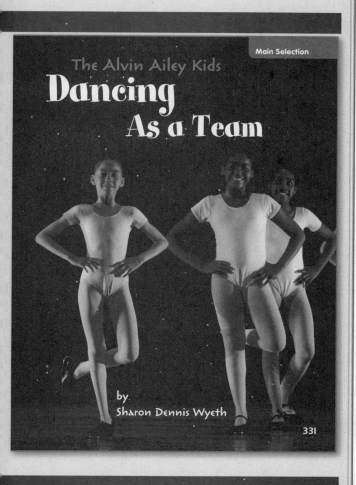

Main Selection

The Alvin Ailey Kids
Dancing As a Team

by
Sharon Dennis Wyeth

331

Each spring the students at Ailey **perform** in front of an audience. The dancers show what they have learned during the year.

Dancing is hard work. The steps have to be done just right. That takes a lot of practice. It's also a team **effort**.

The teachers help the students learn the steps. They try to make the classes fun. The musicians also do their part. The kids have a great time while they are learning.

✔ Summarize
Summarize what you know so far about the Ailey school. Describe the people who learn and work there.

333

Page 333

Photo
- *Look at the two boys in the picture. How can you tell that they are not tap dancing?* (They are not wearing tap shoes.) *They are doing another kind of dance.*

Paragraphs 1 and 2
- *Alvin Ailey students perform, or have a show, each spring. They have to dance in front of an audience. The audience is the people who watch.*

- *The students work together. They have to practice a lot. Do you think they like to perform? Why or why not?* (Question is open.)

Paragraph 3
- *This paragraph tells us about teachers and musicians. Musicians are people who make music. Let's read this paragraph together.*

- *The students have a good time even though they work hard. Who helps make the experience fun?* (the teachers and musicans)

 Dancing at Ailey is a team effort. What other things are a team effort? (Question is open.)

> **Request Assistance**
> Remind children of expressions they can use to request assistance from the teacher or their partners, such as *Can you repeat that, please? Can you show me in the picture?*

Page 334

Whole Page

- *This page is about a boy named Jasper and a girl named Whitney. Point to Jasper. Point to Whitney.*

- *Jasper and Whitney attended, or went to, the Alvin Ailey School in the spring of 2004. Who was nine years old in 2004? (Jasper) Who was ten years old?(Whitney)*

- *Ballet is a special kind of dance. Look at Whitney in the picture. She is dancing ballet. Now look at her shoes. Do they look like tap shoes? (no) Whitney is wearing ballet shoes. They don't make noise. They are soft and quiet.*

- *When Whitney was very young, she saw a ballet performance. Why was it important to her? (She realized that she wanted to dance, too.)*

- *Let's read the last paragraph together.*

 Whitney expresses herself through dance. What are some other ways to express yourself? (art, singing, acting) What do you like to do to express yourself? (Question is open.)

Page 335

Whole Page

- *Point to Whitney in the picture. Who is helping her? (her teacher) Now point to Jasper. He is practicing one of his dance steps.*

- *The spring performance is in two weeks. What are the students doing? (They are getting ready by practicing their steps.)*

- *The students are working hard. How do they feel— bored or excited? (excited)*

- *The students will not be performing at the school. Where will they be performing? (at a real theater)*

- *Who will watch their performance? (their parents and friends)*

Getting Ready in the Spring

Jasper and Whitney attended the Ailey school in the spring of 2004. Jasper was nine years old. Whitney was ten. Jasper started to dance when he was four. When Whitney was very young, she went with her family to a ballet.

"I knew then that I wanted to dance myself," said Whitney. "Dance helps me to express myself."

334

Dance Classes

The girls in Whitney's ballet class practiced their steps. Their teacher, Melanie, helped them. She wanted them to do their best.

"Arms open, girls!" Melanie told them.

Teamwork was a big part of the dance. Everyone had to do the steps at exactly the same time. "You have to dance in two ways on stage, by yourself and with a group," said Melanie.

336

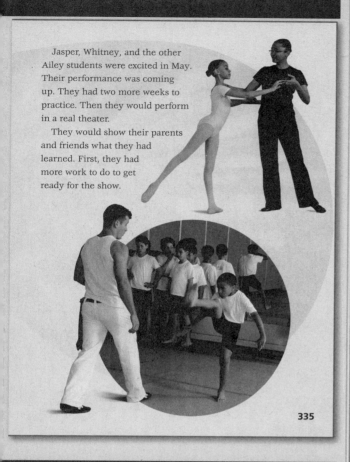

Jasper, Whitney, and the other Ailey students were excited in May. Their performance was coming up. They had two more weeks to practice. Then they would perform in a real theater.

They would show their parents and friends what they had learned. First, they had more work to do to get ready for the show.

335

The same girls also took tap class. The **mood** is different in tap. The music is jazzy! The shoes are noisy!

The girls tapped, stomped, and marched to the music. The dance they were going to perform was long. The students did not always **remember** all the steps. It was also hard to stay together.

"We have some more work to do," said their teacher, Vic. "From the top! 5, 6, 7, 8 smile!" Vic worked for a long time with the girls.

337

Page 336

Photo

- *Look at the three girls at the bottom of the page. Are they dancing tap or ballet?* (ballet)

Text

- *Whitney and her friends are in ballet class. Melanie is there, too. Who is Melanie?* (the teacher)

- *Melanie says, "Arms open!"* (Demonstrate opening arms.)

- *Dancing with a group is hard because everyone has to do everything at the same time. When the teacher says, "Arms open!" everyone has to do it together. Now let's try it again:* Arms open!

Page 337

Whole Page

- *Look at the children in the picture. Are they dancing tap or ballet?* (tap) *Now Whitney and her friends are in tap class. Tap is not like ballet. Ballet is quiet, but tap is _____.* (noisy)

- *The girls practice tap. Let's tap our desktops with our fingers. The girls stomp. (Demonstrate stomping.) Let's stomp next to our desks.*

- *The girls also march. (Demonstrate marching.) Now let's march around the room.*

- *Let's read the last paragraph together.*

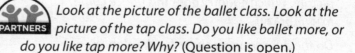 *Look at the picture of the ballet class. Look at the picture of the tap class. Do you like ballet more, or do you like tap more? Why?* (Question is open.)

Analyze Sayings and Expressions

Help children recognize that *From the Top!* is a saying that means "let's start again from the beginning." Discuss the context in which it is used.

The Alvin Ailey Kids: Dancing as a Team

Page 338

Whole Page

- *This is Jasper's favorite class. The students dance in a circle. The name of the dance is capoeira (kah-poo-air-ah).*

- *Look at the boys in the picture. This is how they warm up, or get ready, for the dance. They stretch, kick, and jump.* (Demonstrate each movement as you say the word.)

- *Now stand up and do each movement with me, as I say the word:* stretch, kick, jump. *Be careful not to kick anyone.*

Page 339

Paragraphs 1 and 2

- *The students dance in a circle.* (Draw a circle on the board.) *Two boys are in the middle of the circle.* (Draw two stick figures in the middle of the circle.)

- *How do the dancers in the circle move?* (They kick and move fast.) *What do the rest of the students do?* (They sing and clap to the music.) *The students all take turns.*

- *Let's read the second paragraph together.*

- *What does Jasper like best about dance?* (the beat) *What do you like best about dance?* (Question is open.)

Photo and Text Box

- *Jasper is doing the capoeira, or circle dance, in the picture. Which country does this dance come from?* (Brazil)

- *Do the dancers wear shoes for this dance?* (no)

Jasper's favorite class was capoeira. It is a type of circle dance. To warm up, the boys stretched. They did kicks and jumps.

338

Pages 340–341

Dress Rehearsal

The day of the dress rehearsal arrived. A dress rehearsal is a final practice before the performance. It is held where the show will take place.

The students went to the theater. They thought the stage was huge. The stage manager showed them how to enter and exit the stage properly.

340

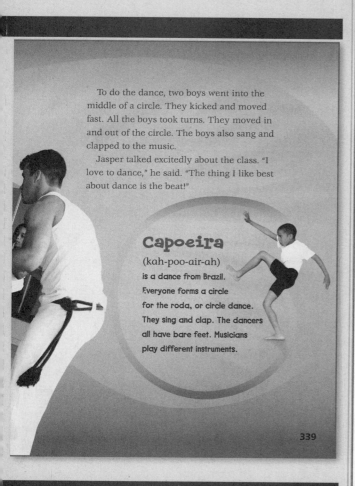

To do the dance, two boys went into the middle of a circle. They kicked and moved fast. All the boys took turns. They moved in and out of the circle. The boys also sang and clapped to the music.

Jasper talked excitedly about the class. "I love to dance," he said. "The thing I like best about dance is the beat!"

Capoeira
(kah-poo-air-ah)
is a dance from Brazil. Everyone forms a circle for the roda, or circle dance. They sing and clap. The dancers all have bare feet. Musicians play different instruments.

339

There were new things to get used to at the dress rehearsal. Moving on the big stage felt different. The lights were also something new.

"Watch your spacing!" said Christine, a ballet teacher. "Remember you are dancing together." The students practiced their dances one last time. The next time they performed, the teachers would not be on stage with them.

341

Page 340

Photo

- *The girls in the picture are not in a classroom. They are in a theater. They are standing on a stage. What will they do there?* (dance, perform)

Text

- *The girls are in a dress rehearsal. A dress rehearsal is a special practice. It is the last practice before their show. The students are on the stage for the first time.*

- Huge *means "very big." Do the students think the stage is small or huge?* (huge)

- *Enter means "go on." Exit means "leave." The dancers learn how to enter and exit the stage.*

Page 341

Text

- *What new things do the students have to get used to at the dress rehearsal?* (the big stage, the lights)

- *Christine helps the students. Who is Christine?* (a ballet teacher) *Christine tells the students to watch their spacing. That means they should make sure there is enough space between dancers. What might happen if they don't?* (They might bump into each other.)

- Will *Christine dance with the class during the concert?* (no) *The students will have to dance by themselves.*

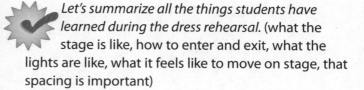 *Let's summarize all the things students have learned during the dress rehearsal.* (what the stage is like, how to enter and exit, what the lights are like, what it feels like to move on stage, that spacing is important)

Page 342

Whole Page

- *Jasper tells about all the people who have helped the students with the show. What two new people helped them at the dress rehearsal?* (the stage manager and the person who helps with the lights)

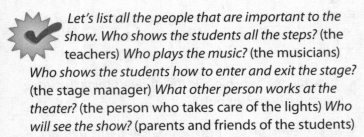 *Let's list all the people that are important to the show. Who shows the students all the steps?* (the teachers) *Who plays the music?* (the musicians) *Who shows the students how to enter and exit the stage?* (the stage manager) *What other person works at the theater?* (the person who takes care of the lights) *Who will see the show?* (parents and friends of the students)

Page 343

Photos

- *Look at the different people at the dress rehearsal. Point to the ballet class. Point to the student doing a kick. Point to the musician.*

- *What are the people doing in each picture?* (Dancers are practicing a dance. A musician is playing music. The students and teachers are talking and hugging.)

Pages 342–343

The dress rehearsal added more people to the team. "Everyone works hard for the performance," said Jasper. "Our teachers make up the dances and teach us the steps. The musicians play the music. Someone else helps with the lights. The stage manager tells everyone where and when to do their jobs. Then we do the dancing."

"The parents help out, too, by coming to watch us. For sure, my family will be there!"

Summarize
Summarize what happened during the dress rehearsal.

342

Pages 344–345

Performance Day

At last, the day of the performance arrived. Backstage, the dancers got ready. Then the audience took their seats.

Lights! Music! The show started! The sound of tapping feet filled the air.

The tap dancers crossed the stage together. Their feet were flying!

344

343

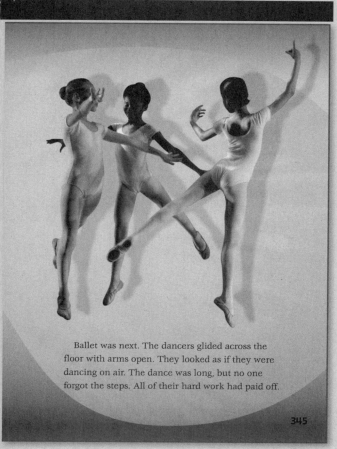

Ballet was next. The dancers glided across the floor with arms open. They looked as if they were dancing on air. The dance was long, but no one forgot the steps. All of their hard work had paid off.

345

Page 344

Text

- *Now it is performance day. The dancers are ready. The audience is ready. It's time for the show.*

- *The show starts. How do people in the audience know?* (They see lights. They hear music and tapping.)

- *The tap dancers enter the stage. Their feet are flying. What do you think that means?* (Their feet are moving very fast.)

Photos

- *Point to the students getting ready. Point to the students on stage.*

Page 345

Whole Page

- *Look at the girls dance. Do you think their dance is easy or hard? Would you like to do it?* (Question is open.)

- *Now the ballet dancers are on stage. They glide, like this.* (Demonstrate gliding with your arm.) *Say* glide *with me and make the gliding movement with your arm.*

The Alvin Ailey Kids: Dancing as a Team

Then the capoeira began. The dancers kicked and jumped. They clapped and sang in the roda.

When the dance was over, the dancers took a bow. The audience cheered. What a great performance!

346

Page 346

Photos

■ *Point to the dancers. Point to the musicians. What kind of instruments do you see in the picture?* (drums)

Text

■ *Now the capoeira begins. The dancers _____.* (Demonstrate kicking and elicit *kick*.) *The dancers _____.* (Demonstrate jumping and elicit *jump*.) *The dancers _____.* (Demonstrate clapping and elicit *clap*.)

■ *The dance ends. The dancers bow.* (Demonstrate bowing.) *The audience cheers.* (Demonstrate cheering.)

■ *Let's take turns bowing and cheering. The children on this side of the room will bow.* (Point to them.) *The children on the other side of the room will cheer.* (Point to them.) *Then we'll switch parts.*

Page 347

Photos

■ *Look at the different people on this page. Are they happy or sad?* (happy)

Text

■ *The show ends. Everyone is excited. The dancers are happy because they did a great job.*

PARTNERS Why were the teachers proud of the students? *(The students did a great job. They remembered the steps. They tried hard.) Talk with your partner about different ways students make teachers happy.*

■ *Jasper and Whitney are very excited about their great performance. Let's read Whitney's words with an excited voice:* It was fun!

■ *Now let's read Jasper's words with an excited voice:* We did it! We all did it together!

The show was over, but the excitement did not end. Backstage, the dancers were happy. They had done a great job.

Their families gave them hugs. Their teachers were very **proud**.

"It was fun!" said Whitney.

"We did it!" said Jasper.

"We all did it together!"

347

Let's make a summary of this story. The students at the Alvin Ailey School learn to _____. (dance) Each year, they have a special show. When is their show? (in the spring) Where is their show? (in a theater) They have to get ready, so they practice a lot. What do we call the last practice before the show? (the dress rehearsal) On the day of the show, parents and friends come to watch. They are the _____. (audience) How does everyone feel at the end the show? (excited, happy, proud)

You'll Sing a Song and I'll Sing a Song

Access Core Content

Teacher Note Pose the questions after you read the paragraph or page indicated.

Page 350

Photo and Title

- *Look at the picture of the children. What are they doing?* (singing)

- *Let's read the title together:* You'll Sing a Song and I'll Sing a Song. *We are going to read the words to a song about music and singing.*

Stanza 1

 The words sing a song *are in the title. How many times do you see them there?* (twice) *Look for them in the lines on this page. With your partner, count how many times you see them.* (five)

- *Point to the word* together *on this page. Together means "at the same time." Let's read the first three lines of the poem together.*

- *Say the word* weather *with me. Sometimes the weather is warm, sometimes it is cold. How is the weather today?*

- *Now let's read the last line together:* In warm or wintery weather. *Wintery means like the winter. How is the weather in the winter?* (cold) *What do you like to do in wintery weather? What do you like to do in warm weather?* (Questions are open.)

- *Let's say this word again:* weather. (Point to the word together.) *Let's say this word again:* together. *Now let's say both words:* weather, together. *Weather and* together *sound similar. They rhyme. Some poems have words that rhyme.*

- *Now let's read the page together. Does the poem sound like a song?* (yes)

Poetry

Genre
Lyrics are the words to a song.

Literary Elements
Alliteration is when the same beginning sound in a group of words is repeated.

Rhythmic Patterns are sounds and words that repeat to give a certain rhythm. Rhyme, rhythm, and repetition help create images in poetry.

You'll Sing a Song and I'll Sing a Song
by Ella Jenkins

You'll sing a song
And I'll sing a song,
Then we'll sing a song together.
You'll sing a song
And I'll sing a song
In warm or wintery weather.

350

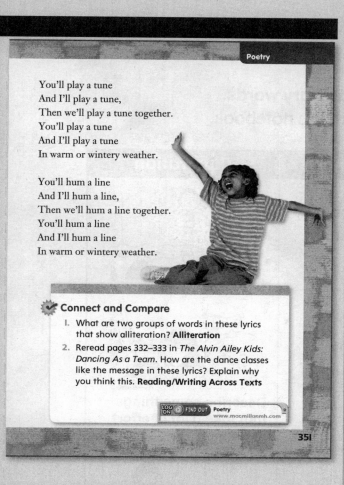

You'll play a tune
And I'll play a tune,
Then we'll play a tune together.
You'll play a tune
And I'll play a tune
In warm or wintery weather.

You'll hum a line
And I'll hum a line,
Then we'll hum a line together.
You'll hum a line
And I'll hum a line
In warm or wintery weather.

Connect and Compare

1. What are two groups of words in these lyrics that show alliteration? **Alliteration**

2. Reread pages 332–333 in *The Alvin Ailey Kids: Dancing As a Team*. How are the dance classes like the message in these lyrics? Explain why you think this. **Reading/Writing Across Texts**

LOG ON · FIND OUT · **Poetry**
www.macmillanmh.com

351

Stanza 2

- *Let's read the first line together:* You'll play a tune. *A tune is a song. You can play a tune on a piano.* (demonstrate) *You can play a tune on a guitar.* (demonstrate) *Let's pretend we're playing a tune together. Choose any instrument you want.*

 Find the words play a tune *on this page and show them to your partner. With your partner, count how many times you see them on this page.* (five)

- *Let's read this part of the poem together.*

Stanza 3

- *This is how I hum* (Demonstrate humming.) *Say* hum *and then hum with me.*

- *Now let's find the words* hum a line *on this page. How many times do you see them?* (five)

- *Let's read this part of the poem together.*

- *Look at the last line of the poem. Look for the letter* w. *How many times do you see it?* (three) *Sometimes a writer uses the same beginning letter or sound several times. It helps the poem sound like a song. Let's read this line together. Listen for the sound of* w.

Name _____

Use the word chart to study this week's vocabulary words.
Write a sentence using each word in your writer's notebook.

Word	Context Sentence	Illustration
perform _____	I feel nervous when I <u>perform</u> in front of people.	
effort _____	Learning to play the piano well takes a lot of <u>effort</u>.	**Describe some things that take a lot of effort to do.**
remember _____	I put my piano music by the door so I would <u>remember</u> it.	
mood _____	The funny song put me in a good <u>mood</u>.	**Which would put you in a bad mood—watching a funny movie or doing extra homework?**
proud _____	I am <u>proud</u> of the painting I made for Mom.	

© Macmillan/McGraw-Hill

Name _____

Read each question and prompt. Discuss the answers with your group. Use your Leveled Reader to find details to support your answers. Then write your answers on the blank lines or on another sheet of paper.

1. Explain why this gift of friendship was called the Statue of Liberty.

   _____

2. Tell about the many people who helped build the statue.

   _____

3. Talk about a problem with the statue and how it was solved.

   _____

4. Explain some of the symbols found on the Statue of Liberty.

   _____

5. What did you find most interesting in this book about the Statue of Liberty?

   _____

6. Write one question about the book to ask your group.

   _____

Abuelo and the Three Bears

Pages 358–359

Prior to reading the selection with children, they should have listened to the selection on **StudentWorks Plus,** the interactive eBook. In addition, selection vocabulary should have been pretaught using the **Visual Vocabulary Resources.**

Access Core Content

Teacher Note Pose the questions after you read the paragraph or page indicated.

Pages 358–359

Title and Illustrations

- *Let's read the title together:* Abuelo and the Three Bears. Abuelo *means "grandfather."* (Point to the picture of the grandfather on page 358.) *Point to the three bears.* (Point to the picture on page 359.)

- *Some of you may know the story of Goldilocks and the three bears. Today we are going to read a story about the three bears, but it is a little bit different. It is a new story of the three bears.*

Page 360

Glossary

- *This word is* glossary. (Point to the word *glossary*.) *A glossary tells us the meaning of words. There are some Spanish words here.*

- *This first word is* Abuelo. *Say it with me.* (As you work through the glossary, ask any Spanish-speaking children to help model pronunciation.) *We already know what* Abuelo *means. It means _____.* ("grandfather")

- *Let's look at the next word,* Osito. *What does* Osito *mean?* ("Little Bear") *Say it with me:* Little Bear.

- *The next word is* frijoles. *What do we call frijoles in English?* (beans) *Raise your hand if you like to eat beans.*

Comprehension

Genre
A Fairytale is a story with made-up characters and events that could not happen in real life.

Visualize
Summarize
As you read, use the Summarize Chart.

Beginning → Middle → End → Summary

Read to Find Out
How does Abuelo entertain Emilio while they wait for his cousins?

358

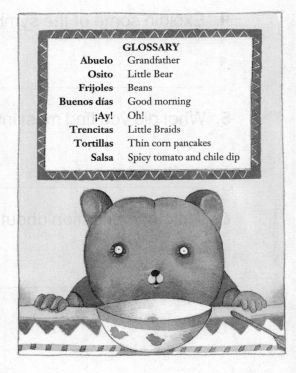

GLOSSARY	
Abuelo	Grandfather
Osito	Little Bear
Frijoles	Beans
Buenos días	Good morning
¡Ay!	Oh!
Trencitas	Little Braids
Tortillas	Thin corn pancakes
Salsa	Spicy tomato and chile dip

360

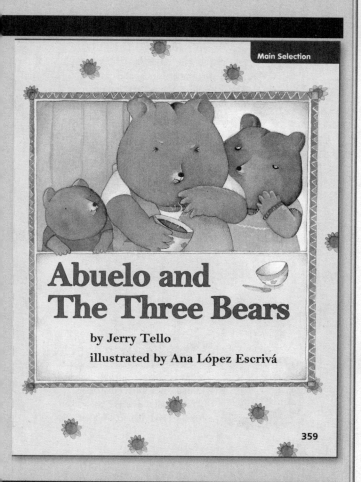

Main Selection

Abuelo and The Three Bears

by Jerry Tello

illustrated by Ana López Escrivá

359

It was a quiet Sunday. Emilio and his grandfather sat on the front porch.

"Abuelo," said Emilio, "do we have to wait much longer? When will everybody get here?"

"Your cousins will **arrive** soon," Abuelo answered, "and we'll have a fine dinner. I'll tell you a story to help pass the time."

361

- *This says* Buenos días. *How do we say* Buenos días *in English? (*Good morning!*) Let's say it all together:* Buenos días! Good morning!

- *The next word is* ay. *When we are surprised, we can say* Ay! *or we can say* Oh!

- *The next word is* trencitas. *In English, we say* braids. (Point to braids if someone in the class is wearing them, or show the picture on page 366.)

- *The next word is* tortillas. *Raise your hand if you like to eat tortillas. Tortillas are good to eat.*

- *The next word is* salsa. *Raise your hand if you like to eat salsa. Salsa is good to eat. It is made from tomatoes.*

 Do you like to eat beans? tortillas? salsa? What kinds of food do you like to eat? Tell your partner three things you like to eat.

Page 361

Illustration

- *In this story, Abuelo tells Emilio a story about the three bears. Point to Abuelo in the picture. Point to Emilio.*

- *Look at Emilio's family. (*Point to people in the background of the illustration.*) Where are they? (*in the kitchen*) What are they doing? (*cooking*)

Text

- *Emilio and Abuelo are sitting on the front porch. A porch is a nice place to sit in front of a house.*

- *Emilio and Abuelo are waiting for Emilio's cousins to arrive, or get to their house. Emilio's cousins are part of his family. Abuelo is going to tell Emilio a story to pass the time, or make time go faster while they wait. Do you like stories? Who tells you stories? (*Question is open.*)*

Page 362

Whole Page

- *Look at Papá Bear. What is he doing?* (He is smelling something.) *He is smelling something good. What might it be?* (Question is open.)

- *Papá Bear, Mamá Bear, and Osito, or Little Bear, lived in the woods. One morning, Papá Bear woke up, and he felt grumpy. Say it with me:* grumpy. *Papá Bear was in a bad mood. When you wake up, are you grumpy or happy?* (Question is open.)

- *Papá Bear smelled something good. He smelled* frijoles, *or beans.*

- *Emilio laughed. He said,* "Bears don't like beans!" *Read it with me:* "Bears don't like beans!" *Abuelo says that all the bears he knows like beans. Do you think he knows any bears?* (no)

Page 363

Whole Page

- *Look at Mamá Bear and Osito. Where are they?* (in the kitchen) *What does Mamá Bear have in her hands?* (a pot of frijoles, or beans)

- *Papá Bear rushed, or ran, to the kitchen. What did he say to Mamá Bear and Osito?* ("Buenos días.") *What does that mean?* ("Good morning.")

Page 364

Illustration

- *Look at Papá Bear eating beans. Is he grumpy or happy now?* (happy)

- *Do you see Papá Bear's napkin? Show it to your partner.*

Once there were three bears who lived in the woods—Papá Bear, Mamá Bear, and their little Osito. One Sunday morning, Papá Bear woke up as grumpy as ever. Then he smelled something good. "Mmmm, frijoles!" he said.

"Abuelo, you're joking!" laughed Emilio. "Bears don't like beans!"
"Well, all the bears I know like frijoles," said Abuelo.

362

Papá Bear sat down at the table and tucked a napkin under his chin. "How are the frijoles? Are they ready yet?" he asked. "Yes," answered Mamá Bear, "but they're still too hot to eat."
"I can't wait," said Papá Bear. "I'm so hungry I could eat an elephant."

"Abuelo," said Emilio, "bears don't eat elephants."
"Emilio," answered Abuelo, "you must never **argue** with a hungry bear."

364

Papá Bear got up and rushed down to the kitchen. "Buenos días," said Papá Bear to Mamá Bear and Osito.

363

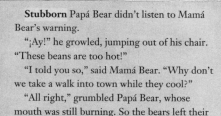

Stubborn Papá Bear didn't listen to Mamá Bear's warning.

"¡Ay!" he growled, jumping out of his chair. "These beans are too hot!"

"I told you so," said Mamá Bear. "Why don't we take a walk into town while they cool?"

"All right," grumbled Papá Bear, whose mouth was still burning. So the bears left their breakfast to cool and went out.

365

Paragraphs 1–2

- *Papá Bear sat down. He put a napkin under his chin. Let's pretend to put a napkin under our chins. He asked Mamá Bear,* "How are the frijoles? Are they ready yet?" *Mamá Bear said,* "Yes, but they're still too _____ to eat." *(hot)*

- *Did Papá Bear want to wait to eat the beans? (no)*

- *Papá Bear didn't want to wait because he was very hungry. He said,* "I'm so hungry I could eat an elephant." *Is an elephant big or small? (Show the meanings of big and small with your hands.) An elephant is very big, isn't it? You have to be very hungry to eat one!*

Paragraphs 3–4

- *Emilio said,* "Abuelo, bears don't eat elephants." *Read it with me:* "Abuelo, bears don't eat elephants." *Is Emilio right? (yes)*

Page 365

Paragraphs 1–2

- *Papá Bear was stubborn. He didn't listen to Mamá Bear. He ate the beans. He growled. (Demonstrate.) He jumped out of his chair. Why did he growl and jump out of his chair? (The beans were very hot.)*

- *Papá Bear said,* "These beans are too hot!" *Read it with me:* "These beans are too hot!"

Paragraphs 3–4

- *Mamá Bear said they should take a walk into town while the beans cooled, or got colder. Papá Bear grumbled,* "All right." *When you grumble something, you say it in a grumpy, or unhappy, way. Let's grumble together, like Papá Bear:* "All right."

In the story about Goldilocks and the three bears, the little girl comes to the house while the bears are out. What do you think will happen in this story?

Page 366

Whole Page

- *Look at the little girl's hair. She has two braids. Point to the braids. Remember, in Spanish, braids are called* trencitas. *What do you think this little girl's name is? Let's read to find out.*

- *What is the little girl's name?* (Trencitas) *That's right, it's Trencitas, just like her braids. Trencitas is going to visit her friend. Who is her friend?* (Osito)

Page 367

Whole Page

- *Emilio says, "Abuelo, the girl in this story is called Goldilocks and she has blond hair."*

- *Abuelo shrugs when he answers. Look at the picture. When you shrug, you raise your shoulders.* (Demonstrate shrugging.) *Let's all shrug like Abuelo.*

Paragraph 2

- *Abuelo tells Emilio, "In my story it was Trencitas with her long black braids who came to visit."*

 *Help me tell a summary of the story, or the most important parts. Abuelo told a story to _____. (Emilio) It was a story about three _____. (bears) One day, Papá Bear woke up. He wasn't happy; he was _____. (grumpy) (Make a grumpy face.) He was also hungry. Mamá Bear made beans, but they were too _____. (hot) (Wave your hand in front of your mouth to indicate heat.) The bear family went for a _____. (walk) (Walk a few steps.) A little girl came to their house. Her name was _____. (Trencitas)*

Just then, in another part of the woods, a girl named Trencitas set out from her house to visit her friend, Osito. She was called Trencitas because she had long black braids.

366

When Trencitas arrived at Osito's house, she **noticed** that the door was open. So she stepped inside and followed her nose until she came to the three bowls of beans.

First Trencitas tasted some beans from the great big bowl, but they were too hot. Then she tasted some from the **medium**-sized bowl, but they were too cold. Finally she tasted some from the little bowl, and they were just right. So she finished them all up.

368

"Abuelo," Emilio called out, "the girl in this story is called Goldilocks and she has blond hair."

"Goldilocks?" Abuelo shrugged. "In my story it was Trencitas with her long black braids who came to visit. And she was hungry, too!"

> **Summarize**
> Use details from the story to summarize what has happened so far.

367

Now Trencitas decided to sit in the living room and wait for the bears to return. She sat in the great big chair, but it was too hard. She sat in the medium-sized chair, but it was too soft. Then she sat in the little chair, and it was just right until… CRASH!

369

Page 368

Illustration

- *Look at the bowls of beans on the table. There are three bowls. Show your partner the big bowl. Show your partner the little bowl. Show your partner the medium-sized, or middle-sized, bowl.*

Text

- *Trencitas arrived at Osito's house. She noticed, or saw, the open door. She went inside. She followed her nose, which means she followed the smell, to find the food. What did she see on the table?* (She saw three bowls of beans.)

- *Trencitas tasted the beans. The beans in the big bowl were too _____.* (hot) *The beans in the medium-sized bowl were too _____.* (cold) *The beans in the little bowl were just _____.* (right) *Trencitas ate them.*

Page 369

Whole Page

- *Look at Trencitas. What happened to her chair?* (It broke, or fell.) *Poor Trencitas!*

- *Trencitas wanted to sit down. She sat in the big chair, but it was too hard.* (Knock on the desk to show the meaning of *hard*.) *She sat in the medium-sized chair, but it was too soft.* (Touch a sweater or other soft object to show the meaning of *soft*.) *She sat in the little chair, and it was just right, but then it broke. Crash! Poor Trencitas!*

- *Let's read this page together.*

Page 370

Whole Page

- *Look at Emilio. Is he happy?* (no) *He isn't happy, he's worried. There is a problem. Why is Emilio worried? Let's read to find out.*

- *Emilio is worried because Trencitas broke the chair. He asks, "Abuelo, what's Trencitas going to do?"*

- *Abuelo says, "Don't worry." Find the words on the page. Let's read them together: "Don't worry!"*

- *Abuelo tells Emilio that Trencitas can fix the chair. She will fix it with glue.* (Hold up a bottle of glue.)

Page 371

Whole Page

- *Look at Trencitas. Where is she?* (in bed) *What is she doing?* (sleeping)

- *Trencitas was sleepy.* (Yawn.) *She went upstairs. She tried the big bed, but it was too scratchy.* (Scratch your arm and make an unpleasant face.) *Say it with me:* scratchy.

- *Next, she tried the medium-sized bed, but it was too lumpy. It had bumps in it.*

- *Then she tried the little bed. It was very little, but it was soft and cozy.* (Hug yourself.) *Say cozy with me as you hug yourself:* cozy. *Trencitas went to sleep.*

PARTNERS *The first bed was scratchy. The second bed was lumpy. The third bed was cozy. What things can you think of that are scratchy, lumpy, or cozy?* (Question is open.)

Non-verbal Cues

Remind children that they can use non-verbal cues to share information when they are not able to do so verbally. Encourage children to use visuals.

"Abuelo, what's Trencitas going to do?" asked Emilio. "She broke her friend's chair."

"Don't worry," Abuelo said. "She'll come back later with glue and leave it like new."

370

When the three bears came home, Papá Bear headed straight to the kitchen to eat his frijoles.

"¡Ay!" he growled when he saw his bowl. "Somebody's been eating my beans."

"And somebody's been eating my beans," said Mamá Bear.

"And there's only one bean left in my bowl," said Osito.

372

Trencitas was feeling very sleepy. She went upstairs to take a rest. First she tried the great big bed, but the blanket was scratchy. Then she tried the medium-sized bed, but it was too lumpy. Finally, she tried the little bed. It was too small, but it was so cozy and soft that Trencitas soon fell asleep.

371

Then the three bears went into the living room.

"¡Ay!" said Papá Bear when he saw that his chair had been moved. "Somebody's been sitting in my chair."

"And somebody's been sitting in my chair," said Mamá Bear.

"And my chair is all over the place!" said Osito.

373

Page 372

Whole Page

- *Look at the picture. The bears have come home. What does Little Bear see?* (His bowl is empty.) *What is Papá Bear looking at?* (the chairs)

- *The three bears came home. Papá Bear saw his bowl. He growled. (Make a growling sound.) Let's read what he said with a growling voice:* "Somebody's been eating my beans."

- *What did Mamá Bear say? Find her words and read them with me:* "And somebody's been eating my beans."

- *Let's read what Osito said in a high voice:* "And there's only one bean left in my bowl."

Page 373

Whole Page

- *The three bears went into the living room. They saw the chairs. What did Papá Bear say? Find his words and read them with me:* "Somebody's been sitting in my chair." (Read with a deep, growling voice.)

- *What did Mamá Bear say?* ("And somebody's been sitting in my chair.")

- *Osito said:* "And my chair is all over the place!" (Read with a high-pitched voice. As you read, move your hand around to show the meaning of *all over the place*.) *Now read his words with me, and use your hand to show that his chair is in pieces all over the room.*

Abuelo and the Three Bears

Page 374

Illustration and Paragraph 1

- *The bears climbed the stairs. Let's pretend we are going upstairs.*

- *Who went first? (Papá Bear) Who went second? (Mamá Bear) Who went last? (Osito)*

- *Look at the bears. What are they looking at? (their beds)*

Paragraphs 2–3

- *Papá Bear looked at his bed. "Somebody's been sleeping in my bed," he said. Find Papá Bear's words and read them with me.*

- *What did Mamá Bear say? ("And somebody's been sleeping in my bed.")*

Page 375

Illustration and Paragraph 1

- *Look at Osito. He sees Trencitas in his bed. Is he mad? Is he afraid? Is he happy?*

- *What did Osito say? Find his words and read them with me: "Look who's sleeping in my bed!" Everybody had a good laugh. That means they were happy and enjoyed laughing.*

- *Why do you think they laughed? (They were surprised to see Osito's friend. They were happy it wasn't a stranger.)*

 What did you think the bears would do when they saw Trencitas? Why? (Question is open.)

Paragraphs 2–5

- *Mamá Bear said they should walk home with Trencitas. Why did she want to do that? (to make sure Trencitas arrived, or got home, safely)*

- *Did Papá Bear want to walk home with Trencitas? Why or why not? (No, he wanted to eat his frijoles.)*

- *Trencitas said, "There'll be beans at my house." Emilio thinks that will make Papá Bear want to go on the walk. Is Emilio right? (yes)*

Pages 374–375

The three bears climbed the stairs to check out the bedrooms. Papá Bear went first. Mamá Bear and Osito followed behind him.

"¡Ay!" said Papá Bear, when he looked in the bedroom. "Somebody's been sleeping in my bed."

"And somebody's been sleeping in my bed," said Mamá Bear.

374

Pages 376–377

When they all arrived at Trencitas's house, they sat down at a long table with Trencitas's parents, grandparents, uncles, aunts, and lots of cousins. They ate pork and fish and chicken and tortillas and beans and salsa so hot it brought tears to their eyes. And they laughed and they shared stories.

376

"Look who's sleeping in my bed!" said Osito. He ran over to Trencitas and woke her up. Then they all had a good laugh.

By now it was getting late. Mamá Bear said they'd walk Trencitas home to make sure she got there safely.

Papá Bear did not like this idea. "Another walk!" he growled. "What about my frijoles?"

"There'll be beans at my house," offered Trencitas.

"I'll bet that made Papá Bear happy," said Emilio.

"You're right," said Abuelo. "Here's what happened next...."

375

Page 376

Whole Page

- *Look at Trencitas's big family. Are they happy or sad?* (happy) *Point to Trencitas in the picture. Then point to Papá Bear, Mamá Bear, and Osito.*

- *Trencitas and the three bears went to Trencitas's house. Her family was there. Let's see who was there: her parents (that means her mother and father); her grandparents (that means her grandmother and grandfather); and her uncles, aunts, and cousins. They are all part of her family.*

- *Everyone ate a lot. What kinds of food did they eat?* (pork, fish, chicken, tortillas, beans, salsa)

- *The salsa was very hot. It brought tears to everyone's eyes. (Gesture to show tears running down your cheeks.) Does hot salsa bring tears to your eyes?*

- *Everybody laughed and told stories. They had a good time.*

Page 377

Whole Page

- *Abuelo told Emilio that Papá Bear had to wait a long time. In the end, though, Papá Bear ate his beans and had a good time.*

- *Who else is waiting a long time?* (Emilio) *Who is he waiting for?* (his cousins) *Will they have a good time, too?* (yes)

"So you see, Emilio," said Abuelo, "Papá Bear had to wait a long time to eat his frijoles. But, in the end, he had a wonderful meal and lots of fun, just as you will when your cousins arrive."

Summarize
How can you summarize this story? Use details from the beginning, middle, and end.

377

Text and Illustrations

- *Abuelo says that Emilio doesn't have to wait anymore. What does he mean?* (The cousins are here.)

- *Look at the picture on page 378. What are Abuelo and Emilio doing?* (waving to cousins)

- *Now look at the picture on page 379. Emilio's cousins are arriving. They are at his house now. They are walking in the door. Point to them.*

- *Let's go back to page 376. What foods did everyone eat at Trencitas's house?* (chicken, pork, beans, tortillas, salsa) *What do tortillas look like?* (thin pancakes) *What color is salsa?* (green or red)

- *Look at the food in the pictures on page 378. Point to the red salsa.*

- *Now look at the picture on page 379. What color is the salsa on this page?* (green) *Point to the frijoles. What's the English word for them?* (beans) *What is the Spanish word for thin corn pancakes?* (tortillas) *Point to them.*

"Is that the end of the story?" Emilio asked.
"Yes," answered Abuelo, "and it's the end of your waiting, too!"

378

379

✔ Let's tell what happened after Trencitas arrived at the bears' house. Trencitas went inside the house. What did she see first? (She saw three bowls of beans.) Trencitas tasted the _____. (beans) The beans in the big bowl were too _____. (hot) The beans in the medium-sized bowl were too _____. (cold) The beans in the little bowl were just _____. (right) Where did Trencitas go next? (She went to the living room.) She saw three _____. (chairs) She sat in the big chair. It was too _____. (hard) She sat in the medium-sized chair. It was too _____. (soft) She sat in the little chair. It was just _____. (right) But then it broke! What did Trencitas do next? (She went upstairs.) What did she see upstairs? (three beds) She tried the big bed. It was too _____. (scratchy) She tried the medium-sized bed. It was too _____. (lumpy) She tried the little bed. It was soft and _____. (cozy) Trencitas went to sleep. The three bears came home. They went to the kitchen. They said, "Somebody has been eating my _____." (beans) Then they went to the living room. They said, "Somebody has been sitting in my _____." (chair) They went upstairs. They saw Trencitas sleeping in the bed. Were they happy or mad to see Trencitas? (They were happy.) Where did they go next? (They went to Trencitas's house.) What did they do there? (They ate dinner with her big family.)

Monitor Oral Production

Remember to model self-corrective techniques on a regular basis as you speak to children. Pretend to mispronounce words and self-correct.

The Three Bears

Access Core Content

Teacher Note Pose the questions after you read the paragraph or page indicated.

Page 382

Title and Introduction

- *Let's read the title together:* The Three Bears. *We are going to read another story about the three bears.*

- *People everywhere like to tell the story of Goldilocks and the three bears. They tell it in different ways.*

- *These are three different books about the three bears.* (Point to book covers.) *There are many more. Today we are going to read a story that is a poem.*

Illustration

- *Look at the picture of the girl near the bottom of the page.* (Point to it.) *Is this Trencitas or Goldilocks?* (Goldilocks) *Is this Baby Bear or Papá Bear?* (Baby Bear) *Where is Goldilocks?* (in bed)

Poem

- *Listen while I read.* (Read with different voices for Goldilocks and Baby Bear.)

- *Baby Bear says to Goldilocks,* "What pretty hair!" *Goldilocks says to Baby Bear,* "What pretty _____!" (fur) *People have hair, and animals have fur. Baby Bear has brown fur.*

- *Goldilocks is sleeping in Baby Bear's bed.*

Page 383

Lines 1–6

- *Goldilocks got lost. She found Baby Bear's house.*

- *Poems often have words that rhyme, or end with the same sound.* Cat *and* bat *rhyme. They both end with* -at. *Now listen for a word that rhymes with* way. (Read lines 4–6.) *What word rhymes with* way? (stay)

Pages 382–383

Language Arts

Genre
Fairy Tales take place long ago and have made-up characters and settings.

 **Literary Element**
Words that Rhyme begin with different sounds but end with the same sound. Rhyme, rhythm, and repetition help create images in poetry.

~THE~ THREE BEARS

by Mary Ann Hoberman
illustrated by Michael Emberly

People have been telling the story *Goldilocks and the Three Bears* all over the world for many years. Below are the names of three different versions of the story. The version you will read next has text that rhymes.

I'm Goldilocks.

    I'm Baby Bear.

What pretty fur!

    What pretty hair!

Why are you here?

    You're in my bed.

382

Pages 384–385

I know the forest
Very well.
I'll take you home.
I'll trace your smell.

Why, Baby Bear,
You're very smart!

    Get out of bed
    And then we'll
    start.

When I get home,
Here's what I'll do:
I'll make some porridge
Just for you.

    Will you add honey
    For a treat?
    (That's my favorite
    Thing to eat.)

I'll add some honey
If you wish.
(You can even
Lick the dish.)

    Yummy yum!
    I love to lick!

384

I'm in your bed?

That's what I said.
Why are *you* here?

I lost my way.
I found your house.
And thought I'd stay.

And then you ate
My porridge up
And drank my milk
Right from my cup.

Why, yes, I did.
You weren't there
And I was hungry,
Baby Bear.

Well, now I'm very
Hungry, too.

Oh, goodness me!
What shall I do?

Where do you live?

Not very far.
A mile or two
From where we are.

383

What comes next?

I'll let you pick.

I pick a picture book
To share.

Why, that is perfect,
Baby Bear!

The Three Bears is
The one we'll do!
You'll read to me!
I'll read to you!

✓ Connect and Compare

1. Which words in this selection rhyme? How do you know? **Rhyme**
2. Think about the baby bear in *Abuelo and the Three Bears*. Compare the baby bear in that story with the baby bear in this version of the story. Use details from the stories to compare the characters. **Reading/Writing Across Texts**
3. Write a poem about a fairy tale you know. Use words that rhyme in your poem. **Rhyme**

385

Lines 7–14

- *Goldilocks was hungry. She ate Baby Bear's porridge—his breakfast. She drank his milk, too. Is Baby Bear happy?* (No, he's mad.)

- *I am going to read. Listen for a word that rhymes with* up. *Say it with me:* up. *Now listen.* (Read lines 7–10.) *What word rhymes with* up? (cup)

- *Let's listen for a word that rhymes with* there. *Say it with me:* there. *Now listen.* (Read lines 11–14.) *What word rhymes with* there? (bear)

Lines 15–22

- *Baby Bear is very hungry because Goldilocks ate his breakfast. Goldilocks says her house is not far—only a mile or two away.* (Explain how long a mile is by using local landmarks. For example, say: *A mile is about how far it is from the school to the* _____.)

Page 384

Lines 1–9

- *Baby Bear says he will take Goldilocks home. He says he will trace her smell. That means he will use his nose to find the way to her house.*

Lines 10–23

- *Goldilocks will make breakfast for Baby Bear at her house. What does Baby Bear want with his breakfast? Why?* (He wants honey. It's his favorite thing to eat.)

- *Will Goldilocks give Baby Bear some honey?* (Yes, he can even lick the dish!)

Page 385

Whole Page

- *Let's read the end of the poem together.*

- *Goldilocks makes Baby Bear some porridge. Then what do they do?* (They read *The Three Bears* to each other.)

 PARTNERS *Were you surprised that Goldilocks and Baby Bear became friends? What would you do with a new friend?* (Questions are open.)

Use the word chart to study this week's vocabulary words.
Write a sentence using each word in your writer's notebook.

Word	Context Sentence	Illustration
medium _____	I picked the <u>medium</u> ice-cream cone.	
stubborn _____	The <u>stubborn</u> puppy would not go for a walk.	**Does a stubborn person listen to advice?**
noticed _____	Sue <u>noticed</u> a hole in her favorite sweater.	
cozy _____	The cat looks <u>cozy</u> sleeping in the chair.	**What is a synonym for cozy?**
arrive _____	The guests <u>arrived</u> at 1:00.	
argue _____	Sam and Tim <u>argued</u> about who could run faster.	

© Macmillan/McGraw-Hill

Read each question and prompt. Discuss the answers with your group. Use your Leveled Reader to find details to support your answers. Then write your answers on the blank lines or on another sheet of paper.

1. How do the animals in the story act like people?

_____

2. What are some tricks that one character played on another?

_____

3. Why was one character so easily tricked by another?

_____

4. How did one character escape the other at the end of the story?

_____

5. What made you laugh the most in this story?

_____

6. Write one question about the book to ask your group.

_____

_____

Music of the Stone Age

Pages 392–393

Prior to reading the selection with children, they should have listened to the selection on **StudentWorks Plus**, the interactive eBook. In addition, selection vocabulary should have been pretaught using the **Visual Vocabulary Resources**.

Access Core Content

Teacher Note Pose the questions after you read the paragraph or page indicated.

Page 392

Whole Page

- *This selection is a nonfiction article. A nonfiction article tells about real people, places, or events.*

  Did the author write this article to tell a make-believe story or to tell about real things? (to tell about real things)

- *The title of this selection is* Music of the Stone Age. *What are the different ways that people today make music?* (They sing. They play guitars, piano, drums, and other instruments.)

- *The Stone Age was a time long, long ago when people lived in caves. Look at the picture of people from a museum exhibit, or display. This is what Stone Age people might have looked like. What are they wearing?* (clothes made out of animal skins)

- *Now let's read aloud the question under the title:* How do we know that people made music thousands of years ago? *What do you think?* (Question is open.)

- *Listen as I read the paragraph aloud to find out about the many kinds of recorded music we listen to. Let's list the different kinds.* (CDs, radio, TV)

- *How will people in the future know what our music is like?* (They will able to listen to recordings of it.)

Pages 392–393

Real World Reading

Comprehension

Genre
Expository text gives information about real people, places, and events.

Ask Questions
Author's Purpose
When you read, you should identify the author's reason for writing the text.

This exhibit shows what people from the Stone Age might have looked like.

Music of the Stone Age

How do we know that people made music thousands of years ago?

Today recorded music surrounds us. You can buy CDs of your favorite music. You can hear singers on the radio. You can even watch them on TV. Thousands of years from now, people will know about our music because we have made recordings of it.

392

Pages 394–395

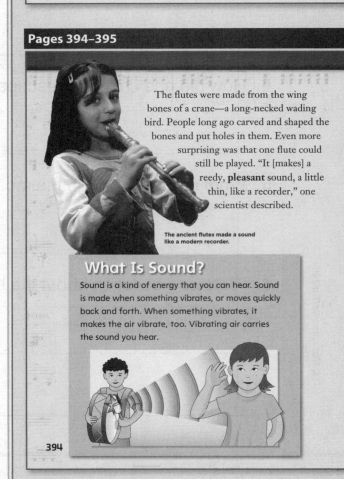

The flutes were made from the wing bones of a crane—a long-necked wading bird. People long ago carved and shaped the bones and put holes in them. Even more surprising was that one flute could still be played. "It [makes] a reedy, **pleasant** sound, a little thin, like a recorder," one scientist described.

The ancient flutes made a sound like a modern recorder.

What Is Sound?

Sound is a kind of energy that you can hear. Sound is made when something vibrates, or moves quickly back and forth. When something vibrates, it makes the air vibrate, too. Vibrating air carries the sound you hear.

394

Thousands of years ago, recording music was **impossible**. So how do we know that people long ago played music? Because scientists have found flutes that are 9,000 years old! The flutes were found in China, in the Yellow River Valley. Here scientists unearthed all sorts of **treasures**, including 36 flutes.

CHINA

Yellow River

Yellow River Valley

This map shows the Yellow River Valley in China, where the flutes were found.

These are some of the ancient flutes found in China. The one in the middle can still be played.

393

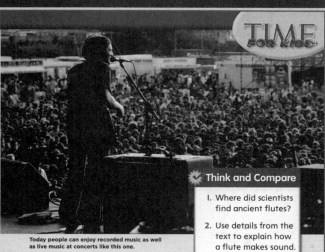

Today people can enjoy recorded music as well as live music at concerts like this one.

No one knows for sure what type of music the people from the Stone Age played. Did it sound like the music of today? Did people have musical **talent** and perform concerts? Did people sing along? We can only wonder what their music might have sounded like!

Think and Compare

1. Where did scientists find ancient flutes?

2. Use details from the text to explain how a flute makes sound.

3. What does the author want readers to learn about in the selection?

4. Why are sculptures from "Frozen Art" and flutes from "Music of the Stone Age" considered treasures?

395

Page 393

Whole Page

- *Say* impossible *with me:* impossible. Impossible *means* "not possible or able." Is it possible for me to walk out the door? (yes) Is it possible for me to fly through the door? (no) It is impossible.

- *It was impossible for people to record music thousands of years ago. They made most tools out of stone. They did know about electricity. How do we know that people played music back then? (People found old flutes.)*

- *Look at the pictures of some ancient, or very old, flutes that people found in China. The one in the middle still works. Point to the flute in the middle.*

- *Now look at the map of China. Point to the Yellow River Valley. That's where the flutes were found.*

Page 394

Whole Page

- *The flutes were made from the bones of a crane. A crane is a water bird with very long wings. People used tools to carve the bones into flute shapes.*

- *When you carve a shape out of something, you cut away the parts you don't need and leave the shape. Pretend you have a big piece of clay and you are carving a flute out of it. (Demonstrate a carving motion.)*

- *The flute from the Stone Age sounds like a recorder. Let's make the sound together. (Demonstrate.)*

- *Listen as I read the last paragraph. What does vibrating, or moving, air carry? (sound)*

Page 395

Whole Page

- *Look at the picture of a live concert. A concert is one or more people playing music for other people. It can be live or recorded.*

- *Was music from the Stone Age always live? (yes) Did people perform, or give, concerts? (We don't know.)*

PARTNERS *Tell your partner what you think music from the Stone Age sounded like. Explain why you think so.* (Question is open.)

Name _____

Use the word chart to study this week's vocabulary words.
Write a sentence using each word in your writer's notebook.

Word	Context Sentence	Illustration
impossible _____	It was <u>impossible</u> to lift the heavy box.	
treasures _____	I put my new necklace in a box with my other <u>treasures</u>.	
talent _____	I think juggling takes a lot of <u>talent</u>.	
pleasant _____	We spent a <u>pleasant</u> day at the beach.	**What would you describe as pleasant?**

© Macmillan/McGraw-Hill

Read each question and prompt. Discuss the answers with your group. Use your Leveled Reader to find details to support your answers. Then write your answers on the blank lines or on another sheet of paper.

1. Tell about sound. What must happen before a sound is made?

   _____

2. Describe how the ear works. Explain the five steps to hearing sounds.

   _____

3. How does sound travel? Give examples.

   _____

4. List two very loud sounds and two very soft sounds.

   _____

5. Talk about your favorite sounds.

   _____

6. Write one question about the book to ask your group.

   _____

   _____

Click, Clack, Moo: Cows That Type

Pages 404–405

Prior to reading the selection with children, they should have listened to the selection on **StudentWorks Plus,** the interactive eBook. In addition, selection vocabulary should have been pretaught using the **Visual Vocabulary Resources.**

Access Core Content

Teacher Note Pose the questions after you read the paragraph or page indicated.

Page 405

Title and Illustrations

- *Think of a story you have read or a movie you have seen that showed characters or places that can't exist in real life. The story you're thinking about probably also had events or actions that couldn't possibly happen in real life because they're just too unusual, or too wild to believe. Give me an example of this kind of story.* (Question is open.) *This kind of story is called fantasy.*

- (Write the word *impossible* on the board, and point to it.) *Say it with me:* Impossible! *That's the main thing about fantasies: they show us characters, events, or things that are impossible. They couldn't happen in real life.*

PARTNERS *Let's read the title of the story together:* Click, Clack, Moo: Cows That Type. *Now look at the illustration on page 405. What are these cows doing?* (They are typing.) *Tell your partner whether you think it would be easy or hard for a cow to type, and why.* (Question is open and may elicit some creative responses, but children's answers should show they understand that in real life, cows can't type at all.)

Pages 404–405

Comprehension

Genre
Fantasy is a story that has made-up characters, settings, or other things that could not happen in real life.

Ask Questions
Cause and Effect
As you read, use your Cause and Effect Chart.

Cause → Effect

Read to Find Out
How do the cows get Farmer Brown to do what they want?

404

Pages 406–407

Farmer Brown has a problem.
His cows like to type.
All day long he hears

Click, clack, **moo.**
Click, clack, **moo.**
Clickety, clack, **moo.**

406

Main Selection

Click, Clack, Moo
Cows That Type
by Doreen Cronin
illustrated by Betsy Lewin

405

At first, he couldn't believe his ears.
Cows that type.
Impossible!

Click, clack, **moo**.
Click, clack, **moo**.
Clickety, clack, **moo**.

407

Page 406

Text

■ *What does Farmer Brown hear all day long? Let's read those lines together:* Click, clack, moo. / Click, clack, moo. / Clickety, clack, moo.

 Let's try to see this scene in our heads, or visualize it. What do you think is making the click, clack, clickety *sound?* (the typewriter, as the cows hit the keys)

■ *How would you feel if you heard that sound all day long?* (Question is open.)

Page 407

Illustration

■ *(Point to Farmer Brown.) How do you think he is feeling?* (Question is open, but responses will include that he's angry, mad, or furious.) *That's right; he is just furious about having to hear all that noise all day long.* (Use facial expressions to illustrate the meaning of *furious*.)

Text

■ *What's that word on page 407 that means that something can't be real? What do you say when you can't believe what you're hearing or seeing? Say it with me:* Impossible!

Request Assistance

Remind children of expressions they can use to request assistance from the teacher or their partners, such as *Can you show me in the picture? Can you show me what it means?*

Page 408

Illustration

- *Now look at Farmer Brown's face. Does it still have that angry look? How would you describe how his face looks in this picture?* (startled or surprised)

Text

- *What's another way of saying* Then he couldn't believe his eyes? ("He couldn't believe that what he was looking at was really there.") *Let's read on to find out what Farmer Brown saw.*

Page 409

Text

- *Why do the cows leave a note for Farmer Brown?* (Because they're cold at night, and they want some electric blankets to keep warm.) *What is an electric blanket?* (a blanket that heats up when you plug it in)

- *Look at the note the cows wrote. Do you think these cows are nice? How can you tell?* (Yes, because they wrote *Dear* and *Sincerely* in the note.)

Pages 408–409

Pages 410–411

Page 410

Text

- *What does it mean to* go on strike? (not to work, to stop working)

- *Workers usually go on strike to get something they want from the owners or managers of the place where they work, or to show they are angry or impatient about something.*

- *These cows are very unusual. What kinds of things have they done so far that ordinary cows don't do in real life?* (They type. They write notes and leave them on the barn door for the farmer. They go on strike.)

Page 411

Illustration

- *Look behind the note on this page at the shadow on the barn wall. Who do you think that is? How can you tell?* (It's Farmer Brown. You can see the outline of his straw hat.)

- *What does he seem to be doing?* (jumping and shaking his fists) *When do we usually jump up and down and shake our fists?* (when we're angry or upset about something)

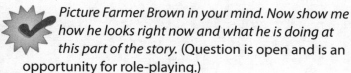 *Picture Farmer Brown in your mind. Now show me how he looks right now and what he is doing at this part of the story.* (Question is open and is an opportunity for role-playing.)

Text

- *What has caused Farmer Brown to be so angry and upset?* (The cows won't give any milk because they are on strike.)

Click, Clack, Moo: Cows That Type

Page 412

Text

- *Those cows really mean it! The farmer hears the sound of their typing in the background, all day long and all night long. In the background means the sound is not right next to him, or up front, but he can always hear it. He can't stand it!*

Page 413

Text

- *So the farmer gets another note. The cows are saying that someone else in the barn is cold and wants electric blankets. Who is that?* (the hens)

- *Those cows are very smart! What do you do when you want something, and you want a better chance of getting it than just trying on your own?* (Question is open, but answers include getting your friends or someone in your family to back you up, to agree with you, and to support you.)

- *The cows are saying that someone else is on their side. They want the farmer to listen to their demand for electric blankets.*

Pages 412–413

"No milk today!" cried Farmer Brown. In the background, he heard the cows busy at work:

Click, clack, **moo**.
Click, clack, **moo**.
Clickety, clack, **moo**.

412

Pages 414–415

The cows were growing impatient with the farmer. They left a new note on the barn door.

Closed.
No milk.
No eggs.

414

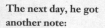

The next day, he got another note:

Dear Farmer Brown,
The hens are cold too.
They'd like electric
blankets.

Sincerely,
The Cows

"No eggs!" cried Farmer Brown.
In the background he heard them.

Click, clack, **moo**.
Click, clack, **moo**.
Clickety, clack, **moo**.

Page 414

Text

- *Who can show me how you look when you are growing impatient, like the cows?* (Question is open. The children's expressions and body language should generally show increasing frustration and impatience.)

- *Let's read the next note the farmer gets. What does the note from the chickens say? Let's read it together:* Closed. No milk. No eggs.

- *When you see a sign that says* closed *on a store window, what does that mean?* (The store is not open. You can't shop there.)

Page 415

Text

- *Who is on strike now?* (The hens and cows are both on strike now.)

Illustration

- *What do the upside-down buckets and stool tell you about what's happening?* (They're not being used because the cows are on strike.)

Page 416

Illustration

- *Just look at the expressions on the faces of these cows!* (Point to the cows in the illustration.) *What do you think they're probably feeling right now?* (Question is open.)

Page 417

Illustration

- *Why is the farmer waving his hands like that?* (Point to the farmer in the illustration. Responses include that he is angry or upset.)

Text

- *Let's read what Farmer Brown says together, using our voices to show how angry he is:* "Cows that type. Hens on strike! Whoever heard of such a thing? How can I run a farm with no milk and no eggs!"

Synonyms and Circumlocution

Remind children that they can ask for synonyms to help clarify words or expressions they do not understand. Ask, *What is another way of saying "furious"?* (very angry)

416

Farmer Brown got out his own typewriter.

Dear Cows and Hens:
There will be no electric blankets.
You are cows and hens.
I **demand** milk and eggs.

Sincerely,
Farmer Brown

418

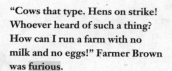

"Cows that type. Hens on strike! Whoever heard of such a thing? How can I run a farm with no milk and no eggs!" Farmer Brown was furious.

Cause and Effect
What is the effect of the hens' strike on Farmer Brown? Use story details to help explain.

417

Duck was a neutral party, so he brought the ultimatum to the cows.

419

Page 418

Text

- *Now Farmer Brown is typing a note to the cows and hens. What does he want?* (milk and eggs)

- *Farmer Brown demands milk and eggs. If I demand that you sit down and be quiet, am I asking in a nice and happy voice, or am I asking in a stern and angry voice?* (I am asking in a stern and angry voice. *Demand* is a very strong word. It shows the farmer is very angry.)

Page 419

Text

- *What do you do when you're not getting along with someone, and things between you seem to be going nowhere? You have to get someone who isn't on either side to help. That's what* neutral *means—"not being on anyone's side."*

- *We know that the word* party *on this page doesn't mean the kind of party we usually think of, with balloons and a cake. It just means another person, or character. Who is the neutral party in this story?* (Duck) *Duck is the messenger, or neutral party. And what's he taking to the cows?* (the note with the farmer's demands, an ultimatum)

- *Let's stop a minute and think about this word,* ultimatum. *If I tell you something for the very last time (grimace to show exasperation), I'm giving you an* ultimatum. *It's the last thing you'll hear from me, and it's your last chance to do something. Say it with me:* ultimatum.

Click, Clack, Moo: Cows That Type

Pages 420–421

Illustration

- *Things are getting serious! Just look at the lock on the barn door! What do you think the other animals could be thinking? (Question is open.)*

With your partner, try to think of who could have put the lock on the door, and tell why you think as you do. (Question is open. The farmer could have put it there to keep other animals from entering the barn and going on strike, too. It could also be the cows and chickens who are on strike who put it there because they don't want the farmer or other nosey animals to barge in and maybe cause trouble.)

Text

- *What does it mean that none of the other animals could understand* Moo*? (The other animals can't understand what the cows are saying.)*

- *We have an expression in English:* I can't understand a word you're saying! *We usually say it when we're confused about what we just heard.*

- *Do you think that cows have their own language? (Question is open.)*

- *How long does Farmer Brown wait for an answer? (all night long)*

Pages 420–421

420

Pages 422–423

Duck knocked on the door early the next morning. He handed Farmer Brown a note:

422

The cows held an emergency meeting. All the animals gathered around the barn to snoop, but none of them could understand Moo.

All night long, Farmer Brown waited for an answer.

Dear Farmer Brown,
We will exchange our typewriter for electric blankets.
Leave them outside the barn door and we will send Duck over with the typewriter.

Sincerely,
The Cows

423

Pages 422–423

Text

- *Now the story gets really good! The cows have an idea about how to fix the problem. What is it?* (The chickens and cows will give the farmer their typewriter if he agrees to give them electric blankets.) *What do you think of their idea?* (Question is open.)

- *Who do you think has a better chance of getting what they want here, the farmer or the cows?* (the cows) *Why do you think so?* (The cows know the farmer wants them to stop typing and will do anything to get rid of the noise.)

Pages 424–425

Text

- *Let's read the sentence on page 420 together to see if things are going to work out between the farmer and the cows:* Farmer Brown decided this was a good deal.

- *Getting a good deal means that someone is offering you something or treating you in some way that is good for you. You can't say no to a good deal!*

Illustration

- *Look at the animals on these pages.* (Point out the blankets on the sleeping cows and hens.) *Do you think that the cows and hens got a good deal?* (Question is open, but responses will include that both the cows and the hens look happy and warm, so they got a good deal.)

Pages 424–425

Pages 426–427

He left the blankets next to the barn door and waited for Duck to come with the typewriter.

425

427

Page 426

Text

- *Something tells me that Farmer Brown's troubles aren't over. Let's read the first line together:* The next morning he got a note:

- *Who is asking Farmer Brown for something now?* (the ducks)

- *What do you think gave the ducks the idea to ask for something?* (They probably got the idea when they saw the farmer giving in to the cows' demands.)

- *What reason do the ducks give in their note for wanting a diving board?* (They say the pond is quite boring.)

 With your partner, brainstorm some things that you would ask for if you were the ducks. What would make your life in the pond more exciting? Tell how your choices would make your life better.

Page 427

Illustration

- *Do you think the farmer gave the ducks what they demanded? How do you know?* (Yes, because the duck is diving off a diving board.)

- *What do you think the ducks offered to the farmer in order to get their diving board?* (Question is open, but guide children's responses to what the farmer wanted most: quiet. Write *Peace and quiet!* on the board, and point to it.)

- *Do you think Farmer Brown's farm will finally be quiet?* (Question is open.)

 With your partner, visualize which animals on the farm might be the next ones to get that typewriter, and write the kind of note they might write. What would you ask for if you were those animals?

Early Ranching in Texas

Access Core Content

Teacher Note Pose the questions after you read the paragraph or page indicated.

Page 430

Title

- *Let's read the title together:* <u>Early Ranching in Texas</u>. Ranching *means "the work on a ranch." A ranch is a type of large farm with animals such as cows, horses, or sheep. Raise your hand if you have seen a ranch.*

Text

- *The people who own ranches are called ranchers. The first ranchers in Texas had cattle.* Cattle *means "a lot of cows together." Say it with me:* cattle.

Photo

- *Look at the picture. Point to the cattle in the picture. Point to their horns. Are those horns long or short?* (long) *What are these cattle called?* (longhorns)

Page 431

Photo

- *Look at this photo. Show your partner the picture of the cowboy. What is the cowboy riding?* (a horse) *Tell me some things the cowboy is wearing.* (Answers will vary.) *What do you see behind the cowboy?* (cattle) *Many cowboys went to work on Texas ranches. On this page, we will learn something about them.*

Paragraph 1

- *Farmers decided to become ranchers because there was a lot of land. A lot of cattle could graze on it.* Graze *means "eat grass." Say it with me:* graze. *Cows graze. Tell me some other animals that graze.* (possible answers: horses, sheep, goats, llamas)

Paragraphs 2–4

- *There were no fences. The cattle could go everywhere. Ranchers needed cowboys to watch the cattle. They put brands, or marks, on the cattle. Then they knew which cattle were theirs. Soon people all over the country wanted beef, or meat, from Texas.*

Would you like to be a cowboy or cowgirl? Why or why not? Tell your partner two reasons.

Social Studies

Genre
Expository text gives information and facts about a topic.

✓ **Text Feature**
Bar Graphs show the relationship between numbers using bars of different lengths.

Content Vocabulary
graze
cowboys
cattle drives

Early Ranching in Texas

By Linda B. Ross

More than 300 years ago, Spanish and Mexican settlers came to Texas. They brought cattle and horses with them and became ranchers.

The word *ranch* comes from the Spanish word *rancho*. These early ranchers raised cattle that were called *longhorns* because of the large size of their horns.

Texas longhorns have horns that measure 4–8 feet from tip to tip.

430

Cattle Trails

Cattle drives moved north from ranches in Texas. They headed to railroads in places like Kansas and Missouri. From there the cattle went by train to the Northeast.

The drives lasted about 25 years. They ended when ranchers built fences around their property. There was no open land for cattle to roam or graze. Then railroads were built in Texas. So ranchers sent their cattle directly to market by train.

Today you can still find many ranches in Texas that raise cattle, and other animals such as horses and sheep. There are also many different kinds of farms typical to the Southwest, including vegetable, fruit, and cotton farms.

Cattle Trails in the 1800s

Kansas City
KS
MO
Red River
OK
AR
TX
Western Trail
Bandera
San Antonio
Gulf of Mexico

City
Cattle trail
Present-day borders are shown

Ranchers used cattle trails from the 1860s to the 1880s.

Area of detail in the United States

432

Social Studies

Texas cowboys came from all over the United States and Mexico.

Over the years new settlers came to Texas. Some of them started out as farmers. However, when they saw the open land where cattle could **graze**, many of them became cattle ranchers.

At first there were no fences separating different ranches. The land was wide open.

By the 1860s, many ranchers hired **cowboys** to help keep track of their cattle. The cowboys branded, or marked, the cattle. They used the rancher's initials or a special design. That way the ranchers knew which cattle belonged to them.

Soon there was a big demand for Texas beef in other parts of the United States. Ranchers were selling their cattle in the Northeast.

431

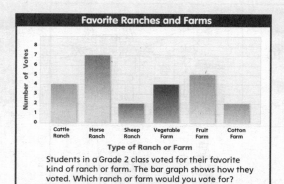

Favorite Ranches and Farms

Students in a Grade 2 class voted for their favorite kind of ranch or farm. The bar graph shows how they voted. Which ranch or farm would you vote for?

Connect and Compare

1. What kind of ranch received the most votes? How many votes did it get? **Bar Graphs**

2. How are the farm animals you read about in *Click, Clack, Moo* different from the animals in this article? **Reading/Writing Across Texts**

Social Studies Activity

Research what cattle ranching is like in Texas today. Tell how it is different from long ago. Use pictures to help explain.

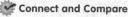  **Science Cattle Ranches** www.macmillanmh.com

433

Page 432

Map

- *Look at the map. Let's read the map title together:* <u>Cattle Trails in the 1800s</u>. *Trails are roads or paths. On this map, the red lines are cattle trails. Show your partner some cattle trails.* (Point to a railroad.) *Lines like this are railroads for trains. Show your partner some railroads.*

- *Cowboys had to take the cattle to the railroads. They used cattle trails. Together with your partner, find San Antonio. Put your finger there, then follow the cattle trail to Abilene.* (Demonstrate for children.)

- *Cowboys put their cattle on the train in Abilene. Then the cattle traveled to places in the Northeast.* (Point to the Northeast on the inset map.)

Paragraphs 1 and 2

- *When the cowboys took the cattle to the railroads, it was called a cattle drive. Say it with me:* cattle drive. *They walked the cattle over open land. But soon people built fences. There was no place for the cattle to walk or graze. Then the railroads came to Texas. It was easy to put the cattle right on the trains. There were no more cattle drives.*

Paragraph 3

- *What animals can we see on Texas ranches today?* (cattle, horses, sheep) *What kinds of farms can we see in Texas?* (vegetable, fruit, cotton) *We use cotton to make clothes, like this.* (Show something made of cotton.)

Page 433

Graph

- (Point to the bar graph.) *This is a bar graph. Bar graphs give information. Each bar shows one kind of information. The height of the bar shows another kind of information.*

- *Let's read the graph title together:* <u>Favorite Ranches</u>. *Students voted for their favorite kind of ranch or farm. This graph shows their answers.*

- *Let's read the types of ranches and farms they voted on.* (Point to and read ranch and farm types.) *Now point to the horse ranch bar. It's the tallest bar. That means the most people voted for it. How many people voted for horse ranch?* (seven) *Find the cattle ranch bar. How many people voted for cattle ranch?* (four)

 Which is your favorite type of ranch or farm? Why? Tell your partner.

Use the word chart to study this week's vocabulary words. Write a sentence using each word in your writer's notebook.

Word	Context Sentence	Illustration
impatient _____	Dad gets impatient when the newspaper is late.	**List what you might do when you feel impatient.**
furious _____	Bill was furious about the mess the dog made.	
neutral _____	Tom doesn't care who wins because he's neutral.	
emergency _____	The fire truck rushed to an emergency.	
demand _____	The police officer demanded that we stop at the corner.	
sincerely _____	I sincerely liked the birthday present.	

© Macmillan/McGraw-Hill

Read each question and prompt. Discuss the answers with your group. Use your Leveled Reader to find details to support your answers. Then write your answers on the blank lines or on another sheet of paper.

1. Tell about the characters in your book, both the animals and the humans.

_____

2. Explain what problem has occurred.

_____

3. How do the animals and humans work together to solve the problem?

_____

4. Tell how the animal characters seem to behave like humans in the book you read. Give examples.

_____

5. Did you find the book to be silly? Did it make you laugh? Share your ideas with your classmates.

_____

6. Write one question about the book to ask your group.

_____

Stirring Up Memories

Pages 440–441

Prior to reading the selection with children, they should have listened to the selection on **StudentWorks Plus**, the interactive eBook. In addition, selection vocabulary should have been pretaught using the **Visual Vocabulary Resources**.

Access Core Content

Teacher Note Pose the questions after you read the paragraph or page indicated.

Pages 440–441

Title and Author

- *Let's read the title of this selection together:* Stirring Up Memories. *Memories are things you remember from the past. I have memories of what I did in class last year. When you stir up memories, you think about things that happened in the past.*

- *The person who wrote this selection is named Pam Muñoz Ryan. (Point to the name.) Pam Muñoz Ryan is an author. She writes children's books. In this selection, Pam tells readers about her memories and about her life as a writer.*

Photos and Captions

- *Let's look at the photographs and read the captions together. (Point to each caption as you read it.)* I moved into this house when I was four years old. *Whose words are these? (They are the words of Pam Muñoz Ryan.)* I had a lot of great friends growing up. *Point to Pam in the photograph. How do you know that is Pam? (The label on the photograph says* Me!*)* Here I am with my favorite doll. *Point to Pam. Point to the doll.* My third-grade class was very big. I'm sitting in the middle and wearing a plaid dress. *Things that are plaid have a pattern made out of crossing lines of color. Point to Pam in the photograph.*

 What kinds of memories do you think Pam will share with readers? (Pam will share memories of growing up.)

Comprehension

Genre
An *Autobiography* is a retelling of someone's life told by that person.

Ask Questions
Draw Conclusions
As you read, use the Conclusion Chart.

Read to Find Out
How does the author use her own life to write stories?

I moved into this house when I was four years old.

Me!

I had a lot of great friends growing up.

440

Growing Up

I grew up in the San Joaquin (wah-keen) Valley in Bakersfield, California. This area is known for its hot, dry summers. It is often more than 100 degrees! When I was a young girl, I stayed cool by taking swimming lessons and eating ice pops. I also rode my bike to the library.

My friends and I liked to eat ice pops during the hot summers in California.

I loved the library for two important reasons. First, I could check out a pile of books and take them home with me. Second, the library was air-conditioned!

442

Stirring Up Memories

by
Pam Muñoz Ryan

Here I am with my favorite doll!

McKINLEY SCHOOL

My third-grade class was very big. I am sitting in the middle and wearing a plaid dress.

441

At my house, I was the oldest of three sisters. Next door to us, there lived another three girls. They were all younger than me, too. Whenever we played together, I was in charge of what we did. I was the director of the play, or the mom in a pretend family. Sometimes I was the doctor who saved their lives!

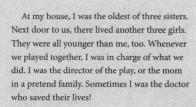

Here I am opening presents at my birthday party with my friends.

443

Page 442

Paragraph 1 and Map

■ *In which city and state did Pam grow up?* (Pam grew up in Bakersfield, California.) *Point to Bakersfield, California, on the map.*

Photo and Caption

■ *Let's read the caption for this photograph together:* My friends and I liked to eat ice pops during the hot summers in California. *What did Pam and her friends like to during the hot California summers?* (They liked to eat ice pops.) *Point to an ice pop in the photograph. Do you like ice pops, too? Why are they good in the summer?* (Ice pops are cold and refreshing.)

Paragraph 2

■ *When a building is air-conditioned, the air inside the building is cooled. Pam loved the library because it was cool in the summer. Why else did she love the library?* (The library had books she could check out and take home.)

Page 443

Text

■ *When you are in charge, you are the leader or the boss. Why was Pam in charge when she played with her sisters and the girls next door?* (Pam was the oldest.)

 What do you like to play when you are in charge? Tell your partner what you like to do.

Photo and Caption

Read the caption of this photograph with me: Here I am opening presents at my birthday party with my friends. *Point to Pam in the photograph. How do you know that girl is Pam?* (Pam says, *Here I am opening presents,* so the girl opening presents in the photograph must be Pam.)

Seek Clarification

Some children may be confused by unfamiliar words. Encourage children to always seek clarification when they encounter a sentence that does not make sense to them.

Page 444

Text

- *When Pam and her cousins played, they pretended that they were in a circus, or at school, or in a jungle. Pam created, or made up, stories as she told her cousins what to do. What stories do you make up when you play?* (Question is open.)

Photo and Caption

- *Look at the photograph and read the caption with me:* I was about 17 years old at this family gathering. I'm second from the right in the back row, holding one of my baby cousins. *Look at the people in the back row. Point to the person on the right.* (Point to the person.) *Now point to the person who is second from the right.* (Point to Pam.) *That person is Pam.*

- *Who else do you think is in the picture? Why do you think that?* (The other people are probably Pam's cousins and maybe her grandmother. The text tells about Pam's grandmother's house and Pam's cousins.)

Page 445

Photo and Caption

- *Let's read the caption below this photograph:* This family party was at my uncle's house. I'm sitting at the table wearing the black sweater. *Point to Pam in the photograph. Use the caption to help you find Pam.*

Text

- *Close your eyes and imagine a kitchen smelling like delicious food. The kitchen is filled with noisy family members having fun. Tell me what you would say if you were there.* (Question is open.)

- *Pam wrote a book called* Mice and Beans. *What is the book about?* (The book is about a big family gathering and a grandmother who loves to cook.) *How are people in the book like Pam's real family?* (Pam's family is big. Her grandmother was always cooking.)

Page 446

Heading

- *Let's read the heading on this page:* Finding an Idea. *We learned about Pam's memories about her childhood. Now we'll learn how she finds ideas for writing.*

I was also the oldest of the 23 cousins in my family. When we had a family party at my grandmother's house, I was the boss again. I would say, "Let's pretend this is a circus or a school or a jungle . . ." Then I would tell everyone what they should do and say. I didn't know it at the time, but I was already **creating** stories!

I was about 17 years old at this family gathering. I'm second from the right in the back row, holding one of my baby cousins.

444

Finding an Idea

Readers always want to know where I get my ideas. I wish I could say that I go to an idea store and buy them. As far as I know, there is no such place.

I like to visit schools. Children always ask me where I get the ideas for my books.

Mrs. Pam Muñoz Ryan

446

This family party was at my uncle's house.
I'm sitting at the table wearing the black sweater.

Some of my favorite **memories** are of those times at my grandmother's house. The kitchen always smelled like onions, garlic, and roasted peppers. There was often a big pot of beans on the stove. A pan of Spanish rice was cooking next to it.

When we were all together, it was crowded and noisy. Sound **familiar**? My story, *Mice and Beans*, is about a big family gathering and a grandmother who loves to cook!

☑ Draw Conclusions
Use details from the text to help draw a conclusion about why Pam Muñoz Ryan's favorite memories are of her grandmother's house.

445

Real-life people like Eleanor Roosevelt (left) and Amelia Earhart (below) sometimes inspire me to write stories.

Sometimes my ideas come from something interesting I might have read about in a book. Sometimes they come from real life, like those times at my grandmother's house. Of course, the clever mice in *Mice and Beans* didn't come from real life. They came from my **imagination**.

447

Text

- *What kinds of ideas would you buy if you could go to a store to buy them?* (Question is open.)

Photo and Caption

- *Read the caption below this photograph with me:* I like to visit schools. Children always ask me where I get the ideas for my books.

☑ *Authors like Pam try to come up with ideas that readers will like. From where might Pam get ideas for books?* (Pam might get ideas from her family.) *Why do you think that?* (The family in *Mice and Beans* is like Pam's own family.)

Page 447

Photos and Caption

- *Let's read the caption for these photographs:* Real-life people like Eleanor Roosevelt (left) (Point to Roosevelt.) and Amelia Earhart (below) (Point to Earhart.) sometimes inspire me to write stories.

- *Eleanor Roosevelt was the wife of a United States president. She was a writer and a speaker, and she helped many people. Amelia Earhart was the first woman to fly a plane across the Atlantic Ocean alone.*

- *When someone inspires you, that person makes you want to do something. Why do you think Eleanor Roosevelt and Amelia Earhart inspired Pam to write?* (They were famous women. They had lives that were interesting to write about.)

- *Point to the book that Pam wrote about Amelia and Eleanor. Let's read the title of that book together:* Amelia and Eleanor Go for a Ride.

Text

- *Pam gets some ideas from real people, such as Eleanor Roosevelt, Amelia Earhart, and her own grandmother. Where did she get the idea for the mice characters in Mice and Beans?* (The idea for the mice came from Pam's imagination.)

PARTNERS *When you use your imagination, you make pictures of things in your mind. What writing ideas have come from your imagination? Tell your ideas to your partner.* (Question is open.)

Page 448

Text

- *Whose birthday is celebrated in* Mice and Beans? (the youngest grandchild's) *When you are the youngest, everyone else is older than you. How does the grandmother get ready for the party for a week?* (The grandmother cleans the kitchen each day.)

Photo, Illustration, and Caption

- *Read this caption with me:* I thought of my grandmother, Esperanza, when I wrote *Mice and Beans*. In the photo above she is holding me when I was a baby. *Point to Pam's real grandmother* (point to Pam's grandmother). *Now point to the grandmother in the book.* (Point to the character.)

Page 449

Photo, Illustration, and Caption

- *Now let's read the caption on this page:* Below is a picture of one of my own family parties. It is my son Tyler's birthday. *Point to the real family birthday party. Whose party is it?* (It is the birthday of Pam's son, Tyler.) *Now point to the party in the book.*

Text

- *When you are tidy, you are very neat and clean. In the story, the grandmother is very tidy because she doesn't want to get mice.*

- *The grandmother makes rice and beans for the party. But the title of Pam's book is* Mice and Beans. *Why is the title funny?* (The word *mice* sounds like *rice*. The grandmother is making rice and beans, but she has mice in her kitchen.)

Page 450

Text

PARTNERS *Have you ever started out with one idea when writing and then changed your idea or added to it as you wrote? Tell your partner what you did.* (Response is open.)

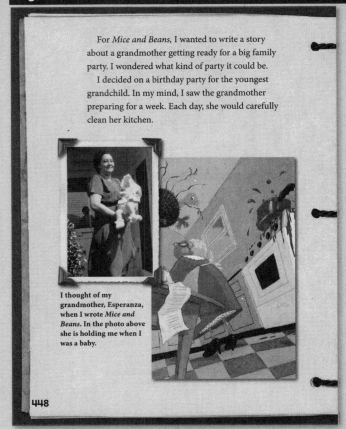

For *Mice and Beans*, I wanted to write a story about a grandmother getting ready for a big family party. I wondered what kind of party it could be.

I decided on a birthday party for the youngest grandchild. In my mind, I saw the grandmother preparing for a week. Each day, she would carefully clean her kitchen.

I thought of my grandmother, Esperanza, when I wrote *Mice and Beans*. In the photo above she is holding me when I was a baby.

448

That's what happens when I'm writing. I start out with one idea. Then, the more I think about it, the more choices I have for the story. Sometimes I try out different ideas on paper. Then I choose the one I like best.

Now that I'm an adult, it's my turn to cook special foods for my friends and family to enjoy.

My Favorite Recipe

Salsa

2 large	tomatoes; seeded and chopped
1 to 2	chile peppers; seeded & chopped
1/3 c	chopped green onions
2 tb	chopped fresh cilantro
2 tb	lime juice
1/4 ts	salt

Combine all ingredients. Mix well and then cover. Refrigerate until serving time.

450

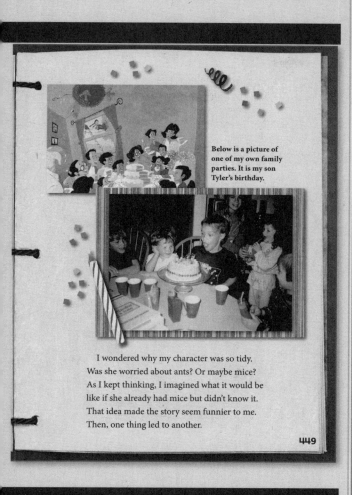

Below is a picture of one of my own family parties. It is my son Tyler's birthday.

I wondered why my character was so tidy. Was she worried about ants? Or maybe mice? As I kept thinking, I imagined what it would be like if she already had mice but didn't know it. That idea made the story seem funnier to me. Then, one thing led to another.

449

Once I've thought of an idea, it's time to start writing.

Many people think that writers look far away to find their stories. The truth is that most writers look within. They stir up memories and then sprinkle them with their imagination.

Draw Conclusions
Use text details and what you know to draw a conclusion about why Pam Muñoz Ryan says most writers look inside themselves for story ideas.

451

Photo and Caption

- *Look at the picture of Pam cooking. Let's read the caption to find out what Pam says about this photograph:* Now that I'm an adult, it's my turn to cook special foods for my friends and family to enjoy.

- *An adult is a grownup. Point to grownup Pam cooking for her friends and family.*

Now point to the recipe card at the bottom of the page. (Point to the card.) *I wonder why the card is on this page. Let's read to find out. The card is titled* My Favorite Recipe. (Point to the words.) *The card shows a recipe for salsa.* (Point to the label Salsa.) *Why do you think the card is shown here?* (Pam wants to share one of her favorite recipes with readers.)

Page 451

Photo and Caption

- *Look at the picture of Pam sitting at her desk. Let's read what she says about this picture:* Once I've thought of an idea, it's time to start writing. *It looks like Pam does some of her writing on a computer. Point to Pam's computer.*

Text

- *Pam says writers stir up memories and then sprinkle them with their imagination. When Pam describes writing in this way, what does it remind you of?* (Pam makes writing sound like cooking.) *When we cook, we also stir things up and sprinkle them with spices, salt, and pepper to make them interesting.*

Synonyms and Circumlocution

Remind children that they can ask for synonyms to help clarify words or expressions they do not understand. Ask, *What is another way of saying "adult"?* (grown up, not a child)

Page 452

Heading

- *Point to the heading on this page and read it with me:* <u>A Writer's Life</u>. *(Point to the heading.)*

Text

- *If you had a glamorous life, you would do things that people think are exciting and very interesting. You might wear fancy clothes and have a fancy car. But Pam's life is not like that. She works at home. She doesn't have to get dressed up.*

Photo and Caption

This photograph shows Pam at home. Let's read what Pam says in the caption: <u>Working at home means I can walk from my breakfast table right to my office.</u> *Do you think it is better for writers to work at home or take a long train ride to an office that is miles away? Why do you think that? (Question is open.)*

Page 453

Photos and Caption

- *Before we read the caption, let's take a look at these photographs of Pam and her dogs. What do you think the dogs' names are? Why do you think that?* (Pam's dogs are Sammie and Buddy. There are dog tags with those names next to the photographs.)

- *Now let's read the caption to find out if we were correct:* <u>Sammie and Buddy keep me company when I want to work and when I want to play.</u> *We were correct. Pam's dogs are named Sammie and Buddy.*

Text

- *What do Pam, Buddy, and Sammie do almost every day?* (They go for a walk in the neighborhood or on the beach.)

- *Imagine that you have two dogs like Buddy and Sammie. What would you do with them every day? Tell your partner what you would do. (Question is open.)*

A Writer's Life

Readers often think that a writer's life is **glamorous** with fancy cars and clothes. For a very few, that might be true, but my life is much different than that.

I work at my home in California, near San Diego. I don't have to dress up to go to work. I don't take long train rides because my desk is in my house. I get up early, eat breakfast, and go straight to my office to write.

Working at home means I can walk from my breakfast table right to my office.

452

For part of the year, the house is mostly quiet. My husband, Jim, and I have four children, two girls and twin boys. The girls are grown up now, but the boys are still in college. They come home during the summer. Since we live near the Pacific Ocean, there is a lot of going back and forth to the beach.

My husband, Jim, and I enjoy taking Buddy and Sammie to the beach.

454

Sammie and Buddy keep me company when I want to work and when I want to play.

BUDDY

I have two friends who love to watch me work. They are my dogs, Buddy and Sammie. Almost every day, I take them for a walk, either in my neighborhood or on the beach.

453

Many of my favorite memories are of times spent at home.

My childhood home

Today when my children are all together in our house for family **occasions**, it is crowded and noisy. It's just like when I was a little girl. Sometimes I even cook rice and beans! During these times, we're creating new memories. Maybe someday they'll give me the idea for another story!

455

Page 454

Text

- *Why is Pam's house mostly quiet for part of the year?* (Pam's children are grown or in college. They are not at always at home with Pam.)

Photo and Caption

- *Read the caption below this photograph with me:* My husband, Jim, and I enjoy taking Buddy and Sammie to the beach. *Who is the man in the photograph?* (He is Pam's husband, Jim.) *Point to Jim in the photograph.*

Page 455

Photos and Captions

- *Read the captions below these photographs with me:* Many of my favorite memories are of times spent at home. (Point to the large photograph.) *The other caption says* My childhood home. (Point to the smaller photograph.) *A childhood home is a home that you live in when you are young, or a child.*

Text

- *Occasions are important or special times. What are some occasions for which Pam's family might get together?* (Pam's family might get together for birthdays, holidays, graduations, weddings, or anniversaries).

 We learned a lot about Pam in this selection. What kind of a person do you think Pam is? Why do you think that? (Pam is a person with a good imagination. She comes up with ideas for stories, and she has written books. Pam is a loving and caring person. She loves and remembers family members, and she includes characters like her family members in her writing.)

What part of Pam's life did you enjoy learning about? Tell your partner what you liked most about this selection. (Responses are open.)

Interactive Question - Response Guide

Brush Dance/ Crayons

Access Core Content

Teacher Note Pose the questions after you read the paragraph or page indicated.

Page 458

Whole Poem

- *Let's read the title of this poem together:* Brush Dance.

- *Close your eyes and imagine a paintbrush dancing across a sheet of paper as it paints a picture. Keep that idea in your mind as we read the beginning of the poem together:* A dot, a blot, a smidge, a smear. / and just a little squiggle here . . .

- *A dot, a blot, a smidge, a smear, and a squiggle are all marks you can make as you paint. A dot is round. A blot looks like a stain. A smidge is just a little, and a smear is spread around. Do you know what a squiggle looks like? Use your hand to make a squiggle in the air.* (Demonstrate a squiggling motion with your hand.)

- *The words* smidge *and* smear *are fun to say. Both words begin with the same sound. Let's say the words again:* smidge, smear. *What sounds do both words begin with?* (Both words begin with /sm/.)

- *Which word at the beginning of the poem rhymes with* dot? (blot) *Remember, words that rhyme end with the same sound. Which word rhymes with* smear? (here)

- *Now let's read the second part of the poem together:* A dab, a dash, a splish, a splat. / that's how Patrick paints a cat!

- *A dab and a dash are also marks.* Splish *and* splat *are sounds that paint makes when it hits the paper. The words* splish *and* splat *sound like the noises they stand for. Let's say* splish *and* splat *again and imagine paint making those sounds as it hits the paper:* Splish! Splat! *With what sound do both words begin?* (Both words begin with /spl/.)

- *What is Patrick painting?* (a cat) *What word in the poem rhymes with* cat? (splat)

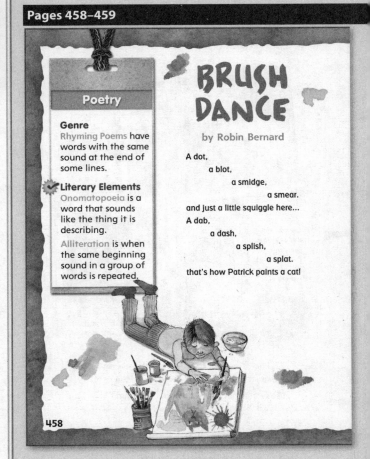

Poetry

Genre
Rhyming Poems have words with the same sound at the end of some lines.

Literary Elements
Onomatopoeia is a word that sounds like the thing it is describing.

Alliteration is when the same beginning sound in a group of words is repeated.

BRUSH DANCE
by Robin Bernard

A dot,
　a blot,
　　a smidge,
　　　a smear.
and just a little squiggle here...
A dab,
　a dash,
　　a splish,
　　　a splat.
that's how Patrick paints a cat!

458

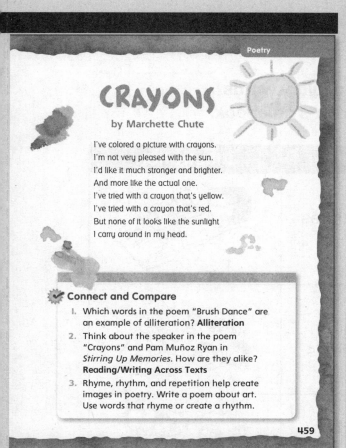

Poetry

CRAYONS
by Marchette Chute

I've colored a picture with crayons.
I'm not very pleased with the sun.
I'd like it much stronger and brighter.
And more like the actual one.
I've tried with a crayon that's yellow.
I've tried with a crayon that's red.
But none of it looks like the sunlight
I carry around in my head.

✔ Connect and Compare

1. Which words in the poem "Brush Dance" are an example of alliteration? **Alliteration**

2. Think about the speaker in the poem "Crayons" and Pam Muñoz Ryan in *Stirring Up Memories*. How are they alike? **Reading/Writing Across Texts**

3. Rhyme, rhythm, and repetition help create images in poetry. Write a poem about art. Use words that rhyme or create a rhythm.

459

- *Now let's read the whole poem together. Listen for words that rhyme, words that begin with the same sounds, and words that sound like noises:* A dot, a blot, a smidge, a smear. / and just a little squiggle here . . . / A dab, a dash, a splish, a splat. / that's how Patrick paints a cat!

Page 459

Whole Poem

- *Read the title of this poem with me:* Crayons. *Close your eyes and imagine what sunlight looks like. Keep that picture in your mind as we read this poem together.*

- *Read the first four lines of the poem with me:* I've colored a picture with crayons. / I'm not very pleased with the sun. / I'd like it much stronger and brighter. / And more like the actual one.

- *The speaker in this poem isn't pleased, or happy, with the sun that he or she colored. Why isn't the speaker pleased?* (The speaker wants the sun to be stronger and brighter in the picture.)

- *What word rhymes with* sun *in these lines of the poem?* (one)

- *Now let's read the second part of the poem together:* I've tried with a crayon that's yellow. / I've tried with a crayon that's red. / But none of it looks like the sunlight / I carry around in my head.

- *What word rhymes with* red *in these lines?* (head)

- *Sometimes it is very hard to draw or paint things in nature, such as sunlight. The colors we see just don't match the colors of the crayons or paints we use! What else in nature might be hard to show with crayons or paint?* (Question is open.)

 Read aloud both poems with a partner. Take turns reading the lines. Tell your partner which poem you like best. Tell your partner why. (Questions are open.)

Use the word chart to study this week's vocabulary words.
Write a sentence using each word in your writer's notebook.

Word	Context Sentence	Illustration
creating _____	Dad is <u>creating</u> pictures for his story.	
familiar _____	The story was <u>familiar</u>. I'd heard it many times.	
occasions _____	Birthday parties are my favorite family <u>occasions</u>.	
memories _____	Looking at my photo album brings back good <u>memories</u>.	**Describe two of your favorite memories.**
imagination _____	I use my <u>imagination</u> to write stories.	**When might you use your imagination?**
glamorous _____	I dressed up like a <u>glamorous</u> movie star.	

© Macmillan/McGraw-Hill

Read each question and prompt. Discuss the answers with your group. Use your Leveled Reader to find details to support your answers. Then write your answers on the blank lines or on another sheet of paper.

1. Explain what a cave is and how it forms.

_____

2. How are formations made?

_____

3. Describe Natural Bridge Caverns.

_____

4. Retell how the Inner Space Cavern was discovered.

_____

5. What objects do the formations in the Caverns of Sonora look like?

_____

6. Write one question about the book to ask your group.

_____

_____

Weekly Planners

Week 1

Selections	Vocabulary		ELL Practice Book
	Key Selection Words/Cognates	Academic Language/Cognates	
Head, Body, Legs: A Story from Liberia	gasped attached frantically swung delicious *delicioso*	reread folk tale linking verb cause *causa* effect *effecto*	• Phonics, pp. 76–77 • Vocabulary, p. 78 • Grammar, p. 79 • Book Talk, p. 80
Watch It Move!			

Week 2

Selections	Vocabulary		ELL Practice Book
	Key Selection Words/Cognates	Academic Language/Cognates	
Officer Buckle and Gloria	buddy tip attention *atención* accident *accidente* enormous *enorme* obeys *obedecer*	monitor read ahead helping verb illustrations *ilustraciones* comprehension *comprensión*	• Phonics, pp. 81–82 • Vocabulary, p. 83 • Grammar, p. 84 • Book Talk, p. 85
Fire Safety			

Week 3

Selections	Vocabulary		ELL Practice Book
TIME FOR KIDS	Key Selection Words/Cognates	Academic Language/Cognates	
A Trip to the Emergency Room	heal aid serious *serio* personal *personal* informs *informar*	events sequence *secuencia* dictionary *diccionario* homophones *homófonos* irregular verb *verbo irregular*	• Phonics, pp. 86–87 • Vocabulary, p. 88 • Grammar, p. 89 • Book Talk, p. 90

Week 4

Selections	Vocabulary		ELL Practice Book
	Key Selection Words/Cognates	Academic Language/Cognates	
A Harbor Seal Pup Grows Up	young mammal hunger rescued examines *examinar* normal *normal*	sequence *secuencia* events *eventos* antonyms *antónimos* poetry *poesía*	• Phonics, pp. 91–92 • Vocabulary, p. 93 • Grammar, p. 94 • Book Talk, p. 95
The Puppy			

Week 5

Selections	Vocabulary		ELL Practice Book
	Key Selection Words/Cognates	Academic Language/Cognates	
Mice and Beans	fetch simmered assembled menu *menú* devoured *devorar*	story structure recipe fantasy *fantasía* reality *realidad* analyze *analizar*	• Phonics, pp. 96–97 • Vocabulary, p. 98 • Grammar, p. 99 • Book Talk, p. 100
Rosa Maria's Rice and Beans			

Student Response Strategies

Use the following strategies to help English Language Learners move to the next proficiency level.

✔ **WAIT** Give children ample time.

- Let children know that they can respond in different ways depending on their levels of proficiency, but all should be encouraged to answer questions related to the main point of the picture or text.

- Allow children to respond in their native language if they are very limited proficient. Ask a more proficient ELL student to repeat the answer in English.

✔ **REPEAT** If the child's response is correct, the teacher can repeat what the child has said. The teacher should repeat in a clear, loud voice that all can hear and at a slower pace.

✔ **REVISE for FORM** Generally the teacher will be repeating what the child has said but with corrections for grammar and pronunciation. The correction can be implicit or explicit (where teacher calls attention to the correction).

✔ **REVISE for MEANING** Teachers should also correct for meaning.

✔ **ELABORATE** Here, the teacher elaborates on a child's response or states the response in another way in order to more fully develop children's comprehension and oral language proficiency.

✔ **ELICIT** Finally, the teacher can also elicit a more comprehensive response from the child by prompting the child for further information.

Newcomers

Basic and Social Language Each week you will be focusing on an important aspect of classroom communication to teach or reinforce with your newcomers. Children will expand and internalize initial English vocabulary by learning and using routine language needed for classroom communication.

Numbers Teach and/or reinforce the numbers 1–20 (or go higher if children are ready). Use the numbers to help children learn and complete the sentence frames *I am _____ years old. How old are you? He is _____. She is _____.*

Likes/Dislikes Teach and/or reinforce the sentence frames *I like _____* and *I don't like _____*. Teach food words, such as foods commonly served in the school cafeteria, to help children complete these sentence frames. Use Photo Cards during the lesson, for example, *I like an (hold up apple Photo Card) apple.*

Pronouns *His/Her* Teach the pronouns his and her using the sentence frames *His hair is _____* and *Her hair is _____*. In addition, teach and/or review the names of *colors* and *body parts*. Provide daily practice, for example, *My notebook is brown. What color is his notebook (point to child's notebook)?*

LOG ON ▶ Have children use **Newcomer Games** to expand and internalize language needed for classroom communication. **www.macmillanmh.com**

Head, Body, Legs

Pages 10–11

Prior to reading the selection with children, they should have listened to the selection on **StudentWorks Plus**, the interactive eBook. In addition, selection vocabulary should have been pretaught using the **Visual Vocabulary Resources**.

Access Core Content

Teacher Note Pose the questions after you read the paragraph or page indicated.

Pages 10–11

Title and Illustrations

- *Read the title of this story with me:* Head, Body, Legs. *What do these words have in common? Why do they all go together?* (They are all parts of a person.) *We are going to read a funny story about the human body.*

- *Look at the pictures on page 11. Point to and name the things on this page with me: arm, leg, head, body.*

 Now, look at the picture on page 10. What is funny about it? Share your ideas with your partner. (It shows arms attached to a head. That is not where arms are on a real person.)

Page 12

Whole Page

- *The story starts:* <u>Long ago, Head was all by himself.</u> *What can Head do by himself in the story?* (He can roll everywhere and eat things on the ground.)

Pages 10–11

Comprehension

Genre
A Folktale is usually a made-up story that takes place long ago.

Reread
Cause and Effect
As you read, use your Cause and Effect Chart.

Cause → Effect
○ → □

Read to Find Out
What causes the body parts to work together?

10

Pages 12–13

Long ago, Head was all by himself.

He had no legs, no arms, no body. He rolled everywhere. All he could eat were things on the ground that he could reach with his tongue.

12

Main Selection

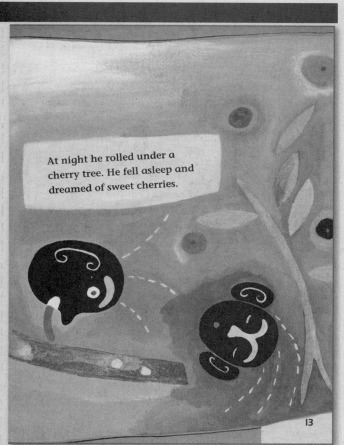

At night he rolled under a cherry tree. He fell asleep and dreamed of sweet cherries.

13

 Head has no legs or arms. What can't he do? (He cannot stand or walk. He cannot reach for things or hold them.)

- *Look at Head in the picture. Is he round like a ball or square like a block?* (round like a ball) *How does that help him get from place to place?* (He is able to roll.)

- *Point to the picture of Head with his tongue out. Say* tongue *with me and point to it. Head can eat only things on the ground that he can reach with his tongue.*

- *Let's brainstorm all the things that Head might find to eat on the ground. Let's see how long we can make our list.* (apples dropped from trees, berries on low bushes)

- *Let's read aloud together what we know about Head so far:* Long ago, Head was all by himself. He had no legs, no arms, no body. He rolled everywhere. All he could eat were things on the ground that he could reach with his tongue.

Page 13

Whole Page

- Cherries are little red berries that grow on trees. *Could Head pick cherries? Why or why not?* (no, because cherries would be too high for his tongue to reach)

- *Let's read this page together:* At night he rolled under a cherry tree. He fell asleep and dreamed of sweet cherries. *Why does Head dream about the cherries?* (They are sweet, and he wants to eat them. But he can't reach them.)

Page 14

Paragraph 1

- *Head is getting tired of eating things on the ground. He wants to be able to reach the cherries. Do you think Head feels happy or sad?* (sad)

- *Let's read together in a sad voice:* One morning Head woke up and thought, "I'm tired of grass and mushrooms. I wish I could reach those cherries."

Paragraph 2

- *Head hits the trunk of the cherry tree in this part of the story. We're going to act out this scene without using any words. One of your fists will be Head, and your other arm will be the tree.*

- *Pretend that your arm is the tree and your fingers are the branches. Bend your left arm at the elbow.* (demonstrate) *Hold the lower part of your arm and your hand straight up.* (demonstrate) *Spread your fingers out.* (demonstrate)

- *Now use your right hand to point to the part of your arm that is the trunk.* (Point to your left forearm.)

- *Make a tree again with your left arm. Make a fist with your right hand.* (demonstrate) *Pretend your fist is Head. Let's show what Head did to try to get the cherries off the tree.* (Demonstrate making a rolling motion with your fist, and bang it into your left arm.)

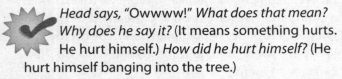 *Head says, "Owwww!" What does that mean? Why does he say it?* (It means something hurts. He hurt himself.) *How did he hurt himself?* (He hurt himself banging into the tree.)

Page 15

Paragraph 1

- *Let's read this page together:* "Who's there?" someone asked.

- *Who do you think is talking to Head?* (Question is open.)

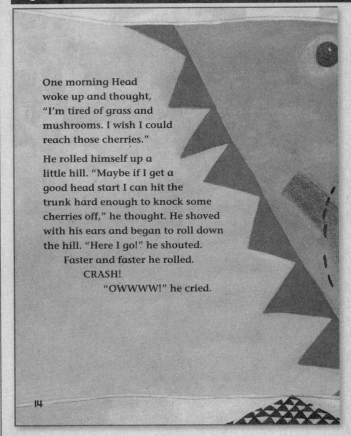

One morning Head woke up and thought, "I'm tired of grass and mushrooms. I wish I could reach those cherries."

He rolled himself up a little hill. "Maybe if I get a good head start I can hit the trunk hard enough to knock some cherries off," he thought. He shoved with his ears and began to roll down the hill. "Here I go!" he shouted. Faster and faster he rolled. CRASH!
"OWWWW!" he cried.

14

Head looked up. Above him **swung** two Arms he had never seen before.

"Look down here," Head said, "and you'll see."

16

"Who's there?"
someone asked.

15

"How can we look?"
asked Arms. "We don't
have eyes."

17

Page 16

Paragraph 1

- *Head looks up and sees something for the first time. What does he see?* (Arms) *How do you think Head feels? Show me with your face.* (Children make surprised expressions.) *Yes, he probably feels surprised.*

- *The author says that the arms swung. They were moving back and forth. Let's swing our arms back and forth.* (demonstrate)

Paragraph 2

- *Head tells Arms to look down. Do you think Arms can look down? Why or why not?* (no, because arms do not have eyes to see)

Page 17

Whole Page

 Arms cannot see. What other things can Head do in the story that Arms cannot? (chew, sing, nod, sneeze, listen)

- *Show me some things that Arms can do that Head cannot.* (clap, grab, point, wave)

Non-verbal Cues

Remind children that they can use non-verbal cues to share information when they are not able to do so verbally. Encourage children to use pantomime or draw.

Page 18

Text

■ *Head has an idea to share with Arms. What kind of voice do we use to share a good idea? (excited) Let's read Head's idea in an excited voice:* <u>"I have an idea. Let's get together. I have eyes to see, and you have hands for picking things to eat."</u>

Arms say yes to Head's idea. Why do they decide to get together? (because they need things from each other; Head needs hands for picking things, and Arms need eyes for seeing.)

■ *Say shoulders with me as you touch your shoulders. (demonstrate) Our arms are connected to our shoulders. Why do the arms in the story have to attach to the head? (because there are no shoulders)*

Page 19

Whole Page

■ *Look at the picture. What is different now? (Arms are attached to Head.) How do you think Head feels? (happy) How do you know? (because he is smiling)*

■ *Head says:* <u>"This is perfect."</u> *What other things could Head say that mean almost the same thing? (This is very good. This is great. This is wonderful. This is just right. Awesome!)*

> **Patterns in Language**
>
> Some grammatical structures, such as past tense "ed," pose difficulties to ELLs. Point out that there are several examples of words ending in *-ed* in this selection, such as *dropped, attached, picked, pushed.* Help children find a pattern.

Pages 18–19

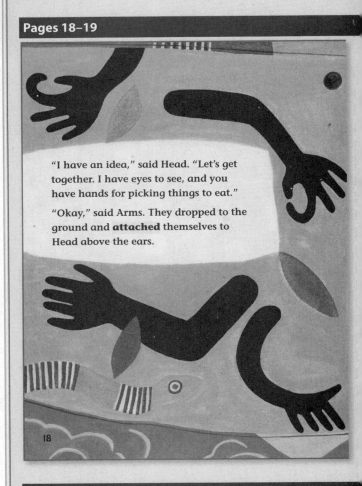

"I have an idea," said Head. "Let's get together. I have eyes to see, and you have hands for picking things to eat."

"Okay," said Arms. They dropped to the ground and **attached** themselves to Head above the ears.

18

Pages 20–21

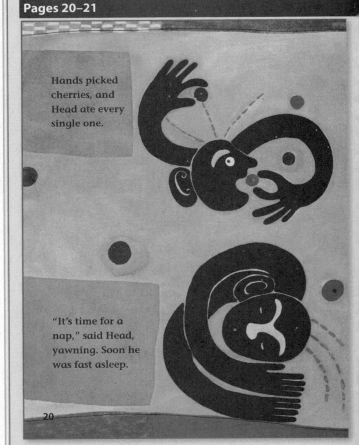

Hands picked cherries, and Head ate every single one.

"It's time for a nap," said Head, yawning. Soon he was fast asleep.

20

"This," said Head, "is perfect."

Cause and Effect
Describe one possible effect of Arms and Head working together.

19

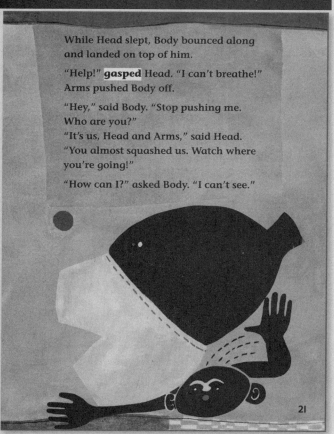

While Head slept, Body bounced along and landed on top of him.

"Help!" **gasped** Head. "I can't breathe!" Arms pushed Body off.

"Hey," said Body. "Stop pushing me. Who are you?"

"It's us, Head and Arms," said Head. "You almost squashed us. Watch where you're going!"

"How can I?" asked Body. "I can't see."

21

Page 20

Illustration and Paragraph 1

- *Look at the picture at the top of the page. What does it show?* (Arms picking cherries and feeding one to Head)

 Take turns with your partner pretending to be Head and Arms. Stoop down behind your table or desk like this. Only your head and arms will show. (demonstrate) Use your head to look up as if you are looking at cherries on a tree. Use your arms to reach up and pretend to pick cherries and feed them to you.

- *Do the hands pick cherries at the top of the tree or at the bottom? How do you know?* (at the bottom, because just a Head and Arms could not reach the top)

Paragraph 2

- *Read the second paragraph together with me, and do what I do:* "It's time for a nap," said Head, yawning. (yawn) Soon he was fast asleep. (Put your hands together to form a pillow. Put your head on your hands, and close your eyes.)

Page 21

Whole Page

- *Body bounced along while Head slept. He bounced up and down like a ball. (Demonstrate bouncing quietly on a desktop with a fist.) Why did he bounce and not walk?* (He had no legs.) *Let's make our hands bounce.*

- *Look at the picture. Body is on top of Arms and Head. Which body part is biggest?* (Body) *Do you think Body is heavy or light?* (heavy)

- *Head gasps and says he cannot breathe when Body lands on him. (Demonstrate gasping.) Let's gasp together.*

- *When something is squashed, it is crushed or made flat. How did Head almost get squashed?* (Body landed on him.) *Why would that squash Head?* (Body is big and heavy, and Head and Arms are small and thin.)

- *When Head tells Body to look where he is going, what does he say?* ("How can I? I can't see.") *How are Body and Arms alike?* (They can't see.)

Page 22

Paragraph 1

- *Head asks Body:* "Why don't you join us?" *Does he mean "Why don't you have fun with us?" or "Why don't you attach yourself to us?"* ("Why don't you attach yourself to us?")

- *A mango is a sweet, juicy fruit that grows on trees.*

 Head wants to eat the sweet mangoes. Why does he have to swim to them? (They are not nearby. They are on the other side of a river.)

Paragraph 2

- *Head is attached to Body at Body's belly button. Turn back to page 21. Look at the picture of Body. Let's point to his belly button.* (Point to the belly button.)

Page 23

Whole Page

- *Look at the picture. How is this person different from a real person?* (A real person's body is attached to its head at the neck. Also, there are no legs.) *Point to where Head should be attached to Body and say the word with me:* neck.

- *Let's read what Head says about the new situation together:* "This is perfect." *Is he right?* (no)

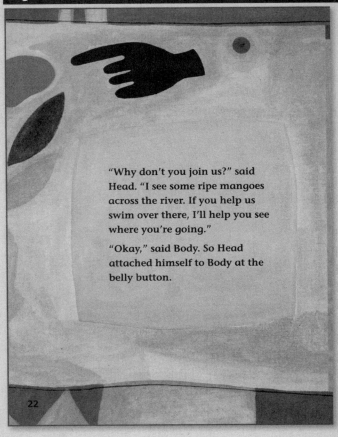

"Why don't you join us?" said Head. "I see some ripe mangoes across the river. If you help us swim over there, I'll help you see where you're going."

"Okay," said Body. So Head attached himself to Body at the belly button.

22

They bounced down the bank into the river.

"Pull right . . . pull left," Head shouted to Arms, who paddled **frantically** against the current.

24

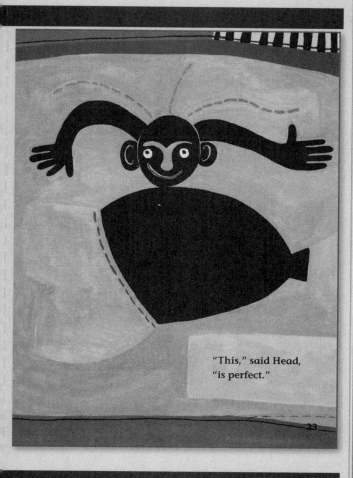

"This," said Head, "is perfect."

23

25

Pages 24–25

Illustrations and Text

- *Look at the pictures. Do you see land or water?* (water) *This is the river that Head, Arms, and Body need to cross.*

- *Head, Arms, and Body bounce down a bank into the river. A bank can be a place to keep money. Or it can be steep land beside water. Which kind of bank do you think this is?* (steep land beside water) *How do you know?* (Head, Arms, and Body bounce into the river.)

- *The water in a river flows in one direction. This is called the current.*

- *A current can be slow and gentle or fast and hard. Why would Arms have to paddle frantically?* (The current must be fast and hard. The water is going one way, and he is trying to go the other way. It is hard to do)

- *Let's act out paddling frantically to see how Arms felt.* (Demonstrate making fast, strong paddling motions with your arms.)

PARTNERS *One partner will tell the other how to paddle. You might say "Paddle slowly," "Paddle frantically," or "Paddle quickly." The other partner will act out the direction. Take turns giving and following the directions.*

Request Assistance

Remind children of expressions they can use to request assistance from the teacher or their partners, such as *Can you show me? Can you draw it, please?*

Pages 26–27

Illustrations and Paragraph 1

- *Look at the pictures. Where are Head, Arms, and Body now?* (on land, near the mango tree)

- *Why do Head, Arms, and Body have to bounce instead of walk to the mango tree?* (They don't have legs.)

Paragraphs 2 and 3

- *Let's read together what Arms did:* Arms stretched as high as they could, but they couldn't quite reach. *Show me what they did.* (Children stretch their arms up high.)

 Head looks for a stick. Why do you think he wants a stick? (to poke the tree and knock down a mango)

- *Head thinks the two legs are sticks!*

Pages 26–27

26

Pages 28–29

Arms grabbed them.
"Let us go!" shouted Legs.

28

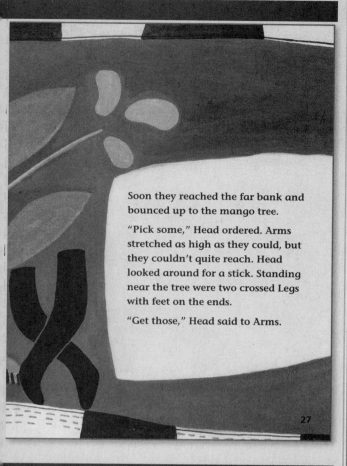

Soon they reached the far bank and bounced up to the mango tree.

"Pick some," Head ordered. Arms stretched as high as they could, but they couldn't quite reach. Head looked around for a stick. Standing near the tree were two crossed Legs with feet on the ends.

"Get those," Head said to Arms.

27

"Who are you?" asked Head.

"We're Legs. We were walking but we bumped into this tree."

29

Whole Page

 Take turns showing your partner things that Legs can do that Head, Arms, and Body cannot. (run, jump, stand on tiptoe, kick)

- *What do you think will happen next?* (Head will attach Legs to Body. He will try to reach the fruit.)

- *Do you think Head will put Legs in the right place on Body? Why or why not?* (no, because he hasn't put any of the other parts in the right place) *Where do you think he might put Legs?* (Question is open.)

Pages 30–31

Illustrations and Text

- *Head wants Legs to join the other Body Parts. Head says he can show Legs where the mangoes are. How does Head know?* (He can see them.)

- Legs say, "Okay." Legs will join the others. Look at the picture on page 31. *Where do Legs attach themselves?* (to the hands) Will this work? (no, because the feet would be at the end of the arms, and feet cannot pick fruit)

- *Let's read the second paragraph on page 31 together.*

- *Where would Legs go if Body were in the middle?* (Legs could go on the top or bottom.) Which would work better? (on the bottom)

- *The parts are starting to realize, or understand, something important. What are they starting to realize?* (that they could work together better if they were in different places)

Pages 30–31

"Join us," said Head. "I have eyes. I can show you where to go, and you can help us reach those mangoes."

"Okay," said Legs. So Legs attached themselves to the hands.

Cause and Effect
What causes Legs to join the other body parts? Use details from the story.

30

Pages 32–33

32

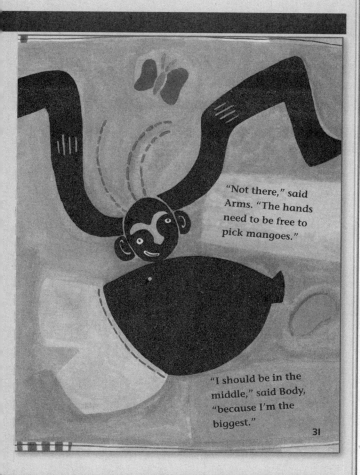

"Not there," said Arms. "The hands need to be free to pick mangoes."

"I should be in the middle," said Body, "because I'm the biggest."

31

"That's right," said Head. "You should be at the bottom, Legs. I'll swing around on top of Body so I can see everything. And Arms, you move to the shoulders."

33

Pages 32–33

Text

- *Let's read this page together.*

- *Will Head's idea work this time? Why or why not?* (yes, because the body parts will be attached the way they are on a real body)

Illustrations

- *What do the pictures on these pages show?* (They show the parts coming apart and going back together the right way.)

PARTNERS

Work together to draw how you think Head, Arms, Body, and Legs will look when they are all put together. Take turns drawing body parts.

Page 34

Text

- *Let's read page 34 together and do what I do:* Everyone slid into place. Legs stood on tiptoe. *(Stand on your tiptoes.)* Body straightened out. *(Stand very tall and straight.)* Arms stretched up and the hands picked a mango. *(Reach up and pretend to pick fruit.)* Head took a bite. *(Pretend to bite into fruit.)*

Page 35

Whole Page

- *Look at the picture on page 35. Head is rubbing his stomach with one hand. Say* stomach *and point to it. What is he doing with his other hand?* (He is holding a mango.)

- *Now let's read the page together and rub our stomachs:* "Mmm, delicious. Now THIS is perfect!"

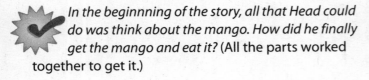

In the beginnning of the story, all that Head could do was think about the mango. How did he finally get the mango and eat it? (All the parts worked together to get it.)

Everyone slid into place. Legs stood on tiptoe. Body straightened out. Arms stretched up and the hands picked a mango. Head took a bite.

34

"Mmm, **delicious**," Head said. "Now THIS is perfect!"

35

- Do you think this story is funny? Tell why or why not. (yes, because it is silly to think of body parts attached this way)

 One partner will cut out a large oval shape like this. (demonstrate) The other partner will cut out a small circle like this. (demonstrate) Each partner will cut out one short rectangle like this. (demonstrate) Each partner will cut out a long rectangle like this. (demonstrate) Now, retell the story using the cutouts. Take turns telling different parts.

Watch It Move!

Access Core Content

Teacher Note Pose the questions after you read the paragraph or page indicated.

Page 38

Special Internet Text Features

- *This article is from the Internet. Let's look at some of the special things about it.* (Point to *Search* at the top of page 38.) *When we search for something, we look for it. This tells us what subject someone searched for to find this article. The box tells what was typed into the computer. Let's read the words together:* Force and Motion.

- *Find this on your page.* (Point to the "Home" icon.) *It is an icon. This icon means we are on the first page of the website where the article appears.*

- *This is an icon for a computer printer.* (Point to the "Print" icon.) *What do you think it means?* (that we can make a paper copy)

- *Point to the icon of an envelope. This means we can e-mail the article to people. We can send it from our computer to theirs.*

Text

- *Let's read the first page of the article together to find out what it tells about force and motion.*

- *What two kinds of force does the article tell about?* (push and pull) *Would dragging a sled be an example of push or pull?* (pull) *Would shoving a box from one place to another be a push or pull?* (push)

- *Let's use our bodies to feel the force of push and pull. Do this.* (Demonstrate putting your hands together, palm-to-palm in front of you. Raise your elbows so that your forearms are parallel to the floor.) *Press your right hand against your left hand. Feel the push.*

- *Now, keep your arms up. Grab your left wrist with your right hand.* (demonstrate) *Tug on your left arm with your right hand. Feel the pull.*

Pages 38–39

Search | Force and Motion

Favorites | History | Search | Scrapbook

Science

Genre
Expository An Internet article gives facts about a topic and is found on the World Wide Web.

Text Feature
The Drop-Down Menu in an Internet article has links to related information on the Web site.

Content Vocabulary
force
friction
gravity

Watch It Move!

Rolling a ball and pulling a wagon are both examples of **force**. Force changes the way an object moves. Force can be a push, like when you roll a ball to a friend. Force can also be a pull, like when you drag a wagon.

38

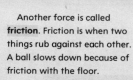

Science

Another force is called **friction**. Friction is when two things rub against each other. A ball slows down because of friction with the floor.

Gravity is a force, too. Hold a ball over your head and let it go. The ball will fall because Earth's **gravity** pulls it down.

Force and Motion Links

For more information about force and motion, check out:

- Experiments in Force and Motion
- The Force of Gravity
- Understanding Friction

 Connect and Compare

1. What other information about force can you link to in this article? **Drop-Down Menus**
2. Think about this article and *Head, Body, Legs: A Story from Liberia*. What kind of force do the arms use to paddle across the river? **Reading/Writing Across Texts**

Science Activity

Research force and motion activities online. Choose an activity and show it to the class. Explain why you chose this activity. Remember to speak at an appropriate pace.

LOG ON ▶ FIND OUT **Science** Force and motion
www.macmillanmh.com

39

Page 39

Whole Page

- *Let's read this page together to find out about two other kinds of force.*

- *We see friction when we roll a ball across the floor. The ball slows down because it rubs against the floor. We see the force of gravity when we drop a ball. Gravity pulls the ball down.*

- *Let's experiment with gravity. Take out a pencil. Hold it over your desk. Now let go. (demonstrate) What happens? Why?* (It falls. Gravity pulls the pencil down.)

- *Now let's experiment with friction. Put the pencil on your desk. Give it a tiny push. (demonstrate) Why does it slow down?* (It rubs against the desk. Friction slows it down.)

- *Point to the box at the top of the page. This shows places to get more information. Let's read together the subjects you could look up:* Experiments in Force and Motion, The Force of Gravity, Understanding Friction. *Put your finger on the one you would use if you wanted to learn more about why things fall to the Earth.*

 Draw a picture that shows one of these kinds of force: push, pull, friction, or gravity. Have your partner look at your picture and tell which kind of force you have drawn.

Name _____

Use the word chart to study this week's vocabulary words.
Write a sentence using each word in your writer's notebook.

Word	Context Sentence	Illustration
gasped _____	We gasped when we saw the size of the huge spider.	**What has made you gasp?**
attached _____	We wondered if a fish would be attached to the hook.	
frantically _____	Jack and I looked frantically for his missing cat.	
swung _____	We watched as the monkey swung from branch to branch.	
delicious _____	Together, we made a delicious meal.	**What would you describe as delicious?**

© Macmillan/McGraw-Hill

Name_____

**Read each question and prompt. Discuss the answers
with your group. Use your Leveled Reader to find
details to support your answers. Then write your
answers on the blank lines or on another sheet of
paper.**

1. How does helping an animal or person lead to getting three wishes
   in the story you read?

   _____

2. Tell about the wishes the main character asks for. Use order words.

   _____

3. Are the wishes wise ones? Give examples.

   _____

4. What happens to the characters who are greedy and ask for too much?

   _____

5. What would you wish for if you had three wishes?

   _____

6. Write one question about the book to ask your group.

   _____

   _____

Officer Buckle and Gloria

Prior to reading the selection with children, they should have listened to the selection on **StudentWorks Plus**, the interactive eBook. In addition, selection vocabulary should have been pretaught using the **Visual Vocabulary Resources**.

Access Core Content

Teacher Note Pose the questions after you read the text indicated.

Pages 46–47

Title and Illustration

- *Listen as I read aloud the title of this story* (point to the title)*: Officer Buckle and Gloria.*

- *Officer is a title, or a special name, for a policeman or a policewoman. Let's say the word* officer *together:* officer. *Point to Officer Buckle in the picture.*

- *Police officers often use dogs to help them in their work. Gloria is a police dog. Point to Gloria.*

 The children in the picture are looking up at Gloria as she jumps and turns in the air. They look surprised at what Gloria can do! Pictures tell us a lot about what is happening in a story. Let's use the pictures in this story to help us understand it.

Page 48

Text

- *What did Officer Buckle know more about than anyone else in Napville?* (safety tips)

- *A tip is a helpful bit of information. Let's name some safety tips we learned when we read "Safety at School."* (Pay attention to the teacher. There should be no running in the halls. Stay together in the halls.)

- *Look at Safety Tip Number 77. This symbol stands for the word* number. (Point to the pound sign.) *Let's read the tip together. As we read, say the words in capital letters a little louder than the other words:* NEVER stand on a SWIVEL CHAIR.

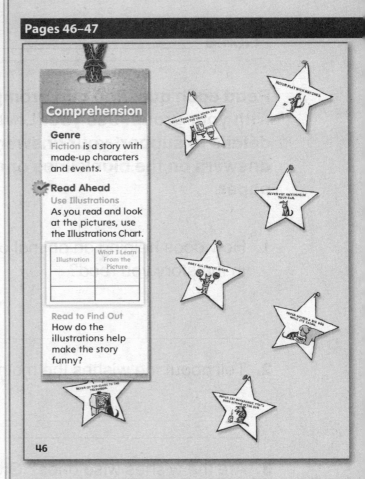

Comprehension

Genre
Fiction is a story with made-up characters and events.

✓ **Read Ahead**
Use Illustrations
As you read and look at the pictures, use the Illustrations Chart.

Illustration	What I Learn From the Picture

Read to Find Out
How do the illustrations help make the story funny?

46

Officer Buckle knew more safety **tips** than anyone else in Napville.
Every time he thought of a new one, he thumbtacked it to his bulletin board.

Safety Tip #77
NEVER stand on a SWIVEL CHAIR.

48

Main Selection

OFFICER BUCKLE
AND
GLORIA

written and illustrated
by Peggy Rathmann

47

Officer Buckle shared his safety tips with the students at Napville School.

Nobody ever listened.

Sometimes, there was snoring.

Afterward, it was business as usual.

Mrs. Toppel, the principal, took down the welcome banner.

"NEVER stand on a SWIVEL CHAIR," said Officer Buckle, but Mrs. Toppel didn't hear him.

49

Illustration

- Look at Officer Buckle in the picture. Point to the swivel chair. A swivel chair has wheels and a seat that turns. What can happen if you stand on a swivel chair? (The chair can move. You can fall.)

- Officer Buckle has a lot of safety tips on his bulletin board! I wonder how he will share those tips with others. Let's keep reading to find out.

Page 49

Text

- With whom did Officer Buckle share his safety tips? (Officer Buckle shared his tips with students at Napville School.)

- It sounds like Officer Buckle wasn't very interesting when he shared his safety tips. Nobody listened. Some people fell asleep and snored! Let's make a snoring noise together. (Demonstrate the noise.)

- After Officer Buckle spoke, it was business as usual. That means that nothing changed after Officer Buckle gave his safety tip speech!

- Let's read aloud what Officer Buckle said to Mrs. Topple: "NEVER stand on a SWIVEL CHAIR." Officer Buckle knows this tip because he fell off a swivel chair himself!

Illustration

- Look at the picture. Point to the principal, Mrs. Toppel, taking down the welcome banner. A banner is like a long sign with a message. Mrs. Topple didn't hear Officer Buckle when he gave her the safety tip.

- Now let's read the sign above the water fountain (point to the sign): Safety is no accident. The sign reminds people at school to follow safety tips and rules.

- Look at all the accidents in the picture! The children aren't paying attention to the sign. Point to each accident as I name it: A student slips on water. A student trips over his shoelaces. A student carries too many books and drops them.

 What safety tips would you give the children in the picture? Name some tips with your partner.

Page 50

Large Illustration

- *Look at Officer Buckle in his police car. Gloria is riding with him. Point to the letter and number K-9 on the car. When you see K-9 on a police car, you know that the police officer in the car works with a police dog.*

Text and Small Illustration

- *Police dogs are taught to do what police officers tell them to do. They obey commands, or follow directions. What command did Officer Buckle give Gloria?* (Officer Buckle told Gloria to sit.)

- *Let's pretend we're Officer Buckle.* (Point to the small illustration.) *Say the command with me as if you are talking to Gloria:* SIT!

Page 51

Text

- *Let's read Safety Tip Number One together:* "KEEP your SHOELACES tied!" *What happened after Officer Buckle gave the children the safety tip?* (The children sat up and stared.)

Large Illustration

The story doesn't tell us why the children sat up and stared, but the picture does. Look at Gloria in the big picture. What is Gloria doing? (Gloria is holding up her paw to show the number one.) *A dog doesn't usually hold up a paw like Gloria is doing. That's why the children sat up and stared at her.*

Small Illustration

- *Look at the small picture. Officer Buckle couldn't see Gloria holding up her paw because she was in back of him. What is Gloria doing when Officer Buckle looks at her?* (Gloria is just sitting.)

Page 52

Text

- *What is Safety Tip Number Two? Let's read the tip aloud together. Remember to say the words in capital letters a little louder than the other words:* "ALWAYS wipe up spills BEFORE someone SLIPS AND FALLS!"

Then one day, Napville's police department bought a police dog named Gloria.

When it was time for Officer Buckle to give the safety speech at the school, Gloria went along.

"Children, this is Gloria," announced Officer Buckle. "Gloria **obeys** my commands. Gloria, SIT!" And Gloria sat.

50

"Safety Tip Number Two," said Officer Buckle.

"ALWAYS wipe up spills BEFORE someone SLIPS AND FALLS!"

The children's eyes popped.
Officer Buckle checked on Gloria again.

"Good dog," he said.

52

Officer Buckle gave Safety Tip Number One:

"KEEP your SHOELACES tied!"

The children sat up and stared.
Officer Buckle checked to see if Gloria
was sitting at **attention**. She was.

51

Officer Buckle thought of a safety tip he
had discovered that morning.

**"NEVER leave a THUMBTACK where
you might SIT on it!"**

The audience roared.

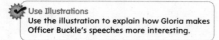
Use Illustrations
Use the illustration to explain how Gloria makes
Officer Buckle's speeches more interesting.

53

- *The children's eyes* popped *after Officer Buckle gave this safety tip. When your eyes* pop, *they get big and wide.* (Demonstrate the expression.) *Show me how you look when your eyes pop.*

- *What did Officer Buckle say when he turned around and checked on Gloria? Let's read his words:* "Good dog." (Point to the words.)

Illustrations

- T*his picture gives us more information about the story. Why did the children's eyes pop? Look at what Gloria is doing.* (The children's eyes popped because Gloria was acting out what would happen if you didn't follow the safety tip.)

- *Now look at the small picture. What was Gloria doing when Officer Buckle looked at her?* (Gloria was just sitting.)

Page 53
Text

- *Read aloud the safety tip on this page with me:* "NEVER leave a THUMBTACK where you might SIT on It!" *The story says that Officer Buckle discovered the tip that morning. How do you think Officer Buckle discovered the tip?* (Officer Buckle probably sat on a thumbtack himself that morning.)

- *The audience, or the children and teachers listening to Officer Buckle, roared when he gave the tip. The word* roared *can mean "growled like an animal." It can also mean "laughed loudly." What does* roared *mean here?* (Roared means "laughed loudly.")

Illustration

- *Officer Buckle still doesn't know what Gloria is doing behind him! Why did the audience roar when he gave the safety tip?* (Gloria was acting out what happens when you sit on a thumbtack. She is funny!)

Tell your partner how Gloria helps Officer Buckle as he gives his tips. (Gloria makes the tips interesting. She is funny, and the children listen to Officer Buckle because they like what Gloria does.)

Page 54

Paragraphs 1 and 2

- *When you say something with plenty of expression, you say it with a lot of feeling. What happened when Officer Buckle said the tips with plenty of expression?* (The children clapped, cheered, and laughed until they cried). *When you laugh until you cry, you laugh so hard that tears come out of your eyes.*

Top Illustrations

- *Look at Gloria in the small pictures at the top of the page. The pictures show us what is happening behind Officer Buckle's back. Why did the children clap, cheer, and laugh when they heard the safety tips?* (The children clapped, cheered, and laughed because Gloria acted out the tips.)

Paragraphs 3 and 4

- *Officer Buckle was surprised because he didn't think his safety tips were funny. What happened after his safety speech?* (There wasn't a single accident.)

Bottom Illustration

- *Point to Officer Buckle in the picture. We can use the picture to figure out how Officer Buckle feels in this part of the story. How do you think he feels?* (Officer Buckle is smiling, so he probably feels happy that the children like his safety tips.)

Page 55

Text

- *What did the children draw on the thank-you letters they sent to the police station?* (The children drew pictures of Gloria on their letters.) *Officer Buckle didn't know that Gloria was acting out the tips, so he thought the pictures showed a lot of imagination.*

Illustrations

- *Look at all the letters that were sent to the police station! The letters are addressed to Gloria and Officer Buckle. Point to the pictures of Gloria on the letters. The children drew Gloria on the letters to show how much they liked what she did.*

Pages 54–55

Officer Buckle grinned. He said the rest of the tips with *plenty* of expression.

The children clapped their hands and cheered. Some of them laughed until they cried.

Officer Buckle was surprised. He had never noticed how funny safety tips could be.

After *this* safety speech, there wasn't a single **accident**.

54

Pages 56–57

His favorite letter was written on a star-shaped piece of paper. It said:

You and Gloria make a good team.

Your friend,
Claire

P.S. I always wear a crash helmet.
(Safety Tip #7)

56

The next day, an **enormous** envelope arrived at the police station. It was stuffed with thank-you letters from the students at Napville School.

Every letter had a drawing of Gloria on it.

Officer Buckle thought the drawings showed a lot of imagination.

Officer Buckle was thumbtacking Claire's letter to his bulletin board when the phones started ringing. Grade schools, high schools, and day-care centers were calling about the safety speech.

"Officer Buckle," they said, "our students want to hear your safety tips! And please, bring along that police dog."

Page 56

Text and Illustration

- *Let's read aloud Officer Buckle's favorite letter:* You and Gloria make a good team. Your friend, Claire. *Point to the picture of Officer Buckle and Gloria that Claire drew.*

- *Claire added something to the letter. Read the note marked P.S. with me:* I always wear a crash helmet. (Safety Tip Number 7). *You use P.S. when you add something to a letter after you have finished writing it.*

- *Point to Claire wearing her crash helmet. When do children wear helmets like this?* (Children wear the helmets when they are riding a bike or skating.) *They wear the helmets to stay safe.*

Page 57

Text

- *What happened while Officer Buckle was thumbtacking Claire's letter to the bulletin board?* (Other people started calling to ask him to speak at their schools.)

- *Let's read together what the people said. Look for the words in quotation marks* (Point to the quotation marks.): "Officer Buckle,". . ."our students want to hear your safety tips! And please, bring along that police dog."

Illustrations

- *Point to Officer Buckle talking on the phone. Now look at the people in the round pictures at the top of the page. These are the people who called Officer Buckle.*

 Pretend that you and your partner are Officer Buckle and one of the people in the pictures. Act out talking on the phone to each other. (Question is open.)

Formal and Informal English

When children encounter a word, such as *Officer,* used in a formal setting in the text discuss other situations in which that word may be used.

Page 58

Text

- *Officer Buckle told his safety tips to a lot of schools! What happened whenever Officer Buckle told his safety tips?* (Children sat up and listened.)

Illustrations

✓ *Take a look at the pictures on this page. What made children sit up and listen when Officer Buckle told his safety tips?* (Children sat up and listened because Gloria acted out the tips.)

- *Point to Gloria acting out a safety tip in each picture.*

Page 59

Text

- *Officer Buckle and Gloria are buddies. That means they are friends. It's fun to have a buddy to share things with!*

Illustrations

- *What is Gloria doing as Officer Buckle gets ice cream?* (Gloria is writing on a piece of paper.) *Yes, Gloria is writing. She is giving the children her autograph. When you give people your autograph, you write your name on paper for them. The children like Gloria so much, they want her autograph!*

- *Now look at Officer Buckle and Gloria eating ice cream together. They really look like buddies in this picture! What would you say to Gloria now if you were Officer Buckle?* (You are a good buddy, Gloria. I like you a lot!)

Pages 60–61

Text

- *When you videotape something, you film it with a camera so it can be shown later.*

- *Let's read aloud Safety Tip Number Ninety-nine:* DO NOT GO SWIMMING DURING ELECTRICAL STORMS! *An electrical storm is a storm with a lot of lightning. What could happen if you went swimming in an electrical storm?* (You could get hit by lightning.)

Officer Buckle told his safety tips to 313 schools. Everywhere he and Gloria went, children sat up and listened.

58

Then one day, a television news team videotaped Officer Buckle in the state college auditorium.
When he finished Safety Tip Number Ninety-nine,

**DO NOT GO SWIMMING DURING
ELECTRICAL STORMS!,**
the students jumped to their feet and applauded.

60

After every speech, Officer Buckle took
Gloria out for ice cream.
Officer Buckle loved having a **buddy**.

59

"Bravo! Bravo!" they cheered.
Officer Buckle bowed again and again.

61

- *After Officer Buckle finished Safety tip Number Ninety-nine, the students jumped to their feet and applauded, or clapped. They cheered:* "Bravo! Bravo!" *Cheering* "Bravo! Bravo!" *is like saying* "Hurray! Hurray!"

- *Pretend you are students in the audience. Jump to your feet, clap, and cheer:* "Bravo! Bravo!" (Participate in the actions and the cheer with children.)

- *What did Officer Buckle do as the students cheered?* (Officer Buckle bowed again and again.)

Illustration

- *Point to Gloria in the picture. What is Gloria doing?* (Gloria is acting out what it is like to get hit by lightening.) *Why were the students cheering?* (The students were cheering for Gloria.)

 Have you ever enjoyed watching something so much that you jumped up and cheered? Tell your partner what you watched and why you cheered. (Question is open.)

Analyze Sayings and Expressions

Help children recognize that *Bravo!* is an expression used to express enthusiasm about something you like. Invite them to share other examples of similar expressions they may know.

Pages 62–63

Text

- *When did Officer Buckle watch himself giving his safety tip speech?* (Officer Buckle watched himself that night on the 10 o'clock news.)

Illustration

The story doesn't tell us how Officer Buckle felt when he watched himself and Gloria on the news, but we can use the picture to find out. *How does Officer Buckle look in the picture?* (Officer Buckle looks surprised and upset.)

- *What did Officer Buckle see on the news that made him surprised and upset?* (Officer Buckle saw what Gloria was doing. He saw that the students were cheering for Gloria and not for him.)

- *Point to Gloria in the picture. What do you think she would say to Officer Buckle if she could talk?* (I'm sorry, Officer Buckle. Please don't be upset!)

Page 64

Text

- *Why did Officer Buckle tell Mrs. Topple that he wasn't giving any more speeches?* (Officer Buckle was not happy. He found out that people liked his speeches because of Gloria. He found out that people did not look at him.)

- *Why did people look at Gloria instead of Officer Buckle?* (Gloria was fun to watch. Gloria did things that other dogs don't do.)

- *What did Mrs. Toppel ask when Officer Buckle said wasn't giving any more speeches? Let's read what she asked:* "How about Gloria? Could she come?"

Illustration

- *Point to Safety Tip Number 100 on Officer Buckle's desk. Listen as I read aloud the tip:* NEVER turn your BACK on a STRANGE DOG.

- *Gloria isn't a strange dog, but why might Officer Buckle feel he shouldn't turn his back on her?* (Officer Buckle knows Gloria will get all the attention if she acts out the safety tips behind his back.)

Pages 62–63

62

Pages 64–65

The next day, the principal of Napville School telephoned the police station.

"Good morning, Officer Buckle! It's time for our safety speech!"

Officer Buckle frowned.

"I'm not giving any more speeches! Nobody looks at me, anyway!"

"Oh," said Mrs. Toppel. "Well! How about Gloria? Could she come?"

64

That night, Officer Buckle watched himself on the 10 o'clock news.

Use Illustrations
What does Officer Buckle find out about his safety speeches? Use the illustrations to explain your answer.

63

Someone else from the police station gave Gloria a ride to the school.

Gloria sat onstage looking lonely. Then she fell asleep. So did the audience.

After Gloria left, Napville School had its biggest accident ever....

65

■ *How do you think Officer Buckle is feeling at this point in the story? Use the picture to help you.* (The look on Officer Buckle's face shows that he is feeling unhappy and upset.)

Page 65

Text and Illustration

■ *What happened when Gloria went to the school without Officer Buckle?* (Gloria just sat on stage looking lonely. Then Gloria and the students fell asleep.) *Gloria couldn't act out the safety tips without Officer Buckle, so she just sat on stage and fell asleep. The students were so bored they fell asleep, too!*

PARTNERS *Have you ever been so bored that you couldn't keep your eyes open? Tell your partner what happened.*

■ *Something big is about to happen in the story next! The last sentence on the page tells us that Napville School had its biggest accident ever. Let's turn the page and read to find out what happened.*

Pages 66–67

Text

- *Let's read this page together. Use a loud voice to say the words in big letters:* It started with a puddle of banana pudding . . . . SPLAT! SPLATTER! SPLOOSH! Everyone slid smack into Mrs. Toppel, who screamed and let go of her hammer.

- *When you slide* smack *into someone, you slide straight into that person. What did Mrs. Toppel do when everyone slid* smack *into her?* (Mrs. Toppel screamed.) *Can you think of other words that mean almost the same as* screamed? (shouted, yelled, cried out)

Illustration

- *Point to the puddle of banana pudding. The children slipped in the banana pudding and slid into Mrs. Topple. Now point to the hammer that Mrs. Topple was holding. Point to the thumbtack, too.*

- *On what kind of chair was Mrs. Topple standing?* (Mrs. Topple was standing on a swivel chair.) *What was Mrs. Topple doing when the big accident took place?* (Mrs. Topple was putting up a banner to welcome Gloria to the school.)

- *What safety tips might Officer Buckle share if he saw what was happening?* (Always wipe up spills before someone slips and falls. Never stand on a swivel chair.)

Page 68

Text

- *Officer Buckle was shocked, or surprised and upset, to find out about the accident at school. How did Officer Buckle learn about the accident?* (The students wrote him letters.)

- *What did Officer Buckle find at the bottom of the pile of letters?* (Officer Buckle found a note written on a paper star.)

Illustration

- *Point to the note written on a paper star. Let's read the note aloud:* Gloria missed you yesterday! Your friend, Claire.

Pages 66–67

It started with a puddle of banana pudding....

SPLAT! SPLATTER! SPLOOSH!

Everyone slid smack into Mrs. Toppel, who screamed and let go of her hammer.

66

Pages 68–69

The next morning, a pile of letters arrived at the police station.
Every letter had a drawing of the accident. Officer Buckle was shocked.

At the bottom of the pile was a note written on a paper star.
Officer Buckle smiled.

The note said:

Gloria missed you yesterday!
Your friend,
Claire
P.S. Don't worry, I was wearing my helmet!
(Safety Tip #7)

68

67

Look at the picture that Claire drew on her note. What happened to the hammer that Mrs. Toppel dropped in the big accident at school? (The hammer hit Claire on the head.)

- *Now let's read the P.S. that Claire added to her note:* P.S. Don't worry, I was wearing my helmet! (Safety Tip Number 7) *What saved Claire from getting hurt?* (Claire was wearing her helmet.)

Page 69

Text

- *How did Officer Buckle and Gloria show that they were still buddies?* (Gloria kissed Officer Buckle on the nose. Officer Buckle patted Gloria on the back.)

- *Let's read Safety Tip Number 101 together:* ALWAYS STICK WITH YOUR BUDDY!

Illustration

- *How do you think Officer Buckle and Gloria felt at the end of the story?* (They were happy to be together again. They were glad to be sharing safety tips with the students again.)

- *The students look happy to have Officer Buckle and Gloria together again, too. Pretend you are the students. Stand and clap for Officer Buckle and Gloria!*

 Do you agree that Safety Tip Number 101 is a good tip to follow? Tell your partner how the tip can help keep you happy and safe.

Gloria gave Officer Buckle a big kiss on the nose. Officer Buckle gave Gloria a nice pat on the back. Then, Officer Buckle thought of his best safety tip yet...

Safety Tip #101

"ALWAYS STICK WITH YOUR BUDDY!"

69

Fire Safety

Access Core Content

Teacher Note Pose the questions after you read the text indicated.

Page 72

Title and Photo

- *Let's read the title of this selection together:* Fire Safety.

- *I see a firefighter in the photograph. Point to the firefighter with me. (Point to the firefighter.) The firefighter is talking to the children about fire safety.*

Paragraph

- *Fire hazards are things that can put us in danger of being hurt or burned from fires. How can you help prevent fires, or stop them from happening? (You can help prevent fires by following fire safety rules.) Learning about fire safety can also help you know what to do if a fire does start.*

Page 73

Heading 1

- *Read aloud this heading with me (Point to the first heading.):* How to Stay Safe from Fires. *The rules below this heading will tell us how to keep fires from happening.*

- *What should you do if you want to cook something? (Ask an adult to help you.) What might happen if you played with electric cords, plugs, or outlets? (You could get a shock. You could start a fire and get burned.)*

Heading 2

- *Now let's read aloud this heading (Point to the second heading.):* Stop! Drop! Roll!

- *What are three words to remember if your clothes catch on fire? (Stop! Drop! Roll!)*

Social Studies

Genre
Expository text gives information about real people, things, or events.

Text Features
Floor Plans are maps that show where all the rooms in a building are.

Content Vocabulary
hazards
route
calm

Firefighters want everyone to be safe. They teach families how to avoid fire **hazards**, which are dangerous items or situations. You can help prevent fires by following fire safety rules. You can also stay safe by knowing what to do if a fire starts nearby.

72

Make a Plan!

You and your family can learn how to stay safe if there is a fire in your home. Make a floor plan of your home. Mark the best ways to get out of the house. Make sure your plan has more than one **route** in case one path gets blocked. Pick a safe place to meet outside. Have fire drills to practice your plan. Practicing will help you stay **calm** and find a safe path to the outside.

Fire Safety Floor Plan

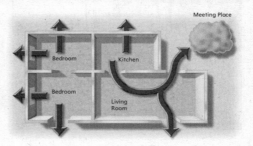

This floor plan shows several ways to get out of a home in case a fire starts.

74

Social Studies

How to Stay Safe from Fire

- Never play with matches or lighters.
- Do not touch lit candles.
- Do not cook unless an adult is with you.
- Be careful around irons, stoves, fireplaces, and grills.
- Never touch electric cords, plugs, or outlets.

Stop! Drop! Roll!

If your clothes catch fire, do these three things right away.

1

2

3

Stop! Running and walking can make fire worse.

Drop! Get down on the ground. Cover your face and eyes.

Roll! Roll over and over until the flames are out.

73

After you are safely out of the house, call 9-1-1 for help. Wait for the firefighters to arrive. Never go back into the house for anything!

Connect and Compare

1. What two escape routes from each bedroom does the floor plan show? **Floor Plan**
2. Think about this article and *Officer Buckle and Gloria*. What are some other safety tips that firefighters might try to teach to students and families? **Reading/Writing Across Texts**

 Social Studies

Draw a floor plan of your home. Show at least two escape routes and your outside meeting place. Give a copy to your family.

  **Social Studies** Fire safety
www.macmillanmh.com

75

- *Why shouldn't you run or walk if your clothes catch on fire?* (Running and walking can make fire worse.) *What do you do when you drop?* (Get down on the ground. Cover your face and eyes.) *How long should you roll?* (Roll over and over until the flames are out.)

 Work with your partner. Practice how to stop, drop, and roll.

Page 74

Headings

- *Read aloud the headings on this page with me* (Point to each heading as you read it.)*:* Make a Plan! Fire Safety Floor Plan.

Text

- *A floor plan is like a map of your house. What should you mark on a floor plan of your home?* (Mark the best ways to get out of the house.) *Why is it important to mark more than one route, or way to travel, on the floor plan?* (If one route gets blocked, you will know another route you can use to get out.)

Floor Plan

- *What does this floor plan show?* (The floor plan shows ways to get out of a home if a fire starts.)

- *Imagine that you are in the living room of this house. Use your finger to show me two ways to get out.*

- *It's important to pick a safe place to meet outside your home. That way, members of your family will know where to find each other. Point to the meeting place on the floor plan.*

Page 75

- *What should you do when you are safely out of the house?* (Call 9-1-1.)

Tell your partner two important things that you learned about fire safety from this selection. (Answers will vary.)

Name _____

Use the word chart to study this week's vocabulary words.
Write a sentence using each word in your writer's notebook.

Word	Context Sentence	Illustration
attention _____	Sam was not paying <u>attention</u> to where he was going.	
buddy _____	I walk to school with my <u>buddy</u> Jack.	
accident _____	Tie your shoelaces so you don't trip and have an <u>accident</u>.	
tip _____	Washing your hands before you eat is a good <u>tip</u> for staying healthy.	
enormous _____	I felt small next to the <u>enormous</u> tree.	**What is a another word for *enormous*?**
obeys _____	My dog <u>obeys</u> me when I tell him to sit.	

© Macmillan/McGraw-Hill

**Read each question and prompt. Discuss the answers
with your group. Use your Leveled Reader to find
details to support your answers. Then write your
answers on the blank lines or on another sheet of
paper.**

1. Describe what you learned about walking safely.

   _____

2. Give examples of the safe ways to ride a bike.

   _____

3. Explain what you should not do on the bus.

   _____

4. Talk about what equipment you need to skateboard safely.

   _____

5. Retell what the book says you should do before crossing the street.

   _____

6. Write one question about the book to ask your group.

   _____

   _____

A Trip to the Emergency Room

Pages 82–83

Prior to reading the selection with children, they should have listened to the selection on **StudentWorks Plus**, the interactive eBook. In addition, selection vocabulary should have been pretaught using the **Visual Vocabulary Resources**.

Access Core Content

Teacher Note Pose the questions after you read the paragraph or page indicated.

Page 82

Paragraph 1

- *A hospital is a place where people go when they are sick or hurt. An emergency room is part of a hospital. People go to the emergency room when they need help right away, or very quickly.*

- *Let's think of a few reasons why someone might go to the emergency room. Let's finish this sentence together: My friend went to the emergency room because she had a _____. (broken arm, cut on the face, bee sting)*

Paragraph 2

- *This paragraph tells us that the people who work in the emergency room keep the hospital running properly. Can a hospital actually run? (Demonstrate running, and then shake your head.) No, the hospital does not run. This sentence means that the people in the emergency room work hard to make sure all the work gets done.*

Photo

- *Look at the picture. These people work at an emergency room. Let's read to find out more about these people.*

Page 83

Whole Page

- *The admissions worker keeps track of patients. When you keep track of someone or something, it means that you know where that person or thing is. Our friend will not get lost!*

Pages 82–83

Real World Reading

A Trip to the Emergency Room
Who works in the emergency room?

Comprehension

Genre
Expository text gives information about real people, things, or events.

Text Structure
Sequence of Events
Sequence is the order in which things happen.

Oh, no! You have a broken bone. Where do you go? To the hospital emergency room, of course. The emergency room can be a busy place. Ambulances and people arrive there during the day and night. People are brought there if they have a **serious** medical problem.

Doctors and nurses work in the emergency room. Their job is to **aid** people who are sick or hurt. Other people help patients, too. They help keep the hospital running properly. Let's meet some of the people who work in a hospital emergency room.

82

Pages 84–85

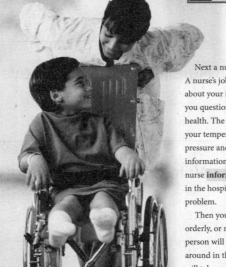

Nurses and Aides

Next a nurse will help you. A nurse's job is to find out about your injury and ask you questions about your health. The nurse will take your temperature and blood pressure and record this information on a chart. The nurse **informs** other people in the hospital about your problem.

Then you will meet an orderly, or nurse's aide. That person will help you get around in the hospital. She will take you to the correct department if you need to get tests done. She may use a wheelchair to take you from one area to another.

84

TIME FOR KIDS

H Admissions Worker

The first person you see in the emergency room is an admissions worker. The hospital needs to keep track of the patients coming into the emergency room. The admissions person checks you in. The adult who is with you will fill out hospital forms. The forms ask for your **personal** information and why you came to the hospital.

83

TIME FOR KIDS

 Doctor

Last, it's time for the doctor to examine you. The doctor checks your injury. He also looks at your chart. He arranges for you to get an X ray if you need one. The doctor knows how to fix your broken bone. He will probably put on a cast so the bone will **heal**. The doctor also decides whether you need to stay in the hospital or if you can go home right away.

So don't worry if you need to go to the emergency room. Now you know about the people who work there and how they will help you feel better.

Think and Compare

1. When do you go to the emergency room?

2. Describe the people you see in an emergency room in the order you meet them.

3. What would happen if the emergency room did not have an admissions worker?

4. How are paramedics similar to doctors? How are they different?

85

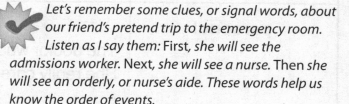

■ The admissions worker checks in our friend with the broken arm. (Write *check in* and *check out* on the board.) *What are some examples of places where you need to check in or check out?* (first day of school, a hotel, a campsite, a sports event)

Page 84

Whole Page

■ *After our friend checks in, another person takes care of her. Who is that?* (a nurse) *Who will help her get from place to place?* (an aide)

■ *An aide, or orderly, may take her around the hospital in a wheelchair. Point to the wheelchair on this page.*

Let's remember some clues, or signal words, about our friend's pretend trip to the emergency room. Listen as I say them: First, she will see the admissions worker. Next, she will see a nurse. Then she will see an orderly, or nurse's aide. These words help us know the order of events.

Page 85

Whole Page

■ *After she sees the admissions worker, the nurse, and the orderly, our friend will see a doctor. A doctor will examine, or look at her carefully, to find out what is wrong.*

■ *Our friend may need an X ray. An X ray is a picture of the inside of the body. Why might the doctor want her to get an X ray?* (to see where the bone is broken)

PARTNERS *Work together with your partner to make a list or draw pictures of the workers you may see if you visit an emergency room. Put your list in the order you will see these workers.*

Monitor Oral Production

Remember to model self-corrective techniques on a regular basis as you speak to children. Pretend to mispronounce words and self-correct.

Name _____

Use the word chart to study this week's vocabulary words. Write a sentence using each word in your writer's notebook.

Word	Context Sentence	Illustration
serious _____	The police officer has a <u>serious</u> look on her face.	**When should you act in a serious way?**
personal _____	The doctor was <u>personal</u>. She really cared.	
aid _____	Nurses give <u>aid</u> to sick people.	
informs _____	The officer <u>informs</u> us about bicycle safety.	**What else might a police officer inform you about?**
heal _____	It took a long time for the cut on my arm to <u>heal</u>.	

Read each question and prompt. Discuss the answers with your group. Use your Leveled Reader to find details to support your answers. Then write your answers on the blank lines or on another sheet of paper.

1. Explain why it is important to work.

_____

2. Describe some of the jobs that were shown in the book.

_____

3. Give examples of what "wants" money earned from working allows people to buy.

_____

4. Give examples of what types of jobs provide a service to people.

_____

5. Share with your classmates what kind of job you want to have someday.

_____

6. Write one question about the book to ask your group.

_____

_____

© Macmillan/McGraw-Hill

A Harbor Seal Pup Grows Up

Pages 94–95

Prior to reading the selection with children, they should have listened to the selection on **StudentWorks Plus**, the interactive eBook. In addition, selection vocabulary should have been pretaught using the **Visual Vocabulary Resources**.

Access Core Content

Teacher Note Pose the questions after you read the paragraph or page indicated.

Pages 95–96

Title and Photos

■ *Read the title of this selection with me:* A Harbor Seal Pup Grows Up. *What kind of animal do you think is in the photograph on page 95?* (seal) *A seal pup is a baby seal.*

Share with your partner anything you know about seals.

Page 96

Chapter Title

■ *This selection has chapters. Let's read the title of the first chapter:* By the Ocean. *What do you know about the ocean and the place where the ocean meets the land?* (Children will share prior knowledge.)

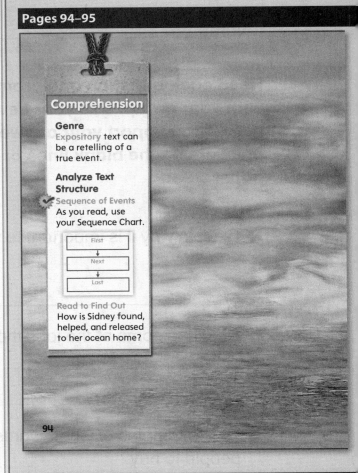

Comprehension

Genre
Expository text can be a retelling of a true event.

Analyze Text Structure
Sequence of Events
As you read, use your Sequence Chart.

First
↓
Next
↓
Last

Read to Find Out
How is Sidney found, helped, and released to her ocean home?

94

Pages 96–97

By the Ocean

The harbor seal pup is 2 weeks old. Her name is Sidney. Sidney stays close to her mother. She drinks her mother's milk.

Waves crash on the rocky beach. Harbor seal families lie in the warm sun.

Sidney and her mother lie in the sun too.

96

A Harbor Seal Pup Grows Up

by Joan Hewett
photographs by Richard Hewett

Main Selection

95

Sidney's mother gets hungry. She dives in the water to catch fish. The water is too cold for Sidney. So Sidney stays on the shore.

97

Paragraph 1

The land near the edge of the ocean is called the coast. A harbor is a place on a coast. A harbor is a safe place for boats to anchor, or park. What does the name harbor seal *tell us about this kind of seal?* (It is found near the coast.)

Paragraph 2

- *Let's read the next part of the page together:* Waves crash on the rocky beach. Harbor seal families lie in the warm sun. *Close your eyes and listen as I read about the beach again. Think about other sounds, sights, and smells you might notice if you were on this beach.* (Reread the paragraph.) *Tell me what you saw, heard, felt, and smelled on your imaginary trip to the beach.* (gulls squawking, salty air, gritty sand)

Page 97

Text

- *This page tells us that the water is too cold for Sidney. What word on page 96 is an antonym, or opposite, for* cold? *(warm)*

Non-verbal Cues

Remind children that they can use non-verbal cues to share information when they are not able to do so verbally. Encourage children to use movement and sounds.

Page 98

Paragraph 2

■ To notice *is to see and pay attention to something. Who do you think might have noticed the seal pup?* (people swimming in the ocean and playing on the beach)

Page 99

Text

■ *Listen to how I read this page:* (low, sad voice) The next day, the pup is still alone. The people call for help. (relieved voice) Sidney is rescued. *Now, read the page with me. Use the same kind of voice I used to show what the sentences mean:* The next day, the pup is still alone. The people call for help. Sidney is rescued.

 Tell me in your own words what has happened so far in this selection. Tell what happened in the order it occurred in the story. (Sidney and her mother were on the rocks. Her mother went into the water to look for food. She did not come back. Sidney was alone for three days. People saw Sidney and got help.)

PARTNERS *Tell your partner what you think the rescuers will do.* (Question is open.)

Page 100

Chapter Title

■ *A new chapter begins on this page. Let's read the chapter title together:* Nursed Back to Health. *We know that a nurse is a person who helps sick people get better. What do you think the action word* nursed *means?* (to take care of sick people or animals so they get better)

The seal pup waits for her mother. She waits for 3 days. She is very hungry.

People notice the seal pup. She is alone. Will her mother come back?

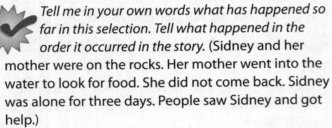

98

Nursed Back to Health

Sidney is brought to a sea **mammal** center.

A scientist named Peter is in charge. Peter takes care of **young** seals. He lifts the thin pup from her cage.

100

The next day, the pup is still alone. The people call for help. Sidney is **rescued**.

Sequence of Events
Think about what has happened so far. Use details from the text to describe how Sidney ends up alone on the beach.

99

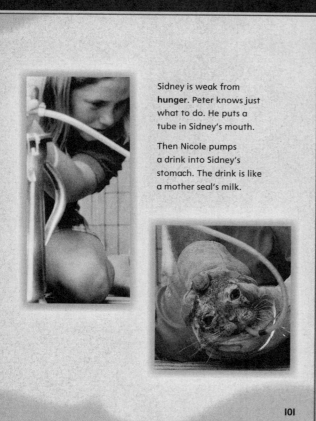

Sidney is weak from **hunger**. Peter knows just what to do. He puts a tube in Sidney's mouth.

Then Nicole pumps a drink into Sidney's stomach. The drink is like a mother seal's milk.

IOI

Text, Choral Reading

- *A scientist is someone who studies the different parts of our world. What are some of the things we have studied in science?* (Question is open.) *Let's read about the scientist who helped Sidney:* A scientist named Peter is in charge. Peter takes care of young seals. He lifts the thin pup from her cage.

- *Let's figure out what it means when the author says* Peter is in charge. *I'll say a sentence to help you figure it out. "Our principal is in charge of our school." What do you think* in charge *means?* (to be the person who decides what others will do)

- *When the author says,* He lifts the thin pup from her cage, *what animal is he talking about?* (Sidney) *Who do you think put her in a cage?* (the rescuers) *Why is she thin?* (Her mother has been gone for three days, so Sydney had nothing to eat.) *What do you think Peter will do?* (get food for Sidney)

Page 101

Whole Page

- *Point to the tube. How is the tube like a straw?* (It is the same shape as a straw. Liquid can go through it.)

Seek Clarification
Some children may be confused by unfamiliar words, such as *stomach*. Encourage children to always seek clarification when they encounter a word or phrase that does not make sense to them. For example, *What does "stomach" mean?*

A Harbor Seal Pup Grows Up

Page 102

Whole Page

- *Why do you think Sidney is tired?* (She is weak. She has not had enough food to eat.)

Look at the picture on page 102. Talk about why it is funny. Talk about why it proves that Sidney was very, very tired. (It is funny to see an animal sleep in its bowl. It shows that she was too tired to even crawl to a comfortable place.) *Now talk about a time you saw an animal do something funny.* (Answers will vary.)

Pages 102–103

Text, Choral Reading

- *We will read aloud how Sidney was before and after her nap. When we read the part about her being tired we will use a tired voice, and make our eyes look sleepy. We will read the part about her waking up with a wide-awake voice and wide-open eyes:* Sidney is full. She is also very tired. She falls asleep. When Sidney wakes up, her eyes are bright. She looks around.

- *Does Sidney feel better after her nap? How do you know?* (Yes, she is strong enough to look around. Instead of tired eyes, her eyes are bright.)

Page 104

Paragraph 1, Choral Reading

- *Let's read aloud what Peter found when he examined Sidney:* Peter examines the pup. Her heartbeat is normal. So is her temperature. She is healthy.

Sidney is full. She is also very tired. She falls asleep.

102

Peter **examines** the pup. Her heartbeat is **normal**. So is her temperature. She is healthy.

Sidney has a full set of teeth. That means she is at least 3 weeks old. Sidney is small for her age.

104

When Sidney wakes up, her eyes are bright. She looks around.

103

Sidney gets her drink 3 times a day. She becomes stronger. Using her flippers, she scoots around.

A child's plastic pool becomes Sidney's playpen. She likes the water. She swims faster and faster.

105

Paragraph 2

- *Why might Sidney be smaller than normal?* (because she didn't get enough food for a while)

 Tell me what has happened since Sidney came to the sea mammal center. (Someone fed her. She took a nap. Peter examined her.)

Page 105

Paragraph 1

- *Does Sidney move around on front and back legs like a dog pup? Explain.* (no, because she has flippers on the front and no legs in the back) *Look back at page 102. Point to Sidney's flippers in the picture.*

Paragraph 2

- *The author tells us that Sidney's pool is like a baby's playpen. A playpen is a place where babies can play without getting hurt. How is her pool different from a playpen?* (The pool is full of water. A playpen is not.)

- *Sidney uses her flippers to move through the water and swim. This page says she swims faster and faster. That means she is getting stronger. Let's pretend to be Sidney. We will use our arms for flippers and move them quickly. When I say, "Go faster!" you will flap your flippers as fast as you can.*

Nicole shows Sidney a fish. Sidney does not want it.

106

Page 106

Text

■ *This page tells us that Sidney looks at the fish but won't take it from Nicole. Sidney's mother left before she taught Sidney how to eat fish. All Sidney knows how to do is drink liquid.*

■ *In her home in the sea mammal center, is Sidney more like a wild animal or like a pet?* (She is a lot like a pet. People take care of her. Wild animals have to take care of themselves.)

Page 107

Text

■ *Why doesn't Nicole give up? Why doesn't she stop trying to feed fish to Sidney?* (Nicole knows it is important for Sidney to learn to eat fish, so she can grow big and strong. Nicole knows Sidney will learn if she keeps trying.)

PARTNERS *Role play what is happening on this page with your partner. First, make some paper cutouts of fish. Then one partner will pretend to be Nicole and wiggle the paper fish. The other partner will pretend to be Sidney. The person pretending to be Sidney will not take the fish at first. Then he or she will take it.*

Page 108

Paragraph 1, Choral Reading

■ *Let's read together what happens when Sidney starts eating fish:* Before long, Sidney wants to eat fish. She waits for her bucket of fish in the morning.

Before long, Sidney wants to eat fish. She waits for her bucket of fish in the morning.

The pup is gaining weight. She no longer needs her healthy drink.

108

Nicole does not give up. Day after day, she wiggles a fish in front of Sidney. Then one day, the pup swallows it.

107

Sidney is 5 weeks old. She has a thick layer of fat. The fat will keep her warm in cold water.

Sidney is ready to be on her own.

> **Sequence of Events**
> Describe the order of events that people take to help Sidney at the sea mammal center.

109

Paragraph 2

- *The author says that Sidney is gaining weight. Is that a good thing or a bad thing? Why?* (a good thing because before she was too thin and weak)

- *Raise your hand if you think Sidney will stay at the sea mammal center. Tell us why.* (because she still needs to grow bigger) *Raise your hand if you think Sidney will not stay at the sea mammal center. Tell us why.* (She is strong enough to go back to the ocean.)

Page 109

Paragraph 1

- *Go back to page 104 to see how old Sidney was when she came to the center. Use that detail to figure out how long she has been at the center.* (two weeks)

Paragraph 2

- *When the author says Sidney is ready to be on her own, does she mean that Sidney will be lonely or that Sidney can take care of herself?* (She can take care of herself.)

Page 110

Chapter Title

- *This is the last chapter. Let's read the title of the chapter together:* Returning to the Ocean. *What do you think this chapter will tell about?* (It will tell about Sidney going back to live in the ocean.)

Text

- *Why does Peter put Sidney in a carrying case?* (so they can move her from the sea mammal center to a boat to put her back in the ocean)

- *The author says the salty air makes Sidney feel excited. Why?* (She knows she is going back to the ocean. She wants to go back to her home and be with other seals.)

Page 111

Paragraph 1

- *Who will say goodbye?* (The scientists from the sea mammal center will say good–bye to Sidney.)

Paragraph 2

- *Read the second paragraph with me and do what I do:* A scientist tips the case. (pretend to tip a case) "Good luck, little one," she says. (Wave good-bye.)

- *Why are the scientists letting Sidney go back to the ocean?* (because she is healthy now; because she can live like other seals live)

 Take turns pretending to be Peter. Tell your partner how you feel about returning Sidney to the ocean. (I will miss Sidney, but I am happy that I helped her get well.)

Pages 110–111

Returning to the Ocean

Peter puts the pup in a carrying case. Other scientists take over. They carry Sidney onto a boat. Sidney is excited by the ocean's salty smell. She shakes the case.

110

Pages 112–113

Sidney slips into the water. She will find other seals. She will catch fish. Sidney will grow up in her ocean home.

112

The boat heads toward an island. When they are almost there, the boat stops. It is time to say good-bye.

A scientist tips the case. "Good luck, little one," she says.

III

113

Pages 112–113

Whole Page

- *Now that Sidney is back in the ocean, how will her life be different from her life in the sea mammal center? Let's make a list on the board.* (Nicole will not feed her. She will catch her own fish for food. She will play with seals, not people.)

- *How is* A Harbor Seal Pup Grows Up *like* A Whale is Saved? (Both were about sea animals that needed to be rescued.) *How are* A Harbor Seal Pup Grows Up *and* A Whale is Saved *different from each other?* (The whale was well and went back into the ocean. The seal was sick and had to stay at the sea mammal center to get well.)

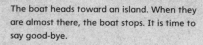 *Let's tell in our own words what happened in this selection. What happened first?* (Sidney's mother went into the ocean and didn't come back. Sidney had no food and got weak. Some people noticed the seal and took her to the sea mammal center.) *What happened next?* (Scientists took care of Sidney. They made her well. They taught her to eat fish, and she grew bigger and stronger.) *What happened last?* (The scientists let Sidney go back into the ocean with the other seals.)

The Puppy

Access Core Content

Teacher Note Pose the questions after you read the paragraph or page indicated.

Pages 116–117

Text, Choral Reading

- *Let's read the poem together. First, let's think about what kind of voice we should use to read it.* (a happy voice because puppies are fun) *Let's read in a happy voice.*

- *Summarize what this poem tells us about what owners need to do to take care of their puppies.* (The poem says that owners must feed puppies and brush their coats. They must give them bones to make their teeth strong and take them for walks.)

- *The poet compares a puppy's brushed coat to silk. Silk is a shiny, soft cloth. Let's say it together:* silk.

Poetry

Genre
Poems can describe things in interesting or unusual ways. Rhyme, rhythm, and repetition help create images in poetry.

✓ **Literary Element**
Similes compare one thing to another. A simile uses the words *like* or *as*.

The Puppy

Anonymous

Call the puppy,
And give him some milk.
Brush his coat
Till it shines like silk.
Call the dog
And give him a bone.
Go for a walk,
Then take him home.

116

Poetry

Connect and Compare

1. What things are compared in the poem? How can you tell that the comparison is a simile? **Simile**

2. Think about how the scientists cared for Sidney in *A Harbor Seal Pup Grows Up*. How is caring for a seal pup like caring for a puppy? How is it different? **Reading/Writing Across Texts**

LOG ON ⊙ **FIND OUT** Poetry Animal care
www.macmillanmh.com

117

- *How would this selection be different if it were an article instead of a poem?* (It would have longer sentences. It would tell more details. It would explain things.)

- *Which line of the poem does the illustration show?* (Go for a walk)

 The poem tells four things a puppy owner needs to do. Each of you will choose two things to draw. Then put the drawings in the order that the poem told about them.

Name _____

Use the word chart to study this week's vocabulary words.
Write a sentence using each word in your writer's notebook.

Word	Context Sentence	Illustration
young _____	The <u>young</u> bird fell from the nest and needed help.	
examines _____	The doctor takes her time when she <u>examines</u> her patient.	
mammal _____	Today in school we learned about <u>mammals</u>.	
normal _____	It is not <u>normal</u> to see a whale on a beach.	
hunger _____	An animal will feel <u>hunger</u> if it can not find food.	
rescued _____	The firefighter <u>rescued</u> the cat from the tree.	**Why might someone need to be rescued at the beach?**

Read each question and prompt. Discuss the answers with your group. Use your Leveled Reader to find details to support your answers. Then write your answers on the blank lines or on another sheet of paper.

1. Explain how the bald eagle got its name.

   _____

2. Give examples of what bald eagles eat.

   _____

3. Describe how and why bald eagles were once endangered.

   _____

4. Explain how bald eagles get food.

   _____

5. Explain how people can help bald eagles.

   _____

6. Write one question about the book to ask your group.

   _____

   _____

Mice and Beans

Pages 124–125

Prior to reading the selection with children, they should have listened to the selection on **StudentWorks Plus**, the interactive eBook. In addition, selection vocabulary should have been pretaught using the **Visual Vocabulary Resources**.

Access Core Content

Teacher Note Pose the questions after you read the paragraph or page indicated.

Pages 124–125

Title

■ *Read the title of this story with me:* Mice and Beans. *What might a story called* Mice and Beans *be about?* (mice who like beans, mice who make something from beans, mice who steal beans)

Illustration

■ *Look closely at the pictures on these pages. I see mice wearing clothes and dancing. How many mice do you see? Let's count them together.* (Point to the mice and count to eight.)

■ *Do you think this story might be about things that can really happen or things that are made up? Tell me why you think that.* (things that cannot really happen because mice don't wear clothes and dance around)

Page 126

Paragraphs 1–2

■ *Let's read the first two paragraphs together to find out who the main characters of this story are.*

■ *Rosa María and Little Catalina are the names of the main characters. We saw mice on page 125. Do you think Rosa María and Little Catalina are mice? Why or why not?* (No, the woman on page 126 is probably Rosa María. She is a person, not a mouse.)

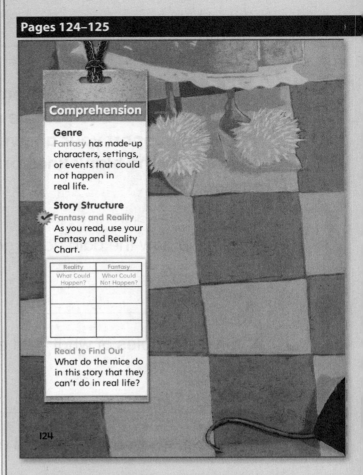

Rosa María lived in a tiny house with a tiny yard. But she had a big heart, a big family, and more than anything, she loved to cook big meals for them.

In one week, her youngest grandchild, Little Catalina, would be seven years old, and the whole family would squeeze into her *casita* for the party.

Rosa María didn't mind because she believed what her mother had always said: "When there's room in the heart, there's room in the house, except for a mouse."

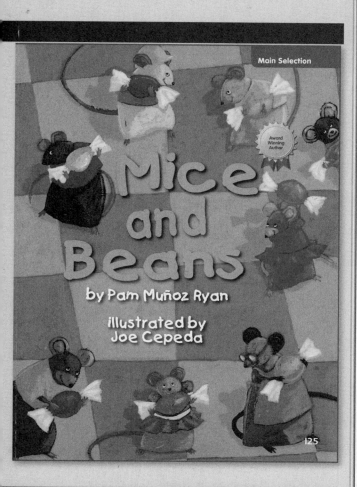

Paragraph 2

- *Let's read paragraph 2 together:* In one week, her youngest grandchild, Little Catalina, would be seven years old, and the whole family would squeeze into her *casita* for the party.

- *What kind of party is Rosa María planning?* (a birthday party) *How do you celebrate a birthday?* (eating cake and ice cream, playing games, giving gifts)

- *When you* squeeze into *something, you try to get something into a small space.*

- *Casita is a Spanish word. Look at the picture on page 127 to help you figure out what it means. What are some English words we could use instead of* casita? (house, home, cottage)

Paragraph 3, Echo Reading

- *I am going to read part of what Rosa María said. Please echo after me:* When there's room in the heart, there's room in the house, EXCEPT for a mouse. *Do you think Rosa María likes mice?* (no)

- *What do you think there is room for in Rosa María's house?* (family and friends) *What does her saying mean?* (When someone loves others, there is room in their heart and room in their house.)

 Families have lots of sayings. Think of some sayings you have heard people say. For example, I have heard people say, "Look before you leap." That means "think before you do something." Tell your partner a saying you have heard. Tell what you think the saying means. (Responses will vary.)

Page 128

Illustration

Look closely at the picture on page 128. Tell your partner what you see. (Rosa María is making a list. There are mice on the floor. There is a mousetrap.)

Page 129

Paragraph 1

- *An enchilada is a corn or flour tortilla rolled up with meat, vegetables, and sauce inside. A tortilla is flat and round, like a pancake. Who has eaten an enchilada? Tell us what was in it.*

- *Let's read together what Rosa María said about rice and beans:* no dinner was complete without rice and beans! *What does this tell you about what Rosa María thinks of rice and beans?* (She likes them very much. She likes to eat them with every meal.) *What food could you eat every day? Tell us using Rosa María's words.* No meal is complete without _____. *I will say one first:* No meal is complete without potatoes.

- *A piñata is a paper decoration in the shape of an animal that is full of candy. Someone hangs it from the ceiling. Then others take turns hitting it with a stick to make the candy fall out.*

Paragraph 2

- *What do you think Little Catalina might have wanted for a birthday present? Let's make a list of ideas.* (game, ball, book, stuffed animal)

128

Monday, Rosa María did the laundry. She washed and ironed her largest tablecloth and the twenty-four napkins that matched. But when she finished, she only counted twenty-three.

"*No importa,*" she said. "It doesn't matter. So what if someone has a napkin that doesn't match? The important thing is that we're all together."

After dinner she swept the floor and checked the mousetrap.

But it was missing.

Didn't I set one last night? she wondered.

She hurried to the cupboard to **fetch** another, and when it was set and ready to **snap,** she turned off the light and went to bed.

130

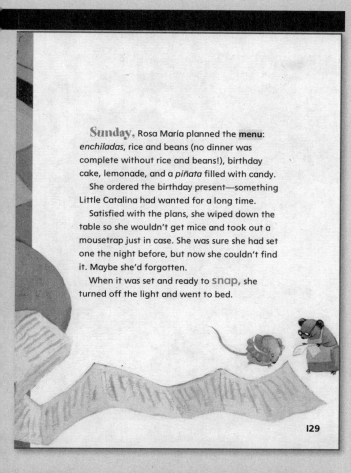

Sunday. Rosa María planned the **menu**: *enchiladas*, rice and beans (no dinner was complete without rice and beans!), birthday cake, lemonade, and a *piñata* filled with candy.

She ordered the birthday present—something Little Catalina had wanted for a long time.

Satisfied with the plans, she wiped down the table so she wouldn't get mice and took out a mousetrap just in case. She was sure she had set one the night before, but now she couldn't find it. Maybe she'd forgotten.

When it was set and ready to **snap**, she turned off the light and went to bed.

129

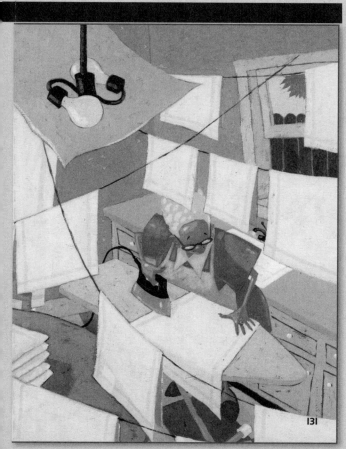

131

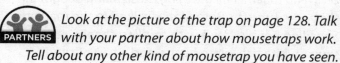
Paragraph 3
- *Why did Rosa María wipe down the table?* (so she would not get mice)

PARTNERS *Look at the picture of the trap on page 128. Talk with your partner about how mousetraps work. Tell about any other kind of mousetrap you have seen.*

- *Do you think Rosa María forgot to set a trap the night before? Why or why not?* (She probably did set a trap because she does not like mice, but something happened to it.)

So far in the story, could everything that has happened also happen in real life? Explain why you think so. (yes; A grandmother could plan a birthday party for her grandchild. She could wipe down her table. She could set mousetraps.)

Page 130

Paragraph 1 and Illustration
- *What clue in the picture on page 130 helps you figure out where the other napkin might be?* (The picture makes us think the mice have taken the other napkin off the line.)

Paragraph 2
- *Let's say together what Rosa María said about the napkin:* No importa. *What do you think it means?* (not important) *What clues did you use to figure it out.* (The word *no* is like not. The word *importa* is like important. Also, the author says: "It doesn't matter." That is the same as saying it is not important.)

Page 131

Illustration
- *What is Rosa María doing?* (She is ironing the tablecloth and napkins.)

Pages 132–133

Paragraph 1

- *Let's read together all the things Rosa María bought for the party:* Tuesday, Rosa María walked to the market. She filled her big bolsa with *tortillas,* cheese, red sauce, white rice, pinto beans, and a bag of candy. She bought a piñata and on her way home she stopped at the pasteleria to order the cake.

- *Look at the picture on page 132. Point to what you think is the big bolsa. How can you tell?* (It is the bag on her arm. The story says Rosa María filled something with the things she got in the market. This looks like something you can fill with things.)

- *What is the turkey-shaped thing Rosa María is carrying on page 132?* (the piñata)

Paragraph 2

- *The first paragraph tells some things Rosa María did on Tuesday. The second paragraph tells more things she did. We'll make a sequence chain on the board to show everything she did on Tuesday.* (shopped for food, bought a piñata, ordered a cake, had dinner, washed dishes, tried to check the mousetrap)

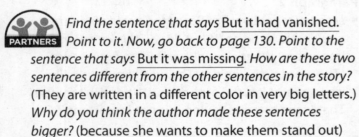 *Find the sentence that says* But it had vanished. *Point to it. Now, go back to page 130. Point to the sentence that says* But it was missing. *How are these two sentences different from the other sentences in the story?* (They are written in a different color in very big letters.) *Why do you think the author made these sentences bigger?* (because she wants to make them stand out)

Pages 132–133

Pages 134–135

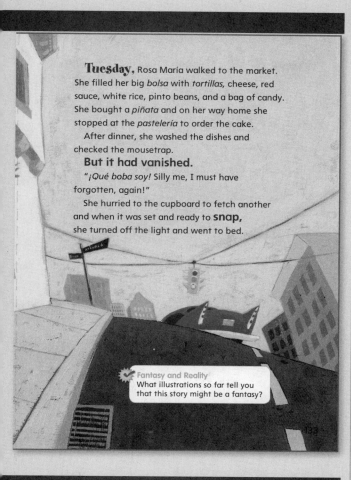

Tuesday, Rosa María walked to the market. She filled her big *bolsa* with *tortillas,* cheese, red sauce, white rice, pinto beans, and a bag of candy. She bought a *piñata* and on her way home she stopped at the *pastelería* to order the cake.

After dinner, she washed the dishes and checked the mousetrap.

But it had vanished.

"*¡Qué boba soy!* Silly me, I must have forgotten, again!"

She hurried to the cupboard to fetch another and when it was set and ready to **snap,** she turned off the light and went to bed.

Fantasy and Reality
What illustrations so far tell you that this story might be a fantasy?

133

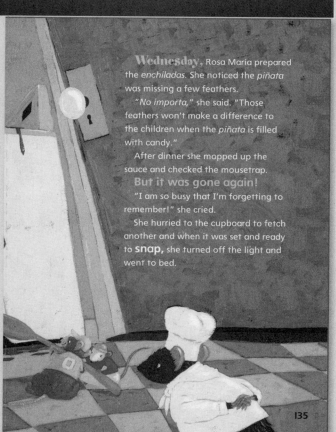

Wednesday, Rosa María prepared the *enchiladas.* She noticed the *piñata* was missing a few feathers.

"*No importa,*" she said. "Those feathers won't make a difference to the children when the *piñata* is filled with candy."

After dinner she mopped up the sauce and checked the mousetrap.

But it was gone again!

"I am so busy that I'm forgetting to remember!" she cried.

She hurried to the cupboard to fetch another and when it was set and ready to **snap,** she turned off the light and went to bed.

135

- *Rosa María said something in Spanish when she saw the mousetrap was gone. Say it with me:* "¡Qué boba soy!" *What other words in the paragraph help you know what that means?* (the words "Silly me")

- *So far in this story, we know some things that Rosa María does not know. Tell me the things that we know that she does not.* (There are mice in her house. They take the mousetraps every night. The mice took her napkin.)

Pages 134–135

Paragraph 1

- *Look back at page 129. How long has Rosa María been working on the party? What clues help you know?* (four days; Page 129 starts with the word *Sunday,* and page 135 starts with the word *Wednesday.*)

- *Rosa María notices the piñata is missing feathers. The word* missing *can have more than one meaning. Which of these sentences uses the word* missing *the same way it is used in this story? I was missing Dad because he was on a trip. My button fell off and was missing.* (second sentence)

Paragraph 5, Choral Reading

- *Let's read together what Rosa María says about forgetting:* "I am so busy that I'm forgetting to remember!" *What does that mean?* (She has so many things to do that she can't remember them all.)

Illustration

Look at the picture. What is happening in the picture that the story does not tell you about? (The mice are watching Rosa Maria. They are wearing clothes and using a big spoon.) *What do these clues tell you about what kind of story this is?* (Mice do not wear clothes or use spoons. This is not something that happens in real life.)

Page 136

Paragraphs 1–2

- *If someone does not know what* frijoles *are, what clue in paragraph 2 helps them figure it out?* (Rosa María says, "The beans will taste just as good …") Frijoles *are beans.*

Last Paragraph, Choral Reading

- *Let's read together the part on this page that we have read over and over in the story:* She hurried to the cupboard to fetch another and when it was set and ready to snap, she turned off the light and went to bed.

- *What is the same about every day that Rosa María works on the party?* (She sets a mousetrap. The mousetrap is missing the next day.)

Page 137

Paragraph 2

- *The author says:* Tomorrow was the big day. *What does this mean?* (The birthday party is tomorrow.)

Paragraph 3

- *Why did Rosa María wrap the cake?* (so it would stay fresh and the mice would not get it)

- *What might have happened if she did not wrap the cake.* (The mice might have eaten it. There would be no cake for the party. She would have to get a new cake or quickly make another one.)

Analyze Sayings and Expressions

Help children recognize that *Heavens!* is an expression used to express frustration and/or surprise. Invite them to share other examples of similar expressions they may know.

Thursday. Rosa María the beans. She searched for her favorite wooden spoon, the one she always used to cook *frijoles,* but she couldn't find it.

"*No importa,*" she said. "The beans will taste just as good if I use another spoon."

She added water all day long until the beans were plump and soft. Then she scrubbed the stove and checked the mousetrap.

But it was nowhere in sight!

"*¡Cielos!*" she said. "Heavens! Where is my mind?"

She hurried to the cupboard to fetch another and when it was set and ready to **snap,** she turned off the light and went to bed.

136

138

Friday, Rosa María picked up the cake and seven candles.

Tomorrow was the big day. Rosa María knew she mustn't forget anything, so she carefully went over the list one last time.

After dinner she wrapped the cake and checked the mousetrap.

She couldn't believe her eyes.

No mousetrap!

"Thank goodness I've got plenty."

She hurried to the cupboard to fetch another and when it was set and ready to **snap,** she turned off the light and went to bed.

137

Saturday, Rosa María cooked the rice. As the workers **assembled** Little Catalina's present, she set the table and squeezed the juiciest lemons from her tree.

"Let's see," she said, feeling very proud. "*Enchiladas,* rice and beans (no dinner was complete without rice and beans!), birthday cake, and lemonade. I know I have forgotten something, but what? **The candles!**"

But she only counted six.

"*No importa,*" she said. "I will arrange the six candles in the shape of a seven and Little Catalina will be just as happy. **Now,** everything is ready."

PARTNERS *We are finding out more and more things that Rosa María does not know. Pretend that your partner is Rosa María. Tell her what you know. (Be careful! You have mice in your house. They are taking some things you bought for your party!)*

Pages 138–139

Text and Illustration

■ *The story says that the workers* assembled *the birthday gift. That means they "put it together." Look at the picture on page 138. What might a gift be that you had to assemble outside? (playground toys, a swing)*

■ *Rosa María did a lot of work on Saturday to get ready for the party. As I say what she did, act it out with me: She cooked the rice, (Pretend to pour rice into a pot and stir it.) set the table, (Pretend to pick up and place several items on a table.) and squeezed the lemons. (Pretend to squeeze lemons.)*

PARTNERS *Rosa María realizes that a candle is missing. She said she would arrange the six candles in the shape of a seven. With your partner, make a drawing to show how she solved the problem. Take turns drawing the candles.*

Pages 140–141

Illustration

- *Look at the picture on page 140. What are the mice looking at?* (the piñata) *What did we say before about a piñata?* (that is it a decoration full of treats)

Text

- *Let's read together page 141:* But was everything ready? *What does this sentence mean?* (Rosa María thinks everything is ready, but maybe there is a problem she doesn't know about yet.)

- *Let's read together the word on the bag on page 141:* dulces. Dulces means "candy" in Spanish. *What do you think is in the bag?* (candy)

- Now let's read together the words on the list that are not crossed out: fill piñata. *What did Rosa María forget to do?* (to fill the piñata with candy)

Pages 142–143

Illustration

- *Look at the picture. I see a lot of things piled up on one another: a container, a toaster, a glass, a cup, a container of milk.* (Point to each as you say them.) *Why have the mice piled up so many things?* (so they can reach the piñata)

- *Look closely at the mice. What do they have in their paws?* (candies) *Are the mice putting candy into the piñata or taking it out of the piñata?* (putting it in)

But WAS everything ready?

Fantasy and Reality
Is this story a fantasy or a realistic story? Use details to explain.

141

143

 Could the things you see happening on page 143 really happen? Explain. (no, because mice are not able to make a tower of things and climb up it to fill a piñata)

■ Why do you think the mice in the story are filling up the piñata? (to help Rosa Maria because she forgot to fill it with candy)

 The mice in this story made a tower of things to reach the piñata. With your partner, brainstorm other ways for the mice to reach the piñata. Since it is a made-up story that could not really happen, you can use made-up ideas that real mice could not do.

Pages 144–145

Illustration

- *Do you think Rosa María's family minds that they are crowded into such a small house? Look at the picture for a clue.* (no, because they all look happy)

Paragraph 1, Choral Reading

- *We'll read together the first paragraph to find out about the day of the party:* That afternoon Rosa María's family filled her tiny casita. They ate the *enchiladas* and rice and beans. They drank the fresh-squeezed lemonade. And they devoured the cake.

Paragraph 2

- *This paragraph tells about Little Catalina's gift. Point to it in the picture on page 144.* (Children point to swing set.) *The author tells us that every cousin had a turn. What did every cousin have a turn doing?* (swinging on the new swing)

- *Let's chant what the children said after they finished swinging. What kind of voices do you think they used to chant?* (excited) *Let's chant with excited voices :* ¡La piñata! ¡La piñata!

 Tell your partner in a complete sentence what the children meant when they chanted: "¡La piñata! ¡La piñata!" (Let's play with the piñata now. We want to see what's in the piñata.)

Paragraph 3

- *Why did the people at the party throw a rope over the branch of the tree?* (They wanted to hang the piñata from the tree.)

Pages 144–145

144

Pages 146–147

Whack! Whack! Little Catalina swung the *piñata* stick.

"Wait!" cried Rosa María as she remembered what she'd forgotten. But it was too late.

Crack! The *piñata* separated, and the children scrambled to collect the candy.

146

That afternoon Rosa María's family filled her tiny *casita*. They ate the *enchiladas* and rice and beans. They drank the fresh-squeezed lemonade. And they **devoured** the cake.

Little Catalina loved her present—a swing set! And after every cousin had a turn, they chanted, *"¡La piñata! ¡La piñata!"*

They ran to the walnut tree and threw a rope over a high branch.

145

How could that be? Rosa María puzzled. I must have filled it without even realizing!

She laughed at her own forgetfulness as she hugged her granddaughter and said, *"Feliz cumpleaños,* my Little Catalina. Happy birthday."

147

Page 146

Paragraph 1

- *I will read what Little Catalina did. You will pretend to be Little Catalina. Pretend to hold a stick and swing at the piñata.* Whack! Whack! Little Catalina swung the piñata stick. *What does* Whack! Whack! *mean?* (It is the sound of the stick hitting the piñata.)

Paragraph 2

- *What does Rosa María realize that she forgot to do? Look back at page 143 if you need a hint.* (put the candy in the piñata)

- *Use your face to show me how Rosa María felt when she saw candy coming out. Why would she feel that way?* (Children show a surprised expression. Rosa María would be surprised because she wouldn't know how the candy got into the piñata.)

Page 147

Paragraph 1

- *First, Rosa María thinks she forgot to fill the piñata. Then she thinks she did fill it but forgot that she filled it. Does Rosa María get upset when she thinks that she forgot she had filled it? How do you know?* (no, because she just laughs)

Non-verbal Cues

Remind children that they can use non-verbal cues to share information when they are not able to do so verbally. Encourage children to use pantomime.

Pages 148–149

Paragraph 1

- *After the party was over Rosa María tidied her kitchen. When we tidy something, we make it clean and neat. Act out some things Rosa María probably did to tidy her kitchen.* (Children may act out sweeping, wiping tables, throwing out trash.)

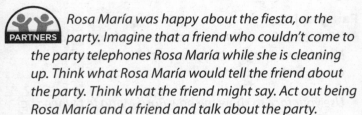 *Rosa María was happy about the fiesta, or the party. Imagine that a friend who couldn't come to the party telephones Rosa María while she is cleaning up. Think what Rosa María would tell the friend about the party. Think what the friend might say. Act out being Rosa María and a friend and talk about the party.*

Paragraph 3

- *What signs of mice does Rosa María probably see? Look back in the story to help you remember the things she was missing as she got ready for the party.* (a napkin, some feathers from the piñata, a candle)

Paragraphs 4–5

- *Let's remember what Rosa María said about mice at the beginning of the story. Look back at the last sentence on page 126 to help you remember. Tell me what she said in your own words.* (There is room in a house for everyone except mice.)

- *How do you think Rosa María felt when she realized there were mice in her house?* (upset and angry) *Let's read what Rosa María said when she realized she had mice. Let's read it in an upset, angry voice:* "¡Ratones!" she cried. "Where are my mousetraps? I will set them all!"

- *The author tells us that Rosa María inched to the floor. Let me show you what* inched *means.* (Demonstrate stooping down to the floor very slowly, bit by bit.) *Let's see if you can inch to the floor.*

Analyze Sayings and Expressions

Help children recognize that *Imagine that!* is an expression used to express slight frustration and/or surprise. Invite them to share other examples of similar expressions they may know.

Pages 148–149

148

Pages 150–151

150

After everyone had gone, Rosa María tidied her kitchen and thought contentedly about the *fiesta*. She pictured the happy look on Little Catalina's face when the candy spilled from the *piñata*. But Rosa María still couldn't remember when she had filled it.

"*No importa*," she said. "It was a wonderful day."

But as Rosa María swept out the cupboard, she discovered the telltale signs of mice!

"*¡Ratones!*" she cried. "Where are my mousetraps? I will set them all!"

She inched to the floor and when she did, something caught her eye.

She looked closer.

Maybe I **didn't** fill the *piñata*, she thought.

149

"Was it possible?" she asked, shaking her head. "Could I have had help?"

Rosa María looked at the leftovers. Too much for one person.

And what was it her mother had always said? "When there's room in the heart, there's room in the house . . . **even** for a mouse."

"*¡Fíjate!* Imagine that!" she said. "I remembered the words wrong all these years."

Besides, how many could there be? Two? Four?

"*No importa*," she said. "It doesn't matter if a few helpful mice live here, too."

Then she turned off the light and went to bed . . .

151

Last Sentence and Illustration

- *Rosa María thought, "Maybe I didn't fill the piñata." What did she find that made her think that? Look at page 148 for a clue.* (She found a piece of candy on the floor.)

Pages 150–151

Paragraph 1

- *Rosa María says, "Could I have had help?" What does she mean? Who does she think helped her? How did they help her?* (She realizes that the mice helped her by filling the piñata when she forgot to do it.)

Paragraph 2 and Illustration

- *Rosa María says that there are too many leftovers. Leftovers are foods that were left over after a meal. What does she do with some of the leftovers? Look at the illustration on page 150 to figure it out.* (She puts some on the floor for the mice to get.)

Paragraphs 3 and 4

- *Let's read the paragraph 3 together:* And what was it her mother had always said? "When there's room in the heart, there's room in the house … even for a mouse." *How is the saying different from the one Rosa María said at the beginning of the story?* (The first one said "except for a mouse," and this one says, "even for a mouse.")

Last Paragraph

- *How was this night different from all the other nights in the story?* (Rosa María did not set a mousetrap.) *Why not?* (She didn't want to catch the mice anymore. They were her friends now.)

Pages 152–153

Whole Story

- *Every time something was missing, Rosa María's thought it was because she forgot to get it. When something is missing from now on, what might she think?* (that the mice have taken it)

. . . and never set another mousetrap again.

✔ *Why can we say this story is a fantasy? Give examples to explain your answer.* (Some of the things in the story could not happen in real life. Mice cannot wear clothes. They cannot make towers to reach piñatas. They cannot fill up piñatas to help someone.)

- *Is Rosa María a good person? Why do you think that?* (yes; because she loves her family, she doesn't get upset about things, she makes great birthday parties)

*You and your partner will pretend to be Little
Catalina. Make a thank you card for Rosa María.
Make a picture on the front that Rosa María would like.
Write a message telling her what you liked about the party.*

■ *How were* Bobo's Celebration *and* Mice and Beans
alike? (Both were about parties. There were special
foods at both parties. Both were about things that
couldn't really happen.)

Rosa María's Rice and Beans

Access Core Content

Teacher Note Pose the questions after you read the paragraph or page indicated.

Page 156

Paragraph 1, Choral Reading

- *This page tells about liquids and solids. Things that you can pour are liquids. What are some foods that are liquids?* (juice, milk, oil) *We cannot pour solids. They are hard. A carrot is an example of a solid. What are some other solid foods?* (apple, potato, cookie)

- *We'll read the first paragraph together to find out the main idea of this selection:* When you cook, you often mix liquids and solids. These different states of matter can change in different ways as you cook them.

Paragraph 2

- *To help us understand this paragraph, we'll think of some examples. The author says that heating some solids makes them brown. Think about how chicken looks before it is cooked. Then think how it turns brown on the outside when someone fries it in a pan.*

- *What are other solid foods that get brown when you cook them?* (French fries)

- *The paragraph also says that some solids become liquid when you heat them. If you heat a solid chocolate bar, it will turn into liquid chocolate syrup. Can you think of another example of a solid that turns into a liquid when you heat it?* (butter, ice)

Page 157

Text

- *This recipe tells how to make rice. Point to the part that tells what you need. I will name each of the things we need. You will say,* solid *or* liquid*:* oil *(liquid),* onion *(solid),* pepper *(solid),* rice *(solid),* broth *(liquid),* tomato sauce *(liquid),* water *(liquid).*

Pages 156–157

Science

Genre
Some *expository* articles give you information about how to make a food or a drink.

✓ **Text Feature**
Written Directions are steps that tell you how to make or do something.

Content Vocabulary
liquids
solids
gas

ROSA MARÍA'S RICE AND BEANS

When you cook, you often mix **liquids** and **solids**, such as when you mix water and flour. These different states of matter can change in different ways as you cook them.

Heating some solids can make them turn brown. Other solids become soft when you heat them. Heating liquids can make them boil. If you boil liquid long enough, it can change its state. It becomes a **gas**, another state of matter.

In the following recipes you will mix solids and liquids to make Rosa María's rice and beans.

156

Pages 158–159

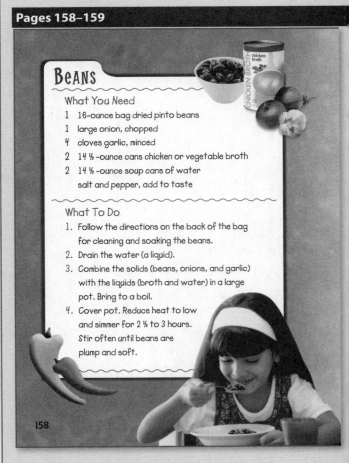

Beans

What You Need

1 16-ounce bag dried pinto beans
1 large onion, chopped
4 cloves garlic, minced
2 14 ½ -ounce cans chicken or vegetable broth
2 14 ½ -ounce soup cans of water
   salt and pepper, add to taste

What To Do

1. Follow the directions on the back of the bag for cleaning and soaking the beans.
2. Drain the water (a liquid).
3. Combine the solids (beans, onions, and garlic) with the liquids (broth and water) in a large pot. Bring to a boil.
4. Cover pot. Reduce heat to low and simmer for 2 ½ to 3 hours. Stir often until beans are plump and soft.

158

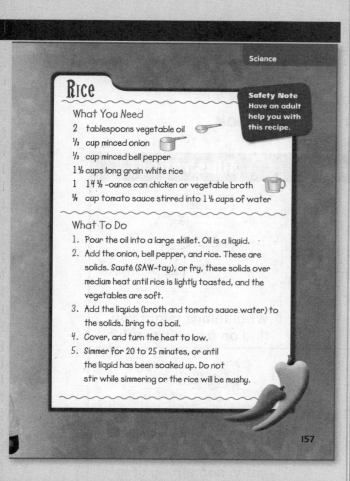

Science

Rice

Safety Note
Have an adult help you with this recipe.

What You Need

2 tablespoons vegetable oil
⅓ cup minced onion
⅓ cup minced bell pepper
1½ cups long grain white rice
1 14 ½ -ounce can chicken or vegetable broth
¼ cup tomato sauce stirred into 1 ½ cups of water

What To Do

1. Pour the oil into a large skillet. Oil is a liquid.
2. Add the onion, bell pepper, and rice. These are solids. Sauté (SAW-tay), or fry, these solids over medium heat until rice is lightly toasted, and the vegetables are soft.
3. Add the liquids (broth and tomato sauce water) to the solids. Bring to a boil.
4. Cover, and turn the heat to low.
5. Simmer for 20 to 25 minutes, or until the liquid has been soaked up. Do not stir while simmering or the rice will be mushy.

157

Solid, Liquid, or Gas?

The same material can be in three different states—solid, liquid, and gas.

1. A solid has a definite size and shape. Ice is a solid. When water freezes, it becomes ice.
2. Liquid takes up space, but it does not have shape. Liquid in a container takes that container's shape. Water is a liquid.
3. Gas does not take up space or have shape. Steam is a gas. When water boils, it turns to steam.

Connect and Compare

1. What should you do to the beans while they are simmering? **Written Directions**
2. Think about the recipes and the story *Mice and Beans*. Rosa María planned a menu for the party. Write a menu that includes the food you would like to have at a party.
Reading/Writing Across Texts

 Science Activity

Think about your favorite recipe. Write the steps and describe the solids, liquids, and gases.

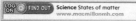 **Science** States of matter
www.macmillanmh.com

159

- Point to the part that tells what you do to make the rice.

- Read step 2 with me.

- Think about what happens to the rice. It becomes toasted. When we toast bread, what happens to the color? (It turns brown.) *So what happens to rice when it becomes toasted?* (It turns brown.)

- On page 156, it says that heating solids makes them turn brown or get soft. Which happens to the rice? (It turns brown.) *Which happens to the onions and peppers?* (They get soft.)

- Now let's read step 5 together to learn what happens to the rice: Simmer for 20 to 25 minutes, or until the liquid has been soaked up. Do not stir while simmering or the rice will be mushy. *During this step, does the solid rice get brown or soft?* (soft)

Page 158

Text

- This is the recipe to make the beans. Let's list the solids together: beans, onion, garlic, salt, pepper. *Let's list the liquids together:* chicken or vegetable broth, water.

Page 159

Text

- Ice, water, and steam are the same material, but they are in three different states. Which is a liquid? (water) *Which is a gas?* (steam) *Which is a solid?* (ice)

- Why do we need to know about solids, liquids, and gases when we cook? (so we'll know what to do to the food to make it turn out the way we want it to)

 Work with your partner to write a recipe. Label each food in the *What You Need* part to show whether it is a solid or liquid.

Name _____

Use the word chart to study this week's vocabulary words.
Write a sentence using each word in your writer's notebook.

Word	Context Sentence	Illustration
menu _____	Yum! The picnic <u>menu</u> listed my favorite foods.	**What things might you find on a picnic menu?**
fetch _____	We went to <u>fetch</u> the food from the house.	**Does *fetch* mean to catch something or to run and bring it back?**
simmered _____	The soup <u>simmered</u> for an hour before it was done.	
assembled _____	We <u>assembled</u> all the food for the picnic.	
devoured _____	Greg <u>devoured</u> his lunch before anyone else.	

© Macmillan/McGraw-Hill

Read each question and prompt. Discuss the answers with your group. Use your Leveled Reader to find details to support your answers. Then write your answers on the blank lines or on another sheet of paper.

1. The characters are getting ready for a party. What kind of party is it?

   _____

2. In each story, the characters go shopping or get ingredients to make something. Tell what the main character in your story had to get.

   _____

3. The stories seem to be about real people. Talk about the details that make your story a fantasy, too.

   _____

4. Describe something in your story that is about math or art.

   _____

5. What did you learn from the story you read? Share with your classmates.

   _____

6. Write one question about the book to ask your group.

   _____

Weekly Planners

Week 1

Selections	Vocabulary		ELL Practice Book
	Key Selection Words/Cognates	Academic Language/Cognates	
The Tiny Seed *Plant Parts*	burst drifts drowns gently neighbor desert *desierto*	summarize context clues draw conclusion *conclusión* pronoun *pronombre* singular *singular* plural *plural*	• Phonics, pp. 101–102 • Vocabulary, p. 103 • Grammar, p. 104 • Book Talk, p. 105

Week 2

Selections	Vocabulary		ELL Practice Book
	Key Selection Words/Cognates	Academic Language/Cognates	
The Ugly Vegetables *The Water Cycle*	scent trade prickly blooming muscles *músculos* aroma *aroma*	summarize sequence *secuencia* events *eventos* pronouns *pronombres*	• Phonics, pp. 106–107 • Vocabulary, p. 108 • Grammar, p. 109 • Book Talk, p. 110

Week 3

TIME FOR KIDS®

	Vocabulary		ELL Practice Book
	Key Selection Words/Cognates	Academic Language/Cognates	
Meet the Super Croc	ancient hopeful unable confirm *confirmar* valid *válido* site *sitio*	summarize monitor adjust reading rate comprehension *comprensión*	• Phonics, pp. 111–112 • Vocabulary, p. 113 • Grammar, p. 114 • Book Talk, p. 115

Week 4

Selections	Vocabulary		ELL Practice Book
	Key Selection Words/Cognates	Academic Language/Cognates	
Farfallina and Marcel *Butterflies*	giggled fluttered peered vanished snuggled recognized *reconocer*	monitor comprehension reread inference *inferencia* contraction *contracción* synonyms *sinónimos*	• Phonics, pp. 116–117 • Vocabulary, p. 118 • Grammar, p. 119 • Book Talk, p. 120

Week 5

Selections	Vocabulary		ELL Practice Book
	Key Selection Words/Cognates	Academic Language/Cognates	
Nutik, the Wolf Pup *Wolves*	beloved promised wiggled gleamed glanced noble *noble*	monitor adjust reading rate inflected verbs base words inference *inferencia*	• Phonics, pp. 121–122 • Vocabulary, p. 123 • Grammar, p. 124 • Book Talk, p. 125

Student Response Strategies

Use the following strategies to help English Language Learners move to the next proficiency level.

✔ **WAIT** Give children ample time.

- Let children know that they can respond in different ways depending on their levels of proficiency, but all should be encouraged to answer questions related to the main point of the picture or text.

- Allow children to respond in their native language if they are very limited proficient. Ask a more proficient ELL student to repeat the answer in English.

✔ **REPEAT** If the child's response is correct, the teacher can repeat what the child has said. The teacher should repeat in a clear, loud voice that all can hear and at a slower pace.

✔ **REVISE for FORM** Generally the teacher will be repeating what the child has said but with corrections for grammar and pronunciation. The correction can be implicit or explicit (where teacher calls attention to the correction).

✔ **REVISE for MEANING** Teachers should also correct for meaning.

✔ **ELABORATE** Here, the teacher elaborates on a child's response or states the response in another way in order to more fully develop children's comprehension and oral language proficiency.

✔ **ELICIT** Finally, the teacher can also elicit a more comprehensive response from the child by prompting the child for further information.

Newcomers

Basic and Social Language Each week you will be focusing on an important aspect of classroom communication to teach or reinforce with your newcomers. Children will expand and internalize initial English vocabulary by learning and using routine language needed for classroom communication.

Articles of Clothing Teach and/or reinforce the names of clothing using the sentence frames *It is a _____* and *I have a _____*. Prompt children to use adjectives and nouns to complete each sentence, for example, *I have a blue shirt*.

Apologies Teach and/or reinforce basic courtesies in English, such as *Excuse me* and *I'm sorry*. Provide situations in which each is used. Model and provide practice opportunities for children throughout the day.

More Place and Position Introduce the sentence frames *Where is the _____? It is _____.* Teach the position and location words *behind, in front of, next to, on the bottom of,* and *on top of.* Model each using classroom objects. Then ask questions about the position of objects, and ask children to respond. Finally, prompt children to ask classmates about the position or location of objects.

LOG ON Have children use **Newcomer Games** to expand and internalize language needed for classroom communication.
www.macmillanmh.com

The Tiny Seed

Prior to reading the selection with children, they should have listened to the selection on **StudentWorks Plus**, the interactive eBook. In addition, selection vocabulary should have been pretaught using the **Visual Vocabulary Resources**.

Access Core Content

Teacher Note Pose the questions after you read the paragraph or page indicated.

Pages 176–177

Illustration

- *Look at this pretty flower. Do you like flowers? Where do you see flowers?* (Answers will vary.)

- *Flowers have parts. Let's look at the parts of this flower. These are petals.* (Point to the petals.) *Say it with me:* petals. *This flower has a lot of petals. Let's count them.* (Point to each petal as you count with children.)

- *This is the stem.* (Point to the stem.) *Say it with me:* stem. *These are leaves.* (Point to the leaves.) *Say it with me:* leaves. *This flower has two leaves.*

Title

- *Let's read the title together:* The Tiny Seed. *A seed is small.* (Hold your index finger and thumb close together to indicate *small*.) *It goes in the ground. It grows and grows and becomes a plant.* (Move your hand up from the ground to indicate growing.)

- *Some seeds are very small. They are tiny. We are going to read about a tiny seed.*

Synonyms and Circumlocution

Remind children that they can ask for synonyms to help clarify words or expressions they do not understand. Ask, *What is another word for "autumn"?* (fall)

Comprehension

Genre
Informational Fiction is a made-up story that may give information about a real-life topic.

Summarize
Draw Conclusions
As you read, use your Conclusions Chart.

Fact Fact
Conclusion

Read to Find Out
What does the tiny seed need to grow?

176

It is Autumn.
A strong wind is blowing. It blows flower seeds high in the air and carries them far across the land. One of the seeds is tiny, smaller than any of the others.
Will it be able to keep up with the others?
And where are they all going?

178

Main Selection

The Tiny Seed

177

One of the seeds flies higher than the others.
Up, up it goes! It flies too high and the sun's rays
burn it up. But the tiny seed sails on with the others.

Draw Conclusions
How does the wind help
the seed?

179

Page 178

Illustration

- *Look at the trees. The wind is blowing the trees.* (Sway your arms back and forth like trees in the wind and make a blowing sound.) *Look at the seeds. Point to the smallest one. The wind is blowing the seeds.*

Text

- *It's autumn, or fall. Summer is finished. The wind blows seeds high in the air.* (Hold your hand high.) *The wind carries them far.* (Hold your hand high and move it from left to right to indicate distance.)

- *One seed is tiny.* (Point to the tinest seed.) *Can the tiny seed keep up with the other seeds? Let's read more to find out.*

Page 179

Illustration

- *Look at the sun. The sun has rays.* (Point to the rays.) *Say it with me:* rays. *The sun's rays are very hot. Do you see a seed very close to the sun's rays? Show your partner. What is happening to the seed?* (It's on fire.)

PARTNERS *Do you see the tiny seed on this page? Show your partner.*

Text

- *One seed flies higher than the other seeds.* (Hold one hand at face level and hold the other hand up higher.) *It burns up. It's on fire. Why does the seed burn up?* (It flies close to the sun.)

- *The tiny seed keeps going. It sails on—it flies—with the other seeds.*

- *Let's read the last line together:* But the tiny seed sails on with the others.

Page 180

Illustration

Look at this mountain. What's on top of the mountain? (snow and ice) *It's very cold there. Do you see the seed on top of the mountain? Show your partner. Show your partner. Tell your partner where the tiny seed is now.*

Text

- *One seed lands on a mountain.* (Make one hand land on the other.) *The mountain is icy. That means it is cold and covered with ice. The ice never melts. It never gets warm.*

Let's talk about the seed on the mountain. The mountain is a cold place. Can the seed grow there? (no) *Why not?* (It's cold.) *The story tells us this fact about the seed: It can't grow in a cold place. This fact can help us draw a conclusion. What kind of place does a seed need to grow?* (a warm place)

- *The other seeds fly on, or keep going. Let's read the last line together:* But the tiny seed does not go as fast as the others.

Page 181

Illustration

- *Look at the seeds. They fly on. They fly faster than the tiny seed.*

Page 182

Illustration

- *Look at this water. This is the ocean. Do you like to play in the ocean? Do you think a seed likes to be in the ocean? Why or why not?* (Questions are open.)

- *The tiny seed flies low.* (Hold one hand close to the ground.) *The other seeds fly high.* (Hold one hand high.) *The tiny seed does not fly as high as the others.*

Another seed lands on a tall and icy mountain. The ice never melts, and the seed cannot grow. The rest of the seeds fly on. But the tiny seed does not go as fast as the others.

180

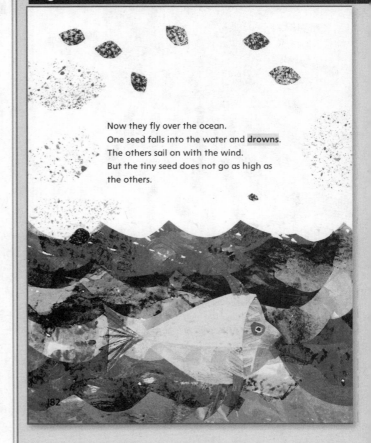

Now they fly over the ocean. One seed falls into the water and **drowns**. The others sail on with the wind. But the tiny seed does not go as high as the others.

182

181

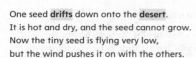

One seed **drifts** down onto the **desert**.
It is hot and dry, and the seed cannot grow.
Now the tiny seed is flying very low,
but the wind pushes it on with the others.

183

Text

- *The seeds fly over the ocean.* (Hold one hand out flat to represent the ocean and move the other above it to represent the seeds flying over.)

- *One seed falls.* (Drop one hand.) *It can't swim. It can't live in the water. So it drowns. Say it with me: drowns. The other seeds keep going high in the air.*

- *Let's read the last line together:* But the tiny does not go as high as the others.

Page 183

Illustration

- *Now the seeds fly over the desert. The desert is hot and dry. It doesn't rain much in the desert. Many things cannot grow in the desert.*

Text

- *One seed drifts down.* (Drift one hand down.) *The desert is hot and dry. The seed can't grow.*

 Let's talk about the seed in the desert. The desert is a dry place. Can the seed grow there? (no) *Why not?* (It's too dry. It doesn't rain.)

- *The tiny seed flies low.* (Hold one hand low.) *But it keeps going with the other seeds.*

Patterns in Language

Some grammatical structures, such as comparisons, pose difficulties to ELLs. Point out that there are several examples of comparisons using the construction *as . . . as,* such *as fast as* and *as high as.* Help children find a pattern.

Page 184

Illustration

- *Look at this bird. What is it eating?* (a seed) *Do you see the tiny seed? Show your partner. Do you think the bird will eat the tiny seed, too?* (Question is open.)

Text

- *The wind stops. The seeds fall down gently.* (Make one hand fall gently on the desk.) *They don't fall hard.* (Make one hand fall hard on the desk.) *They fall gently, like this.* (Repeat *gently* gesture.) *Say it with me:* gently.

- *A bird eats one seed. It doesn't eat the tiny seed. Why doesn't it eat the tiny seed?* (The tiny seed is so small that the bird can't see it.)

- *Let's read the last line together:* It is so small that the bird does not see it.

Page 185

Illustration

- *Do you see snow falling? Show your partner. It isn't autumn any more. Now it's winter.*

- *Look at this mouse. What is it doing?* (eating a seed)

- *The seeds and the mouse aren't on the grass. They are under the ground.* (Hold one hand under the other.)

Text

- *It's winter. The seeds are in the earth, under the ground. Snow falls and covers them.* (Move your fingers down to imitate falling snow, then rest that hand on top of the other for cover.)

- *A hungry mouse eats one seed. The tiny seed lies very still; it doesn't move. The mouse doesn't see the tiny seed. Sit still like the tiny mouse. Don't move!* (Demonstrate sitting still and encourage children to imitate you.) *Now the mouse can't see you.*

- *Let's read the last line together:* But the tiny seed lies very still and the mouse does not see it.

Pages 184–185

Finally the wind stops and the seeds fall **gently** down on the ground. A bird comes by and eats one seed. The tiny seed is not eaten. It is so small that the bird does not see it.

Pages 186–187

Now it is Spring.

After a few months the snow has melted. It is really Spring! Birds fly by. The sun shines. Rain falls. The seeds grow so round and full they start to **burst** open a little. Now they are not seeds any more. They are plants. First they send roots down into the earth. Then their little stems and leaves begin to grow up toward the sun and air. There is another plant that grows much faster than the new little plants. It is a big fat weed. And it takes all the sunlight and the rain away from one of the small new plants. And that little plant dies.

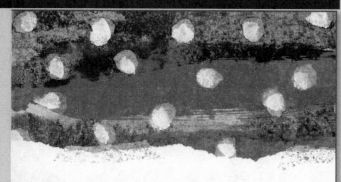

Now it is Winter.

After their long trip the seeds settle down. They look just as if they are going to sleep in the earth. Snow falls and covers them like a soft white blanket. A hungry mouse that also lives in the ground eats a seed for his lunch. But the tiny seed lies very still and the mouse does not see it.

185

The tiny seed hasn't begun to grow yet.
It will be too late! Hurry!
But finally it too starts to grow into a plant.

Page 186

Illustration

PARTNERS
Look at the pictures. (Point to the illustrations on pages 186 and 187.) *It isn't winter now. It's spring. How do you know it's spring and not winter? Tell your partner.* (It isn't snowing; it's raining. There are birds. There are flowers. It looks warm.)

- *Let's remember the parts of a plant. These are stems.* (Point to the stems.) *These are leaves.* (Point to the leaves.) *One part of the plant is under the ground.* (Point to the roots.) *These are roots. Say it with me:* roots.

Text

- *It's spring now. The snow is gone. The sun is shining. Rain is falling.* (Move your fingers down like falling raindrops.) *The seeds grow. Now they are plants. Their roots grow down.* (Point to the roots.) *Their stems and leaves grow up.* (Point to the stems and leaves.)

- *One plant is very big.* (Point to the weed.) *This little plant* (point to the little plant) *dies, it can't live, because the big plant takes all the sun and rain.*

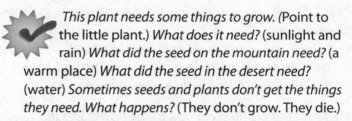
This plant needs some things to grow. (Point to the little plant.) *What does it need?* (sunlight and rain) *What did the seed on the mountain need?* (a warm place) *What did the seed in the desert need?* (water) *Sometimes seeds and plants don't get the things they need. What happens?* (They don't grow. They die.)

Page 187

Text

- *First, the tiny seed doesn't grow like the other seeds. It's late. But then it starts to grow.*

Illustration

- *The tiny seed is starting to grow.* (Point to the smallest plant on page 187.) *How many leaves does it have?* (one)

Page 188

Illustration

- *Look at this big foot stepping on the plant. Poor plant! It can't grow anymore.*

Text

- *It's warm. The children play outside. They like the springtime. One child walks on the plants. Why do you think he does that?* (He probably doesn't see them.)

- *The child breaks one of the plants.* (Mime breaking a pencil in two.) *Read the last sentence with me:* He breaks one! Now it cannot grow any more.

 The plants like the spring. They like the warm weather. Do you like to play outside in the warm weather? Tell your partner three things you like to do outside in the warm weather. (Responses will vary.)

Page 189

Illustration

- *Look at this tiny plant.* (Point to the small plant.) *It came from the tiny seed. It's still growing. How many leaves does it have now?* (two)

Page 190

Illustrations

- *The tiny plant is still growing.* (Direct children's attention to the illustrations on pages 190 and 191.) *How many leaves does it have now?* (three)

- *Look at this big flower.* (Point to the flower.) *It's the neighbor of the tiny plant. Neighbors live close by each other. Say it with me:* neighbor. *Do people live close by your house? They are your neighbors.*

- *The tiny plant has three leaves. How many leaves does the other plant have? Let's count.* (Point to each of the seven leaves as you count with the children.)

The warm weather also brings the children out to play. They too have been waiting for the sun and spring time. One child doesn't see the plants as he runs along and—Oh! He breaks one! Now it cannot grow any more.

188

The tiny plant that grew from the tiny seed is growing fast, but its **neighbor** grows even faster. Before the tiny plant has three leaves the other plant has seven! And look! A bud! And now even a flower!

190

189

Text

- *The tiny plant is growing fast.* (Move your hand up from floor to indicate growing.) *Its neighbor, the big plant, is growing even faster.*

- *The tiny plant has three leaves. How many leaves does its neighbor have?* (Count together.) *It has seven leaves. And it has a flower, too!*

Page 191

Illustration

- *Look at this boy's hand. What is he going to do?* (Pick the flower.)

Text

- *What's happening? We hear footsteps.* (Walk a few steps making footstep sounds.) *A hand reaches down and picks the flower.* (Reach down and mime picking a flower.) *A boy picks the flower. Will he keep it for himself or give it to a friend?* (give it to a friend)

But what is happening? First there are footsteps.
Then a shadow looms over them. Then a hand
reaches down and breaks off the flower.
A boy has picked the flower to give to a friend.

191

Pages 192–193

Illustrations

▪ *Look at this flower.* (Point to the tall flower.) *It's very tall.* (Hold your hand up as high as possible.) *Have you ever seen a flower this tall?* (Question is open.)

Text

▪ *It's summer. The tiny plant is alone. It grows and grows. It grows very tall.* (Hold your hand close to the ground and move it higher and higher as you talk.) *It's taller than everything. It's taller than the* people. (Point to the people.) *It's taller than the* trees. (Point to the trees.) *It's taller than the* house. (Point to the house.)

▪ *Everybody wants to see this tall flower. It is a giant flower. That means it is very, very big. Say it with me:* giant.

✦ *Let's stop here and remember the story. In the beginning, there were many seeds. In the spring, they started to _____.* (grow)*They became plants. The big weed took all the sun and _____.* (rain) *One plant died. A person stepped on another plant and it _____.* (broke) *A boy picked a _____.* (flower) *The tiny seed grew and grew. It became a giant _____.* flower)

Pages 192–193

It is Summer.

Now the tiny plant from the tiny seed
is all alone. It grows on and on. It doesn't stop.
The sun shines on it and the rain waters it.
It has many leaves. It grows taller and taller.
It is taller than the people. It is taller than
the trees. It is taller than the houses.
And now a flower grows on it. People come
from far and near to look at this flower.
It is the tallest flower they have ever seen.
It is a giant flower.

192

Pages 194–195

All summer long the birds and bees and butterflies come visiting. They have never seen such a big and beautiful flower.

194

Pages 194–195

Illustrations

- *Different animals come to visit the tall flower. There are birds.* (Point to the birds.) *There are butterflies.* (Point to the butterflies.) *Say it with me:* butterflies. *There are bees.* (Point to the bees.) *Say it with me:* bees.

 How many birds are there in the pictures? Count them with your partner. Then count the butterflies. Count the bees.

Text

- *Birds and bees and butterflies visit the flower.* (Point to each animal as you name it.) *They think the flower is very big and very beautiful. Do you think the flower is beautiful?* (Question is open.)

Pages 196–197

Illustration

PARTNERS *Summer is over. Now it is autumn again. Look at the picture. How do you know it's autumn now? Tell your partner.* (The leaves are different colors. The leaves fall off the trees.)

- *Look at the trees. Look at the leaves in the air. The wind is blowing.* (Sway arms back and forth like trees in the wind.) *Help me make the wind blow.* (Encourage children to imitate your gesture.)

- *Look at the flower. Look at its petals. Some of its petals came off. Do you see a petal in the air? Show your partner.*

Text

- *It's autumn. It's cooler now. The wind carries red and yellow leaves. The wind carries petals. The leaves and petals sail; they fly in the air. Some fall to the ground.* (Move your hand across in front of you for *sail*, then drop it for *fall*.)

Pages 198–199

Illustrations

- *There are a lot of seeds. Point to some of them. Is the wind blowing?* (yes) *How do you know the wind is blowing?* (The seeds are in the air. The seeds are flying. The flower is moving.)

- *The seeds come from here.* (Point to the center of the plant.) *This is the pod. Say it with me:* pod. *The pod is a part of the plant. It holds the seeds.*

196

The wind blows harder. The flower has lost almost all of its petals. It sways and bends away from the wind. But the wind grows stronger and shakes the flower. Once more the wind shakes the flower, and this time the flower's seed pod opens. Out come many tiny seeds that quickly sail far away on the wind.

198

Now it is Autumn again.

The days grow shorter. The nights grow cooler. And the wind carries yellow and red leaves past the flower. Some petals drop from the giant flower and they sail along with the bright leaves over the land and down to the ground.

Draw Conclusions
Use details from the text to help draw a conclusion about what may happen to the flower next.

197

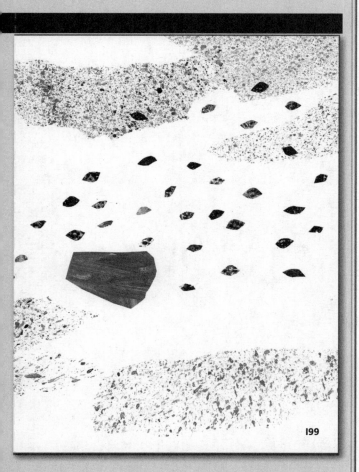

199

Text

- *The wind blows. The flower sways in the wind. Say and do it with me:* sway. (Hold your arm up and sway it. Encourage children to imitate your gesture.)

- *The flower bends in the wind. Say and do it with me:* bend. (Bend your wrist down.)

- *The flower shakes in the wind. Say and do it with me:* shake. (Shake your arm.)

- *The seed pod opens. Do it with me.* (Hold up a fist then burst it open.) *The seeds come out. They fly away with the wind. The whole story is starting over!*

Let's remember the story of the tiny seed. First it was a tiny seed. Then it grew and grew and became a giant plant. We know a fact about the seeds in the picture: They came from the plant that grew from the tiny seed plant. What do you think will happen to these seeds? (They will grow into giant plants.)

Plant Parts

Access Core Content

Teacher Note Pose the questions after you read the paragraph or page indicated.

Pages 202–203

Title

■ *Let's read the title together:* Plant Parts. *We are going to read about parts of plants. We already read about some plant parts. A flower is a plant part. What other plant parts do you remember?* (stem, petals, leaves, pod, seeds, roots)

Text

■ *A plant grows from a small seed into a big plant. A plant needs each part to grow. It also needs light. Where does the light come from?* (the sun)

■ *A plant also needs minerals. Say it with me:* minerals. *Minerals are like food for the plant. Minerals are in the soil. Soil is another word for* dirt.

Illustration and Labels

■ *Look at these tomatoes.* (Point to the tomatoes on page 203.) *Raise your hand if you like to eat tomatoes. Tomatoes grow on a plant like this.* (Point to the plant on page 202.)

■ *These boxes give us information about the tomato plant.* (Point to the labels around the illustration.)

■ *This word says* roots. (Point to the word in the box.) *Find the box that has the word* roots. *This box has an arrow. Follow the arrow with your finger.* (demonstrate) *What does the arrow show us?* (the roots) *This box tells us information about the roots. Let's read it together.*

■ *The roots are under the ground. They hold the plant. It doesn't fall.*

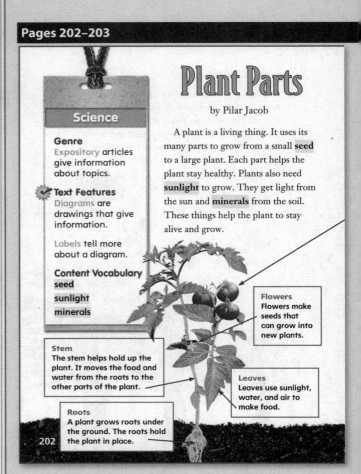

Science

Genre
Expository articles give information about topics.

Text Features
Diagrams are drawings that give information.

Labels tell more about a diagram.

Content Vocabulary
seed
sunlight
minerals

Plant Parts
by Pilar Jacob

A plant is a living thing. It uses its many parts to grow from a small **seed** to a large plant. Each part helps the plant stay healthy. Plants also need **sunlight** to grow. They get light from the sun and **minerals** from the soil. These things help the plant to stay alive and grow.

Flowers
Flowers make seeds that can grow into new plants.

Stem
The stem helps hold up the plant. It moves the food and water from the roots to the other parts of the plant.

Leaves
Leaves use sunlight, water, and air to make food.

Roots
A plant grows roots under the ground. The roots hold the plant in place.

202

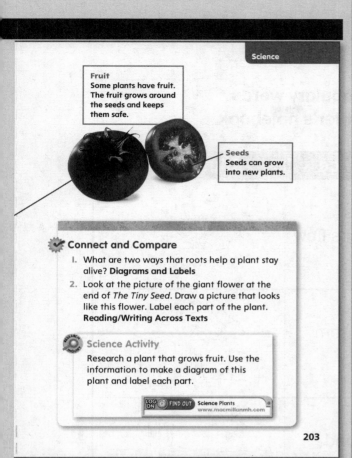

Science

Fruit
Some plants have fruit. The fruit grows around the seeds and keeps them safe.

Seeds
Seeds can grow into new plants.

Connect and Compare

1. What are two ways that roots help a plant stay alive? **Diagrams and Labels**

2. Look at the picture of the giant flower at the end of *The Tiny Seed*. Draw a picture that looks like this flower. Label each part of the plant. **Reading/Writing Across Texts**

Science Activity

Research a plant that grows fruit. Use the information to make a diagram of this plant and label each part.

 Science Plants
www.macmillanmh.com

203

- *This word is* stem. *(Point to the word in the box.) Find the box that has the word* stem. *Find the arrow. Follow the arrow to the stem with your finger. This box tells us information about the stem. Let's read it together.*

- *The stem moves food and water from the roots to the other parts of the plant. (Trace the route of food and water from roots through both stems.)*

- *This word is* leaves. *(Point to the word in the box.) Find the box that has the word* leaves. *Find the arrow and follow it to the leaf with your finger. Let's read this box together.*

- *The leaves make food for the plant.*

- *This word is* flowers. *(Point to the word in the box.) Find the box that has the word* flowers. *Find the arrow. Follow the arrow to the flower with your finger. Let's read it together.*

- *The flowers make seeds.*

- *This word is* fruit. *(Point to the word in the box on page 203.) Find the box that has the word* fruit. *Find the arrow and follow it to the fruit with your finger. Let's read this box together.*

- *The fruit grows around the seeds. The seeds are inside the fruit.*

- *This word is* seeds. *(Point to the word in the box.) Find the box that has the word* seeds. *Follow the arrow to the seeds with your finger. Let's read this box together.*

- *The seeds make new plants.*

- *Each part of the plant has a job. I am going to say a job. You tell me the part of the plant that does that job. They hold the plant in the ground. (roots) They move food and water through the plant. (stems) They make food for the plant. (leaves) They make seeds. (flowers)*

PARTNERS *Let's find the different plant parts. Show your partner the stem. Show your partner the roots. Show your partner some leaves. Show your partner the flower. Show your partner the fruit. Show your partner the seeds.*

Name _____

**Use the word chart to study this week's vocabulary words.
Write a sentence using each word in your writer's notebook.**

Word	Context Sentence	Illustration
burst _____	The seed pod burst open, and the seeds flew out.	
drifts _____	A leaf drifts down from the tree.	
desert _____	The desert is hot and dry.	
drowns _____	Do not drown the plant with water.	
gently _____	I gently picked some flowers in the garden.	**When else would you need to do something gently?**
neighbor _____	Our neighbor next door has many plants.	**What is the name of your neighbor?**

© Macmillan/McGraw-Hill

Read each question and prompt. Discuss the answers with your group. Use your Leveled Reader to find details to support your answers. Then write your answers on the blank lines or on another sheet of paper.

1. Describe some things that plants need to live.

   _____

2. Name the parts of a plant. Explain how those parts help the plant to grow.

   _____

3. Explain where pollen comes from and what it does.

   _____

4. Tell what can harm plants.

   _____

5. Explain what leaves do.

   _____

6. Write one question about the book to ask your group.

   _____

   _____

The Ugly Vegetables

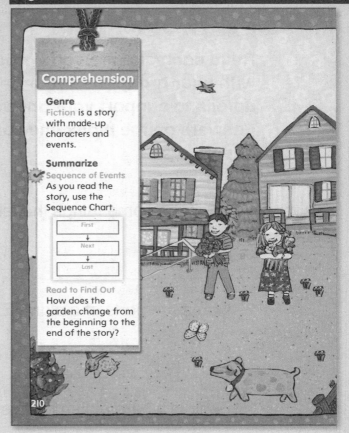

Pages 210–211

Prior to reading the selection with children, they should have listened to the selection on **StudentWorks Plus**, the interactive eBook. In addition, selection vocabulary should have been pretaught using the **Visual Vocabulary Resources**.

Access Core Content

Teacher Note Pose the questions after you read the paragraph or page indicated.

Pages 210–211

Title and Illustration

- *Let's read the title together:* The Ugly Vegetables. *A carrot is a vegetable. Lettuce is a vegetable.*

I like carrots. What kinds of vegetables do you like? Name some vegetables with your partner.

- *Look at the first picture. The children are holding flowers. Flowers are growing out of the ground, too. Point to them.*

- *Look at the mother and daughter in the other picture. They have shovels.* (Point to the shovels.) *Say it with me:* shovels. *They are using the shovels to dig.*

Page 212

Whole Page

- *The girl helps her mother start a garden. Do they start in the winter or spring?* (spring) *Is it hard work or easy work to dig a garden?* (hard work)

- *The girl sees little animals called worms.* (Point to the worms.) *Say it with me:* worms. *Worms live in the dirt. They wriggle, like this.* (Wriggle your fingers.) *Say and do it with me:* wriggle. *(Repeat the gesture and encourage children to imitate you.)*

- *The neighbor, Mrs. Crumerine, is digging, too.* (Point to the neighbor.) *She uses a small shovel.*

- *Let's read the last three lines together.*

Pages 212–213

In the spring I helped my mother start our garden. We used tall shovels to turn the grass upside down, and I saw pink worms wriggle around. It was hard work. When we stopped to rest, we saw that the neighbors were starting their gardens too.

"Hello, Irma!" my mother called to Mrs. Crumerine. Mrs. Crumerine was digging too. She was using a small shovel, one that fit in her hand.

"Mommy," I asked, "why are we using such big shovels? Mrs. Crumerine has a small one."

"Because our garden needs more digging," she said.

212

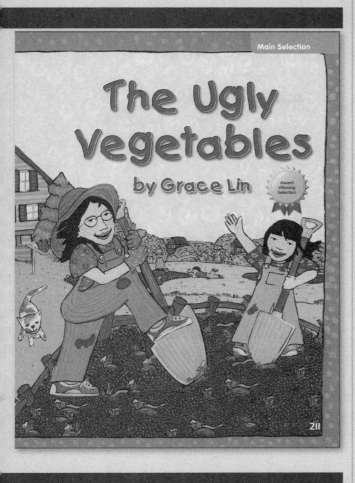

Main Selection

The Ugly Vegetables

by Grace Lin

Award Winning Selection

211

I helped my mother plant the seeds, and we dragged the hose to the garden. "Hi, Linda! Hi, Mickey!" I called to the Fitzgeralds. They were sprinkling water on their garden with green watering cans.

"Mommy," I asked, "why are we using a hose? Linda and Mickey use watering cans."

"Because our garden needs more water," she said.

213

Page 213

Illustration

- *Look at this hose.* (Point to the hose.) *Say it with me:* hose. *We use a hose to water a garden.* (*These are watering cans.* Point to the watering cans.) *Say it with me:* watering cans. *We also use watering cans to water a garden.*

Paragraph 1

- *The girl and her mother plant seeds. They put seeds in the ground. The seeds need water. What do the girl and her mother use to water the seeds?* (the hose)

- *The girl says hi to her neighbors, Linda and Mickey Fitzgerald.* (Point to the children.) *Linda and Mickey have watering cans.*

- *The Fitgeralds use watering cans to sprinkle water on the garden, like this.* (Mime sprinking water with a watering can on a few plants in an imaginary garden.) *Let's pretend to sprinkle water on some plants with a watering can.* (Encourage children to imitate you.)

Paragraphs 2 and 3

- *Let's read the last three lines together.*

The girl and her mother made a garden. Let's remember what they did first, second, and third. First, they used shovels to _____. (dig) *Second, they planted _____.* (seeds) *Third, they watered the seeds with a _____.* (hose)

Request Assistance

Remind children of expressions they can use to request assistance from the teacher or their partners, such as *Can you show me in the picture?*

Then my mother drew funny pictures on pieces of paper, and I stuck them into the garden.

"Hello, Roseanne!" my mother called across the street to Mrs. Angelhowe.

"Mommy," I asked, "why are we sticking these papers in the garden? Mrs. Angelhowe has seed packages in her garden."

"Because our garden is going to grow Chinese vegetables," she told me. "These are the names of the vegetables in Chinese, so I can tell which plants are growing where."

214

Page 214

Illustration

■ *Look at this seed package on a stick .* (Point to the marigold seed package in the corner of the page.) *It has flower seeds inside.*

■ *After people plant seeds, they sometimes put the empty packages in the garden.* (Point to the seed packages in the small garden.) *That helps them remember the kinds of seeds they planted.*

■ *The girl is holding some papers on sticks. Point to them. Let's read to find out what they are.*

Paragraphs 1–3

■ *The mother writes something on pieces of paper. Then she says hello to her neighbor, Mrs. Angelhowe. Where does the girl stick the pieces of paper?* (in the garden)

■ *The girl says:* "Mommy, why are we sticking these papers in the garden?" (Point to the papers.) "Mrs. Angelhowe has seed packages in her garden." (Point to the seed packages.)

Paragraph 4

■ *Is the girl's mother growing flowers or vegetables?* (vegetables) *She is growing Chinese vegetables.*

■ *The mother is writing the Chinese names of the vegetables on the paper. Why is she writing the names?* (so that she can remember the kinds of seeds she planted)

Page 215

Illustration

■ *The seeds in the girl's garden are beginning to grow.* (Point to the girl's sprouting garden.) *Do the stems look like leaves or like grass?* (like grass)

■ *Look at the neighbor's garden.* (Point to the neighbor's garden) *Do the stems look like little leaves or like grass?* (like little leaves)

Soon all the neighbors' gardens were **blooming**. Up and down the street grew rainbows of flowers.

216

One day I saw our garden growing. Little green stems that looked like grass had popped out from the ground.

"Our garden's growing!" I yelled. "Our garden's growing!"

I rushed over to the neighbors' gardens to see if theirs had grown. Their plants looked like little leaves.

"Mommy," I asked, "why do our plants look like grass? The neighbors' plants look different."

"Because they are growing flowers," she said.

"Why can't we grow flowers?" I asked.

"These are better than flowers," she said.

215

The wind always smelled sweet, and butterflies and bees flew everywhere. Everyone's garden was beautiful, except for ours.

217

Text

- *The little girl is excited and happy. Why does she feel this way?* (Her garden is growing.) *Let's read the second paragraph together in an excited voice:* "Our garden's growing!" I yelled. "Our garden's growing!"

- *What are the neighbors growing?* (flowers) *The little girl wants to grow flowers in her garden, too. What is growing in the girl's garden?* (vegetables)

- *Let's read the last two lines together.*

Page 216

Illustration

- *Look at all those pretty flowers. They're different colors. What colors do you see?* (purple, pink, yellow, orange)

- *This woman is picking flowers.* (Point to the woman picking flowers.) *What are other people doing?* (playing, sleeping, reading, climbing)

Text

- *All the flowers are blooming. That means they are opening up.* (Open up your hands to show blooming flowers.) *Say and do it with me:* blooming. (Lead children in opening up their hands.)

- *The flowers are many colors. The street looks like a rainbow, with many pretty colors.*

Page 217

Illustration

- *Look at this flower garden. Is it pretty or ugly?* (pretty) (Point to the vegetable garden.) *Look at this vegetable garden. The girl thinks it is ugly.*

- *This animal is a butterfly.* (Point to the butterflies.) *Say it with me:* butterfly. *This animal is a bee.* (Point to the bee near the top of page 216.) *Say it with me:* bee. *Do butterflies and bees like flowers?* (yes)

 There are many nice things in the picture. I see a rabbit. What do you see? Show and tell your partner three things. (Responses will vary.)

Text, Choral Reading

- *Let's read this page together.*

Page 218

Illustration

- The flower gardens had many colors. *What color do you see the most in the vegetable garden?* (green)

- *Look at the girl. Is she happy or sad?* (sad) *Is the mother happy or sad?* (happy)

Text

- *The girl does not like her garden. Let's read the first sentence together in an unhappy voice:* Ours was all dark green and ugly.

- *The girl asks:* "Why didn't we grow flowers?" *What does the mother answer.* ("These are better than flowers".) *The girl looks again. She still does not like what she sees.*

- *Many of the leaves are wrinkled, like this.* (Crumple a piece of paper and show children the wrinkles.) *Say it with me:* wrinkled.

- *The stems are prickly. When you touch a prickly stem, it hurts. Say it with me:* prickly.

Page 219

Whole Page

- *The vegetables grow. Some are big and lumpy.* (Point to one of the plants that are both yellow and green.) *Some are thin and green with bumps.* (Point to the thin green plant in front of the pink flower.)

- *Some are icky yellow.* (Point to one of the yellow plants.) *Say it with me:* icky yellow. *We say* icky *when something is very ugly.*

- *Let's read the last sentence together:* They were ugly vegetables.

Formal and Informal English

When children encounter a colloquial or informal word in the text, discuss other ways of saying the same word with more formal language. For example, *icky / repulsive*

Ours was all dark green and ugly.
"Why didn't we grow flowers?" I asked again.
"These are better than flowers," Mommy said again.
I looked, but saw only black-purple-green vines,
fuzzy wrinkled leaves, **prickly** stems, and a few little
yellow flowers.
"I don't think so," I said.
"You wait and see," Mommy said.

218

Sometimes I would go over to the neighbors' and look
at their pretty gardens. They would show the poppies and
peonies and petunias to me, and I would feel sad that our
garden wasn't as nice.

220

Before long, our vegetables grew. Some were big and lumpy. Some were thin and green and covered with bumps. Some were just plain icky yellow. They were ugly vegetables.

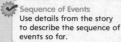

Sequence of Events
Use details from the story to describe the sequence of events so far.

219

One day my mother and I picked the vegetables from the garden. We filled a whole wheelbarrow full of them. We wheeled them to the kitchen. My mother washed them and took a big knife and started to chop them.

221

Let's talk about the changes in the garden. The seeds started to grow. First, they looked like _____. (grass) (Point to the grass on page 215.) *Then, they had wrinkled* _____ (leaves) *and prickly* _____. (stems) (Point to the leaves and stems on page 218.) *Now they are ugly* _____. (vegetables)

Page 220

Whole Page

- *There are different kinds of pretty flowers in the picture. Which ones do you like best?* (Responses will vary.)

- *The girl looks at the flowers in her neighbors' gardens. She sees poppies, peonies, and petunias. Why does the girl feel sad?* (Her garden isn't as nice as her neighbor's gardens.)

Page 221

Illustration

- *The vegetables are ready to eat now. They are in a wheelbarrow.* (Point to the wheelbarrow in the picture.) *Say it with me:* wheelbarrow.

Text

- *The girl and her mother pick the vegetables.* (Mime picking vegetables.) *They put the vegetables in the wheelbarrow. Let's pretend to pick vegetables and put them in a wheelbarrow.* (Mime the actions and encourage children to imitate you.)

- *Where do the mother and daughter take the vegetables?* (to the kitchen)

- *The mother washes the vegetables and she chops them, or cuts them into pieces. Let's pretend to chop vegetables.* (Mime chopping, using the side of your hand, and encourage children to imitate you.)

Page 222

Illustration

- *Look at this vegetable.* (Point to the vegetable in the girl's hand.) *It isn't smooth like the table.* (Run your hand along a table surface.) *It's bumpy.*

- *Now look at the shape of the vegetable. Is it straight like a pencil, or is it curled?* (Trace a curl in the air.) (It's curled.) *Say and do it with me:* curled. (Repeat the curling gesture and have children imitate you.)

Paragraph 1

- *When the mother cuts the vegetables, she uses all her muscles.* (Show your biceps.) *Say and do it with me:* muscles. (Show your biceps again and encourage children to imitate you.) *The vegetables are hard, like this.* (Knock on a table.)

Paragraph 2

- *The mother gives her daughter a bumpy, curled vegetable.* (Point to the bumpy, curled vegetable.) *She tells her the Chinese name. She says the Chinese names for all the vegetables.* (If there are Chinese children in the class, ask if they know these vegetables.)

Page 223

Illustration

- *Point to the girl. She is playing a game of ball with her neighbor, Mickey. Point to Mickey.*

Text

- *The girl plays with Mickey outside. She smells an aroma. Say it with me:* aroma. *An aroma is a very good or pleasing smell. All the neighbors smell the aroma.*

 Flowers smell nice. Tell your partner three other things that smell nice. (Responses will vary.)

Pages 222–223

"Aie-yow!" she said when she cut them. She had to use all her **muscles**. The vegetables were hard and tough.

"This is a sheau hwang gua," Mommy said, handing me a bumpy, curled vegetable. She pointed at the other vegetables. "This is shiann tsay. That's a torng hau."

> Sequence of Events
> Describe how the girl's mother prepares the vegetables. Put the steps in the correct sequence.

222

Pages 224–225

The wind carried it up and down the street. Even the bees and the butterflies seemed to smell the **scent** in the breeze.

224

I went outside to play. While I was playing catch with Mickey, a magical **aroma** filled the air. I saw the neighbors standing on their porches with their eyes closed, smelling the sky. They took deep breaths of air, like they were trying to eat the smell.

223

I smelled it too. It made me hungry, and it was coming from my house!

225

Page 224

Illustration

■ *Look, everybody smells the nice aroma.* (Run your finger along the "aroma" in the illustration.) *Let's read to find out what it is.*

Text

■ *The scent moves up and down the street. The butterflies and bees smell it too. What carries the pretty smell?* (the wind)

■ *Now we know three words that have the same meaning:* aroma, smell, scent. *Say them with me:* smell, aroma, scent.

Page 225

Whole Page, Choral Reading

■ *Let's read this page together:* I smelled it too. It made me hungry, and it was coming from my house!

■ *The aroma makes the girl feel hungry. Do you think the aroma comes from food?* (yes)

Text

- *The girl follows the aroma to her house. What does her mother put on the table?* (soup)

- *The girl tastes the soup. Does she like it?* (yes) *How do you know she likes it?* (She says that it is good. She smiles.)

Paragraphs 4–7

- *Did the mother use pretty flowers to make the soup?* (no) *What did she use?* (the ugly vegetables)

Illustration

 Look at the soup. What colors do you see? Show and tell your partner.

Page 228

Illustration

- *Look at the picture on this page and the next page. Point to all the flowers.*

- *Now point to the dog. What is it doing?* (eating soup) *All the neighbors are eating soup, too. Do they like it?* (yes) *How do you know they like it?* (They're smiling. They look happy.)

Paragraph 1

- *All the neighbors are at the door. What are they holding?* (flowers)

When I followed it to my house, my mother was putting a big bowl of soup on the table. The soup was yellow and red and green and pink.

"This is a special soup," Mommy said, and she smiled.

She gave me a small bowl full of it and I tasted it. It was so good! The flavors of the soup seemed to dance in my mouth and laugh all the way down to my stomach. I smiled.

"Do you like it?" Mommy asked me.

I nodded and held out my bowl for some more.

"It's made from our vegetables," she told me.

Then the doorbell rang, and we ran to open the door.

226

All our neighbors were standing at the door holding flowers.

"We noticed you were cooking." Mr. Fitzgerald laughed as he held out his flowers. "And we thought maybe you might be interested in a **trade**!"

We laughed too, and my mother gave them each their own bowl of her special soup.

228

227

My mother told them what each vegetable was
and how she grew it. She gave them the soup recipe
and put some soup into jars for them to take home.
I ate five bowls of soup.

It was the best dinner ever.

229

Paragraphs 2–3

- *Mr. Fitzgerald says that he noticed that the girl's mother was cooking. Do you think that he saw her cooking, or did he figure it out some other way?* (He figured it out some other way.) *He smelled the soup!*

- *Mr. Fitzgerald holds out the flowers and says that he is interested in a trade. When you make a trade, you give something to get something else. Say it with me:* trade. *Mr. Fitzgerald wants to trade flowers for soup. Does he get soup?* (yes) *Do all the neighbors get soup?* (yes)

Page 229

Whole Page

- *The mother tells the neighbors about the vegetables. She gives them the soup recipe. A recipe tells how to make something. She also gives them soup to take home.*

- *How many bowls of soup does the girl eat?* (five)

- *Before, the girl didn't like the ugly vegetables. Does she like them now?* (yes) *How do you know she likes them?* (She says: It was the best dinner ever. She's smiling in the picture.)

Pages 230–231

Illustration

Show your partner a flower garden in the picture. Show your partner a vegetable garden. Show your partner a shovel. Show your partner a butterfly.

Paragraph 1

- *The next spring, the mother and daughter plant vegetables, and they plant flowers, too. What do the neighbors plant?* (the same thing; vegetables and flowers)

Paragraph 2

- *Everybody plants Chinese vegetables next to their flowers.*

- *The seeds start to grow. Some look like grass. Those aren't flowers. They are _____.* (vegetables)

- *Some look like leaves. Those aren't vegetables. They are _____.* (flowers)

- *Soon the flowers are blooming; they open up.* (Open up your hands like blooming flowers.)

- *Soon there is an aroma, a good smell in the air. It isn't the flowers. What is it?* (soup)

- *Let's talk about the things that happened in the story in order. First, the mother and daughter made a garden. What did they do first—dig with shovels or plant seeds?* (dig with shovels)

- *Then, the garden grew. What did the girl see in her garden first—ugly vegetables or little green stems?* (little green stems)

- *What did the girl see in the neighbors' gardens first—pretty flowers or little green leaves?* (little green leaves)

Pages 230–231

The next spring, when my mother was starting her garden, we planted some flowers next to the Chinese vegetables. Mrs. Crumerine, the Fitzgeralds, and the Angelhowes planted some Chinese vegetables next to their flowers.

Soon the whole neighborhood was growing Chinese vegetables in their gardens. Up and down the street, little green plants poked out of the ground. Some looked like leaves and some looked like grass, and when the flowers started blooming, you could smell soup in the air.

230

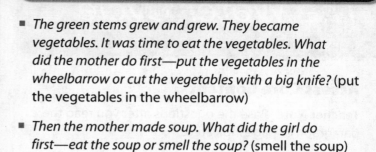

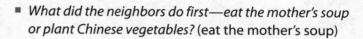

- *The green stems grew and grew. They became vegetables. It was time to eat the vegetables. What did the mother do first—put the vegetables in the wheelbarrow or cut the vegetables with a big knife?* (put the vegetables in the wheelbarrow)

- *Then the mother made soup. What did the girl do first—eat the soup or smell the soup?* (smell the soup)

- *What did the neighbors do first—eat the mother's soup or plant Chinese vegetables?* (eat the mother's soup)

231

The Water Cycle

Access Core Content

Teacher Note Pose the questions after you read the paragraph or page indicated.

Page 234

Photo

- *Look at all these leaves. (Point to the leaves.) Do you see water drops on them? Show your partner the water drops.*

Title

- *Let's read the title together: The Water Cycle. We will learn how water changes to vapor and then changes back to water again. This is called a cycle. In a cycle, things happen in a certain order. Each thing leads to the next. The things happen over and over again in the same order.*

Text

- *We can find water in the ocean. Tell me two more places where we can find water.* (rivers and lakes)

- *The sun heats the water, and the water turns into vapor. Say it with me: vapor. When water turns into vapor, we say the water evaporates. Say it with me: evaporates. Can we see water vapor in the air?* (no)

Page 235

Paragraph 1

- *The air cools the water vapor. The vapor turns back into water drops. We call this condensation. Say it with me: condensation.*

- *Clouds may look like soft pillows in the sky. But clouds are really made out of many water drops.*

Paragraphs 2 and 3

- *The water drops may fall from the sky as rain. If the air is very cold, the drops may freeze, or turn to ice. Then they may come down from the sky as snow, sleet, or hail.*

- *Rain, snow, sleet, and hail are all made out of water drops. When the drops fall from the sky, they fill up the oceans, lakes, and rivers with water.*

Science

Genre
Expository text gives information and facts about a topic.

Text Feature
Step-by-Step Directions tell you the steps for how to do something or make something.

Content Vocabulary
evaporate
water vapor
condensation

The Water Cycle

by Linda B. Ross

Water can be found all around us in oceans, rivers, and lakes, and even on the ground. When the sun shines down, it heats up the water. Then the water will **evaporate** and become a gas called water vapor. **Water vapor** floats in the air, but we can't see it.

234

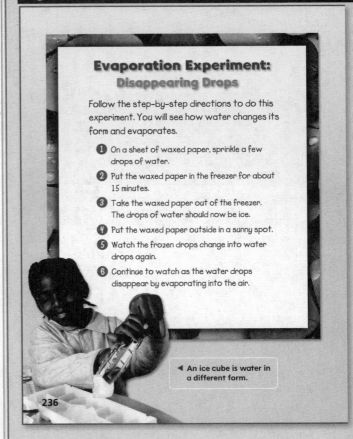

Evaporation Experiment:
Disappearing Drops

Follow the step-by-step directions to do this experiment. You will see how water changes its form and evaporates.

1. On a sheet of waxed paper, sprinkle a few drops of water.
2. Put the waxed paper in the freezer for about 15 minutes.
3. Take the waxed paper out of the freezer. The drops of water should now be ice.
4. Put the waxed paper outside in a sunny spot.
5. Watch the frozen drops change into water drops again.
6. Continue to watch as the water drops disappear by evaporating into the air.

◄ An ice cube is water in a different form.

236

When water vapor rises in the air, it cools off and changes into tiny drops of water. This is called **condensation**. As the tiny drops get bigger and come together, they form clouds.

When the water drops get too heavy, they come down as rain. If the air happens to be very cold, then snow, sleet, or hail may fall.

Rain, snow, sleet, and hail are all forms of water. This water wets the earth and fills our oceans, rivers, and lakes once again. That is how the water cycle keeps going. It is a journey that never ends.

How the Water Cycle Works

Condensation occurs when water vapor forms clouds.

Water falls as rain, snow, sleet, or hail.

Water evaporates.

Oceans / Lakes / Rivers / Groundwater

235

Water is an important part of our environment. All living things—plants, animals, and people—need water to live.

The water cycle helps water move through our environment.

 Connect and Compare

1. What happens in step 5 of the experiment? What do the water drops become? **Step-by-Step Directions**

2. Think about this selection and *The Ugly Vegetables*. What smell floated through the air? Explain how this happened. **Reading/Writing Across Texts**

Science Activity

As a class, we will make a list of ways we can conserve water. Choose one example and illustrate a poster showing how people can save water.

 **Science** Water Cycle www.macmillanmh.com

237

Diagram

- *Let's read the title together:* How The Water Cycle Works. *The arrows show what happens next in the cycle.*

- *Point to the water at the bottom of the diagram. With your finger, follow the arrows as we read the steps in the water cycle together.*

 What special clothes do people wear when it rains? What special clothes do people wear when it snows? Tell your partner.

Page 236

Heading

- *Listen while I read the heading:* Evaporation Experiment: Disappearing Drops. *Now read it after me. An experiment is a test to discover or prove something. This experiment is to prove how water evaporates, or disappears, into the air.*

Text and Photo

 (Point to numbered steps.) *These steps tell us what to do first and what to do next. They tell us the right order to do the parts of the experiment. Let's read the steps together.*

- *The first step says to put drops of water on a piece of paper. What does the second step say?* (Put the paper in the freezer.)

- *Think about snow, sleet, and hail. In the freezer, the water turns to ice. Look at the photo at the bottom of the page. What is the girl doing?* (removing an ice cube from a tray) *Let's read the caption together.*

- *Next, we take the paper out and put it in the sun. We watch the ice turn back to water. What happens in the last step?* (We watch the water disappear, or evaporate.) *The water turns to vapor. It's in the air, but we can't see it.*

Page 237

Photo

- *Do you think these children like the rain? How do you know?* (They like it. They are smiling.)

Text

- *Why is water important?* (All living things need water to live.) *Why is the water cycle important?* (It helps water move through the environment.)

Name _____

Use the word chart to study this week's vocabulary words.
Write a sentence using each word in your writer's notebook.

Word	Context Sentence	Illustration
scent _____	Roses have a sweet <u>scent</u>.	**Is a scent something you see or something you smell?**
trade _____	She <u>traded</u> a large plant for some apples.	
muscles _____	He has strong <u>muscles</u>.	
prickly _____	This plant has a <u>prickly</u> stem.	
blooming _____	One flower is <u>blooming</u>.	
aroma _____	I love the <u>aroma</u> of our vegetable soup.	**What aroma do you like?**

Read each question and prompt. Discuss the answers with your group. Use your Leveled Reader to find details to support your answers. Then write your answers on the blank lines or on another sheet of paper.

1. Tell what you learned about the history of tomatoes.

   _____

2. Explain what conditions tomatoes need to grow.

   _____

3. List what foods come from tomatoes.

   _____

4. Tell your classmates what your favorites are.

   _____

5. Explain why tomatoes are good for you.

   _____

6. Write one question about the book to ask your group.

   _____

   _____

Meet the Super Croc

Pages 244–245

Prior to reading the selection with children, they should have listened to the selection on **StudentWorks Plus**, the interactive eBook. In addition, selection vocabulary should have been pretaught using the **Visual Vocabulary Resources**.

Access Core Content

Teacher Note Pose the questions after you read the paragraph or page indicated.

Page 244

Title

■ *Read the title with me:* Meet the Super Croc. *Now, let's read the question under the title:* Did a crocodile the size of a school bus once live on Earth? *Why do you think the author started with this question?* (to get people interested in the article)

Illustration and Paragraph

■ *Look at the picture at the bottom of page 244. It shows what this giant crocodile looked like. Imagine a car parked beside the animal. Would the car be shorter, longer, or the same size as this crocodile?* (shorter because the crocodile was as long as a school bus)

■ *The crocodile's jaws were about five feet long. That's as long as this!* (Use your hand to show five feet in relation to your height.) *These are my jaws.* (Point to your jaws.) *Point to the jaws in the picture.*

Page 245

Illustrations

■ *Look at the pictures of crocodiles at the bottom of page 245. These crocs are alive today. Let's compare them to "Super Croc."*

■ *Point to the light-colored crocodile. This kind of crocodile is from Australia. Look at the line that says,* Length. *It tells that the crocodile can be as long as 23 feet long. Rememer that a "Super Croc" could be up to 50 feet long. Is an Australian crocodile longer or shorter than a "Super Croc"?* (shorter).

Pages 244–245

Real World Reading

Comprehension

Genre
Expository text gives information about real people, things, or events.

Adjust Reading Rate
Summarize
To summarize a selection, you tell only the most important ideas without retelling the whole selection.

Meet the Super Croc

Did a crocodile the size of a school bus once live on Earth?

What kind of animal was it? Its body was about 40 feet long. That's about the size of a school bus. Its jaws were about 5 feet long. That's about as long as some people are tall! It had about 100 teeth.

Name: *Sarcosuchus imperator* ("Super Croc")
Length: Up to 50 feet
Weight: About 17,500 pounds
Lived: About 110 million years ago

244

Pages 246–247

Paul Sereno shows the skull of "Super Croc."

Paul Sereno, a scientist, was the leader of a team of scientists who found the bones of the animal. They discovered them at a **site** in Niger, a country in Africa.

Sereno and his team were **hopeful** the bones belonged to a kind of giant crocodile from the time of the dinosaurs. But they weren't sure. The whole team needed to study the bones before they could **confirm** their theory. They compared the bones to the bodies of crocodiles living today. If the bones were similar, the theory would be **valid**.

AFRICA
NIGER Site of discovery
Agadez

These maps show the country in Africa where "Super Croc" fossils were found.

246

This powerful creature hid in the water, waiting for an animal to come to the river for a drink. Any animal that was grabbed by those teeth would be **unable** to get away.

Don't worry! This toothy giant is no longer alive today. It lived about 110 million years ago, when dinosaurs roamed Earth. That's about 105 million years before human beings were around.

This drawing shows what scientists think "Super Croc" looked like.

Name: Australian crocodile
Length: Up to 23 feet
Weight: About 2,000 pounds
Lived: Alive today

Name: American alligator
Length: Up to 20 feet
Weight: About 1,300 pounds
Lived: Alive today

245

- *Look at the picture of the alligator on the right. Let's read what it says above the picture. What is similar about the two animals?* (They are similar in length.)

Paragraphs 1 and 2

- *Let's pretend to be a "Super Croc." Pretend to hide under the water. Pretend to see an animal at the edge of the water. Watch it with your big eyes. Now, chomp with your big pointy teeth.*

- *Giant crocodiles lived during the time of dinosaurs. What do you know about dinosaurs? Describe animals a "Super Croc" would have seen as it wandered around.* (Children will share prior knowledge about dinosaurs.)

Page 246

Whole Page

- *Find the map of Africa. Point to the dark part in the map on the left. It shows where Sereno found the bones. The map in the middle shows a close up of the place.*

PARTNERS *How might you feel if you had been Paul and found the bones? Tell your partner what you might have said.* (Responses will vary.)

Page 247

Paragraph 1

- *What proved that the bones belonged to a kind of giant crocodile?* (The proof was that the bones were like the bones of crocodiles living today.)

Whole Article

Summarize, or retell, what you learned about "Super Croc." ("Super Croc" was a kind of giant crocodile that lived during the time of the dinosaurs. Paul Sereno discovered some "Super Croc" bones in Africa.)

The shape of the head and skull bones gave Sereno and his team the proof they were looking for. The **ancient** bones belonged to a "Super Croc" that lived at the same time the dinosaurs lived on Earth.

Sereno made copies of the bones to keep in the United States. The original bones were sent back to the country of Niger. If you want to see the real "Super Croc," the bones are on display in a museum there.

A young boy checks out the model of "Super Croc."

Think and Compare

1. What type of bones did Paul Sereno find?

2. What steps were taken to prove Sereno's theory?

3. How would you summarize this selection?

4. Compare the creature described in "Boy Finds Fossils!" with "Super Croc." How are they the same? How are they different?

247

Use the word chart to study this week's vocabulary words.
Write a sentence using each word in your writer's notebook.

Word	Context Sentence	Illustration
ancient _____	Dinosaurs lived in an <u>ancient</u> time.	
hopeful _____	Carla is <u>hopeful</u> that she will make a basket.	**What are you hopeful of doing some day?**
unable _____	We were <u>unable</u> to visit the museum.	
confirm _____	Use a dictionary to <u>confirm</u> how a word is spelled.	
valid _____	This answer is not <u>valid</u>.	3 + 3 = 6 1 + 1 = 2 2 + 2 = 5 X
site _____	We found a lot of pottery at this <u>site</u>.	

Read each question and prompt. Discuss the answers with your group. Use your Leveled Reader to find details to support your answers. Then write your answers on the blank lines or on another sheet of paper.

1. Describe the difference between a fossil and a living fossil.

   _____

2. Tell why scientists think horseshoe crabs have lived for so long.

   _____

3. Explain why discovering more living fossils is important.

   _____

4. Share with your classmates some fun facts you've learned about sharks.

   _____

5. Talk about some facts you learned about crocodiles.

   _____

6. Write one question about the book to ask your group.

   _____

   _____

Farfallina and Marcel

Pages 256–257

Prior to reading the selection with children, they should have listened to the selection on **StudentWorks Plus**, the interactive eBook. In addition, selection vocabulary should have been pretaught using the **Visual Vocabulary Resources**.

Access Core Content

Teacher Note Pose the questions after you read the paragraph or page indicated.

Pages 256–257

Title

- *The title of this story is* Farfallina and Marcel. (Point to the title.) *Farfallina and Marcel are the names of the main characters. Say them with me:* Farfallina and Marcel.

Illustration

- *We can see the main characters in the picture. Point to the bird. Point to the caterpillar.*

Page 258

Text and Illustration

- *Rain splashes and splatters. That means it's falling and bouncing off of things like the pond and the leaf.*

- *Look at the picture. Farfallina is on her leaf. Is Farfallina the caterpillar or the bird?* (the caterpillar) *Point to the dry part of the leaf. That's what Farfallina is eating.*

- *Let's read the fifth and sixth lines together:* "Hey," said a little voice. "You're eating my umbrella." *Look at the picture. Who is talking to Farfallina?* (the bird) *The bird is called Marcel.*

Formal and Informal English

When children encounter a colloquial or informal word in the text, discuss other ways of saying the same word with more formal language. For example, *Hey! / Excuse me.*

Pages 256–257

Comprehension

Genre
Fantasy is a story that has made-up characters, settings, or other things that could not happen in real life.

Reread
Make Inferences
As you read, use your Inference Chart.

What I Read → What I Know
Inference

Read to Find Out
How do you know Farfallina and Marcel are good friends?

256

Pages 258–259

The rain fell all morning.
It splattered on the pond and
splashed on Farfallina's leaf.
She found a dry spot and ate it.
"Hey," said a little voice.
"You're eating my umbrella."
Farfallina **peered** over the edge.
A small gray bird was huddled underneath.

258

Main Selection

Farfallina & Marcel

by Holly Keller

257

- *An umbrella keeps us dry when it rains. We stand under it.* (Draw a stick figure with an open umbrella.) *Marcel tells Farfallina to stop eating his umbrella. What do you think the umbrella is?* (the leaf) *How do you know?* (That's what Farfallina is eating.)

 Let's figure out why Marcel calls the leaf an umbrella. Do we stand under an umbrella or on top of it to stay dry? (under it) *Look at the picture. Is Marcel under the leaf or on top of it?* (under it) *What will happen to Marcel if Farfallina eats the leaf?* (He will get wet.)

- *Farfallina hears Marcel, but she doesn't know who is talking. So she peers, or looks, over the edge of the leaf.* (Point to the edge.) *What does she want to see?* (who is talking) *What does she see?* (Marcel, a small gray bird)

- *Marcel is huddled underneath the leaf. That means he is curled up under it.* (Demonstrate huddling.) *Let's stand and then bend down and huddle.*

- *It's raining. Why do you think Marcel is huddling?* (to fit better under the leaf so he won't get wet)

Page 259

Whole Page

- *Look at the picture. Do Farfallina and Marcel look friendly or angry?* (friendly) *They are becoming friends.*

- *Farfallina likes Marcel's soft feathers and gentle eyes. She slides down to be with him. What does Marcel like about Farfallina?* (her smile and pretty colors)

PARTNERS *Talk with a partner about new friends you have made. What kinds of things make you want to be friends with someone?* (Question is open.)

Farfallina liked his soft feathers and his gentle eyes.
"I'm Farfallina," she said,
and she slid down to the ground.
"My name is Marcel," said the bird.
He liked Farfallina's smile and her pretty colors.

259

Page 260

Text

- *The rain turns to drizzle. Farfallina wants to play now. Do you think* that drizzle is light rain or heavy rain? (light rain)

- *Farfallina wants to hide. Who does she want to look for her?* (Marcel)

- *This game is called* hide-and-seek *or* hide-and-go-seek. *One person hides, and others look for the person. When the hiding person is found, someone else hides. Does Marcel want to play the game?* (yes)

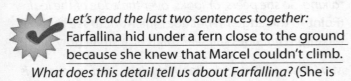 *Let's read the last two sentences together:* Farfallina hid under a fern close to the ground because she knew that Marcel couldn't climb. *What does this detail tell us about Farfallina?* (She is kind. She plays fair. She is a good friend.)

Illustration

- *Farfallina hides under a fern. Look at the picture. What do you think a fern is?* (a kind of plant)

Page 261

Whole Page

- *Marcel is kind, too. What does he know about the way Farfallina moves?* (He knows that she moves slowly.) *So he doesn't want to go far.*

- *Look at the picture. Where is Marcel hiding?* (behind the tree) *Is Marcel close to Farfallina or faraway?* (He is close to her. She is in front of the tree.)

Page 262

Text

- *An inch is a very small distance.* (Use two fingers to demonstrate.) *Farfallina is very small. She inches her way up Marcel's back. That means she moves up his back slowly, inch by inch.*

The rain turned to drizzle, and Farfallina wanted to play.
"I'll hide and you find me," she said.
Marcel agreed.
Farfallina hid under a fern close to the ground
because she knew that Marcel couldn't climb.

260

"I can take you for a ride on the pond," said Marcel.
Farfallina inched her way up to Marcel's back.
"You tickle," said Marcel, and he slipped into the water.
Farfallina **giggled**.
"There's so much to see," she said.
Farfallina and Marcel played together every day.
They liked the same games, and they liked each other.

262

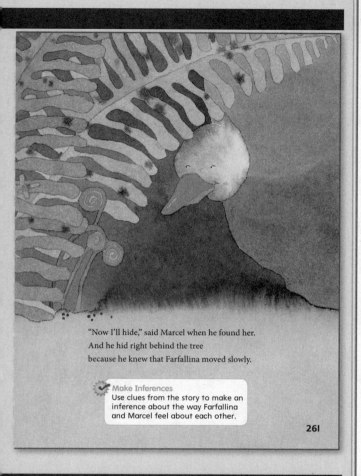

"Now I'll hide," said Marcel when he found her.
And he hid right behind the tree
because he knew that Farfallina moved slowly.

> **Make Inferences**
> Use clues from the story to make an inference about the way Farfallina and Marcel feel about each other.

261

But one day Farfallina was not herself.
"I'm not sick," she told Marcel, "just a little uncomfortable.
I need to climb up onto a branch and rest for a while."
"I'll wait for you," Marcel called as Farfallina made
her way up the tree.
Marcel watched until Farfallina was completely
out of sight. Then he settled himself in the grass
and waited.

263

- *Let's read the first three lines together:* "I can take you for a ride on the pond," said Marcel. Farfallina inched her way up to Marcel's back. "You tickle," said Marcel, and he slipped into the water.

- *Is Farfallina big and heavy or small and light?* (small and light) *She is so small and light that Marcel feels like he's being tickled. Let's use one hand to tickle our other hand.* (demonstrate)

- *Is going across the pond something Farfallina can do by herself?* (no) *Does she need Marcel's help to do it?* (yes) *Why?* (because she cannot swim but Marcel can)

 Farfallina and Marcel like to do the same kinds of things. Tell your partner things you like to do. Find at least one thing you both like to do.

Page 263

Whole Page

- *The author tells us that one day Farfallina was not herself. I will say two things it could mean. Stand up when you hear the one that tells what was happening with Farfallina: She was pretending to be someone else. She was not feeling like she usually did.* (second idea)

- *She was uncomfortable. Would you feel good if your shoes or clothes were too small?* (no) *You would feel uncomfortable.*

- *Farfallina doesn't know why she feels uncomfortable. So she goes up the tree to rest. Point to her in the picture.*

- *Marcel watches her until she is out of sight. If something is out of sight, you can't see it. Look at my hand.* (Hold up your hand.) *Now, I will put my hand out of sight.* (Put your hand in a pocket or behind your back.) *Now, you try it. Put your book out of sight.*

- *Marcel settles himself in the grass. That means he plans to be there for a while. What is he waiting for?* (for Farfallina to feel better and come down)

Page 264

Text

- *Look at the picture. What is Marcel doing?* (looking up at the tree and calling to Farfallina)

- *Night came and then morning. How long does Marcel sit by the tree?* (all day and all night) *Does Farfallina answer when he calls to her?* (no)

- *When you worry, you think something bad has happened or will happen. Marcel feels worried and lonely. What do you think Marcel is worried about?* (that something bad has happened to Farfallina)

- *When you are lonely, you want to be with a friend or relative. For whom is Marcel lonely?* (Farfallina)

- *Look at the picture. What is Marcel doing?* (looking up at the tree and calling to Farfallina)

Page 265

Whole Page

- *Time goes by. The afternoons are longer now. Is the weather warmer or colder?* (warmer)

- *Marcel looks at his reflection in the water. He sees himself. Look at the picture and point to Marcel's reflection. Where else could you see a reflection of yourself?* (in a mirror)

PARTNERS *Look at the picture of Marcel on page 264. Look at his picture on page 265. Talk with your partner about them. How has Marcel changed?* (His color is different. He is bigger.) *Did this happen in one night, or has time passed?* (Time has passed.)

Pages 264–265

Night came and then morning,
but Farfallina didn't come down.
Marcel called to her, but she didn't answer.
He was very worried and terribly lonely.

264

Pages 266–267

He went back to the tree every day to look
for Farfallina, but she was never there.
And after a while he gave up.
At the top of the tree Farfallina was **snuggled**
in a blanket of glossy silk.
She was growing too.

266

Weeks went by.
The afternoons grew longer and warmer,
and Marcel went to the pond.

He was growing, and when he looked
at his reflection in the water,
he hardly **recognized** himself.

265

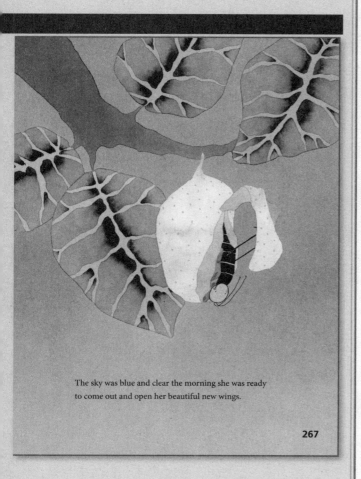

The sky was blue and clear the morning she was ready
to come out and open her beautiful new wings.

267

Paragraph 1

- *It has been many weeks since Marcel saw Farfallina. Marcel comes to the tree every day to look for Farfallina. Does he ever see her* (no) *Do you think he feels fine about it or sad?* (sad) *Do you think he will keep coming back or give up?* (Responses will vary.)

- *Let's read paragraph 1 together:* He went back to the tree every day to look for Farfallina, but she was never there. And after a while he gave up.

Paragraph 2 and Illustration

- *The author tells us where Farfallina is. She is hanging from a branch. Point to her.*

- *Farfallina is snuggled in a blanket of glossy, or shiny, silk. When you snuggle in a blanket, you feel warm and cozy. Look at the picture. Farfallina is snuggled in a kind of blanket.*

Whole Page

- *Let's read this page together:* The sky was blue and clear the morning she was ready to come out and open her beautiful new wings.

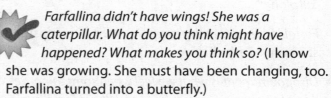 *Farfallina didn't have wings! She was a caterpillar. What do you think might have happened? What makes you think so?* (I know she was growing. She must have been changing, too. Farfallina turned into a butterfly.)

Monitor Oral Production

Remember to model self-corrective techniques on a regular basis as you speak to children. Pretend to mispronounce words and self-correct.

Page 268

Whole Page

- *Farfallina floats down to see Marcel. She is so light that she is almost carried by the air. Let's pretend we are butterflies and float around the room. (Lead students in gently floating around the room with their arms outstretched.*

- *Look at Farfallina as a butterfly. Point to her wings. She is waiting for Marcel. Farfallina thinks she will see Marcel. Does she know how long she has been gone?* (no)

- *Farfallina spends the night waiting. Does Marcel come the next day?* (no) *How does Farfallina feel now feel?* (confused and tired*) Where does she go—back to the tree or to the pond?* (She goes to the pond.)

Page 269

Text and Illustration

- *The pond is smooth. The only ripples, or lines, are the ones made by the goose as he swims. Point to the ripples in the picture.*

- *The goose is swimming in solitary circles. Do you see any other animals in the pond?* (no) *Solitary means "all alone."*

- *Farfallina shivers with disappointment. (Demonstrate shivering.) Let's all shiver.*

- *Disappointment is what we feel when something we want to happen does not happen. Why is Farfallina feeling disappointment?* (She hoped to find her bird friend at the pond, but she doesn't see him there.)

 Who do you think the goose is? (Marcel) *What makes you think so?* (We saw Marcel when he grew up.) *Why doesn't Farfallina know who the goose is?* (because she was in the tree and didn't see how Marcel looked when he grew up)

Pages 268–269

She had no idea how long she had been up in the tree, and she floated down to find Marcel.
"I'll just wait," said Farfallina when she didn't see him, and she sat on a flower.
Night came and then morning, but Marcel wasn't there.
Farfallina was tired and confused.
She **fluttered** around a bit and went to the pond.

> **Make Inferences**
> Use details from the text to make an inference about why Farfallina needs to spend time alone in the tree.

268

Pages 270–271

She went to the pond every day to look for the small gray bird named Marcel, but he never came.
One morning the goose stopped his silent rounds and spoke to her.
"You must like it here," he said.
Farfallina fluttered a bit.
"I've been waiting for a friend," she said sadly, "but I don't think he'll come."

270

The pond was glassy smooth
except for the ripples
made by a large, handsome goose
who was swimming in solitary circles.
Farfallina shivered with disappointment.

269

Marcel liked her smile and her brilliant colors.
"I know how you feel," he said. "I lost a friend too.
She just **vanished** into thin air."
Farfallina liked his sleek feathers and his gentle eyes.
"A ride around the pond might cheer you up,"
Marcel said.
Farfallina thought it would, and she settled
herself on Marcel's back.

271

Page 270

Text

■ *Look at the picture. What is happening?* (Farfallina and Marcel are talking to each other.)

■ *Let's read what Marcel finally says to Farfellina and how she answers him:* "You must like it here," he said. Farfallina fluttered a bit. "I've been waiting for a friend," she said sadly, "but I don't think he'll come."

 Why doesn't Marcel recognize his friend Farfallina? (because he hasn't seen her all grown up before; because he hasn't seen her as a butterfly)

Page 271

Text

■ *In the beginning of the story, Marcel and Farfallina became friends. Now they are becoming friends again. Did they like each other in the beginning?* (yes) *Did Marcel take Farfallina for a ride on his back?* (yes) *Are the same things happening now?* (yes)

 Pretend with your partner to be Marcel and Farfallina at the pond. You don't know that you are old friends yet. What do you say to each other as you play? Make up your own words. Take turns being each character.

Page 272

Text, Choral Reading

■ Let's read this page together.

■ *Show me with your face how you think Marcel feels when the butterfly says her name.* (Children should look surprised and happy.)

Page 273

Whole Page

Marcel beats the water with his wings and swims around in circles. What does this tell us about his feelings? (He is happy.) *What actions might a person do to show the same feelings?* (clap, jump up and down)

■ *Look at the picture. Marcel's wings are wet from beating the water. You can see the drops of water in the air. Point to them.*

■ *Marcel and Farfallina laugh. What do they think is funny?* (that they had been looking for each other when they were already together)

Pages 272–273

"It's funny," Marcel said, "but I feel as though I've known you a long time."
"I was just thinking the same thing," said Farfallina.
"My name is Farfallina. What's yours?"

272

Pages 274–275

By evening they had explained everything, and they fell asleep smiling at the stars.

274

Marcel stopped suddenly.
He beat the water with his strong wings.
Then he swam round and round and round.
"It's me Farfallina," he shouted. "It's me, Marcel!
Is that really you?"
"It is," Farfallina shouted back.
They looked at each other and laughed.

273

275

Pages 274–275

Text

■ *Let's read this page together:* By evening they had explained everything, and they fell asleep smiling at the stars.

■ *What do Marcel and Farfallina have to explain to each other?* (how they changed) *Why do they have to explain that?* (because they are different kinds of animals and do not know the changes the other one went through)

 Pretend to be Marcel and Farfallina. Explain everything to each other.

■ *Look at the picture on page 275. What are Marcel and Farfallina doing?* (sleeping and smiling at the stars)

Page 276

Whole Page

- *Farfallina and Marcel spend the summer playing together. Why does Marcel have to be careful not to fly too fast?* (because a butterfly cannot fly as fast as a goose)

- *Farfallina doesn't hide in the flowers now. Why would that make the game too hard for Marcel?* (She is so brightly colored that she would look like one of the flowers)

PARTNERS *Pretend to be Marcel and Farfallina. Make friendship cards for each other. The partner pretending to be Marcel will make a card telling why he likes Farfallina. The partner pretending to be Farfallina will make a card telling why she likes Marcel.*

Page 277

Illustration

- *Look at the picture. The leaves are red and gold. What time of year is it?* (fall, autumn)

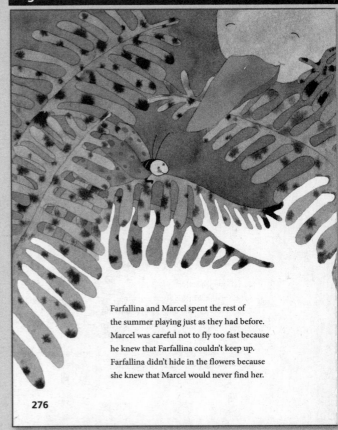

Farfallina and Marcel spent the rest of the summer playing just as they had before. Marcel was careful not to fly too fast because he knew that Farfallina couldn't keep up. Farfallina didn't hide in the flowers because she knew that Marcel would never find her.

276

And when the leaves on the trees around the pond turned red and gold, they decided to go south.

Together.

277

Text

- *Let's read what happens at the end of the story, using a happy voice:* And when the leaves on the trees around the pond turned red and gold, they decided to go south. Together.

- *The friends decide to go south in the fall. Why is that a good idea?* (because it will be warmer and more comfortable for them in the south)

- ✔ *The story is about being good friends. What are some things you can figure out about being a good friend from what happens in the story?* (Good friends are kind to each other. Good friends like to do things together.)

Butterflies

Access Core Content

Teacher Note Pose the questions after you read the paragraph or page indicated.

Page 280

Paragraph 1, Choral Reading

- *Let's read the first paragraph together to find out what this article is about.* Butterflies come in all shapes and sizes. Some are big and some are small. Some have bright spots and some have other markings like dark patterns on their wings.

Tell your partner about butterflies you have seen. What colors were they? What were they doing? (Responses will vary.)

Paragraph 2 and Photo

- *This paragraph tells us about two kinds of butterflies. Point to the Monarch butterfly on page 280. Point to the part that is orange. Point to the part that is black. Touch some of the white dots with your finger. Point to the Skipper butterfly on page 281.*

Page 281

Diagram

- *All butterflies have the same parts. Let's read the name of each part together as we point to it:* wings, antennae, head, legs.

- *All butterflies have wings. What other animals have wings?* (birds, flies, bees)

- *The antennae are long and skinny. How many antennae does a butterfly have?* (two)

- *Which body parts can butterflies use to get from place to place?* (wings and legs)

Pages 280–281

Monarch Butterfly

Science

Genre
Expository text gives information and facts about a topic.

Text Features
Illustrations are drawings that help readers understand information.

Captions explain what is shown in the illustrations.

Content Vocabulary
patterns
stages
hatches

Butterflies

Butterflies come in all shapes and sizes. Some are big and some are small. Some have bright spots and some have other markings like dark patterns on their wings.

The Monarch and the Skipper are two kinds of butterflies. The Monarch is bigger and more colorful than the Skipper. The Monarch is bright orange and black. It has white spots. The Skipper is brown and has clear spots.

Although these two butterflies look different, they have the same body parts as all other butterflies.

280

Pages 282–283

How Butterflies Grow and Change

All butterflies become adults in the same way. Every butterfly's life has four steps, or **stages**, of development.

Stage 1: Egg

A butterfly begins life as an egg. The egg is about the size of the top of a pin. It is usually laid on a leaf. The egg is sticky, so it stays on the leaf.

Stage 2: Larva

When the egg **hatches**, a caterpillar comes out. This part of the butterfly's life is called the larva stage. When the caterpillar is large enough, it hooks itself onto a leaf or branch.

Stage 3: Pupa

The caterpillar makes a hard shell or case to live in. It usually stays inside the shell for a few weeks. This is called the pupa stage. Inside the shell the caterpillar grows and changes.

282

Science

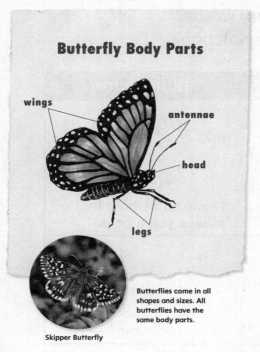

Butterfly Body Parts

wings

antennae

head

legs

Skipper Butterfly

Butterflies come in all shapes and sizes. All butterflies have the same body parts.

281

Stage 4: Adult

When the shell breaks open, the caterpillar has completely changed into a butterfly. This is the adult stage. After its wings are dry, the butterfly is ready to fly away.

 Connect and Compare

1. Reread page 281. What is the same about all butterflies?
   Illustrations and Captions

2. Use text from this selection and *Farfallina and Marcel* to help explain why Marcel does not know who Farfallina is. Use the names of at least two of the stages of a butterfly's life in your answer. **Reading/Writing Across Texts**

Science Activity

Use an encyclopedia to research two types of butterflies that live in your state. Tell how they are alike and different.

LOG ON ▶ FIND OUT **Science** Animal Growth
www.macmillanmh.com

283

Pages 282–283

Introductory Paragraph

■ *This section is called* How Butterflies Grow and Change. *Let's read the first paragraph under the heading together:* All butterflies become adults in the same way. Every butterfly's life has four steps, or stages, of development.

■ *Let's think about how people go through stages, too. The first stage is a baby. Then what stage is next?* (child) *The third stage is a teenager. What stage is last?* (adult)

Stages

■ *Farfallina is a caterpillar when Marcel meets her. What stage is that?* (larva)

■ *Look back through* Farfallina and Marcel. *Find the picture of Farfallina in the pupa stage. What page is it on?* (page 266)

■ *Think about Farfallina at the end of the story. What stage is that?* (adult)

Name _____

Use the word chart to study this week's vocabulary words. Write a sentence using each word in your writer's notebook.

Word	Context Sentence	Illustration
giggled _____	Kim and Rosa giggled at the playful puppy.	**Name something that makes you giggle.**
fluttered _____	A butterfly fluttered from flower to flower.	
peered _____	The cat peered from under the bed.	
recognized _____	I cannot recognize the person in the mask.	
vanished _____	The seal slipped into the ocean and vanished.	
snuggled _____	The baby ducks snuggled together next to their mother.	**What animals have you seen snuggled together?**

Read each question and prompt. Discuss the answers with your group. Use your Leveled Reader to find details to support your answers. Then write your answers on the blank lines or on another sheet of paper.

1. Explain how you know that your book is a fantasy story.

   _____

2. Tell about the main character. What is happening to this character during the story?

   _____

3. What real information is in this fantasy story? Tell three things you learned.

   _____

4. Tell the group about the illustration you like best. Tell why you like it.

   _____

5. Describe the most exciting event of the story. How did it make you feel?

   _____

6. Write one question about the book to ask your group.

   _____

Nutik, the Wolf Pup

Pages 290–291

Prior to reading the selection with children, they should have listened to the selection on **StudentWorks Plus**, the interactive eBook. In addition, selection vocabulary should have been pretaught using the **Visual Vocabulary Resources**.

Access Core Content

Teacher Note Pose the questions after you read the paragraph or page indicated.

Page 291

Title and Illustrations

- *Let's read the title together:* Nutik, the Wolf Pup. *Nutik is the name of the young wolf in this story. A baby wolf is called a pup. Which other animals have babies called pups—dogs or cats?* (dogs) *Dogs can be pets, but wolves are wild animals.*

- *In this story, though, a boy and a wolf become friends. Point to the boy in the picture. His name is Amaroq. Now point to Nutik, the wolf pup.*

- *Look at what the boy is wearing in the picture. Do you think the weather is cold or warm?* (cold) *The story takes place way up north in the Arctic.*

- *This is an area called the tundra. It is flat with very few trees. The ground in the tundra is also frozen most of the year.*

Pages 290–291

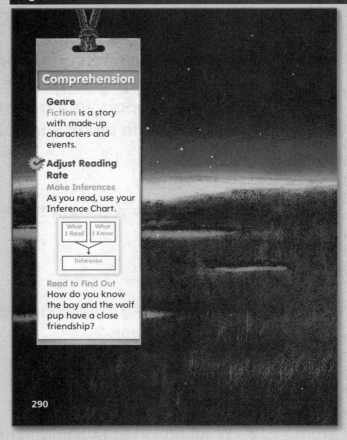

290

Pages 292–293

292

Main Selection

Nutik, the Wolf Pup

by Jean Craighead George
illustrated by Ted Rand

Award Winning Author

291

In an Eskimo village at the top of the world lived a lively little boy. He was not very old, but he could run as fast as a bird's shadow.

When he ran, his father, Kapugen, the great hunter, caught him and lifted him high over his head.

When he ran, his mother, Ellen, caught him and hugged him closely.

When he ran, his big sister, Julie, caught him and carried him home to tell him wolf stories.

293

Pages 292–293

Illustration

- *Look at the picture. Point to the boy. Point to his mother and father. The boy also has a big sister, Julie, but we can't see her in the picture.*

Paragraph 1, Choral Reading

- *The boy lives at the top of the world. This is another way to say that he lives in the far north.* (Point out the area on a map or globe.)

- *The boy lives in an Eskimo village, just like the girl we read about in My Home in Alaska.*

- *The boy is also lively, or has a lot of energy. He goes as fast as a bird's shadow. Do birds fly fast?* (yes) *A bird's shadow goes where the bird goes, so it must be fast like the bird. If the boy moves as fast as a bird's shadow, is he fast or slow?* (fast)

- *Now let's read the first paragraph together:* In an Eskimo village at the top of the world lived a lively little boy. He was not very old, but he could run as fast as a bird's shadow.

Paragraphs 2–4

- *The author does not tell us how the people in the boy's family feel about him. We can figure out how they feel by their actions. What are the boy's parents doing?* (lifting him high, hugging him) *How do you think they feel about him?* (They love him.)

- *Nutik's big sister, Julie, catches him when he runs and carries him. She tells him wolf stories. Do you think she is a good big sister? Why or why not?* (She's a good big sister because takes the time to play with him and to tell him stories.)

Page 294

Whole Page

- *Julie tells her brother about the time she was lost on the tundra. We learned about the* tundra *in* My Home in Alaska. *Is the land snowy or green?* (snowy) *What is one kind of animal that lives in the tundra?* (a wolf)

- *Julie was starving when she was lost. That means that she didn't have the food she needed to live. A pack, or group, of wolves took care of her. What did the noble, or good, leader of the pack share with her?* (food)

- *Julie's parents named her brother after the leader of the pack. Her brother and the leader are both called Amaroq.*

- *Julie's parents will think of the wolf when they call their son's name Why would they want to remember the wolf?* (because he saved Julie's life) *Was the wolf noble and kind?* (yes) *Perhaps they also want their son to be noble and kind like the wolf.*

Page 295

Whole Page

- When an animal is sickly, it is weak like someone sick. *Let's read the first paragraph together:* One day Julie came home with two pups. They were hungry and sickly. She put one in Amaroq's arms.

- *Julie tells Amaroq to feed and to* tend *the pup. When we* tend *something, we take care of it. Tell some things Julie and Amaroq might need to do to* tend *the wolf pups.* (find a place for them to sleep, keep them warm, feed them)

- *Julie and Amaroq will take care of the pups until they are fat and well. What will happen then?* (The pack of wolves will come and get them.)

- *Amaroq hugs and kisses the pup. How do you think he feels about it?* (He loves it already.)

She told him how a wolf pack had saved her life when she was lost and starving on the vast tundra. The wolf pack's **noble** black leader had shared his family's food with her.

The wolf's name was Amaroq.

The little boy's name was Amaroq.

294

"Amaroq," Julie said when she saw this, "do not come to love this wolf pup. I have **promised** the wolves we will return the pups when they are fat and well."

Amaroq looked into Nutik's golden eyes. The wolf pup licked him and wagged his tail. Julie frowned.

"Don't fall in love, Amaroq," she warned again, "or your heart will break when the wolves come and take him away."

"No, it won't," he said.

> **Make Inferences**
> Use details from the story to make an inference about whether Amaroq will begin to love the wolf pup.

296

One day Julie came home with two pups. They were hungry and sickly. She put one in Amaroq's arms.

"Feed and tend this pup," she said. "His name is Nutik. I will feed and tend the other pup. I named her Uqaq. When they are fat and well, the wolves will come and get them."

Amaroq hugged his pup. He felt the little wolf heart beat softly. He kissed the warm head.

295

Julie gave Amaroq a bottle of milk to feed to his pup. Amaroq wrapped Nutik in soft rabbit skins, and they snuggled down on the grizzly-bear rug.

Every day Amaroq fed Nutik many bottles of milk, bites of raw meat, and bones to chew.

When the moon had changed from a crescent to a circle and back again, Nutik was fat. His legs did not wobble. His fur **gleamed**. He bounced and woofed. When Amaroq ran, Nutik ran.

297

Page 296

Whole Page

- *Julie sees Amaroq hug and kiss the pup. What is Julie afraid will happen?* (She is afraid that Amaroq will love the pup too much to let him go back to his family.)

- *Look at the picture. Do you think Amaroq likes the pup?* (yes)

 Talk with your partner. How is the wolf pup like a small dog? (He licks Amaroq and wags his tail.) *How is taking care of the wolf like taking care of any pet? How is it different?* (Responses will vary.)

Page 297

Paragraph 3

- *The moon changes from a crescent to a circle and back again. This is what a crescent moon looks like.* (Draw a crescent moon on the board.) *It changes into a circle, or full moon, which looks like this.* (Draw a full moon on the board.)

- *Then the moon changes back to a crescent moon.* (Point to the crescent moon.)

- *The moon changes shape as time passes. It usually takes almost a month to change from a crescent moon to a full moon and back to a crescent moon. This means that Amaroq has cared for Nutik for almost a month.*

 Nutik is fat and healthy now. His fur gleams, or looks shiny. How do you think Amaroq feels about Nutik now? (He probably really loves him now.) *Do you think he will want to give up the pup?* (no)

Request Assistance

Remind children of expressions they can use to request assistance from the teacher or their partners, such as *Can you repeat that, please? Can you show me?*

Page 298

Text

- *For half the year, the Arctic area has long periods of light with no darkness. Then, during the other half, it has darkness with no light. A nickname for this part of the world is* Land of the Midnight Sun.

- *It is never dark. Amaroq and Nutik play whenever they want and fall asleep when they are tired.*

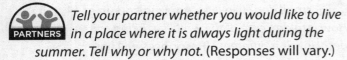 *Tell your partner whether you would like to live in a place where it is always light during the summer. Tell why or why not.* (Responses will vary.)

- *Owls usually are awake at night. Now Amaroq and Nutik wake up to the sounds of the owlets, or baby owls. When do you think Amaroq and Nutik get up?* (at night) *Point to the snowy owlets in the bottom picture, and say their sound after me:* hiss. (Make a raspy sound.)

- *Amaroq and Nutik sleep when the snowy geese are awake. Point to the snowy geese in the top picture and say their sound after me:* gabble .

Page 299

Illustration

- *We call the sound that a wolf makes a* howl. *It sounds something like this:* (Imitate a wolf's howl.) *What does the picture on this page show?* (Amaroq is trying to howl like Nutik.) *Pretend you are Amaroq. Try to* howl *like you think Nutik* howled.

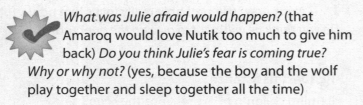 *What was Julie afraid would happen?* (that Amaroq would love Nutik too much to give him back) *Do you think Julie's fear is coming true? Why or why not?* (yes, because the boy and the wolf play together and sleep together all the time)

Summer came to the top of the world. The sun stayed up all day and all night for three beautiful months.

Because of this, Amaroq and Nutik lived by a different clock.

They fell asleep to the gabble of baby snow geese. They awoke to the raspy hiss of snowy owlets.

They ate when they were hungry. They slept when they were tired, and they played wolf games in shadow and sun. They were never apart.

298

"Don't fall in love with Nutik," Julie warned again when the midnight sun was riding low. "I hear the wolves calling. Soon they will come for their pups." She looked at him. "Be strong."

"I am strong," he answered. "I am Amaroq."

300

299

One morning Amaroq and Nutik were tumbling on the mossy tundra when the wolf pack called. They were close by.

"Come home. Come home," they howled.

Nutik heard them.

Uqaq and Julie heard them.

Amaroq heard them. He got to his feet and ran.

Nutik stopped listening to the wolves and ran after him.

Amaroq led Nutik as fast as a falling star. He led him down a frost heave. He led him around the village schoolhouse. He led him far from the wolves.

301

Page 300

Whole Page

- *Again on this page, Julie tells Amaroq not to fall in love with Nutik. Why do you think she tells him the same thing over and over?* (to remind him that the wolves are coming for Nutik)

 Pretend that you and your partner are Julie and Amaroq. You are having the same conversation they are having on this page. Take turns being each character and reading the lines.

Page 301

Top Half of Page

- *Do you think the wolves really said,* "Come home"? (no) *What do you think the author meant when she said* "Come home," they howled? (that they were howling for Uqaq and Nutik, and Julie knew it meant they wanted the young wolves to come with them)

Last Paragraph, Choral Reading

- *Let's read together what Amaroq does when he hears the wolves call for Uqaq and Nutik:* Amaroq led Nutik as fast as a falling star. He led him down a frost heave. He led him around the village schoolhouse. He led him far from the wolves.

- *Amaroq runs* as fast as a falling star. *A falling star is a star that shoots across the sky, like this.* (Use your hand to show how a falling star shoots across the sky.) *Falling stars are fast, like Amaroq.*

- *Why does Amaroq run?* (He wants to take Nutik away from the other wolves so that Nutik will not leave him.) *Does Nutik want to go with the other wolves? How do you know?* (no, because Nutik runs after Amaroq instead of toward the other wolves)

- *Show me how Nutik probably looks as he runs. Use your body and face.* (Lead children in running in place quickly. Children should show sad, scared, or determined expressions.)

Page 302

Paragraphs 2–3

■ *We will read aloud what Julie and Amaroq say to each other. One half of our group will read Julie's part. The other half will read Amaroq's part.* (Designate groups.) *Read Julie's part:* "Uqaq has returned to her family. The wolves came and got her. Nutik is next." *Now read Amaroq's part:* "I am very tired." .

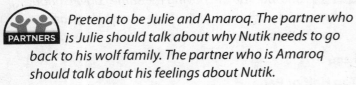 *Pretend to be Julie and Amaroq. The partner who is Julie should talk about why Nutik needs to go back to his wolf family. The partner who is Amaroq should talk about his feelings about Nutik.*

■ *Nutik wiggles into the sleeping bag with Amaroq. Why do you think Nutik does this?* (Nutik loves Amaroq and wants to stay with him.)

Page 303

Whole Page

■ *Remember that we talked about a time when it was always light where Julie and Amaroq live. Now, the position of the sun has changed. It is always dark.*

■ *The wolves come to the village. What do they want?* (They want Nutik to come with them.)

Pages 302–303

After a long time he led Nutik home. Julie was at the door.

"Uqaq has returned to her family," she said. "The wolves came and got her. Nutik is next."

"I am very tired," Amaroq said, and he rubbed his eyes.

Julie put him to bed in his bearskin sleeping bag. When Julie tiptoed away, Nutik **wiggled** into the sleeping bag too. He licked Amaroq's cheek.

302

Pages 304–305

Nutik crawled out of Amaroq's sleeping bag and gently awakened him. He took his hand in his mouth and led him across the room. He stopped before Amaroq's parka. Amaroq put it on. Nutik picked up a boot. Amaroq put on his boots.

Nutik whimpered at the door.

Amaroq opened it. They stepped into the cold.

304

The sun set in August. The days grew shorter until there was no day at all. Now it was always nighttime.
In the blue grayness of the winter night the wolves came to the edge of the village.
When everyone was sleeping, they called to Nutik.

303

The wolves were prancing and dancing like ice spirits on the hill.
Nutik took Amaroq's mittened hand and led him toward his wolf family. The frost crackled under their feet. The wolves whispered their welcome.

305

Page 304

Whole Page

- *Nutik wakes up and crawls out of Amaroq's sleeping bag. What makes Nutik wake up?* (He hears the wolves calling for him.)

- *Nutik wakes up Amaroq and leads him to his parka and boots. Then he whimpers, or makes a little crying sound, at the door. What is he trying to say?* (They have to go outside to be with the wolves.)

Page 305

Whole Page

- *The wolves are dancing and prancing. Let's dance and prance around the room.* (Lead children.) *Do you think the wolves are happy or sad?* (happy)

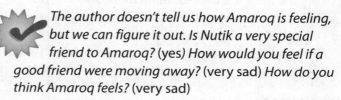 *The author doesn't tell us how Amaroq is feeling, but we can figure it out. Is Nutik a very special friend to Amaroq?* (yes) *How would you feel if a good friend were moving away?* (very sad) *How do you think Amaroq feels?* (very sad)

- *Nutik leads Amaroq by his mittened hand toward his wolf family. Why do you think Nutik is taking Amaroq to his family?* (Question is open.)

Page 306

Text

- *Amaroq stops. What does he realize?* (that Nutik is taking Amaroq to his wolf home and that he wants Amaroq to stay there) *What does Amaroq say?* (that he can't go with Nutik)

Illustration

- *What does the picture show? Pay special attention to Amaroq and Nutik's faces.* (They love each other very much. It is hard to say goodbye.)

Page 307

Whole Page

Amaroq turns and walks away from Nutik. *Does he think it is the best thing for his friend?* (yes) *What does Amarok say to himself?* ("I am very strong.") *What does he mean?* (He means he is strong enough to do the right thing even though it is hard.)

Page 308

Whole Page

- *Amaroq is sad. Tears keep welling up in his eyes. Welling up means "filling up with tears." When you cry, your eyes well up, or fill up, with tears. Why is he so sad?* (because Nutik is gone)

- *Amaroq is too sad to eat. He goes back to his sleeping bag. What does he find there?* (Nutik) *Look at the picture. How does Amaroq feel now?* (very happy)

- *The author tells us that Amaroq cries the wolf's name joyfully. What else might Amaroq have said? Tell me in the kind of voice Amaroq would have used.* (I am so happy you are back! I missed you so much!)

Suddenly Amaroq stopped. Nutik was taking him to his wolf home.

"No, Nutik," he said. "I cannot go with you. I cannot live with your family." Nutik tilted his head to one side and whimpered, "Come."

"You must go home alone," Amaroq said, and hugged his **beloved** wolf pup for a long time.

306

Amaroq did not eat lunch. When Kapugen took him out to fish, he did not fish. Tears kept welling up. He ran home to hide them in his bearskin sleeping bag.

It was surprisingly warm.

Up from the bottom and into Amaroq's arms wiggled the furry wolf pup.

"Nutik," Amaroq cried joyfully. He hugged his friend and **glanced** at Julie. Instead of scolding him, she stepped outside.

308

Then he turned and walked away. He did not run. Nutik did not chase him.

"I am very strong," Amaroq said to himself.

He got home before his tears froze.

Amaroq crawled into his bearskin sleeping bag and sobbed. His heart was broken after all.

At last he fell asleep.

Julie awoke him for breakfast.

"I don't want to eat," he told her. "Last night the wolves came and took Nutik away."

"You are a strong boy," she said. "You let him go back to his family. That is right."

✓ Make Inferences
Use evidence from the text to make an inference about why Amaroq let Nutik return to his family.

307

"Dear wolves," she called across the tundra. "Your beautiful pup, Nutik, will not be coming back to you. He has joined our family.

"Amaroq loves Nutik. Nutik loves Amaroq. They are brothers now. He cannot leave."

As if listening, the wind stopped blowing. In the stillness Julie called out clearly and softly:

"I shall take care of him as lovingly as you took care of me."

And the wolves sang back, "That is good."

309

- Amaroq glances, or looks quickly, at Julie. He think she will scold, or yell, at him. What does she do instead? (go outside)

Page 309

Whole Page

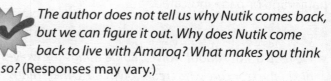 The author does not tell us why Nutik comes back, but we can figure it out. Why does Nutik come back to live with Amaroq? What makes you think so? (Responses may vary.)

- Julie tells the wolves that Amaroq and Nutik are brothers now. She means that they love each other as much as brothers do. Nutik will now be treated as a member of the family.

- Let's read the last three paragraphs together: As if listening, the wind stopped blowing. In the stillness Julie called out clearly and softly: "I shall take care of him as lovingly as you took care of me." And the wolves sang back, "That is good."

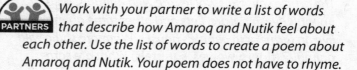 Work with your partner to write a list of words that describe how Amaroq and Nutik feel about each other. Use the list of words to create a poem about Amaroq and Nutik. Your poem does not have to rhyme.

PARTNERS

Non-verbal Cues

Children have seen you using non-verbal cues to convey meaning. When needed, encourage them to use visuals when talking to a partner so they can better express themselves.

Wolves

Access Core Content

Teacher Note Pose the questions after you read the paragraph or page indicated.

Page 312

- *We read a story about wolves. Some things the wolves did in the story are what real wolves do. Other things the wolves did were made-up. Now, we'll read an article that tells facts about wolves.*

- *The article is from an* encyclopedia. *An* encyclopedia *is a big book, or a set of many books. It gives facts and other information about different topics.*

Paragraph 1, Choral Reading

- *Let's read the first paragraph aloud to learn some facts about wolves.*

- *The article says that wolves are wild animals. Wild animals live in nature. Pets and other tame animals live on farms or in people's houses. What are some wild animals?* (tigers, wolves, squirrels) *What are some tame animals?* (cats, dogs, cows)

Photo

- *Look at the biggest wolf in the picture. Point to the wolf's long legs. Point to its large feet. Point to its powerful jaws.*

Paragraph 2

- *A habitat is where an animal lives. What do we know about the habitat of the wolves in* Nutik, the Wolf Pup*?* (Nutik and the other wolves live in a cold, snowy place in the north.)

Page 313

Heads

- *The heads on this page help us know that the page will tell about two things. Point to each head as you read it with me:* Habitat, Food.

Pages 312–313

Science

Genre
Expository An encyclopedia article gives information and facts about a topic.

Text Features
Encyclopedia entries may have several sections. Headings tell what information is found in each section.

Content Vocabulary
habitats
roam
prey

WOLVES

Wolves are wild animals that are related to the dog family. They look similar to dogs, but they have longer legs and larger feet. They also have more powerful jaws.

Wolves live in different areas, or **habitats**. Some wolves are gray. Others are almost black. Wolves that live in northern Alaska are white. All wolves have long, bushy tails.

312

Pages 314–315

Life Cycle

The female wolf gives birth to pups in the spring. First she finds or digs a den. Often she will use the same den year after year. The cubs cannot see or hear when they are born. Their mother stays with them for about three weeks. During this time the male brings food for the mother to eat.

After about a month, the pups can eat meat. All of the pack members hunt food for them. The female hunts, too. Another pack member takes care of the pups while she is away. By fall the pups have learned to hunt. They are ready to travel with the pack.

314

Habitat

Wolves live in forest or mountain habitats. Wolves need lots of land because they move around a lot. They **roam**, or travel, 20 miles a day to look for and find food.

Wolves are endangered animals. They used to live all over North America, but now they live only in northern forests and Alaska.

Food

Wolves are hunters. They have a good sense of smell. This helps them find their **prey**. Wolves that live in forests eat mice, rabbits, deer, and moose. Wolves in Alaska also eat caribou or oxen. Finding food is not easy for wolves. Sometimes they must follow a herd for several days. They swallow food in large pieces without chewing. Wolves can eat 20 pounds of meat at one time.

313

Encyclopedia entries often have words in dark print called headings. These summarize what the following section will be about.

The Pack

Wolves live in family groups called packs. A pack may have 7 or 8 wolves. One male is the leader of the pack. He has a female mate. Their children are part of the pack, too. A pack may also have an aunt or an uncle.

Connect and Compare

1. In which section would you find information about where wolves live? What did you learn about in the section with the heading "Food"? **Headings**

2. Think about the encyclopedia entry and *Nutik, the Wolf Pup*. How would Nutik's life have been different if he had never left his pack? **Reading/Writing Across Texts**

Science Activity

Research a type of wolf. Write facts about what the wolf looks like and where it lives. Share with your class. Remember to speak clearly at an appropriate pace.

Science Wolves
www.macmillanmh.com

315

Habitat

- *When there are not many of a kind of animal left, we say the animal is* endangered. *What might cause an animal to be* endangered? (being hunted, sickness)

Food

- *What does Amaroq feed Nutik? You can look back in the story to help you remember.* (milk, meat, bones) *Listen as I read the section about the food that wolves eat.* (Read aloud.) *Does Nutik eat some of the same things as real wolves?* (Yes, he eats meat.)

Page 314

Life Cycle

- *Let's read the head for this page together:* Life Cycle. *Another way to say this is* life steps. *This part will tell about some of the steps a wolf goes through as it grows up.*

PARTNERS *Make a timeline with your partner.* (Demonstrate each step as you give directions.) *Draw a line. Above the line on the left side write* Spring. *Leave a space, and then write* Three Weeks *above the line. Leave another space, and write* One Month *above the line. Leave a lot of space. At the end of the line write* Fall.

- *Work with your partner to talk about what you have learned about each step*

Page 315

The Pack

- *Near the end of the story,* Nutik the Wolf Pup, *the wolves come to get Nutik to join their pack. Let's read this section aloud to find out more about wolf packs.*

- *A pack is a family group with a leader. How is our class like a pack?* (It is like a family, and it has a teacher as the leader.)

Name _____

**Use the word chart to study this week's vocabulary words.
Write a sentence using each word in your writer's notebook.**

Word	Context Sentence	Illustration
beloved _____	I hug my <u>beloved</u> grandfather.	
promised _____	We <u>promised</u> that we'd be friends forever.	
wiggled _____	I <u>wiggled</u> into last year's shirt.	
gleamed _____	The ice <u>gleamed</u> in the bright sun.	 **Name something else that gleams in the sun.**
glanced _____	I <u>glanced</u> quickly at the dog as I walked past.	
noble _____	The queen looked <u>noble</u> as she sat on the throne.	

Read each question and prompt. Discuss the answers with your group. Use your Leveled Reader to find details to support your answers. Then write your answers on the blank lines or on another sheet of paper.

1. Share with your classmates what you learned about the life of a dolphin calf.

   _____

2. Explain how a dolphin mother keeps her calf safe while she hunts for food.

   _____

3. Describe how dolphins use sound waves.

   _____

4. Tell about the dolphin's body.

   _____

5. Explain why it is important for dolphins to live in groups.

   _____

6. Write one question about the book to ask your group.

   _____

Week 1

Selections	Vocabulary		ELL Practice Book
	Key Selection Words/Cognates	Academic Language/Cognates	
Dig Wait Listen: A Desert Toad's Tale *The Sonoran Desert*	burrow beyond warning lengthy distant *distante*	possessive nouns purpose generate questions adjective *adjetivo* author *autor*	• Phonics, pp. 126–127 • Vocabulary, p. 128 • Grammar, p. 129 • Book Talk, p. 130

Week 2

Selections	Vocabulary		ELL Practice Book
	Key Selection Words/Cognates	Academic Language/Cognates	
Splish! Splash! Animal Baths *Ant and Grasshopper*	puddles nibble itches preen handy beast *bestia*	inflectional nouns generate questions articles *artículos* compare *comparar* contrast *contrastar*	• Phonics, pp. 131–132 • Vocabulary, p. 133 • Grammar, p. 134 • Book Talk, p. 135

Week 3

	Vocabulary		ELL Practice Book
TIME FOR KIDS	Key Selection Words/Cognates	Academic Language/Cognates	
A Way to Help Planet Earth	hardest remains trouble extinct *extinto* conservation *conservación*	generate questions multiple-meaning words problem *problema* solution *solución*	• Phonics, pp. 136–137 • Vocabulary, p. 138 • Grammar, p. 139 • Book Talk, p. 140

Week 4

Selections	Vocabulary		ELL Practice Book
	Key Selection Words/Cognates	Academic Language/Cognates	
Super Storms *It Fell in the City*	beware prevent uprooted destroy grasslands violent *violento/-a*	compound words cause *causa* effect *efecto* visualize *visualizar* adjectives *adjetivos*	• Phonics, pp. 141–142 • Vocabulary, p. 143 • Grammar, p. 144 • Book Talk, p. 145

Week 5

Selections	Vocabulary		ELL Practice Book
	Key Selection Words/Cognates	Academic Language/Cognates	
Pushing Up the Sky *Getting to Know Joseph Bruchac*	signal randomly agreed gathered jabbing	adverb problem *problema* solution *solución* visualize *visualizar*	• Phonics, pp. 146–147 • Vocabulary, p. 148 • Grammar, p. 149 • Book Talk, p. 150

Student Response Strategies

Use the following strategies to help English Language Learners move to the next proficiency level.

✔ **WAIT** Give children ample time.

- Let children know that they can respond in different ways depending on their levels of proficiency, but all should be encouraged to answer questions related to the main point of the picture or text.

- Allow children to respond in their native language if they are very limited proficient. Ask a more proficient ELL student to repeat the answer in English.

✔ **REPEAT** If the child's response is correct, the teacher can repeat what the child has said. The teacher should repeat in a clear, loud voice that all can hear and at a slower pace.

✔ **REVISE for FORM** Generally the teacher will be repeating what the child has said but with corrections for grammar and pronunciation. The correction can be implicit or explicit (where teacher calls attention to the correction).

✔ **REVISE for MEANING** Teachers should also correct for meaning.

✔ **ELABORATE** Here, the teacher elaborates on a child's response or states the response in another way in order to more fully develop children's comprehension and oral language proficiency.

✔ **ELICIT** Finally, the teacher can also elicit a more comprehensive response from the child by prompting the child for further information.

Newcomers

Basic and Social Language Each week you will be focusing on an important aspect of classroom communication to teach or reinforce with your newcomers. Children will expand and internalize initial English vocabulary by learning and using routine language needed for classroom communication.

Addresses and Phone Numbers Help children memorize their phone numbers and addresses. Write each on an index card. Have children practice throughout the week. Ask, *What is your phone number? Where do you live?*

Question Words Continue to work with Newcomers to understand and use basic classroom language. Emphasize the use of question words *Who, What, Where, Why, When, How,* and *Which* in this and upcoming weeks. Assess Newcomers' language abilities to

determine appropriate next steps for instruction.

More Likes/Dislikes Teach and/or reinforce the sentence frames *I like* _____ and *I don't like* _____ . Teach game words, such as games commonly played in the school playground or at home, including sports and board games, to help children complete these sentence frames.

LOG ON ▶ Have children use **Newcomer Games** to expand and internalize language needed for classroom communication.
www.macmillanmh.com

Dig, Wait, Listen: A Desert Toad's Tale

Pages 332–333

Prior to reading the selection with children, they should have listened to the selection on **StudentWorks Plus**, the interactive eBook. In addition, selection vocabulary should have been pretaught using the **Visual Vocabulary Resources**.

Access Core Content

Teacher Note Pose the questions after you read the paragraph or page indicated.

Pages 332–333

Illustration

- *A toad is an animal. It looks like a frog. Say it with me:* toad. *Point to the toads in the picture. Let's count them together:* one toad, two toads, three toads.

- *This is a desert.* (Point to the desert and cacti behind the title.) *Say it with me:* desert. *The desert is a special kind of place. It doesn't rain very often in the desert.*

- *The desert has a lot of sand.* (Point to it.) *Say it with me:* sand. *Where else can you find sand?* (at a beach, in a sandbox)

Title

- *Let's read the first part of the title together:* Dig, Wait, Listen. Dig *means "to make a hole in the ground." These toads are in a hole in the ground.* (Point to the toads.) *They had to dig to make the hole.*

- *Let's read the second part of the title together:* A Desert Toad's Tale. *A tale is a story. We are going to read a story about a toad who lives in the desert.*

Pages 332–333

Comprehension

Genre
Fiction is a made-up story that may give facts about a real topic.

Ask Questions
✓ Author's Purpose
As you read, use your Author's Purpose Chart.

```
[Clue]  [Clue]
     ↓
[Author's Purpose]
```

Read to Find Out
What do you learn about the toad?

332

Pages 334–335

Deep in the desert, under the sand, the spadefoot toad waits. She waits...for the sound of rain.

334

Main Selection

DIG
WAIT
LISTEN

**A DESERT
TOAD'S TALE**

BY APRIL PULLEY SAYRE
ILLUSTRATED BY BARBARA BASH

333

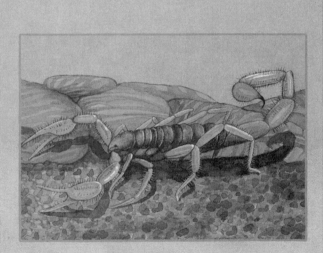

Skitter, skitter, scratch.
She hears soft sounds.
Is this the rain at last?

No. It's the scorpion overhead,
crawling slowly past.
Skitter, scratch!

335

Page 334

Illustration
- *Look at the toad. What is it doing?* (sitting, sleeping, waiting) *Is the toad under the sand or on top of the sand?* (under the sand)

- *There are many different kinds of toads. This one is called a spadefoot toad. It has special feet for digging.*

Text
- *The toad waits under the sand. What does she wait for?* (the sound of rain)

- *Let's read the last line together:* She waits...for the sound of rain.

Talk with your partner about the sound of rain. What does a lot of rain sound like? What does a little rain sound like? Do you like the sound of rain? (Questions are open.)

Page 335

Illustration
- *Look at the animal in the picture. It's a scorpion. Say it with me: scorpion. A scorpion is a small desert animal. It makes a soft sound when it walks.*

Paragraph 1
- *The toad hears a soft sound, a quiet sound.* Skitter, skitter, scratch, *like this.* (Scratch your fingernails lightly on a desktop.) *Let's read it together:* Skitter, skitter, scratch.

- *Let's read the last line together:* Is this the rain at last? *Is* skitter, skitter, scratch *the sound of rain?* (no) *What do you think is making this soft sound?* (the scorpion)

Paragraph 2
- *The soft sound is made by the scorpion overhead.* Overhead *is made up of the words* over *and* head. (Write *over + head* on the board.) *The toad hears the scorpion over, or above, her head.*

- *The scorpion is crawling slowly on the ground. That means it is moving slowly, close to the ground. Where is the toad?* (under the ground; in the hole)

Page 336

Illustration

- *Look at the top picture. Point to the toad. Point to the feet of some other animals.*

- *Those feet are very hard, like this desk.* (Knock on a desk.) *They are called hooves. Say it with me:* hooves. *Many different animals have hooves. Horses and cows have hooves.*

- *The hooves in the top picture belong to these animals.* (Point to the bottom picture.) *These animals are called peccaries. Say it with me:* peccaries. *Peccaries live in the desert.*

 Peccaries have hard hooves. What sound do you think they make? Tell your partner.

Paragraph 1

- *The toad hears big sounds. Read the top part of the page with me:* Thunk, thunk, thunk. Clink, clunk, clink, clunk. Sounds shake the soil. *Soil is another word for dirt or ground. Is this the sound of rain?* (no)

Paragraph 2

- *The sound is made by a herd, or group, of peccaries. Their hooves make a big sound on the ground. They sound like a hammer.*

Page 337

Illustration

- *Look at the animal. What is it doing?* (jumping, leaping, hopping) *What sound do you think it makes when it hops?* (Question is open.)

Paragraph 1

- *The toad is under the ground. What sound does the toad hear now?* (Pop, pop, pop.)

- *Let's read the last line of paragraph 1 together:* Is this the rain at last? *Does the toad want the rain to come?* (yes)

Pages 336–337

Thunk, thunk, thunk.
Clink, clunk,
clink, clunk.
Sounds shake the soil.

But it's only a herd of peccaries.
Their hooves hammer the ground.

336

Pages 338–339

Will the rain *ever* come?
The desert's so hot, so dry!
And the toad's been waiting
so many months in her
basement **burrow** home.

Author's Purpose
Why does the author include information about other desert animals?

338

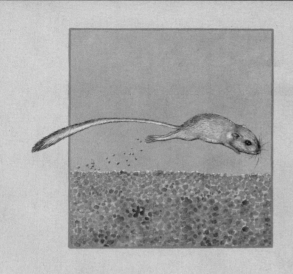

Pop, pop, pop.
What's that sound now?
Is this the rain at last?

No, it's a rat,
hopping in **lengthy** leaps
like a tiny kangaroo.

337

Tap, tap, tap!
Could this be it?
Is this the rain at last?
No, it's a gila woodpecker
tapping on a tall green cactus.

339

Paragraph 2

- *The rat is making the sound as it jumps and hops. It makes lengthy leaps. That means it makes very long jumps, like a tiny, or small, kangaroo.*

- *Let's read this paragraph together:* No, it's a rat, hopping in lengthy leaps like a tiny kangaroo.

Page 338

Illustration

- *Look at the toad in the picture. What is she doing?* (waiting or listening)

Text

- *The desert is very hot and very dry. The toad waits for the rain. She waits for a long time in her burrow. That's the hole where she lives.* (Point to the toad in her burrow.) *Say* burrow *with me:* burrow.

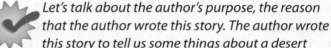

Let's talk about the author's purpose, the reason that the author wrote this story. The author wrote this story to tell us some things about a desert animal. What animal is it? (toad)

- *What do we know about the toad so far?* (She lives in a burrow in the desert. She digs. She listens. She waits for the rain.) *Why does the toad wait for the rain? We don't know yet. We have to keep reading to find out.*

Page 339

Illustration

- *Look at that bird. It's a woodpecker. Say it with me:* woodpecker. *It has a long beak.* (Point to its beak.) *Look at this desert plant.* (Point to the cactus.) *It is called a cactus. Say it with me:* cactus.

Text

- *The woodpecker hits the cactus with its beak. What sound does it make?* (Tap, tap, tap!)

Page 340

Illustration

- *This is a footprint.* (Point to the footprint.) *Who do you think made it—an animal or a person?* (a person) *It's a person's boot. Boots walk on the sand. What sound do you think they make?* (Responses will vary.)

Paragraph 1

- *The toad hears a loud sound. Let's read the first three lines together:* The toad feels the ground begin to shake. Then a crunch, crunch, crunch that's loud.

- *Crunch, crunch, crunch is a fun sound. Cookies crunch. Crackers crunch. What other foods crunch?* (apples, cold cereal)

- *The toad hears* crunch, crunch, crunch. *Let's read the last line together:* Is this the rain? *Do you think* crunch, crunch, crunch *is the sound of rain?* (no)

Paragraph 2

- Crunch, crunch, crunch *is the sound of the park ranger walking. Park rangers work in the desert. They take care of the animals and the plants. They have to walk a lot in the desert.*

Page 341

Illustration

- *Look at the snake in the picture. It is called a rattlesnake. Say it with me:* rattlesnake. *What sound do you think it makes?* (Responses will vary.)

Paragraphs 1 and 2

- *Now the toad hears* tsk, tsk, tsk. *Is it the rain?* (no)

- *It's a rattlesnake. The rattlesnake's sound warns, or tells, everyone not to come near it. Let's read the warning together:* STAY AWAY! *What do you think might happen if you go near a rattlesnake?* (The snake might bite you; the snake might hurt you.)

Pages 340–341

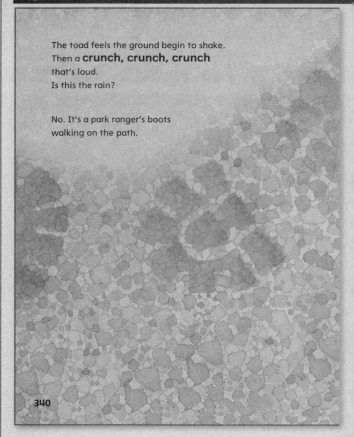

The toad feels the ground begin to shake.
Then a **crunch, crunch, crunch**
that's loud.
Is this the rain?

No. It's a park ranger's boots
walking on the path.

340

Pages 342–343

Surely that rumbling…
that rumble, rumbling….
Surely that's the rain…?
Not yet.
It's the thunder of a **distant** storm.
But perhaps the rain is near.

342

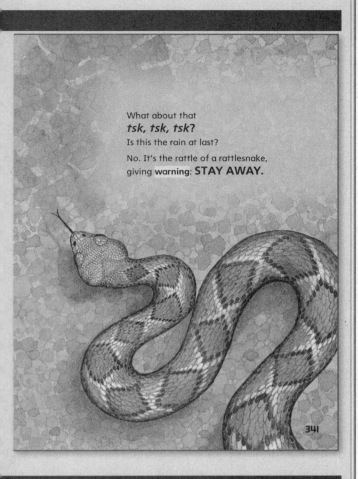

What about that
tsk, tsk, tsk?
Is this the rain at last?
No. It's the rattle of a rattlesnake,
giving warning: STAY AWAY.

341

Plip, plop, **plip,** plop.
Plip, plop, **plop!**
Is this the rain at last?
Plop **thunk.** Plop **thunk.**
Plop **thunk** *gussssshhhhhhh!*
It is rain!

The toad hears it.
She digs.

343

Page 342

Illustration

■ *Look at all the clouds.* (Point to the storm clouds.) *Is it going to rain?* (yes)

■ *Sometimes when it rains, there's a big storm. You see lightning in the sky.* (Make a zigzag motion.) *You hear a big sound, boom!*

■ *Sometimes, when the storm is far away, the boom is small. It sounds like rumbling. It makes this sound:* rumble, rumble, rumble. (Say it with a soft voice.)

Text

■ *The storm is distant. That means it's faraway. But we can hear it rumbling.*

 The author writes about the rumbling sound for a reason. If the toad can hear rumbling, will there be sun or rain? (rain) *The author wants us to know that rain is finally coming to the desert.*

Page 343

Illustration

■ *Look at the picture. What is happening?* (It's raining.)

■ *Look at the toad. Where do you think she is going?* (up to the ground to see the rain)

Paragraph 1

■ *The toad hears a sound. It's the rain! Let's read the first two lines together:* Plip, plop, plip, plop. Plip, plop, plop!

■ *The rain makes more sounds. Let's read them together.* Plop thunk. Plop thunk. Plop thunk gussssshhhhhhh!

Paragraph 2

■ *The toad digs. Does she dig up toward the rain?* (Point up.) *Or does she dig down, away from the rain?* (Point down.) (She digs up toward the rain.)

Dig, Wait, Listen:
A Desert Toad's Tale

Page 344

✓ *Let's summarize the story so far. The toad is waiting for _____. (rain) She hears the soft sound of a _____ (scorpion), a herd of _____ (peccaries), a hopping _____ (rat), a tapping _____ (woodpecker), the boots of a _____ (ranger), and the rattle of a _____ (rattlesnake). She finally hears rain.*

Illustration

■ *Look at the toad.* (Point to the toad.) *Is she in her hole or out in the rain?* (out in the rain) *She isn't waiting anymore. How do you think the toad feels now?* (happy)

Paragraph 1

■ *The rain is coming down hard now. Let's read the last sentence together:* Heavy rain pounds the desert floor. *That means that heavy rain hits the ground hard. Do you think the sounds are quiet or loud now?* (loud)

PARTNERS *These words tell us the sound of the rain falling in the desert.* (Write the words *plop, thunk,* and *gush* on the board.) *Read them with me:* plop, thunk, gush. *Find these words on this page. Read them to your partner. Then listen to your partner read to you.*

Paragraph 2

■ *The toad pushes.* (Push hands.) *Then she pops out of the sand.* (Use one hand to represent the hole in the sand and jump the other hand out of it.) *She's in the open air now. That means she is outside.*

Page 345

Paragraphs 1 and 2

■ *The toad hears* bleat, bleat, bleat. *Does the rain ever sound like that?* (no) *Male spadefoot toads are making those sounds.*

■ *Male means "boy." What sounds do male toads make?* (bleat, bleat, bleat) *What do those sounds mean?* ("Here, come here!")

Synonyms and Circumlocution

Remind children that they can ask for synonyms to help clarify words or expressions they do not understand. Ask, *What is another way of saying "make it"?* (survive, live)

Pages 344–345

Plop **thunk.**
Plop **thunk.**
Plop **thunk** *gussssshhhhhh!*
Heavy rain pounds the desert floor.

Push, push, and the toad pops right out, into the open air.

344

Pages 346–347

Plop **thunk,** plop **thunk,** plop **thunk** *gussssshhhhhh!*

346

Bleat, bleat, bleat!
The toad hears loud bleats.
Is that the rain sound too?

No. It's male spadefoot toads,
calling: Here, come here!

Plop **thunk**. Plop **thunk**.
Plop **thunk**
gussssshhhhhhh!
The toad hops in a puddle.
She lays her eggs,
like beads of glass.

345

Two days later, the eggs hatch. Wriggling and
wiggling in their puddle home, the tadpoles
are here at last!

347

Paragraph 3

■ *The toad hops in a puddle. A puddle is a little pool of water on the ground. It comes from the rain. Say* puddle *with me:* puddle. *The toad lays her eggs in the puddle. The eggs are very, very small.*

Page 346

Illustration

■ *Look at all this water. This is the puddle. The toad laid her eggs here. It is still raining. Look at the rain hitting the water.*

Text

■ *Let's read the sound of the rain together.* Plop thunk, plop thunk, plop thunk *gussssshhhhhhh!*

Page 347

Illustration

■ *Look at all these little animals in the puddle.* (Point to the tadpoles.) *They came from the toad's eggs.*

■ *The little animals are the toad's babies. Do these animals look like the toad?* (no) *They will grow, and they will look like the toad later. They are called tadpoles. Say it with me:* tadpoles.

Text

■ *A few days after the toad lays her eggs, the eggs hatch. That means the eggs open up and the tadpoles come out of the eggs.*

■ *The tadpoles wriggle and wiggle.* (Hold your arm out and wiggle it.) *Say and do it with me:* wriggle and wiggle. (Repeat the gesture and encourage the children to imitate you.)

■ *Now let's read this page together:* Two days later, the eggs hatch. Wriggling and wiggling in their puddle home, the tadpoles are here at last!

PARTNERS Take turns with your partner to tell what is happening on this page of the story.

Pages 348–349

Illustrations

- *Look at this tadpole.* (Point to the first picture in the series.) *Does it have a tail?* (yes) *Does it have legs?* (no)

- *The tadpole grows.* (Point to the second picture.) *Look at it now. Does it still have a tail?* (yes) *How many legs do you see?* (one) *What else is different?* (the eyes)

- *The tadpole grows more.* (Point to the third picture.) *How many legs do you see now?* (four)

- *The tadpole grows more.* (Point to the fourth picture.) *Now it has dark spots, or circles on it.* (Point to them) *What else is different?* (the color) *Does it look like a toad now?* (yes)

Text

- *The tadpoles eat and grow. They get legs. The puddle starts to dry. That means that the water is going away. Will the toads make it—will they live?*

- *Yes, they will live. Now they have legs. They can use their legs to crawl. They crawl out of the puddle. They can use their legs to leap, or jump. They leap into the desert.*

- *Let's read the last sentence on page 349 together:* They rest, then LEAP into the desert beyond.

Monitor Oral Production

Remember to model self-corrective techniques on a regular basis as you speak to children. Pretend to mispronounce words and self-correct.

Pages 348–349

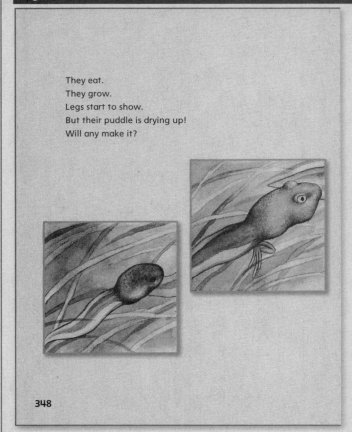

They eat.
They grow.
Legs start to show.
But their puddle is drying up!
Will any make it?

348

Pages 350–351

350

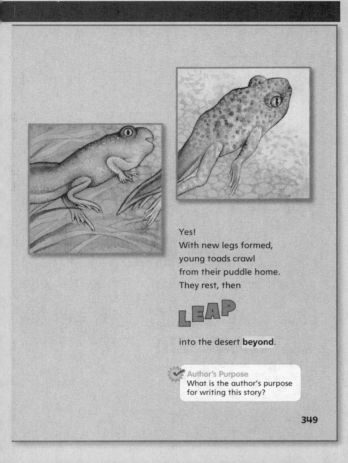

Yes!
With new legs formed,
young toads crawl
from their puddle home.
They rest, then

LEAP

into the desert **beyond.**

Author's Purpose
What is the author's purpose
for writing this story?

349

Pages 350–351

Illustrations

- *This is the desert after the rain. It looks different now. Point to the grass. Point to the flowers. After the rain, things grow in the desert.*

- *Look at all those toads! Some of them have tails. Point to a toad with a tail. These toads will lose their tails soon. Some toads have already lost their tails. Point to a toad without a tail.*

- *All the toads are jumping around the desert. What sound do you think they make when they jump? (Question is open.)*

Text

- *The toads jump. What sound do they make? (Thump, thump, thump.) The toads are tiny. Does that mean they are big or little? (little)*

- *Let's read this page together:* Thump, thump, thump. Hundreds of tiny toads jump. The rain has made the desert green.

Thump, thump, thump.
Hundreds of tiny toads jump.
The rain has made the desert green.

351

Dig, Wait, Listen:
A Desert Toad's Tale

Yet it won't be long till the desert's dry,
and toads dig down deep with their
spadefoot feet, to wait for that sound...
that marvelous sound,
the sound of the desert rain.

352

Page 352

Illustration

- *Look at that toad. Is she going up to the rain or down under the sand?* (down under the sand)

- *This toad is in a hole in the sand.* (Point to the toad on page 353.) *What do we call the hole where the toad lives?* (burrow). *Let's say it together:* burrow.

Text

- *Soon the desert will be dry again. The rain will stop. The toads will dig down under the sand. Then they will wait. What will they wait for?* (the sound of the rain)

- *The sound of the desert rain is marvelous. That means the sound is special and wonderful.*

The toad waits and waits for the sound of rain. That may be why the sound seems so marvelous. Talk with your partner about special things you've waited for that finally came. (Responses will vary.)

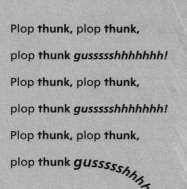

Plop **thunk,** plop **thunk,**

plop **thunk** *gusssssshhhhhhh!*

Plop **thunk,** plop **thunk,**

plop **thunk** *gusssssshhhhhhh!*

Plop **thunk,** plop **thunk,**

plop **thunk** *gusssssshhhhhh!*

353

Page 353

Whole Page

- *The toads wait to hear this sound:* plop, thunk, gusssssshhhhhhh. *Let's read the first two lines together:* Plop thunk, plop thunk, plop thunk gusssssshhhhhhh

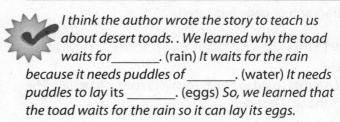 *I think the author wrote the story to teach us about desert toads. . We learned why the toad waits for*_____. (rain) *It waits for the rain because it needs puddles of* _____. (water) *It needs puddles to lay its* _____. (eggs) *So, we learned that the toad waits for the rain so it can lay its eggs.*

- *What are some other things we learned about the toad?* (It lives under the sand. Its babies are called tadpoles. Its babies don't have legs. Its babies swim in the puddle.)

- *We also learned some things about the desert because it is the toad's home. Does it rain much in the desert?* (no) *Is there a lot of sand in the desert?* (yes) *When is the desert green?* (after the rain)

The Sonoran Desert

Access Core Content

Teacher Note Pose the questions after you read the paragraph or page indicated.

Page 356

Title

- *Listen as I read the title. Then let's read it together:* The Sonoran Desert.

Paragraph 1

- *The Sonoran Desert is in Mexico, California, and Arizona. It is very, very big.*

- *This is a very big number.* (Write the number 100,000 on the board and point to it.) *It's one hundred thousand. Say it with me:* one hundred thousand. *The Sonoran Desert is this size—100,000 square miles.*

- *The Sonoran Desert is very dry. In some places it doesn't rain for one or two years. In other places there are sometimes big rainstorms.*

Paragraph 2

- *The Sonoran Desert has a high temperature. Say it with me:* temperature. *A high temperature means that it's very hot.*

- *Let's say this number together:* one hundred. (Write the number 100 on the board and point to it.) *The temperature in the Sonoran Desert is sometimes more than 100 degrees Fahrenheit. That's very, very hot.*

- *In winter, the desert isn't as hot, but it isn't freezing either.* Freezing *means "very cold."*

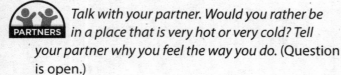 *Talk with your partner. Would you rather be in a place that is very hot or very cold? Tell your partner why you feel the way you do.* (Question is open.)

Paragraph 3

- *Desert animals and plants can survive in the desert. They have special ways to live there. Can people survive, or live, without water?* (no) *We need water every day. But desert plants and animals can survive with very little water.*

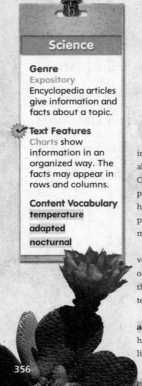

Science

Genre
Expository
Encyclopedia articles give information and facts about a topic.

Text Features
Charts show information in an organized way. The facts may appear in rows and columns.

Content Vocabulary
temperature
adapted
nocturnal

The Sonoran Desert

The Sonoran Desert is a dry area in the American Southwest. It covers about 100,000 square miles in parts of California, Arizona, and Mexico. Some parts of the Sonoran Desert may not have rain for one or two years. Other parts have sudden summer rainstorms more frequently.

Summer in the Sonoran Desert is very, very hot. The **temperature** is often more than 100 degrees during the day. Even in the winter, the temperature is usually above freezing.

Desert plants and animals have **adapted** to life in the desert. They have special ways to survive with very little water and in very hot weather.

356

Sonoran Desert Animals

Name	Type of Animal	What It Eats
black-chinned hummingbird	bird	flowers, nectar, nuts
coyote	mammal	small animals, insects, plants
ground snake	reptile	insects
horned toad	reptile	plants, insects
roadrunner	bird	insects, lizards, snakes
Sonoran Desert toad	amphibian	insects, mice

The animal name is in the first column.

Information about the animal is in the row.

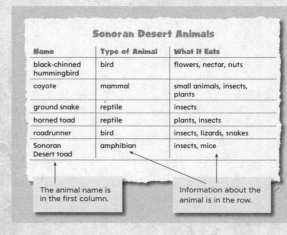

358

Science

Plants

The Sonoran Desert has many different kinds of cactus plants. Cactus plants can live a long time without rain.

Cactus plants store water in their thick stems. They also have thick, waxy leaves that help keep in water. Cactus roots grow close to the top of the ground. When it does rain, the roots can soak up the water very quickly.

357

Animals

Like desert plants, desert animals can live without much rain. Most desert animals do not have to drink water. They get the water they need from their food.

Many desert animals are **nocturnal**. This means they come out to find food only at night, when it is cool. During the hot days, these animals hide in the shade or underground. Staying cool helps animals keep water in their bodies.

Connect and Compare

1. Which desert animals eat insects? Which desert animals eat only plants? **Chart**
2. Think about this encyclopedia article and *Dig, Wait, Listen.* How is the spadefoot toad like the other animals of the Sonoran Desert? **Reading/Writing Across Texts**

 Science Activity

Use an encyclopedia or other references to research desert plants. Make a chart that gives two facts for each plant.

LOG ON · FIND OUT **Science** Desert Facts
www.macmillanmh.com

359

Page 357

Whole Page

- *Look at the plants in the pictures. They are all cactus plants. A cactus has parts like other plants.* (Write on the board: *roots, stems, leaves*)

- *Let's read these words together:* roots, stems, leaves. *Which part of the plant is under the ground?* (the roots) *Which part of the plant holds the plant up?* (Hold your forearm up straight.) (the stem) *Cactus plants have roots, stems, and leaves.*

- *Cactus plants hold water in their leaves and stems. They can hold water for a long, long time. Their roots are close to the top of the ground. They can soak up, or drink, the rainwater very quickly.*

Page 358

Chart

- *Let's read the title of the chart together:* Sonoran Desert Animals. *This chart tells us about animals in the Sonoran Desert.*

- *The first column tells the name of the animal. What does the second column tell?* (the type of animal) *What does the third column tell?* (what the animal eats)

- *Let's read the first animal name together:* black-chinned hummingbird. *What kind of animal is it? Look in the second column.* (It's a bird). *What does this bird eat? Look in the third column.* (flowers, nectar, and nuts) *Nectar is the liquid inside a flower. It's like juice for bugs and animals!*

Page 359

Paragraph 1

- *Desert animals can live a long time without rain. They don't drink often. How do they get water when they need it?* (from plants)

Paragraph 2

- *Many desert animals are nocturnal. Say it with me:* nocturnal. *Nocturnal animals come out at night to find their food. The desert is cool at night. It's hot in the day. Nocturnal animals rest or sleep during the day. Where do they rest and sleep?* (in the shade or underground)

Use the word chart to study this week's vocabulary words.
Write a sentence using each word in your writer's notebook.

Word	Context Sentence	Illustration
burrow _____	I saw a rabbit run into its <u>burrow</u> and hide.	**Which animal lives in a burrow—an eagle or a gopher?**
beyond _____	We are not allowed to go <u>beyond</u> the fence.	
warning _____	When a cat hisses, it is a <u>warning</u> sign to leave it alone.	
lengthy _____	There was a <u>lengthy</u> wait to get into the park.	**If a wait is lengthy, is it long or short?**
distant _____	I can see the <u>distant</u> stars.	

© Macmillan/McGraw-Hill

**Read each question and prompt. Discuss the answers
with your group. Use your Leveled Reader to find
details to support your answers. Then write your
answers on the blank lines or on another sheet of
paper.**

1. Tell what you learned about the Sonoran Desert.

_____

2. Describe where the Sonoran Desert is and how this desert is different
from some other deserts.

_____

3. Give examples of animals that live in the Sonoran Desert.

_____

4. Describe how different animals survive in the desert.

_____

5. Give examples of plants that live in the desert. Tell how they survive.

_____

6. Write one question about the book to ask your group.

_____

_____

Splish! Splash! Animal Baths

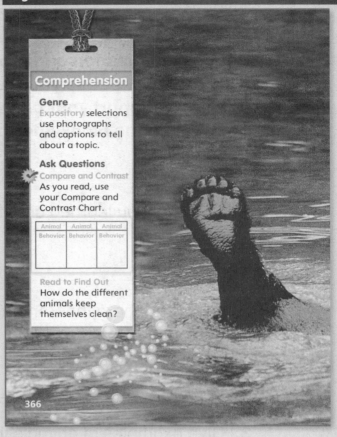

Comprehension

Genre
Expository selections use photographs and captions to tell about a topic.

Ask Questions
Compare and Contrast
As you read, use your Compare and Contrast Chart.

Animal Behavior	Animal Behavior	Animal Behavior

Read to Find Out
How do the different animals keep themselves clean?

366

Pages 366–367

Prior to reading the selection with children, they should have listened to the selection on **StudentWorks Plus**, the interactive eBook. In addition, selection vocabulary should have been pretaught using the **Visual Vocabulary Resources**.

Access Core Content

Teacher Note Pose the questions after you read the paragraph or page indicated.

Pages 366–367

Title and Photo
- *The title of this selection is* Splish! Splash! Animal Baths. *When animals or people splash in the water, the water goes in all different directions! What does the word* splish *sound like?* (splash) Splish *is a made-up word that sounds like* splash.

Photo
- *Look at the picture. What is the bear doing?* (taking a bath) *Do you think the bear likes baths?* (yes)

Pages 368–369

Text
- *People use water to clean themselves. How do you use water to clean yourself?* (wash face, wash hands, take a bath, brush teeth) *Some animals clean themselves with water, too.*

- *This page has some funny words on it:* Splish! Splash! Squirt! Squirt! *These are sounds that water makes. These are also things you can do in water or with water. Let's read them together, using our voices to make them sound like water:* Splish! Splash! Squirt! Squirt!

SPLISH! SPLASH!

Take a bath.
Brush your teeth clean.

And think of the animals.

They clean themselves, too.

Squirt!

An elephant sprays water over its back.

Squirt!!

Baby will get a shower, too.

368

- Now, let's read the first part of the page together. It tells us what the selection is all about: Splish! Splash! Take a bath. Brush your teeth clean. And think of the animals. They clean themselves, too.

 Tell your partner about times you have seen animals cleaning themselves. Tell what animals you saw. Tell how they cleaned themselves. (Cats and dogs lick themselves clean. Birds splash in puddles or in birdbaths.)

Photo

- *The elephants are using water to get clean. The elephants use their trunks to spray water. The elephant's trunk is its long nose. Point to the trunks of the elephants in the picture.*

 Think about how elephants get clean. Is it more like taking shower or taking a bath? (taking a shower) We use a shower to spray water on us. What do elephants use? (their trunks)

Non-verbal Cues

Remind children that they can use non-verbal cues to share information when they are not able to do so verbally. Encourage children to use pantomime or draw.

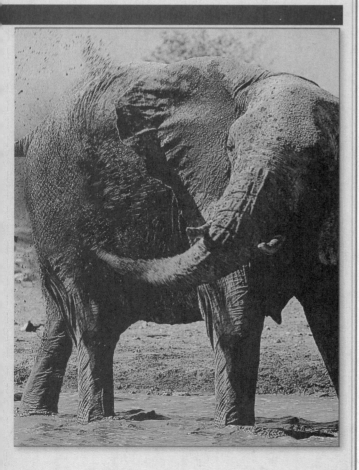

Pages 370–371

Photo

- *Look at the picture. What do you think the pig is doing?* (Question is open.)

Text

- *Let's read the first sentence together to find out what the picture has to do with animal baths:* Pigs take their baths in thick, brown mud.

- *The second sentence on this page is fun to read. Listen as I read it aloud:* They soak, slog, snort … and seem to smile. *What sound do a lot of the words begin with?* (the sound of *s*) That's what makes the sentence fun to read.

- Soak, slog, *and* snort *are words that tell us what the pigs do in the mud. The pigs soak. That means they spend a lot of time just lying in the wet mud.*

- Slog *means to "move around slowly."* (Demonstrate moving slowly and with great effort, as though through mud or snow). *The pigs have to work hard to move because the mud is so thick.*

- Snort *is the sound that pigs make.* (demonstrate) *Let's make the sound together.*

- *The mud is fun for pigs. It is also a good way for them to get cool and to get rid of itches.*

- *Let's think about ways a pig's bath is different from a person's bath. People take baths in* _____. (water) *Pigs take baths in* _____. (mud) *People take baths to get* _____. (clean) *Pigs take baths to cool their skin and to get rid of* _____. (itches)

Pages 370–371

370

Pages 372–373

Birds take baths in puddles. Or shower under sprinklers or waterfalls.

372

Pigs take their baths in thick, brown mud. They soak, slog, snort ... and seem to smile. Mud cools their skin. And best of all, it gets rid of **itches**, as well.

371

Once clean, they **preen**— smoothing, fluffing, and straightening their feathers. That's like hair brushing for you.

Compare and Contrast
How does the way a bird takes a bath differ from the way a pig does?

373

Photo

■ *Look at the small picture. What kind of animal is it?* (bird) *What is the bird doing?* (taking a bath)

Text

■ *Birds take baths or showers. Some birds take baths in puddles. Some birds take showers under* sprinklers. *Sprinklers are things people use to spray water on grass and other plants.*

■ *Some people put birdbaths in their yards. This gives birds a place to bathe. A birdbath looks like a swimming pool for birds.*

Whole Page

■ *After a shower or a bath, birds preen. That's what the birds in the picture are doing.*

■ *When birds come out of water, their feathers are wet and flat. What do the birds do to dry off and to look better?* (They smooth, fluff, and straighten their feathers.) *That's called preening.*

 Pretend that you and your partner are birds. Your arms are your wings. You've just had a bath or shower. Now it's time to preen. Use your fingers to fluff, smooth, and straighten the feathers on your wings.

Patterns in Language

Some grammatical structures, such as the ending -*ing,* may pose difficulties to ELLs. Point out that there are several examples of words ending in -*ing* that describe actions animals do, such as *smoothing, fluffing, straightening.* These actions can also be described as *making smooth, making fluffy, making straight.* Help children find a pattern.

Page 374

Photo

- *Look at the picture. This animal is a duck. Let's be sure you know parts of the duck that will help you understand this page. Point to the duck's tail. Point to a feather. Point to the duck's beak. A duck's beak is called a* bill.

Text

- *A duck spreads oil on its feathers to keep the rain off. The oil makes the water run off the feathers. That's how a duck waterproofs itself. What do we use to waterproof ourselves, or keep dry?* (raincoat, umbrella, boots)

- Soggy *means "wet." The ducks don't want to be soggy, and cold.*

- Ducky *is an old-fashioned word that means "good." The author says that it wouldn't be* ducky *if ducks got soggy and cold. Do you think it would be ducky for you to get soggy and cold?* (no)

Page 375

Whole Page

- *This bear is rubbing his back against a tree.* (Demonstrate rubbing your back against the wall.) *Is the bear doing a silly dance or getting rid of itches and bugs?* (getting rid of itches and bugs)

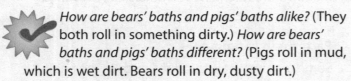 *How are bears' baths and pigs' baths alike?* (They both roll in something dirty.) *How are bears' baths and pigs' baths different?* (Pigs roll in mud, which is wet dirt. Bears roll in dry, dusty dirt.)

Ducks do extra work. They spread oil on their feathers. This special oil waterproofs them. Without it, ducks would get soggy and cold … which wouldn't be *ducky* at all!

374

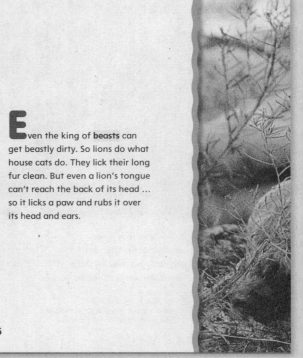

Even the king of **beasts** can get beastly dirty. So lions do what house cats do. They lick their long fur clean. But even a lion's tongue can't reach the back of its head … so it licks a paw and rubs it over its head and ears.

376

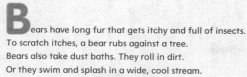

Bears have long fur that gets itchy and full of insects. To scratch itches, a bear rubs against a tree. Bears also take dust baths. They roll in dirt. Or they swim and splash in a wide, cool stream.

375

377

Pages 376–377

Photo

- *This is a picture of a lion. What is the lion doing?* (licking itself) *Point to the lion's tongue. Point to the lion's feet. Lions' feet are called* paws. *Say it with me:* paws.

Text

- *The first sentence talks about the* king of beasts. *The lion is called the* king of beasts. *A beast is a large animal with four feet.*

- *Let's read this page together:* Even the king of the beasts can get beastly dirty. So lions do what house cats do. They lick their long fur clean. But even a lion's tongue can't reach the back of its head . . . so it licks a paw and rubs it over its head and ears.

- *Lions clean themselves by licking. What house pet cleans itself that way, too?* (a cat)

PARTNERS *Pretend that you and your partner are lions, and do what they do. Don't really lick your hands, though. Just pretend to lick them. Then use them to rub the backs of your heads and your ears.*

Pages 378–379

Photo

- *These animals are a kind of ape called a* chimpanzee. Chimp *is a shorter way to say* chimpanzee.

Text

- *Chimps use their fingers to pull things from their fur. What kinds of things might get stuck in a chimp's fur?* (sticks, bugs, leaves)

- *Pretend you are a chimp. Use your fingers to comb things out of the fur on your arms.* (demonstrate)

- *Let's read page 379 together:* <u>Chimps bite and pull bugs and leaves from their family and friends' fur. What are good buddies for?</u>

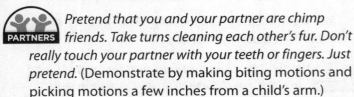 *Pretend that you and your partner are chimp friends. Take turns cleaning each other's fur. Don't really touch your partner with your teeth or fingers. Just pretend.* (Demonstrate by making biting motions and picking motions a few inches from a child's arm.)

Page 380

Photo

- *There are two kinds of animals in this picture: a giraffe and a bird called an oxpecker. Point to the giraffe on this page. Point to one of the oxpeckers. Why do you think the oxpeckers are on the giraffe?* (They want a ride. They're cleaning the giraffe.)

Text

- *The article says that the oxpeckers are* <u>hanging around</u>. *Let me use that phrase in another sentence to show what it means.* On sunny days, I like to *hang around* my yard and work on the garden. *Does* hang around *mean "run around" or "stay in one place"?* (stay in one place)

A comb might come in **handy** for cleaning a chimpanzee's fur. But chimps don't have combs, so fingers work fine.

378

Oxpeckers, a type of bird, spend their time hanging around. Where? On the bodies of giraffes. Giraffes don't seem to mind. Oxpeckers peck away ticks. They get a meal, and the giraffe gets clean.

380

Chimps bite and pull bugs and leaves from their family's and friends' fur. What are good buddies for?

379

- The author says that the birds help giraffes with ticks. The word tick has more than one meaning. A tick can be the sound a clock makes: tick tock, tick tock. A tick can also be a tiny bug. Which one fits here? (tiny bug)

- Do you think that it would be easy for a giraffe to clean its own neck? (no) Oxpeckers help giraffes by cleaning them. How does that help oxpeckers? (They get food.)

Page 381

Photo

- There are two kinds of animals in this picture: a hippopotamus and some fish. Hippo is a short way of saying hippopotamus. Point to the hippo on this page. Point to the fish.

Text

- On this page, we read that hippos wade in rivers and in ponds. That means the hippos walk through the water.

- The author says that fish nibble, or eat, algae off hippos. Algae are tiny living things that live in water. They are like plants, but they don't have leaves or roots.

- Let's read the last four sentences of this page together: Fish nibble algae off a hippo's skin. Does it tickle the hippo? Only hippos know. And they won't say.

- Why does the author say: Only hippos know. And they won't say. (because hippos can't talk) The author is saying this to be funny.

Hippos have helpers, too. But these helpers are under water, in the rivers and ponds where hippos wade. Fish **nibble** algae off a hippo's skin. Does it tickle the hippo? Only hippos know. And they won't say.

381

Pages 382–383

Photo

- *What kind of animal do you see in this picture?* (fish)
Fish live in water. Do you think they need to get clean?
(Question is open.)

Paragraph 1

- *Listen as I read the first two sentences aloud:* Fish don't take baths. They live in water. But some do try to stay clean. *What might get on a fish to make it dirty?* (algae, sand, insects)

- *Let's read the rest of the paragraph together:* Big fish wait in line—not for a carwash, but for a cleaner fish. Cleaner *can mean "more clean."* Cleaner *can also mean "someone who cleans." Which meaning fits this sentence?* (someone who cleans) *A cleaner fish is a fish that cleans other fish.*

The author compares fish waiting in line for the cleaner fish to cars waiting in line for a carwash. Let's show how these two things are alike. One partner will draw a line of cars at a carwash. The other partner will draw a line of fish waiting for a cleaner fish to clean them. Share your pictures. Talk about how they are alike.

Paragraph 2

- *The cleaner fish cleans bigger fish by biting things off the big fish's scales.* Scales *are the small, hard pieces that cover a fish's body. Point to a scale on the fish in the picture.*

Pages 382–383

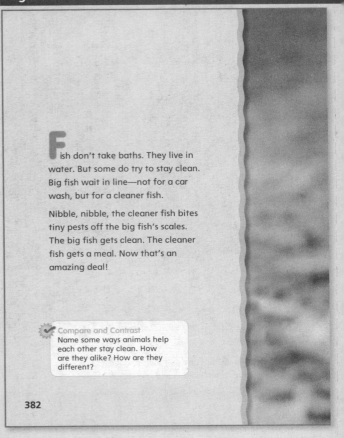

Fish don't take baths. They live in water. But some do try to stay clean. Big fish wait in line—not for a car wash, but for a cleaner fish.

Nibble, nibble, the cleaner fish bites tiny pests off the big fish's scales. The big fish gets clean. The cleaner fish gets a meal. Now that's an amazing deal!

> **Compare and Contrast**
> Name some ways animals help each other stay clean. How are they alike? How are they different?

382

Pages 384–385

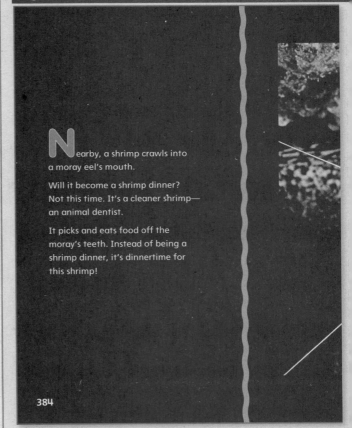

Nearby, a shrimp crawls into a moray eel's mouth.

Will it become a shrimp dinner? Not this time. It's a cleaner shrimp— an animal dentist.

It picks and eats food off the moray's teeth. Instead of being a shrimp dinner, it's dinnertime for this shrimp!

384

383

385

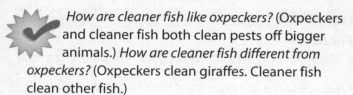

How are cleaner fish like oxpeckers? (Oxpeckers and cleaner fish both clean pests off bigger animals.) *How are cleaner fish different from oxpeckers?* (Oxpeckers clean giraffes. Cleaner fish clean other fish.)

Pages 384–385

Photo

■ *Look at the picture. There are two kinds of animals in this picture: an eel and a shrimp. The bigger animal is the eel. Point to the eel and say it with me:* eel. *The smaller animal is the shrimp. Point to the shrimp and say it with me:* shrimp.

Paragraphs 1–2

■ *What does the author mean when she asks:* Will it become a shrimp dinner? (Will the eel eat the shrimp?)

■ *The eel isn't going to eat the shrimp. What is the shrimp going to do in the eel's mouth?* (The shrimp is going to clean the eel's teeth.)

Paragraph 3

■ *Let's read the last sentence together:* Instead of being a shrimp dinner, it's dinnertime for this shrimp! *Tell me in your own words what this means.* (The eel will not eat the shrimp. The shrimp eats what is on the eel's teeth.)

Pages 386–387

Photos

- *What animals are in these pictures?* (elephant, chimps)

- *Let's read the last page together:* Now that you've heard about animal baths and animal dentists, and how animals splish, splash, peck, and preen . . . it's time to take your bath. Splish and splash. And think of the animals. They, too, are getting clean.

 Which animal's bath is most like your bath or shower? Why? (Responses will vary.)

Now that you've heard about animal baths and animal dentists, and how animals splash, splash, peck, and preen ... it's time to take *your* bath.

Splish and splash.

And think of the animals. They, too, are getting clean.

387

- Let's look through all the pictures and think about some of the different animals. Which ones clean themselves in water? (bears, elephants, birds) *Which ones clean themselves with mud or dirt and dust?* (pigs, bears)

- *Which ones preen?* (birds) *Which ones lick themselves clean?* (lions) *Which ones help other animals?* (chimps, oxpeckers, cleaner fish, shrimp)

Tell your partner three facts you learned about animal baths that you did not know before. (Answers will vary.)

Interactive Question - Response Guide

Ant and Grasshopper

Access Core Content

Teacher Note Pose the questions after you read the paragraph or page indicated.

Page 390

Title, Characters, and Setting

- *The title of this play is* Ant and Grasshopper. *It comes from a fable, or story, by Aesop. Aesop lived a long time ago. A fable is a story with a moral, or lesson.*

- *Lets find out about the characters. (Point to the word* Characters *under the title.) The narrator talks about the setting and tells what is happening. The main characters are Ant and Grasshopper. Point to the ant in the picture. Point to the grasshopper.*

- *Now let's find out about the setting. (Point to the word* Setting *under the title.) This play takes place on an ant hill in a meadow. A* meadow *is a grassy field. An* ant hill *is a little pile of dirt.*

- *Point to the* ant hill *in the picture. Point to the hole at the top of the hill. Ants go down the hole to their home.*

Scene 1

- *Let's read the first part of the play together. I will read the narrator's part. One half of the group will read Ant's part. The other half will read Grasshopper's part. (Designate groups, and read aloud.)*

- *It's a beautiful summer day. Most of the insects are gathering food. That means they are collecting food from different places and bringing it home. What does Grasshopper want to do?* (play leaf hop with Ant)

- *Ant says he doesn't have time to play games. What does he have to do instead?* (put away food for winter)

- *Grasshopper says there is no rush. He thinks there is plenty of time, and that he does not have to hurry. Is he right?* (Responses will vary.)

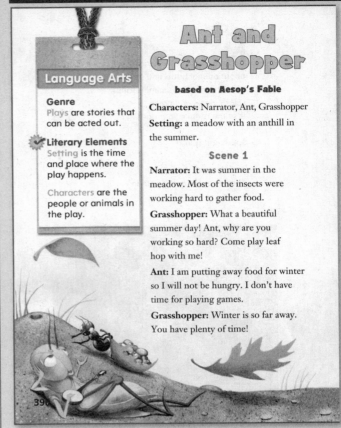

Language Arts

Genre
Plays are stories that can be acted out.

✓ Literary Elements
Setting is the time and place where the play happens.

Characters are the people or animals in the play.

Ant and Grasshopper

based on Aesop's Fable

Characters: Narrator, Ant, Grasshopper

Setting: a meadow with an anthill in the summer.

Scene 1

Narrator: It was summer in the meadow. Most of the insects were working hard to gather food.

Grasshopper: What a beautiful summer day! Ant, why are you working so hard? Come play leaf hop with me!

Ant: I am putting away food for winter so I will not be hungry. I don't have time for playing games.

Grasshopper: Winter is so far away. You have plenty of time!

390

Language Arts

Ant: Winter lasts as long as summer. You have to be ready! I think you should save some food.

Grasshopper: I'll do it next week. There is no rush.

Narrator: Week after week, Ant worked. Week after week, Grasshopper played leaf hop.

Scene 2

Narrator: Soon winter came. The meadow was covered with snow. There was no food to be found.

Grasshopper: Ant, please help me. I am cold and hungry.

Ant: Oh, Grasshopper, you did not plan. I will give you some food, but next summer you must gather food for yourself.

Narrator: Ant gave Grasshopper some food. Ant also taught Grasshopper an important lesson!

Connect and Compare

1. Why is the setting of the play important to the characters' feelings and actions? **Setting**

2. Think about this play and the selection *Splish! Splash!* How do the animals in both selections get what they need? **Reading/Writing Across Texts**

LOG ON · FIND OUT **Language Arts** Fables
www.macmillanmh.com

391

Take turns playing Ant and Grasshopper with your partner. Make up your own words. What would you want to do on a beautiful summer day if you were Grasshopper? What would you say to Grasshopper if you were Ant?

Page 391

Scene 2

- *Let's read the rest of the play together.* (Read the rest of the play using the same groups.)

- *Winter comes, and snow covers the meadow. This means that there is snow on top of all the grass. Can Grasshopper find any food?* (no) *Is he warm and full or cold and hungry?* (cold and hungry)

- *Grasshopper asks Ant to help him. Does Ant give him food?* (yes) *Ant also teaches Grasshopper a lesson.*

- *Will Grasshopper play all the time next summer?* (no) *What will Grasshopper do?* (gather his own food; plan for the winter)

You and your partner will pretend to be Ant and Grasshopper again. Talk about your plans for gathering food next summer.

Name _____

**Use the word chart to study this week's vocabulary words.
Write a sentence using each word in your writer's notebook.**

Word	Context Sentence	Illustration
beasts _____	We saw many different <u>beasts</u> at the zoo.	**How are the words *beasts* and *animals* the same? How are they different?**
puddles _____	The fox lapped water from the <u>puddle</u>.	
nibble _____	The mouse <u>nibbles</u> on a big piece of cheese.	**Give examples of things you might nibble on.**
itches _____	I have <u>itches</u> all over from bug bites.	
preen _____	My cats like to <u>preen</u> each other.	
handy _____	A step stool is a <u>handy</u> tool.	

© Macmillan/McGraw-Hill

Name_____

Read each question and prompt. Discuss the answers with your group. Use your Leveled Reader to find details to support your answers. Then write your answers on the blank lines or on another sheet of paper.

1. Describe what giraffes look like.

   _____

2. Tell where giraffes live and what helps them survive there.

   _____

3. Describe what a giraffe's tongue looks like and what it is used for.

   _____

4. Explain why giraffes have such long necks and legs.

   _____

5. Tell why giraffes seldom sit down.

   _____

6. Write one question about the book to ask your group.

   _____

   _____

A Way to Help Planet Earth

Pages 398–399

Prior to reading the selection with children, they should have listened to the selection on **StudentWorks Plus**, the interactive eBook. In addition, selection vocabulary should have been pretaught using the **Visual Vocabulary Resources**.

Access Core Content

Teacher Note Pose the questions after you read the paragraph or page indicated.

Page 398

Photo and Title

- *Look at all the plastic bottles. Sometimes water comes in plastic bottles. Raise your hand if you drink water out of a plastic bottle. We all use a lot of plastic bottles.*

- *Let's read the title and question together:* A Way to Help Planet Earth: What can everyone do to help keep Earth clean? *We have to work together, and everyone can help.*

Paragraph 1

- *Our environment is the world around us. People who work on environmental conservation try to keep our planet healthy. Say it with me:* conservation.

- *Conservation also involves helping plants and animals. Some plants and animals are in danger. They might become extinct, which means that they might die out or stop living on Earth. Say it with me:* extinct.

Paragraph 2

- *Trash is a big problem. That means that every day there is more and more trash. We might run out of places to put it. We might not have any more places for our trash.*

Pages 398–399

Comprehension

Genre
Expository text gives information about real people, things, or events.

Text Structure
Problem and Solution
A problem is something that needs to be worked out. A solution is the steps taken to solve a problem.

Plastic bottles are piled high at recycling centers.

Real World Reading

A Way to Help Planet Earth

What can everyone do to help keep Earth clean?

Keeping Earth healthy is an important job. That's what environmental **conservation** is all about. People who do that job are working to keep the air, land, and water clean. They are also working to keep endangered plants and animals from becoming **extinct**.

One of the **hardest** jobs is solving the problem of trash. The **trouble** with trash is that it keeps piling up. We could run out of places to put it.

398

Pages 400–401

1 Plastic bottles are separated from other trash.

2 Sanitation trucks collect the recyclables.

3 Plastics are taken to a recycling center.

4 Bottles are crushed into small pieces.

Here's how it works. People save their plastic bottles. A special recycling truck picks the bottles up and takes them to the recycling center. Here the bottles are crushed into small pieces. Then the small pieces of plastic are melted down. The melted plastic is sent to a factory.

At the factory, the old plastic is made into something new. It may become a new bottle or maybe a new rug. It may become a backpack or even a slide at a playground!

5 A factory turns recycled plastic into something new and useful.

400

A lot of our trash comes from plastic. Soda, juice, water, shampoo—these all come in plastic bottles. Too much plastic is one of our worst trash problems. When a plastic bottle becomes trash, it **remains** trash for hundreds of years. That's because plastic doesn't change much as it gets old.

Is there a better way to deal with plastic? Yes! We can recycle it.

When we recycle, we take something that's been used and turn it into something new. An old plastic bottle can stay old and become trash. Or that old plastic bottle can be recycled and become something new.

People recycle plastic and glass at home and at school.

399

A teacher and students visit a recycling center.

Sometimes there's not much kids can do to help solve our planet's problems. But kids can do a lot about trash. Recycling is one way all people, young and old, can make a big difference!

Think and Compare

1. Where are plastics melted down?

2. What happens when something is recycled?

3. How does recycling help solve a problem with our environment?

4. Prairies are smaller, some animals are endangered, and too much plastic is being thrown away. How have humans caused these problems?

401

Page 399

Paragraph 1

■ *What kinds of plastic bottles are in the trash?* (soda, juice, water, shampoo) *Does plastic trash fall apart and disappear, or does it stay on Earth for a long time?* (It stays on Earth.)

 Tell your partner three kinds of plastic bottles you see at home or school. (Answers will vary.)

Paragraphs 2 and 3

■ *We don't have to put plastic in the trash. We can recycle it. Say it with me: recycle. Does recycle mean to throw something away or to make something new out of it?* (to make something new out of it)

Photos and Caption

■ *Look at the three pictures on the side of the page. Are the people putting things in the trash?* (no) *What are they doing?* (recycling)

Page 400

Paragraphs 1 and 2

■ *People save plastic bottles. A truck picks up the bottles. Where does it take them?* (to the recycling center)*At the recycling center, the bottles are crushed into pieces. Say it with me: crushed.*

■ *Then the plastic goes to a factory. There, old plastic is made into new things. What are some of these things?* (a new bottle, a rug, a backpack,a playground)

Photos

■ *Point to each picture as I tell about it. People separate plastic bottles, or take them away, from other trash. Trucks pick up the bottles. Trucks bring the bottles to the recycling center. The bottles are crushed. A new playground is made from old plastic.*

Page 401

Whole Page

■ *Everyone can help Earth. Everyone can recycle. What other things do people recycle?* (Question is open.)

The main idea is that trash is a big problem for Earth, but everyone can do something about it. What kind of trash is a big problem? (plastic) *What can people do about it?* (recycle)

Name _____

Use the word chart to study this week's vocabulary words. Write a sentence using each word in your writer's notebook.

Word	Context Sentence	Illustration
conservation _____	Wild animals are safer living on the <u>conservation</u> land.	
remains _____	The crust is all that <u>remains</u> of my sandwich.	
trouble _____	The car's flashing lights showed that it was in <u>trouble</u>.	 **What can you do when you are in trouble?**
extinct _____	Dinosaurs used to roam the earth, but now they are <u>extinct</u>.	
hardest _____	The third problem is the <u>hardest</u> one to answer.	 **What is the hardest thing you've had to learn?**

Name_____

**Read each question and prompt. Discuss the answers
with your group. Use your Leveled Reader to find
details to support your answers. Then write your
answers on the blank lines or on another sheet of
paper.**

1. Give examples of the ways we use oil.

   _____

2. Describe what happens when there is an oil spill.

   _____

3. Tell what happens to animals when they are covered in oil.

   _____

4. Describe the biggest oil spill in the United States. Don't forget to
   mention how much money and how many people it took to clean it up.

   _____

5. Explain how people can help clean up the oil when there is a spill.

   _____

6. Write one question about the book to ask your group.

   _____

Super Storms

Prior to reading the selection with children, they should have listened to the selection on **StudentWorks Plus**, the interactive eBook. In addition, selection vocabulary should have been pretaught using the **Visual Vocabulary Resources**.

Access Core Content

Teacher Note Pose the questions after you read the paragraph or page indicated.

Pages 410–411

Title

- *Let's read the title of this book together:* Super Storms. Super *can mean "wonderful" or "excellent." It can also mean "big and strong." Which meaning do you think goes with storms?* (big and strong) *Why?* (Storms are not wonderful, but they can be big and strong.)

Photos

- *Look at the stormy sky in the picture. Point to the clouds. Point to the lightning.*

 Think about stormy skies you have seen. Tell your partner about them.

Seek Clarification

Some children may be confused by unfamiliar words, such as *surface*. Encourage children to always seek clarification when they encounter a word or phrase that does not make sense to them. For example, *Can you explain "surface," please?*

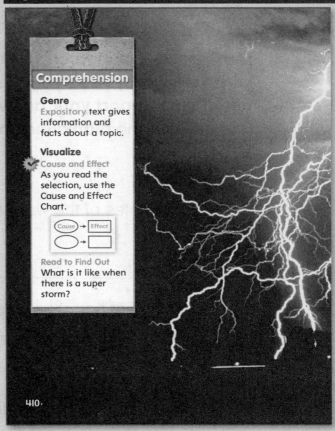

Comprehension

Genre
Expository text gives information and facts about a topic.

Visualize
Cause and Effect
As you read the selection, use the Cause and Effect Chart.

Cause → Effect

Read to Find Out
What is it like when there is a super storm?

410

The air around us is always moving and changing. We call these changes weather.

412

Page 412

Photo

■ *Look at the picture on page 412. The sky is blue, but rain is falling from clouds. Now look at the small picture on the next page. Dark and heavy storm clouds have moved overhead.*

Text

■ *Let's read the first paragraph together:* The air around us is always moving and changing. We call these changes weather. *Storms are the kind of weather we're going to read about.*

Page 413

Whole Page

■ *A storm is a sudden change in weather. That means that the weather changes very quickly.*

■ *Point to the word* thunderstorm. *What two words do you see in it?* (thunder *and* storm) *Let's make a sound like thunder.* (Demonstrate by saying "Boom!" and have the children imitate the sound.)

■ *Heavy rains fall in a thunderstorm. Big thunderstorms can drop millions of gallons of water in a minute.*

■ *Families often buy milk and juice in gallon containers. Imagine someone pouring out a million containers of milk in a minute! There would be a flood of milk. It would cover everything!*

Storms are sudden, **violent** changes in the weather.

Every second, hundreds of thunderstorms are born around the world. Thunderstorms are heavy rain showers. They can drop millions of gallons of water in just one minute.

Cause and Effect
What is the effect of a powerful thunderstorm?

413

Pages 414–415

Whole Page

- Bolt *is another word for flash. Point to a bolt of lightning on each page.*

- *Degrees tell how hot or cold something is. Put your finger on the number on this page that tells how hot lightning is. Read the number with me: 50,000 degrees.*

- *Lightning is hotter than the surface, or outside, of the sun. It can destroy, or ruin, a tree or small house. If something is hit by lightning, it might burn.*

- *A forest is a place with lots of trees. How do you think lightning starts a fire in a forest?* (Lightning is very hot. It hits a tree, which starts a fire. Then the fire spreads to other trees.)

- *Grasslands are flat places that are covered with grass. Lightning can start fires in grasslands, too.*

PARTNERS *You and your partner will draw two pictures. One will draw what it might look like if lightning hit a tree. The other will draw what it might look like if lightning hit a building. Share and talk about your drawings.*

Pages 414–415

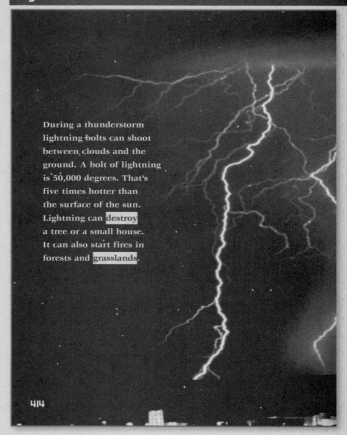

During a thunderstorm lightning bolts can shoot between clouds and the ground. A bolt of lightning is 50,000 degrees. That's five times hotter than the surface of the sun. Lightning can destroy a tree or a small house. It can also start fires in forests and grasslands.

414

Pages 416–417

416

415

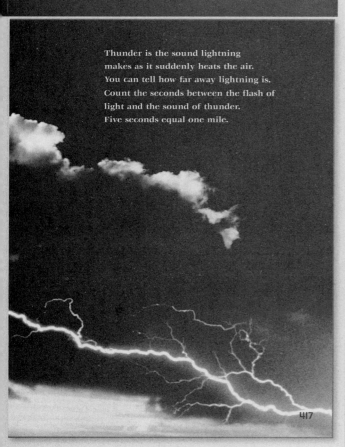

Thunder is the sound lightning
makes as it suddenly heats the air.
You can tell how far away lightning is.
Count the seconds between the flash of
light and the sound of thunder.
Five seconds equal one mile.

417

Pages 416–417

Whole Page

- *Lightning heats the air suddenly, or very quickly. What is thunder?* (the sound lightning makes)

- *Let's read the last four lines together:* You can tell how far away lightning is. Count the seconds between the flash of light and the sound of thunder. Five seconds equal one mile.

- *I will flash the lights. We will pretend that is a bolt of lightning. When the lights flash, start counting like this: "One, and two, and three and four and five." Then I will say "Boom!" Pretend that is thunder.* (Do what you have described, saying "Boom!" when children count five seconds.)

- *Put up the number of fingers to show me how many seconds you counted. How many miles away was the lightning?* (one)

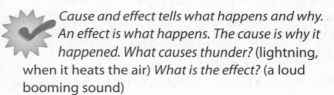 *Cause and effect tells what happens and why. An effect is what happens. The cause is why it happened. What causes thunder?* (lightning, when it heats the air) *What is the effect?* (a loud booming sound)

Pages 418–419

Paragraph 1 and Large Photo

- *Let's read the first paragraph together to find out about a kind of weather called hail:* Hailstones are chunks of ice that are tossed up and down by the winds of some thunderstorms.

- *Look at the big picture. What do you see on the ground?* (small hailstones)

Paragraph 2

- *When something is destroyed, it is ruined. What can hailstones destroy?* (crops) *Crops are fruit and vegetables.*

- *Hailstones are made of ice. Do you think they are hard or soft?* (hard) *Hailstones can damage, or hurt, buildings and cars. They can break windows on buildings. They can dent, or push in, the metal on cars.*

Small Photo and Caption

- *Look at the small picture on page 419. The words underneath the picture are called the caption. Let's read the caption together:* Hail can be the size of a marble or larger than a baseball.

- *Why is there a baseball in the picture?* (to show how big the hail is) *Are the hailstones in the picture bigger than the baseball or a little smaller?* (a little smaller)

Page 420

Photo

- *What do you see in the picture?* (fallen trees) *The thunderstorms uprooted some of the trees, or pulled them from the soil along with their roots. Other trees were snapped in two, which means they were broken into two pieces.*

Pages 418–419

418

Pages 420–421

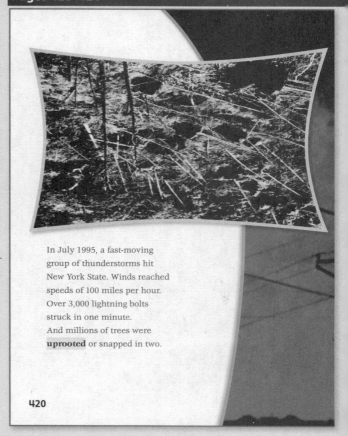

In July 1995, a fast-moving group of thunderstorms hit New York State. Winds reached speeds of 100 miles per hour. Over 3,000 lightning bolts struck in one minute. And millions of trees were **uprooted** or snapped in two.

420

Hailstones are chunks of ice that are tossed up and down by the winds of some thunderstorms.

Nearly 5,000 hailstorms strike the United States every year. They can destroy crops and damage buildings and cars.

Hail can be the size of a marble or larger than a baseball.

419

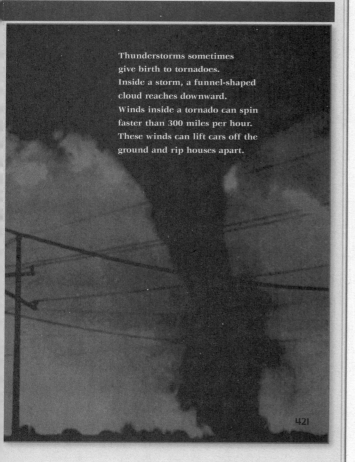

Thunderstorms sometimes give birth to tornadoes. Inside a storm, a funnel-shaped cloud reaches downward. Winds inside a tornado can spin faster than 300 miles per hour. These winds can lift cars off the ground and rip houses apart.

421

Text

- *On the highway, a car may go 60 miles per hour. The winds in one storm in New York State were 100 miles per hour. Was that faster or slower than a car on the highway?* (faster)

 Take turns with your partner saying words to describe the storm this page tells about. (scary, dangerous, fast) *Talk with your partner about how people might have felt during this storm.* (scared)

Page 421

Whole Page

- *What kind of storms have we read about so far?* (thunderstorm, hailstorm) *This page tells about another kind of storm. It tells about tornadoes. Say the word with me: tornado.*

 Let's read the first sentence on this page together: Thunderstorms sometimes give birth to tornadoes. *Thunderstorms sometimes make tornadoes happen. Which is the cause?* (thunderstorms) *Which is the effect?* (tornadoes)

- *A funnel shape is wider at the top and thinner at the bottom, like this.* (Roll a piece of paper into a funnel.) *The winds in a tornado spin in a funnel shape. Point to the funnel shape in the picture.*

- *Let's use our pointer fingers to show how the winds in a tornado spin.* (Demonstrate using your index finger to trace a funnel shape in the air.) *Should we make our fingers go fast or slow? Why?* (fast, because tornadoes spin fast)

Request Assistance

Remind children of expressions they can use to request assistance from the teacher or their partners, such as *Can you repeat it, please? Can you say it with other words?*

Photos

Look at the pictures. *What do you think caused all this damage?* (a tornado) *Name some of the things the tornado destroyed.* (cars, trees, houses)

Text

■ *This page talks about the states east of the Mississippi River. Let's find the Mississippi River on a map.* (Point to the river.) *These states are east of the river.* (Indicate that section of the map.)

■ *There are a lot of numbers on this page. Let's read them together:* 1,000; 1974; 150; 13; 300; 5,000; 10,000.

■ *I'm going to ask some questions about this page. Answer them with the correct number.*
  • *About how many tornadoes are there in the United States each year?* (1,000)
  Let's talk about the year 1974 now.
  • *About how many tornadoes were there east of the Mississippi River?* (150)
  • *How many states were hit by those tornadoes?* (13)
  • *About how many people were killed?* (300)
  • *About how many people were hurt?* (5,000)
  • *About how many homes were destroyed?* (10,000)

Text

■ *An alert is a warning that danger is coming. Why are early alerts about tornadoes important?* (so that people can get to a safe place before a storm hits)

422

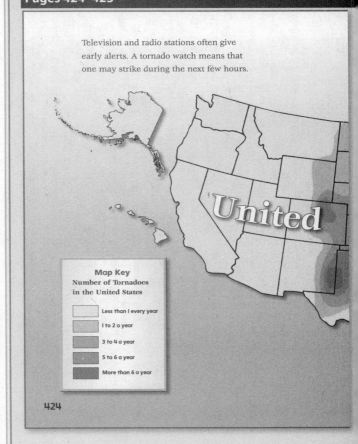

Television and radio stations often give early alerts. A tornado watch means that one may strike during the next few hours.

United

Map Key
Number of Tornadoes in the United States

	Less than 1 every year
	1 to 2 a year
	3 to 4 a year
	5 to 6 a year
	More than 6 a year

424

More than 1,000 tornadoes strike the United States each year. Most of them form during spring and summer. In April 1974, nearly 150 tornadoes struck 13 states east of the Mississippi River. More than 300 people were killed and 5,000 were injured. Nearly 10,000 homes were destroyed.

423

A warning means a tornado has been seen by people or on radar. During a tornado warning you should find shelter in a basement or closet.

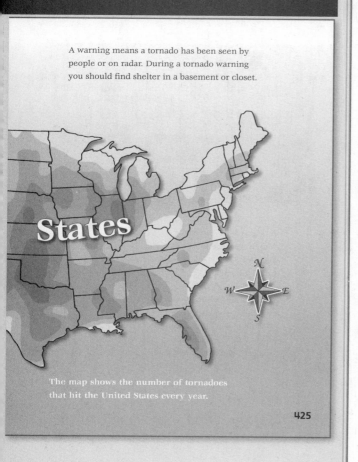

States

The map shows the number of tornadoes that hit the United States every year.

425

- People turn on a television or radio if it looks like a storm is coming. What can they find out about the storm? (if it is big and when it might happen)

- During a tornado, it's important to stay in a safe place. What would be a safe place? (a closet or a basement)

- A tornado watch means that a tornado may strike. What does a tornado warning mean? (Someone has actually seen a tornado.)

 You and your partner will take turns pretending to be weather reporters. Alert people that there is a tornado warning. Tell what that means. (A tornado is coming, and someone has seen it.) *Tell what to do to stay safe.* (Stay in a basement or closet.)

Map and Caption
- Look at the map. It shows the number of tornadoes that hit the United States every year.

- Look at the key. It tells us that the darkest areas on the map have the most tornadoes each year. Point to an area on the map that has more than 6 tornadoes a year.

- Here is our area on the map. (Point to it.) Point to our area on your map. Now look at the Map Key on page 424. How many tornadoes does it say happen in our area each year? (Answer will vary depending on your location.)

Page 426

Text

- *This page tells about another kind of storm. The storm is called a hurricane. Say the word with me:* hurricane.

- *Hurricanes are the deadliest, or most dangerous, storms in the world. Many people die in hurricanes each year. What makes hurricanes so dangerous?* (Fast winds make hurricanes so dangerous.)

Photo and Caption

- *Let's look at the small picture and read the caption:* This photograph of a hurricane was taken in space looking at Earth. *Point to the eye of the hurricane. It is the quiet center of the storm.*

- *Is the storm over when the winds suddenly stop blowing?* (no) *You are probably in the eye of the storm.*

Page 427

Photo

- *Look at the picture. What is happening?* (a storm or a hurricane) *I see palm trees in the picture. Point to the palm trees. Palm trees often grow close to the ocean. This storm is probably close to the ocean.*

Text

- *Hurricanes start over the ocean. When do most hurricanes happen?* (during the summer and fall)

- *High waves can wash away beaches, boats, and houses. That means that the waves can carry these things out to sea. The heavy rains can cause floods.*

- *The winds are so strong that they make a howling sound, like this.* (demonstrate) *Let's make a howling sound together. What can these strong winds uproot, or pull up?* (trees and telephone poles)

One partner will draw a picture of what a beach area might look like during a hurricane. One partner will draw a picture of what a beach area might look like after a hurricane. Share and talk about your picture with your partner.

This photograph of a hurricane was taken in space looking at Earth.

Hurricanes are the deadliest storms in the world. They kill more people than all other storms combined. Hurricanes stretch for hundreds of miles. They have winds of between 74 and 200 miles per hour. The eye of a hurricane is the quiet center of the storm. Inside the eye, the wind stops blowing, the sun shines, and the sky is blue. But **beware**, the storm is not over yet.

> **Cause and Effect**
> What kind of damage does a powerful hurricane cause?

426

In August 1992, Hurricane Andrew smashed into Florida and Louisiana. Over 200,000 people were left homeless.

In the Pacific Ocean, hurricanes are called typhoons. In April 1991, a typhoon hit the country of Bangladesh. Over a million homes were damaged or destroyed. More than 130,000 people died.

428

Hurricanes are born over warm ocean waters from early summer to mid-fall. When they finally reach land, their pounding waves wash away beaches, boats, and houses.

Their howling winds bend and uproot trees and telephone poles. Their heavy rains cause floods.

427

Blizzards are huge snowstorms. They have winds of at least 35 miles per hour. Usually at least two inches of snow fall per hour. Temperatures are at 20 degrees or lower. Falling and blowing snow make it hard to see in a blizzard.

429

Page 428

Whole Page

- *Hurricane Andrew hit Florida and Louisiana in 1992. After the hurricane, more than 200,000 people were left homeless. Why were they without homes?* (The hurricane destroyed their homes.)

- *In the second paragraph, there is another word for hurricane. Let's read the first sentence together to find out what it is:* In the Pacific Ocean, hurricanes are called typhoons.

- *Let's find the Pacific Ocean and the country of Bangladesh on a map.* (Point them out on a map.)

Page 429

Text

- *All the storms we have read about so far are rainstorms. Now we will read about blizzards. A blizzard is a really big snowstorm, with strong winds and heavy snow.*

- *Two inches of snow fall each hour during some blizzards. Let's figure out how much snow would fall in a blizzard that lasted 10 hours. We'll let each of our fingers stand for one hour. We'll count by 2s on our fingers to figure out how much snow that would be.* (Lead children in counting by 2s to 20.)

- *Why is it hard to see in a blizzard?* (because so much snow is falling and blowing all around)

Photo

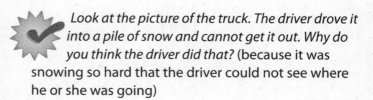 *Look at the picture of the truck. The driver drove it into a pile of snow and cannot get it out. Why do you think the driver did that?* (because it was snowing so hard that the driver could not see where he or she was going)

Page 430

Paragraph 1

- *The author tells about a major blizzard. The word* major *can mean "a leader in the army" or "big and important." Which meaning makes sense in the sentence?* (big and important)

- *The 1993 blizzard happened on the East Coast. Let's look back at the map on pages 424–425. This is the East Coast.* (Guide the children in tracing the East Coast.)

Paragraph 2

- *Let's read the first sentence of this paragraph together:* Millions of people lost power and spent days in dark, cold homes.

 Lost power *means that the electricity stopped working. What happened when the electricity stopped working?* (The lights did not work. People could not use their heaters. It was cold and dark.)

Page 431

Photo

- *Look at the picture. What kind of storm do you see?* (tornado) *What other kinds of storms did we read about?* (thunderstorms, hurricanes, blizzards)

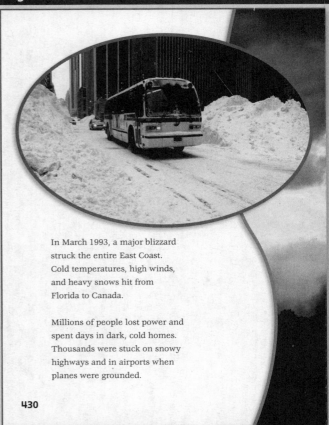

In March 1993, a major blizzard struck the entire East Coast. Cold temperatures, high winds, and heavy snows hit from Florida to Canada.

Millions of people lost power and spent days in dark, cold homes. Thousands were stuck on snowy highways and in airports when planes were grounded.

430

No one can prevent storms. But weather reports can predict and warn us when a storm may hit. The more prepared we are, the safer we will be when the next one strikes.

431

Text, Choral Reading

- *Let's read this page together:* No one can prevent storms. But weather reports can predict and warn us when a storm may hit. The more prepared we are, the safer we will be when the next one strikes.

- *When you prevent something, you stop it from happening. Can anyone prevent storms?* (no) *How do weather reports help people?* (Weather reports predict storms and warn people.)

- *Find the word* hit *on this page to talk about a storm. There is another word on the page that means the same thing as* hit. *What is it?* (strike) *So a storm can hit, or a storm can strike.*

- *Let's talk about some ways to be safe in all kinds of storms.* (Listen to weather reports. Stay indoors. Do what our parents say. Go to a safe place.)

 PARTNERS *Tell your partner about different kinds of storms that you have seen. Whom were you with? What did you do to stay safe?* (Questions are open.)

It Fell in the City

Access Core Content

Teacher Note Pose the questions after you read the paragraph or page indicated.

Page 434

Illustration and Title

■ *Look at the picture. What is on the cars and the branches of the trees?* (snow) *Is it still falling?* (no) *The snow already fell. Now let's read the title of the poem together:* It Fell in the City.

Stanzas 1 and 2

■ *Let's read the first stanza together. Notice the two words that the poet repeats, or says more than once. What are they?* (*It* and *fell*) *What fell?* (snow) *How long was it falling?* (all night long) *The poet wants us to picture that.*

■ *Now listen as I read the first two stanzas together. Listen for the line that repeats three times. What is it?* (All turned white.) *What made everything turn white?* (the snow)

Stanzas 3 and 4

■ *Now let's read the next two stanzas together. Let's pretend that we have a paintbrush with white paint on it. Each time we say* All turned white, *let's move our paintbrush like this.* (Pretend to move a paintbrush horizontally across a canvas in front of you.)

■ *Look at the last two lines of the poem. Where else did we see the words* it fell? (in the first stanza) *Where did we see the words* through the night? (in the first stanza) *What do these words make us think of?* (the snowstorm that turned everything white)

Poetry

Genre
Poems can describe a place by using strong words.

Literary Elements
Repetition is when a word or phrase appears two or more times in a poem.

Rhyme, rhythm, and repetition help create images in poetry.

Word Choice is important in a poem. Poets choose words carefully to give poems a certain feeling or mood.

It Fell in the City
by Eve Merriam

It fell in the city,
It fell through the night,
And the black rooftops
All turned white.

Red fire hydrants
All turned white.
Blue police cars
All turned white.

Green garbage cans
All turned white.
Gray sidewalks
All turned white.

Yellow NO PARKING signs
All turned white.
When it fell in the city
All through the night.

434

Poetry

Connect and Compare

1. What phrases are repeated in this poem? Why do you think the author uses so many color words? **Repetition and Word Choice**

2. Think about this poem and *Super Storms*. Which kind of storm is described in this poem? Use details to explain how you know. **Reading/Writing Across Texts**

LOG ON FIND OUT **Poetry Weather**
www.macmillanmh.com

435

Whole Poem

■ *Count how many times the poet repeats the word* white. (six) *Why do you think she repeats* white *six times?* (because that is what we notice most about snowstorms, how everything is white)

■ *What other color words does the poet use?* (black, red, blue, green, gray, yellow) *Close your eyes. Listen as I read the poem to you again. Try to see the colors in your mind.* (Read the poem aloud.)

Photo

Look at the pictures that go with this poem. Point to the child on the sled. Pretend that you and your partner are outside after a snowstorm. How do things look, feel, and sound? What would you like to do? (Questions are open.)

Use the word chart to study this week's vocabulary words.
Write a sentence using each word in your writer's notebook.

Word	Context Sentence	Illustration
violent _____	The violent storm made trees bend and break.	**Name a word that means the opposite of *violent*.**
beware _____	We were told to beware of the storm, so we stayed indoors.	**Name something to beware of.**
prevent _____	An umbrella prevents you from getting wet.	
uprooted _____	The storm uprooted a tree in front of our house.	
destroy _____	Our roof was destroyed by the wind.	
grasslands _____	Cows graze in the grasslands.	

Read each question and prompt. Discuss the answers with your group. Use your Leveled Reader to find details to support your answers. Then write your answers on the blank lines or on another sheet of paper.

1. How is the wild weather predicted in your story? Give two or more examples.

   _____

2. Give three examples of what the storm does to cause damage.

   _____

3. Does the main character in your story make a risky decision? Explain what happens.

   _____

4. What problem is solved in the story you read?

   _____

5. Choose a character to describe. Tell why you admire or do not admire the character.

   _____

6. Write one question about the book to ask your group.

   _____

Pushing Up the Sky

Pages 442–443

Prior to reading the selection with children, they should have listened to the selection on **StudentWorks Plus**, the interactive eBook. In addition, selection vocabulary should have been pretaught using the **Visual Vocabulary Resources**.

Access Core Content

Teacher Note Pose the questions after you read the paragraph or page indicated.

Pages 442–443

Title
- *Let's read the title of the selection together:* Pushing Up the Sky.

- *This is pushing.* (Hold both hands up and push upwards as if pushing up the sky.) *Say and do it with me:* pushing. (Encourage children to imitate the gesture.) *We're pushing up the sky!*

Illustration
- *Look at the people and animals in the picture. How many people are there?* (two) *Point to the bear. Point to the deer.*

- *The people and animals are holding sticks.* (Point to the sticks.) *What are they doing with those sticks?* (They're pushing up the sky.)

Page 444

Illustration and Paragraph 1
- *Look at the picture. The people who lived here were called Snohomish. Say it with me:* Snohomish. *They lived in a part of our country that is now the state of Washington.* (Point to it on a map.)

- *Look at the fish hanging from the line.* (Point to the fish.) *The people ate fish. They found fish in the ocean.* (Point to the water.) *Where else did they find food?* (on the shore)

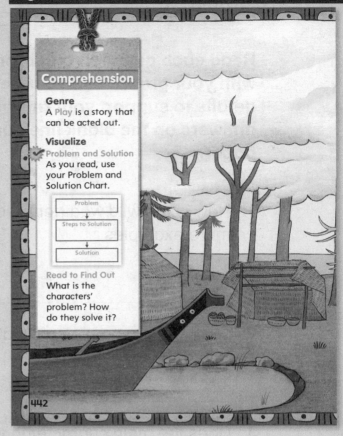

Pages 442–443

Comprehension

Genre
A Play is a story that can be acted out.

Visualize
Problem and Solution
As you read, use your Problem and Solution Chart.

Problem

↓

Steps to Solution

↓

Solution

Read to Find Out
What is the characters' problem? How do they solve it?

442

Pages 444–445

SNOHOMISH

The Snohomish people lived in the area of the Northwest that is now known as the state of Washington. They fished in the ocean and **gathered** food from the shore. Their homes and many of the things they used every day, such as bowls and canoe paddles, were carved from the trees.

Like many of the other peoples of the area, they also carved totem poles, which recorded the history and stories of their nation. *Pushing Up the Sky* is a Snohomish story carved into a totem pole in Everett, Washington.

444

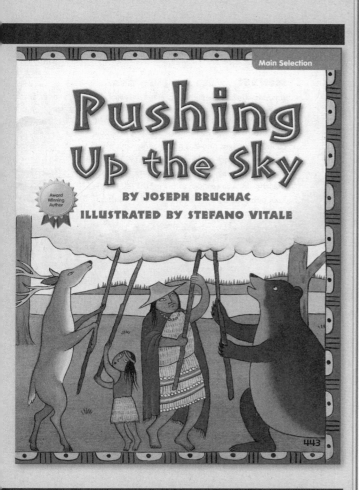

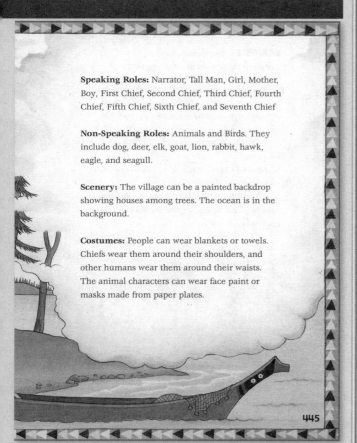

Speaking Roles: Narrator, Tall Man, Girl, Mother, Boy, First Chief, Second Chief, Third Chief, Fourth Chief, Fifth Chief, Sixth Chief, and Seventh Chief

Non-Speaking Roles: Animals and Birds. They include dog, deer, elk, goat, lion, rabbit, hawk, eagle, and seagull.

Scenery: The village can be a painted backdrop showing houses among trees. The ocean is in the background.

Costumes: People can wear blankets or towels. Chiefs wear them around their shoulders, and other humans wear them around their waists. The animal characters can wear face paint or masks made from paper plates.

- *The people carved, or cut, many things out of trees. They made canoes, which are small boats. (Point to the canoe.) Say it with me: canoes. They made paddles to make the canoes go. (Point to the paddles.) Say it with me: paddles.*

Paragraph 2

- *The Snohomish people also carved totem poles like this. (Point to the totem pole.) What do you see on the totem pole? (pictures) The pictures tell a story. We are going to read one of these stories.*

Page 445

Speaking Roles

- *This story is in the form of a play. We will hear different people speak. One person is a narrator. Say it with me: narrator. The narrator helps tell the story.*

- *There are a lot of chiefs in the play. Say it with me: chief. A chief is a leader. The number one chief is called First Chief. The number two chief is called Second Chief. What is the number three chief called? (Third Chief) How many chiefs are there in all? (seven)*

Non-Speaking Roles

- *There are also animals and birds in the play. They play non-speaking roles, which means they don't speak. The birds are a hawk, an eagle, and a seagull. One animal is an elk. An elk is like a big deer. What other animals speak in the play? (dog, deer, goat, lion, rabbit)*

Scenery

- *Scenery is like a big picture. It goes on the stage behind the actors. It shows the place for the play.*

- *The place for this play is a village, or small town. Look at the pictures. Is the village in a very dry place or near the ocean? (near the ocean) What else do you see in the village? (houses, trees)*

Costumes

- *Costumes are special clothes. The chiefs wear blankets on their shoulders. (Point to your shoulders.)*

- *What do the animal characters wear on their faces? (paint or masks)*

Page 446

Illustration

- *Look at the totem pole. I see a bird at the top of the totem pole. Point to it. I can also see faces of people and other animals.*

PARTNERS *Look at how close the cloud is to the woman's head. Look at the tall man on the next page. He bumped his head. Would you like the sky to be that close to the earth? Tell your partner how you feel and why.* (Question is open.)

Scene 1

- *Scene 1 is the first part of the play. This play begins in the village.*

Narrator

- *A long time ago, the sky* (Point up.) *was very close to the earth.* (Hold your hand down low.) *People could jump into it.* ("Jump" one hand off the other, up high.) *How did people get to the sky if they were not good jumpers?* (They climbed up trees.)

Page 447

Whole Page

- *The tall man hits his head on the sky.* (Point to him.) *Let's read his words together:* Oh, that hurt! I just hit my head on the sky again.

- *The girl throws her ball up into the sky.* (Mime throwing a ball up.) *It doesn't come down.*

- *The mother is looking for her son.* (Point to the woman on page 446.) *He is climbing a tree up into the sky. He is looking for his arrow.* (Point to the quiver of arrows.) *An arrow looks like this.* (Draw an arrow on the board.) *Say it with me:* arrow.

- *Let's read the last line together:* The sky is too close!

Synonyms and Circumlocution

Remind children that they can ask for synonyms to help clarify words or expressions they do not understand. Ask, *What is another way of saying "close"?* (near)

SCENE 1: A Village Among Many Tall Trees
Tall Man, Girl, Mother, and Boy stand onstage.

Narrator: Long ago the sky was very close to the earth. The sky was so close that some people could jump right into it. Those people who were not good jumpers could climb up the tall fir trees and step into the sky. But people were not happy that the sky was so close to the earth. Tall people kept bumping their heads on the sky. And there were other problems.

446

SCENE 2: The Same Village
The seven chiefs stand together onstage.

Narrator: So people decided something had to be done. A great meeting was held for all the different nations. The seven wisest chiefs got together to talk about the problem.

First Chief: My people all think the sky is too close.

Second Chief: A very good job was done of making the world.

Third Chief: That is true, but the sky should have been put up higher. My tall son keeps hitting his head on the sky.

448

Tall Man: Oh, that hurt! I just hit my head on the sky again.

Girl: I just threw my ball, and it landed in the sky. I can't get it back.

Mother: Where is my son? Has he climbed a tree and gone up into the sky again?

Boy: Every time I shoot my bow, my arrows get stuck in the sky!

All: THE SKY IS TOO CLOSE!

447

Fourth Chief: My daughter keeps losing her ball in the sky.

Fifth Chief: People keep going up into the sky when they should be staying on the earth to help each other.

Sixth Chief: When mothers look for their children, they cannot find them because they are up playing in the sky.

Seventh Chief: We are **agreed**, then. The sky is too close.

All: WE ARE AGREED.

Problem and Solution
Describe the problem that the characters must solve.

449

Pages 447–448

Illustration

- *All of these people are chiefs. How many chiefs do you see?* (seven)

- *Scene 2 is the second part of the play. We will hear the seven chiefs speak.*

Narrator

- *The people decide that something has to be done about the sky.*

- *There is a great meeting for all the different nations, or groups of people. Each nation has a chief, or leader. Which chiefs get together to talk about the problem— the wisest or the most foolish?* (the wisest)

Dialogue

- *First Chief says that his people think the sky is too close. Does Second Chief think the world was made well or poorly.* (It was made well.) *What does Third Chief think?* (It was made well, but the sky is too close.)

- *What do we learn from Third Chief about his son?* (His tall son keeps bumping his head on the sky.)

- *Fourth Chief tells about his daughter's problem. What does she keep losing in the sky.* (her ball) (Let's pretend to throw a ball up into the sky and act surprised when it doesn't come back down.)

- *Fifth Chief is upset that people keep going up to the sky. What does he think they should do, and why?* (stay on the earth to help each other) *Sixth Chief says that children play in the sky. Why is that a problem?* (Their mothers can't find them.)

- *The seven chiefs all agree. They have the same idea. The sky is too close. Let's read the last line together:* <u>We are agreed.</u>

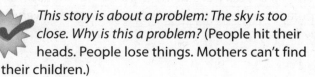

This story is about a problem: The sky is too close. Why is this a problem? (People hit their heads. People lose things. Mothers can't find their children.)

Page 450

Illustration
- *Look at the chiefs. Are they all there?* (Count off the chiefs with the children, using ordinal numbers.) (Yes, all seven chiefs are there.)

Dialogue
- *The chiefs want to fix the problem. They look for a solution.*
- *One chief wants to push up the sky.* (Push your hands upwards.)
- *One chief says that the sky is heavy.* (Mime pushing up something heavy.) *Let's pretend we are trying to push up the heavy sky.*
- *One chief wants to ask the birds and animals for help.*

 I will ask you some questions. Together with your partner, find the answers on this page.

Which chief says, Let's push up the sky? (Seventh Chief)
Which chief says, The sky is heavy? (Third Chief)
Which chief says, We will ask the bird and animals to help? (Sixth Chief)

Page 451

Illustration
- *This animal looks like a deer, but it's bigger. It's an elk.* (Point to the elk.) *The elk has antlers.* (Point to the antlers.) *Say it with me:* antlers.

Dialogue
- *The chiefs tell how the animals also have problems with the sky. The elk's antlers always get caught, or stuck, in the sky.* (Point to the elk's antlers.) *The birds hit their wings on the sky.* (Point to the bird's wing.)
- *First Chief has an idea. Let's read what he says together:* We will cut tall trees to make poles. We can use those poles to push up the sky. *Poles are big sticks. Everyone will push up the sky with poles.*

Second Chief: What can we do?

Seventh Chief: I have an idea. Let's push up the sky.

Third Chief: The sky is heavy.

Seventh Chief: If we all push together, we can do it.

Sixth Chief: We will ask the birds and animals to help. They also do not like it that the sky is so close.

450

SCENE 3: The Same Village

*All the people, except Seventh Chief, are gathered together. They hold long poles. The Birds and Animals are with them. They all begin pushing **randomly**. They are **jabbing** their poles into the air. (The sky can be imagined as just above them.)*

Girl: It isn't working!

Boy: The sky is still too close.

Fifth Chief: Where is Seventh Chief? This was his idea!

Seventh Chief (entering): Here I am. I had to find this long pole.

Problem and Solution
Identify the steps the characters take to solve their problem.

452

Second Chief: The elk are always getting their antlers caught in the sky.

Fourth Chief: The birds are always hitting their wings on it.

First Chief: We will cut tall trees to make poles. We can use those poles to push up the sky.

Fifth Chief: That is a good idea. Are we all agreed?

All: WE ARE ALL AGREED.

451

First Chief: Your plan is not good! See, we are pushing and the sky is not moving.

Seventh Chief: Ah, but I said we must push together.

Fifth Chief: We need a **signal** so that all can push together. Our people speak different languages.

Seventh Chief: Let us use YAH-HOO as the signal. Ready?

All: YES!

453

- *All the chiefs agree. They say it's a good idea. Let's read the last line together:* We are all agreed.

Page 452

Illustration

- *Look at all the poles. (Point to the poles.) What are the people and animals trying to do with them?* (push up the sky)

Scene 3

- *Scene 3 is the third part of the play. Where does it take place?* (in the same village) *All the animals and most of the people are here. Which person is missing?* (Seventh Chief)

- *The animals and people are pushing randomly. Say it with me:* randomly. *That means they are all pushing at different times. They are not pushing together.*

- *They are also jabbing, or poking, like this. (Jab a finger upwards.) Say and do it with me:* jabbing. *(Encourage children to imitate the gesture.)*

Dialogue

- *The girl and the boy say that the plan is not working. Everyone is pushing, but the sky is still close. Why are they looking for Seventh Chief?* (because it was his idea)

Page 453

Whole Page

- *First Chief says that the plan is not good. The plan is not working. What will solve the problem? Seventh Chief says they must push together. Fifth Chief says they need a signal. Say it with me:* signal.

- *A signal tells everyone to begin. Then they can push together. What signal will they use?* (yah-hoo)

- *When Seventh Chief says* YAH–HOO, *everyone will push up the sky. Let's try it. When I say the signal, pretend to push up the sky with poles.*

Page 454

Illustration

- *Look at the picture on both pages. It's nighttime. The people are looking up at the sky. I see stars in the sky. (Point to the stars.) Say it with me: stars. I see the moon. (Point to the moon.) Say it with me: moon.*

Dialogue

- *Seventh Chief calls the signal:* YAH-HOO! *Everyone calls:* YAH-HOO! *Do they push up their poles at the same time or at different times?* (at the same time) *How many times do they push in all?* (four)

- *The mother and son talk as they push. The mother is excited. Now she won't lose her _____. (son) The son is excited, too. Now he won't lose his _____. (arrows)*

- *First Chief says:* We have done it! *They have pushed up the sky. Let's read the last line together:* We have done it!

Page 455

Whole Page

- *Everyone worked together and pushed the sky up. At night, now, they look up at the sky. What do they see there?* (stars)

- *When the people pushed up the sky with poles, they made holes, like this. (Poke a few holes in a sheet of paper with a pencil.) At night, the stars shine through the holes. (Hold the paper up, and look up at it as if you are looking up at the sky.)*

- *The people are happy. They don't bump their heads on the sky now. And at night they can see the stars.*

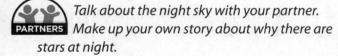 *Talk about the night sky with your partner. Make up your own story about why there are stars at night.*

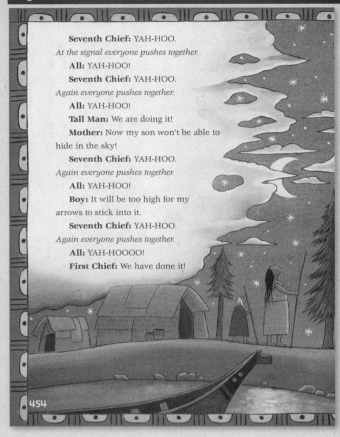

Seventh Chief: YAH-HOO.
At the signal everyone pushes together.
All: YAH-HOO!
Seventh Chief: YAH-HOO.
Again everyone pushes together.
All: YAH-HOO!
Tall Man: We are doing it!
Mother: Now my son won't be able to hide in the sky!
Seventh Chief: YAH-HOO.
Again everyone pushes together.
All: YAH-HOO!
Boy: It will be too high for my arrows to stick into it.
Seventh Chief: YAH-HOO.
Again everyone pushes together.
All: YAH-HOOOO!
First Chief: We have done it!

454

Narrator: So the sky was pushed up. It was done by everyone working together. That night, when everyone looked overhead, they saw many stars in the sky. The stars were shining through the holes poked into the sky by the poles of everyone who pushed it up higher. No one ever bumped his head on the sky again. And those stars are there to this day.

455

This story is about a problem: The sky is too close. The people find a solution, a way to stop the problem. What is the solution? (to push up the sky with poles)

■ *The first time, the solution doesn't work. The people push randomly. Say it with me:* randomly. *The sky does not go up. This is a problem. Seventh Chief has a solution to this problem. What is his solution?* (Everyone should push together.)

Non-verbal Cues

Remind children that they can use non-verbal cues to share information when they are not able to do so verbally. Encourage children to draw.

Getting to Know Joseph Bruchac

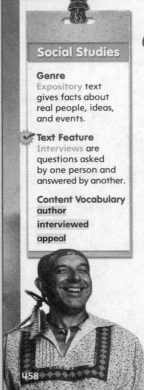

Access Core Content

Teacher Note Pose the questions after you read the paragraph or page indicated.

Page 458

Photo and Title

- *Look at the picture. This man's name is Joseph Bruchac. He is a Native American, just like the people in the play* Pushing Up the Sky. *Does he look like a happy man or a sad man?* (a happy man)

- *Let's read the title together:* Getting to Know Joseph Bruchac. *We are going to read about Joseph Bruchac. We are going to learn some things about him.*

Paragraph 1

- *Joseph Bruchac is an author. Say it with me:* author. *An author writes stories. Joseph Bruchac wrote* Pushing Up the Sky.

- *We are going to read an interview with Joseph Bruchac. Say it with me:* interview. *An interview is when you ask somebody a set of questions and the person answers them. You might ask about the person's work or life.*

- *You can read an interview. When you read* Q, *that means question. When you read* A, *that means answer.*

First Question and Answer

- *Joseph Bruchac writes Native American stories. They appeal to people. That means people like them. Joseph Bruchac says that Native American stories are fun to hear. They also teach good lessons.*

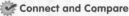

Social Studies

Q: Why do you write plays?
A: I write plays for two reasons. The first is that many teachers told me it was hard to find good Native American plays for kids. The second reason is that I love to give kids the chance to take part in a story.

Q: Which of your stories do you like the best?
A: My favorites are the stories with monsters and scary events in them. One of these is *Skeleton Man*. I like this scary story because it shows how even a child can beat a monster if she does the right thing!

✓ **Connect and Compare**

1. What is one reason Joseph Bruchac writes plays? **Interview**
2. Think about this interview and *Pushing Up the Sky*. Explain why this may be one of Joseph Bruchac's favorite stories. **Reading/Writing Across Texts**

🔍 **Social Studies Activities**

With a partner, find and read another play by Joseph Bruchac.

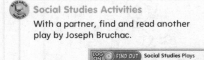

LOG ON · FIND OUT **Social Studies Plays**
www.macmillanmh.com

459

Page 459

Illustration
- *Look at the picture. What do you see?* (a totem pole)

Second Question and Answer
- *Joseph Bruchac writes Native American plays. He writes them because there was a need for them. Teachers told him they couldn't find good Native American plays for their kids. What is another reason that he writes them?* (so kids can act out the stories)

Third Question and Answer
- *Does Joseph Bruchac like funny stories or scary stories?* (scary stories)

- *Raise your hand if you like funny stories. Raise your hand if you like scary stories. Raise your hand if you like sad stories.*

 Joseph Bruchac likes a scary story called Skeleton Man. *It has a monster in it, but the child beats it. Tell your partner the name of a story that you like and why you like it.*

Use the word chart to study this week's vocabulary words. Write a sentence using each word in your writer's notebook.

Word	Context Sentence	Illustration
signal _____	Dark clouds may be a <u>signal</u> that rain is on the way.	**What signals do you see or hear every day?**
randomly _____	The teacher <u>randomly</u> pulled names out of the hat.	
agreed _____	Liz <u>agreed</u> to walk the dog for me.	
gathered _____	Ana <u>gathered</u> flowers from the garden.	**Why might a group of people be gathered?**
jabbing _____	Branches kept <u>jabbing</u> me as I walked along the path.	

Read each question and prompt. Discuss the answers with your group. Use your Leveled Reader to find details to support your answers. Then write your answers on the blank lines or on another sheet of paper.

1. What is the genre of this story? Explain how you know.

_____

2. The Sky has a special problem to solve. Tell how the problem is solved in your story.

_____

3. Pretend you are one of the characters. Act out a few lines for the group.

_____

4. Describe something new you learned from the book you read.

_____

5. Tell the group about something that surprised you in the story.

_____

6. Write one question about the book to ask your group.

_____

_____

Oral Language Proficiency Benchmark Assessment

About the Assessment

The Oral Language Proficiency Benchmark Assessment can be given at different points throughout the year to monitor children's oral language proficiency growth. It is suggested that this oral language assessment be administered three times a year. You may wish to administer the test to all of your children, or to those children who have been scored as Beginning, Intermediate, and Advanced in the speaking portion of your state test.

How to Administer the Assessment

Work with children individually. Use the prompts on pages R5-R6. Ask one question at a time, recording the children's answers. Continue asking questions until the children are not able to respond. The guidelines at the bottom of the second page of the Story-Card Prompts/Student Response Sheet will help you to evaluate children's oral language proficiency at this time of year. The first time you administer the assessment, you may wish to model the responses after children give their responses. Model how each question could be answered, using complete sentences, restating, rephrasing, or elaborating on children's responses.

Student Profiles

Use the results of this assessment to monitor children's growth and determine areas in which to focus instruction for each student. Note children's progress on the Oral Language Proficiency Benchmark Record Sheet on page R7 to chart their oral language development throughout the year.

Dolphin Rescue

✂ -

Dolphin Rescue

✂ -

3

Dolphin Rescue ✂

4

Dolphin Rescue ✂

Dolphin Rescue

⑤

Dolphin Rescue

⑥

GRADE 2

Prompts	Student Responses
Card 1: Let's look at this picture. What do you see?	
Card 1: Where are the boys? What things in the picture tell you where they are? What is the younger boy pointing to?	
Card 1: Point to the fin in the water. What animal is this? Why do you think the boys look surprised?	
Card 2: What is the animal in the water? Where do those animals usually live?	
Card 2: What is the older boy doing? Who do you think he is calling? Why?	

Prompts	Student Responses
Card 3: Who are the people in the brown pants? Why do you think they came there? What are they pulling out of their truck?	
Card 4: What are the rangers doing in the raft? What are the people in the truck doing? Why?	
Card 5: What did the people in the raft do? Why? What do you think they will do with the dolphin?	
Card 6: Where is the dolphin now? Why do you think the rangers moved the dolphin?	
All Cards: Let's look at all the cards together. Tell me a story about what is happening in the cards.	

Review children's responses to the prompts. Use the following as a guide to identify children's language proficiency level at this point.

Beginning: Uses few or no words; gestures or points to respond to prompts.

Intermediate: Uses words, short phrases, and sentences to respond to prompts.

Advanced: Uses sentences to respond to prompts; responses are more detailed; all prompts are addressed.

Oral Language Proficiency Benchmark Assessment Record Sheet

Student Name	Beginning of Year	Middle of Year	End of Year

© Macmillan/McGraw-Hill

Acknowledgments

Volume I

The publisher gratefully acknowledges permission to reprint the following copyrighted materials:

"Abuelo and the Three Bears" by Jerry Tello, illustrations by Ana López Escrivá. Copyright © 1997 by Scholastic Inc. Reprinted with permission of Scholastic Inc.

"Babu's Song" by Stephanie Stuve-Bodeen, illustrated by Aaron Boyd. Text copyright © 2003 by Stephanie Stuve-Bodeen. Illustrations copyright © 2003 by Aaron Boyd. Reprinted by permission of Lee & Low Books, Inc.

"Bella Had a New Umbrella" by Eve Merriam from BLACKBERRY INK. Text copyright © 1985 by Eve Merriam. Reprinted with permission of William Morrow.

"Brush Dance" from POCKET POEMS by Robin Bernard. Text copyright © 2004 by Robin Bernard. Reprinted by permission of Penguin Putnam Books for Young Readers.

"Cat Kisses" by Bobbi Katz. Copyright © 1974 by Bobbi Katz. Reprinted with permission of the author.

"Click, Clack, Moo: Cows That Type" by Doreen Cronin, illustrated by Betsy Lewin. Text copyright © 2000 by Doreen Cronin. Illustrations copyright © 2000 by Betsy Lewin. Reprinted with permission from Simon & Schuster Books for Young Readers, an imprint of Simon & Schuster Children's Publishing Division.

"Crayons" from READ-ALOUD RHYMES FOR THE VERY YOUNG by Marchette Chute. Text copyright © 1974 by Marchette Chute. Reprinted by permission of Random House, Inc.

"Mr. Putter and Tabby Pour the Tea" by Cynthia Rylant, illustrated by Arthur Howard. Text copyright © 1994 by Cynthia Rylant. Illustrations copyright © 1994 by Arthur Howard. Reprinted with permission from Harcourt, Inc.

"My Name Is Yoon" by Helen Recorvits, illustrated by Gabi Swiatkowska. Text copyright © 2003 by Helen Recorvits. Illustrations copyright © 2003 by Gabi Swiatkowska. Reprinted with permission from Frances Foster Books, a division of Farrar, Straus and Giroux.

"One Grain of Rice: A Mathmatical Folktale" by Demi. Copyright © 1997 by Demi. Reprinted with permission of Scholastic Press, an imprint of Scholastic Inc.

"The Three Bears" from YOU READ TO ME, I'LL READ TO YOU: VERY SHORT FAIRY TALES TO READ TOGETHER by Mary Ann Hoberman, illustrated by Michael Emberley. Text copyright © 2004 by Mary Ann Hoberman. Illustrations copyright © 2004 by Michael Emberley. Used by permission of Little, Brown and Company.

"Doña Flor: A Tall Tale About A Giant Woman with a Big Heart" by Pat Mora, illustrated by Raul Colón. Text copyright © 2005 by Pat Mora. Illustrations copyright © 2005 by Raul Colón. Reprinted with permission of Random House, Inc.

"You'll Sing a Song and I'll Sing a Song" from THE ELLA JENKINS SONG BOOK FOR CHILDREN by Ella Jenkins. Text copyright © 1966 by Ella Jenkins. Reprinted with permission from Oak Publications (A Division of Embassy Music Corporation).

"You-Tú" from POCKET POEMS by Charlotte Pomerantz. Text copyright © 1960 by Charlotte Pomerantz. Reprinted with permission from Dutton Children's Books, a division of Penguin Young Readers Group.

ILLUSTRATIONS
Cover Illustration: Luciana Navarro Powell

10–27: Ed Martinez. 38–61: Arthur Howard. 62–63: Marisol Sarrazin. 64: Arthur Howard. 104: Daniel Del Valle. 110–111: Jason Wolff. 112–139: Gabi Swiatkowska. 146–147: Stacy Schuett. 148–149: Karen Dugan. 158–159: Rob Schuster. 160–189: Aaron Boyd. 198–199: Richard Torrey. 200–231: Raul Colon. 234: Daniel Del Valle. 250–251: Dominic Catalano. 252–279: Demi. 280–283: Valerie Sokolova. 290–311: Daniel Del Valle. 317: Anthony Lewis. 319: Doreen Gay-Kassel. 331: Kritina Rodanas. 352: Daniel Del Valle. 356–359: Jayoung Cho. 358–380: Ana Lopez Escriva. 382–385: Michael Emberly. 404–429: Betsy Lewin. 432: Peter Siu. 444: Beth G. Johnson. 462–463: Cecile Schoberle.

PHOTOGRAPHY
All photographs are by Ken Karp for Macmillan/McGraw-Hill (MMH) except as noted below.

iv: Blend Images/Alamy. v: (t) Siri Stafford/Getty Images; (c) George Ancona. vi: Joanna B. Pinneo/Aurora Photos. vii: Russell Kord/Alamy. viii: (tl) Richard Cummins/Corbis; (cl) Beatriz Schiller/Macmillan McGraw-Hill. ix: (tl) Pete Saloutos/Corbis; (bl bc) Courtesy Pam Munoz Ryan; (br) Steve Thanos Photography/Macmillan McGraw-Hill. 2-3: Blend Images/Alamy. 4–5: (bkgd) Wetzel & Company. 4: (b) Terry Vine/Patrick Lane/Getty Images. 5: (br) Notman/Library of Congress, LC-USZ62-13123. 6–7: Hutchings Stock Photography/digital light source. 8: (tr) Ariel Skelley/Corbis; (bl) Royalty-free/Corbis. 9: David Hanover/Stone/Getty Images. 11: Ed Martinez. 26: (tr) Cheron Bayna; (cl) Deborah Chabrian. 28: Sam Toren/Alamy. 29: Hans Georg Roth/Corbis. 30–31: (t) Imagebroker/Alamy. 30: (b) Blend Images/Alamy. 31: (t) Gary Conner/PhotoEdit. 32: Mike Powell/Getty Images. 33: Burke/Triolo/Brand X Pictures/Getty Images. 34–35: Ariel Skelley/Corbis. 36: (t) Burke/Triolo Productions/Brand X Pictures/Getty Images; (bl) Tim Ridley/DK Images; (bc) Erwin Bud Nielsen/Photolibrary. 37: Jim Cummins/Taxi/Getty Images. 60: Michael Papo. 64: Steve Cole/Getty Images. 65: Asia Images/Getty Images. 66–67: Siri Stafford/Getty Images. 68: (bkgd) Craig D. Wood/Panoramic Images; (t) Harald Sund/The Image Bank/Getty Images. 69: (t) Joseph Scherschel/Time Life Pictures/Getty Images; (b) Digital Vision/PunchStock. 70: North Wind Picture Archives. 71: Landing at Jamestown, 1607 (color litho), English School (17th century), Private Collection/The Bridgeman Art Library. 72: (tl) Dover Publications; (b) North Wind Picture Archives. 73: Keith Weller/USDA. 74: Panoramic Images/Getty Images. 76: Stockbyte/Getty Images. 77: (bkgd) Bet Noire/Shutterstock; (cr) PhotoLink/Getty Images; (bl) C Squared Studios/Getty Images. 78–79: Laura Dwight/Omni-Photo Communications. 80–81: (t) Digital vision/Getty Images. 80: (b) Richard T. Nowitz/Corbis. 81: (t) Digital vision/Getty Images; (cr) Myrleen Ferguson Cate/Photo Network/Alamy. 83–101: George Ancona. 102: Macmillan McGraw-Hill. 103: George Ancona. 106: Dennis MacDonald/PhotoEdit. 107: Tony Hutchings/Getty Images. 108–109: Ariel Skelley/Getty Images. 138: Courtesy Farrar, Strauss & Giroux. 140: (t) Dynamic Graphics/IT Stock Free/Alamy. (b) Brand X Pictures/PunchStock. 141: Jeff Greenberg/Alamy. 142: (b) Joe Hermosa/AP Images; (inset) Burke Triolo Productions/Getty Images. 143: Chris Rogers/Corbis. 144: David Young-Wolff/PhotoEdit. 145: Dave King/Dorling Kindersley/Getty Images. 152–153: Joanna B. Pinneo/Aurora Photos. 154–155: Digital Vision/PunchStock. 154: (b) Mitch Wojnarowicz/Amsterdam Recorder/The Image Works. 155: (br) Underwood & Underwood/Corbis. 156–157: Gabe Palmer/Corbis. 158: (bl) Photodisc/Getty Images; (bc) Ron Chapple/Thinkstock/Alamy. 159: Jeff Greenberg/PhotoEdit. 188: (t) Courtesy Stephanie Bodeen; (b) Courtesy Aaron Boyd. 190–193: (t b) PhotoDisc Green/Getty Images. 190: (bl) Tim Davis/Corbis. 191: (bkgd) Tim Davis/Corbis; (c) Photodisc Green/Getty Images. 192: (c) Jim Zucherman/Corbis. 193: (tr) Joe McDonald/Corbis. 194: Sean Justice/Corbis. 195: Marc Romanelli/Royalty Free/AGEfotostock. 196–197: Robert Michael/Corbis. 230 (t) Cheron Bayna; (b) Courtesy Raul Colon. 232–233: Dmitri Kessel/Time Life Pictures/Getty Images. 234: Juice Images/AGEfotostock. 235: David Buffington/Getty Images. 236–237: Russell Kord/Alamy. 238: VI/Alamy. 239: Comstock/PunchStock. 240: Robert Francis/Robert Harding Travel/Photolibrary. 241: Dave G. Houser/Corbis. 242–243: San Jacinto Museum of History. 244: Howie McCormick/AP Images. 246: Digital Vision. 247: (bkgd) Bet Noire/Shutterstock; (bl) C Squared Studios/Getty Images; (br) Ryan McVay/Getty Images; (cr) PhotoLink/Getty Images. 248–249: Jeff Greenberg/PhotoEdit. 278–279: Wetzel & Company. 278: (t) Courtesy Simon & Schuster. 284: Jade Albert Studio/Getty Images. 285: Dorling Kindersley/Getty Images. 286–287: The Granger Collection, New York. 288: (t) Photodisc Green/Getty Images; (bl) Courtesy George Greenwood. 289: Courtesy Sue Gregory. 290–311: (bkgd) Wetzel & Company. 292: (cl) Royalty Free/Corbis; (cr) Chris Collins/Corbis; (b) Ingram Publishing/Alamy. 293: (t) Image Farm; (b) Brown Brothers. 294: (c) Gibson Stock Photography. 295: (t) David Toase/Photodisc/Getty Images. 296: (c)

Acknowledgments

Volume I

Jerry Schad/Photo Researchers; (cr) The Granger Collection, New York. 297: (c) The Granger Collection, New York. 298: (t) Image Farm; (b) Courtesy Newark Public Library. 299: (c) North Wind Picture Archives. 300: (c) Culver Pictures; (b) Courtesy The Newark Public Library. 301: (t) Corbis; (b) John Frank Nowikowski. 302: (t) Image Farm; (b) The Granger Collection, New York. 303: (c) George Washington Carver All -University Celebration,1998, Iowa State University. 304: (t cr) Bettmann/Corbis; (b) Brand X Pictures/Burke/Triolo Productions/Getty Images. 305: (t) Lars Klove/Getty Images; (c) Bettmann/Corbis. 306: (t) Image Farm; (b) Time Life Pictures/Getty Images. 307 308: (b) Courtesy Patricia E. Bath, M.D. 309: (t) Courtesy Patricia E. Bath, M.D. 310: (t) Image Farm; (tl) Courtesy Jim Haskins. 311: (t) David Toase/Photodisc/ Getty Images. 312: (t) Image Farm; (c) The Granger Collection, New York. 313: (tl) Courtesy George Greenwood; (tr) Image Farm. 314: Stockbyte/ Getty Images. 315: Michael Newman/PhotoEdit. 316–317: (t) Dorling Kindersley/Getty Images; (b) AsiaPix/Getty Images. 322–323: Richard Cummins/Corbis. 324: (b) Rubberball/AGEfotostock. 324–325: (l) Farinaz Taghavi/Getty Images; (2) Wetzel & Company. 325: (br) Pictorial Press Ltd/Alamy. 326-327: Bob Daemmrich/PhotoEdit. 328: (l) Comstock/ Getty Images; (b) Paul Slocombe/Next Century Images. 329: (t) Digital Vision Ltd./Getty Images; (b) Ingram Publishing/Alamy. 330–347: (bkgd) Beatriz Schiller/Macmillan McGraw-Hill. 348: Courtesy Sharon Dennis Wyeth. 349: Beatriz Schiller/Macmillan McGraw-Hill. 350-351: (bkgd) Wetzel & Company. 350: (b) BananaStock/Alamy. 351: (c) Photodisc Green/Getty Images. 352: Image 100/Royalty Free/Corbis. 353: Ed Zurga/ AP Images. 354-355: Dirk Anschutz/Getty Images. 380: Courtesy Jerry Tello. 386: Image DJ/Royalty Free/AGEfotostock. 387: Stockdisc/ PunchStock. 388–389: Pete Saloutos/Corbis. 390: (t) Richard T. Nowitz/ Corbis; (c) Michael Kooren/Reuters; (b) Richard T. Nowitz/Corbis. 391: Peter Charlesworth/On Asia; (br) Image Farm. 392: (t) Volker Steger/ Nordstar/Photo Researchers; (b) Jose Luis Pelaez, Inc./Corbis. 393: Institute of Cultural Relics and Archaeology of Henan Province/AP Images. 394: Vicky Alhadeff/Lebrecht Music and Arts Photo Library.

395: Toby Jacobs/Lebrecht Music and Arts Photo Library. 396: Ariane Kadoch/Dallas Morning News. 398: William Howard/Stone/Getty Images. 399: (cr) C Squared Studios/Getty Images; (l) Tracy Montana/ PhotoLink/Getty Images; (bkgd) Bet Noire/Shutterstock. 400–401: Masterfile. 428: Courtesy Simon and Schuster. 430–431: (bkgd) Arthur S. Aubry/Getty Images; (t) Library of Congress, LC-DIG-ppmsca-08795. 430: (b) North Wind Picture Archives. 434: MTPA Stock/Masterfile. 435: Rachel Epstein/PhotoEdit. 436–437: Tim Hall/Getty Images. 438: (bkgd) Wetzel & Company; (c) Susan Werner. 439: (bkgd) Wetzel & Company; (tr) Steve Thanos Photography/Macmillan McGraw-Hill. 440–441: (bkgd) Silver Editions 440: (t b) Courtesy Pam Munoz Ryan; (bl) Silver Editions. 441: (t b) Courtesy Pam Munoz Ryan. 442: (cl) Silver Editions; (cr) Courtesy Pam Munoz Ryan. 443: (bl) Silver Editions; (bc) Courtesy Pam Munoz Ryan. 444, 445, 446: Courtesy Pam Munoz Ryan. 446: (br) Silver Editions. 447: (tl) Stock Montage/SuperStock; (tr) Bettmann/Corbis; (c) Macmillan McGraw-Hill. 448: Courtesy Pam Munoz Ryan. 449: (t cl) Silver Editions; (c) Courtesy Pam Munoz Ryan. 450 through 455: Steve Thanos Photography/Macmillan McGraw-Hill. 451: (br) Silver Editions. 453: (tr bl) Silver Editions. 454: (br) Silver Editions. 455: (tl) Silver Editions; (b) Courtesy Pam Munoz Ryan. 456, 457: Courtesy Pam Munoz Ryan. 460: Richard Hutchings/Photo Researchers. 461: Tom Stewart/Corbis. 464: Joe Atlas/Royalty Free/ AGEfotostock. 465: Digital Vision/Getty Images. 468: (l) J. David Andrews/Masterfile; (r) Lori Adamski Peek/Getty Images. 469: (t) Ariel Skelley/Masterfile; (b) U.S. Fish & Wildlife Service/Dick Bailey. 470: Joeseph Sohm-Visions of America/Getty Images. 471: Ariel Skelley. 472: Nigel Cattlin/Photo Researchers. 473: (t) Corbis; (b) W Productions/ Getty Images. 474: Steve Allen/Brand X Pictures/AGEfotostock. 475: Taxi/ Getty Images. 476: Dick Bailey/U.S. Fish & Wildlife Service. 477: Photo Spin/Getty Images. 478: Brand X Pictures/PunchStock. 479: Royalty-Free/ Corbis. 480: Lori Adamski Peek/Getty Images. 481: Davis Barber/ PhotoEdit. 483: (c) David Young-Wolff/PhotoEdit; (b) Ken Cavanagh/ Macmillan McGraw-Hill.

Text permissions plus photo and illustration credits for the reduced pages can also be found at the back of the Student Book.

Acknowledgments

Volume 2

The publisher gratefully acknowledges permission to reprint the following copyrighted materials:

"Dig Wait Listen: A Desert Toad's Tale" by April Pulley Sayre, illustrated by Barbara Bash. Text copyright © 2001 by April Pulley Sayre. Illustrations copyright © 2001 by Barbara Bash. Reprinted by permission of HarperCollins Publishers.

"Farfallina and Marcel" by Holly Keller. Copyright © 2002 by Holly Keller. Reprinted with permission from Greenwillow Books, an imprint of HarperCollins Publishers.

"A Harbor Seal Pup Grows Up" by Joan Hewett and Richard Hewett. Text copyright © 2002 by Joan Hewett. Photographs copyright © 2002 by Richard Hewett. Reprinted with permission from Carolrhoda Books, Inc., a division of Lerner Publishing Group.

"Head, Body, Legs: A Story from Liberia" by Won-Ldy Paye and Margaret H. Lippert, illustrated by Julie Paschkis. Text copyright © 2002 by Won-Ldy Paye and Margaret H. Lippert. Illustrations copyright © 2002 by Julie Paschkis. Reprinted with permission from Henry Holt and Company, LLC.

"It Fell in the City" from BLACKBERRY INK by Eve Merriam. Text copyright © 1985 by Eve Merriam. Reprinted by permission of William Morrow and Company.

"Mice and Beans" by Pam Muñoz Ryan, illustrated by Joe Cepeda. Text copyright © 2001 by Pam Muñoz Ryan. Illustrations copyright © 2001 by Joe Cepeda. Reprinted by permission of Scholastic Press, a division of Scholastic Inc.

"Nutik, the Wolf Pup" by Jean Craighead George, illustrated by Ted Rand. Text copyright © 2001 by Julie Productions, Inc. Illustrations copyright © 2001 by Ted Rand. Reprinted with permission from HarperCollins Publishers.

"Officer Buckle and Gloria" by Peggy Rathmann. Text and illustrations copyright © 1995 by Peggy Rathmann. Reprinted with permission from G.P. Putnam's Sons, a division of Penguin Putnam Books for Young Readers.

"The Puppy" from RING A RING O' ROSES: FINGER PLAYS FOR PRESCHOOL CHILDREN. Reprinted with permission from Flint Public Library.

"Pushing Up The Sky" from PUSHING UP THE SKY by Joseph Bruchac. Text copyright © 2000 by Joseph Bruchac. Reprinted by permission of Penguin Putnam Books for Young Readers.

"Splish! Splash! Animal Baths" by April Pulley Sayre. Copyright © 2000 by April Pulley Sayre. Reprinted by permission of The Millbrook Press, Inc.

"Super Storms" by Seymour Simon. Text copyright © 2002 by Seymour Simon. Reprinted by permission of SeaStar Books, a division of North-South Books, Inc.

"The Tiny Seed" by Eric Carle. Copyright © 1987 by Eric Carle Corp. Reprinted with permission from Aladdin Paperbacks, an imprint of Simon & Schuster Children's Publishing Division: NY

"The Ugly Vegetables" by Grace Lin. Text and illustrations copyright © 1999 by Grace Lin. Reprinted by permission of Charlesbridge Publishing.

ILLUSTRATIONS
Cover Illustration: Luciana Navarro Powell

8–9: Diane Greenseid. 10–37: Julie Paschiks. 44–45: Diane Greenseid. 46–71: Peggy Rathmann. 74: Robert Schuster. 115: Richard Hewitt. 116–117: Jo Parry. 122–123: Bernard Adnet. 124–155: Joe Cepeda. 162–163: Pam Thompson. 164–165: Cindy Revell. 176–201: Eric Carle. 204: Daniel Del Valle. 210–233: Grace Lin. 243: Grace Lin. 254–255: Marisol Sarrazin. 256–279: Holly Keller. 281–283: Andrea Tachiera. 284: Daniel Del Valle. 290–311: Ted Rand. 310: (bc) Ted Rand, (br) Wendell Minor. 311: Ted Rand. 317–319: Daniel Del Valle. 321: Greg Harris. 332–355: Barbara Bash. 360: Jenny Vainisi. 390–391: Rex Barron. 440–441: Laura Ovreset. 442–459: Stephano Vitale. 462–463: Deborah Melmon.

PHOTOGRAPHY
All photographs are by Ken Karp for Macmillan/McGraw-Hill (MMH) except as noted below.

iv: A. Ramey/PhotoEdit. v: (tl) Jupiter Images/Comstock; (cl) Richard Hewett. vi: R. Ian Lloyd/Masterfile. vii: Maria Stenzel & Mark O. Thiessen/National Geographic Stock. viii: (tl) Glow Images/Alamy; (bl) Courtesy Peter Arnold, Inc. ix: (tl) Barbara Stitzer/PhotoEdit; (cl) Keith Kent/Science Photo Library/Photo Researchers. 2–3 A. Ramey/PhotoEdit. 4–5: (l) Geostock/Getty Images; (2) Getty Images/Blend Images. 4: (b) Mark Karrass/Corbis. 5: (br) Brand X Pictures/PunchStock. 6–7: Corbis/PunchStock. 36: (t) Courtesy Won-Ldy Paye; (b) Courtesy of Julie Paschkis. All rights reserved. Used with permission. 38–39: Comstock/PunchStock. 40: Tom Grill/Corbis. 41: Larry Bones/AGEfotostock. 42–43: Jack Sauer/AP Images. 70: Courtesy Peggy Rathmann. 72: Kathy McLaughlin/The Image Works. 73: (t) Geri Engberg/The Image Works; (others) Richard Hutchings/PhotoEdit. 74: Photodisc Green/Getty Images. 75: Michael Newman/PhotoEdit. 76: David Nagel/Allsport Concepts/Getty Images. 77: (t) Alaska Stock LLC/Alamy; (c) Ablestock/Hemera Technologies/Alamy. 78–79: Jupiter Images/Comstock. 80: (t) Keith Brofsky/Photodisc/Getty Images; (b) Suzanne Dunn/The Image Works. 81: Pete Saloutos/Corbis. 82: Ryan McVay/Photodisc/Getty Images. 83–85: Adamsmith/Taxi/Getty Images. 86: Corbis. 88: Ryan McVay/Photodisc/Getty Images. 89: (bkgd) Bet Noire/ShutterStock; (r) C Squared Studios/Getty Images; (l) Ryan McVay/Getty Images. 90–91: Texas Parks & Wildlife Department/AP Images. 92: Tony Savino/The Image Works. 94–115: Richard Hewett. 114: (tl) Courtesy Joan Hewett. 118: Lori Adamski-Peek/Jupiter Images. 119: Larime Photo/Dembinsky Photo Associates. 120–121: Aflo Foto Agency/Alamy. 154–155: (bkgd) Wetzel & Company. 154: (t) Susan Werner. 156–157: (b) Masterfile. 158: (tl) Simon Smith/DK Images; (tc) Rachel Epstein/PhotoEdit; (tr) Andy Crawford/DK Images; (b) Jose Luis Pelaez, Inc./Corbis. 160: Rubberball/Alamy. 161: Rachel Epstein/PhotoEdit. 168–169: R. Ian Lloyd/Masterfile. 170–171: (bkgd) Brand X Pictures/PunchStock. 170: (b) David C Tomlinson/Getty Images. 171: (b) North Wind Picture Archives. 172–173: (c) Wolfgang Kaehler/Alamy. 174: Masterfile Royalty-Free. 175: Douglas Peebles/Corbis. 200: John Dolan. 202, 203: Macmillan McGraw-Hill. 204: Laura Dwight/PhotoEdit. 205: C Squared Studios/Photodisc Green/Getty Images. 206–207: Blend Images/PunchStock. 208–209: (b) David Young-Wolff/PhotoEdit. 208: (t) John A. Rizzo/Getty Images. 209: (c) Jose Luis Pelaez, Inc./Corbis. 232: Courtesy Grace Lin. 234–235: Panoramic Images/Getty Images. 236: (bl) Michael Newman/PhotoEdit; (bkgd) Panoramic Images/Getty Images. 237, 238: Masterfile. 239: (tl) Picture Arts/Corbis; (tc) Royalty-Free/Corbis. 240–241: Maria Stenzel & Mark O. Thiessen/National Geographic Stock. 242: Norbert Wu. 243: Marcos Brindicci/Reuters. 245: (bl) Edward Degginger/Bruce Coleman Inc.; (br) Millard H. Sharp/Photo Researchers. 246: Mike Hettwer. 247: Will Burgess/Reuters. 248: Courtesy David Krause/Madagascar Ankizy Fund. 250: Ross Whitaker/The Image Bank/Getty Images. 251: (l) Ryan McVay/Getty Images; (br) C Squared Studios/Getty Images; (tr) PhotoLink/Getty Images; (bkgd) Bet Noire/ShutterStock. 252-253: Martin Harvey/Gallo Images/Corbis. 278: Courtesy Holly Keller. 280: Frank Greenway/DK Images. 281: Stephen Dalton/NHPA. 284: Michael Newman/PhotoEdit. 285: Patricia Doyle/Getty Images. 286–287: Jeffrey L. Rotman/Getty Images. 288–289: (bkgd) Charlie Munsey/Corbis. 288: (b) Bryan & Cherry Alexander Photography/Alamy. 289: (t) Robert van der Hilst/Corbis. 310: (t) Courtesy Jean Craighead George; (b) Courtesy Ted Rand. 312–313: (bkgd) Art Wolfe/Stone/Getty Images. 313: (t) David A. Northcott/Corbis. 314: Jeff Lepore/Photo Researchers. 315: Tom Brakefield/Corbis. 316: Richard Hutchings/PhotoEdit. 320–321: (b) John Pontier/Earth Scenes. 320: (c) Scott Camazine/Photo Researchers. 321: (t) Daemon Becker. 324–325: Glow Images/Alamy. 326–327: (bkgd) Maureen Perez/iStockphoto. 326: (b) F. Lukasseck/Masterfile. 327: (br) Bob Daemmrich/Corbis. 328–329: Theo Allofs/Corbis. 330–331: (t) Norbert Rosing/National Geographic/Getty Images. 330: (b) Vince Streano/Corbis. 331: (tr) Ariel Skelley/Corbis. 354: (t) Courtesy April Pulley Sayre; (b) Courtesy Barbara Bash. 356: Stan Osolinski/Dembinsky Photo Associates. 357: (t) Joe McDonald/Corbis; (b) David Muench/Corbis. 358: George H.

Text permissions plus photo and illustration credits for the reduced pages can also be found at the back of the Student Book.

Acknowledgments

Volume 2

H. Huey/Corbis. 359: (bl) Bill Lea/Dembinsky Photo Associates; (br) Daril Gulin/Dembinsky Photo Associates. 360: Photodisc Green/Getty Images. 361: Beth Davidow/Getty Images. 362–363: Rolf Nussbaumer/Alamy. 364–365: (b) Lee Cates/Getty Images. 365: (t) Craig Tuttle/Corbis. 366–367: Courtesy Peter Arnold, Inc. 368-369: Peter Weimann/Animals Animals. 370–371: Ralph Reinhold/Animals Animals. 372–373: (bkgd) Tim Fitzharris/Minden Pictures. 372: (b) Gerard Lacz/Animals Animals. 374: Frans Lanting. 375: Robert Winslow/Animals Animals. 376–377: Mitch Reardon/National Audubon Society Collection/Photo Researchers. 378–379: Gunter Ziesler/Peter Arnold. 380: Frans Lanting. 381: Gregory Ochocki/National Audubon Society/Photo Researchers. 382–383: Allan Power/National Audubon Society/Photo Researchers. 384–385: Mike Severns/Getty Images. 386: Mark Phillips/National Audubon Society/Photo Researchers. 387: Frans Lanting/Minden Pictures. 388: (tl) Frans Lanting; (tr) Courtesy April Pulley Sayre. 389: Peter Weimann/Animals Animals. 392: Ross Whitaker/The Image Bank/Getty Images. 393: Tim Davis. 394–395: Barbara Stitzer/PhotoEdit. 396: (t) Gloria H. Chomica/Masterfile; (b) Jim Brandenburg/Minden Pictures; (inset) Judy Griesedieck. 397: ZSSD/Minden Pictures. 398–399: (b) Reed Kaestner/Corbis. 399: (t) Walter Bibikow/The Image Bank/Getty Images; (c) Felicia Martinez/PhotoEdit; (b) Photodisc/Getty Images. 400–401: (b) Courtesy Landscape Structures Inc. 400: (t) Comstock/Alamy; (c) Karl Weatherly/Corbis; (bc) Mark Gibson/Photolibrary; (bl) Hank Morgan/Photo Researchers. 401: (t) Arthur Tilley/Taxi/Getty Images. 402: Marko Kokic/IFRC. 404: Ryan McVay/Photodisc/Getty Images. 405: (bkgd) Bet Noire/ShutterStock; (tr) PhotoLink/Getty Images; (br) Gabe Palmer/Alamy. 406–407: Warren Faidley/Weatherstock. 408–409: (bkgd) Ron Sanford/Corbis. 408: (b) Ellen Ozier/Reuters/Corbis. 409: (t) Mark J. Thomas/Dembinski Photo Associates. 410–411: Keith Kent/Science Photo Library/Photo Researchers. 412–413: (bkgd) George Post/Science Photo Library/Photo Researchers.

413: (c) Jim Reed/Photo Researchers. 414–415: Kent Wood/Science Source/Photo Researchers. 416–417: Kul Bhatia/Photo Researchers. 418–419: (bkgd) NOAA Central Library, OAR/ERL/National Severe Storms Labratory; (c) Howard Bluestein/Photo Researchers. 420–421: (bkgd) Science VU/Visuals Unlimited. 420: (t) Nancie Battaglia/Nancie Battaglia Photography. 422–423: (bkgd) Bettmann/Corbis. 423: (t) Paul Buck/AFP/Getty Images. 426–427: (bkgd) Annie Griffiths Belt/National Geographic Stock. 426: (t) NOAA/NESDIS/Science Source/Photo Researchers. 428–429: (bkgd) James L. Amos/Corbis. 428: (t) Joel Sartore/National Geographic Stock. 430–431: (bkgd) Howard Bluestein/Photo Researchers. 430: (t) Richard Drew/AP Images. 432–433: (bkgd) George Post/Photo Researchers. 432: (t) Courtesy Seymour Simon. 433: (c) Kent Wood/Science Source/Photo Researchers. 434–435: Bettmann/Corbis. 436: Laura Dwight/PhotoEdit. 437: Richard Hutchings/PhotoEdit. 438–439: Roger Ressmeyer/Corbis. 456: (t) Courtesy Joseph Bruchac; (b) Courtesy Stefano Vitale. 458: Courtesy Joseph Bruchac. 460: Stephen Marks/The Image Bank/Getty Images. 461: Michael Newman/PhotoEdit. 464: Richard T. Nowitz/Corbis. 465: (t) Courtesy Tom and Anne Moore; (b) Ken Karp/Macmillan McGraw-Hill. 468: (bl) Stone/Getty Images; (br) Peter Griffith/Masterfile. 469: (t) Mark Tomalty/Masterfile; (b) Bruce Heinemann/Getty Images. 470: Mira/Alamy. 471: (c) Digital Vision Ltd.; (b) Mark Tomalty/Masterfile. 472: Bruce Heinemann/Getty Images. 473: Jeff Greenberg/AGEfotostock. 474: (c) Paul A. Souders/Corbis; (b) David Buffington/Getty Images. 475: Peter Griffith/Masterfile. 476: Elmar Krenkel/zefa/Corbis. 477: Spencer Grant/PhotoEdit. 478: (c) Stone/Getty Images; (b) Paul Barton/Corbis. 479: Eric and David Hosking/Corbis. 480: Theo Allofs/zefa/Corbis. 481: (c) Kevin Dodge/Masterfile; (b) Brand X Pictures/Picturequest. 482: Richard Hutchings/Workbookstock. 483: Randy Faris/Corbis. 484: (t) Ian Shaw/Alamy; (b) Dale Wilson/Masterfile. 485: Martin Rugner/AGEfotostock.

© Macmillan/McGraw-Hill

Text permissions plus photo and illustration credits for the reduced pages can also be found at the back of the Student Book.